SILAS WRIGHT

BY

JOHN ARTHUR GARRATY, M.A.

Assistant Professor of American History
Michigan State College

SUBMITTED IN PARTIAL FULFILLMENT OF THE REQUIREMENTS
FOR THE DEGREE OF DOCTOR OF PHILOSOPHY
IN THE
FACULTY OF POLITICAL SCIENCE
COLUMBIA UNIVERSITY

NUMBER 552

NEW YORK
1949

COPYRIGHT, 1949

BY

COLUMBIA UNIVERSITY PRESS

PRINTED IN THE UNITED STATES OF AMERICA

———

Published in Great Britain, Canada, and India

by

GEOFFREY CUMBERLEGE

OXFORD UNIVERSITY PRESS
London, Toronto, and Bombay

To

MOTHER and JOE

PREFACE

SILAS WRIGHT'S own letters have provided the framework for this biography. As one of the most prominent politicians of the Jackson era his correspondence touched upon many important personages and issues first in New York State and then in the nation as a whole.

But Wright was a completely unpretentious man, which accounts in part for the undeservedly minor space allotted to him in today's histories. It is certainly true that he did not consider his correspondence to be the property of posterity. He kept no copies of his own letters and with a few exceptions destroyed his incoming mail as soon as he had attended to it. So his biographer must rely principally on the letters which he wrote to others. Thus, while there is no single major source of Wright manuscripts, many hundreds of his letters can be found today in various collections in the Eastern states.

I wish here to express appreciation to the many people at the following institutions who made this material available to me: The New York Public Library, the New York Historical Society, the New York State Library, St. Lawrence University, the Ogdensburg, New York, Public Library, the Massachusetts Historical Society, the Historical Society of Pennsylvania, the Library of Congress. I was also permitted to see some Wright papers owned by Mr. Harry F. Landon, of Watertown, New York. Besides allowing me to use this material, Mr. Landon, who has devoted much time to the study of Wright's life, made many valuable suggestions and has read the manuscript of this work. For all this I am deeply grateful. I wish also to thank Professor John A. Krout, of Columbia University, who has supervised the preparation of this study, Professor Dumas Malone, of Columbia, who has read the manuscript and seen it through the press and Professor Harry J. Brown, of Michigan State College, who has given freely of both his time and valued advice.

My wife, Joan Perkins Garraty, has been of constant assistance. A large share of whatever value this book may have is the result of her keen critical sense and hard work.

JOHN A. GARRATY

MICHIGAN STATE COLLEGE
FEBRUARY 27, 1949

CONTENTS

CHAPTER I
YOUNG LAWYER

" I am as ever lazy, almost out of business, poor, merry and sad by turns
and love my friends and—pity my enemies."
Wright to his brother Pliny, May 15, 1822.

There was a man named Silas Wright, and he was a his-
toric sight. He was a good man, and he had a Simitary and a
Grange named after him, and when he was here he lived at
the Tea Cozy.

To the child in the grade school at Canton, New York, who
wrote this simple biography, the name of Silas Wright is probably as well known as that of George Washington or Abraham
Lincoln, for in that North Country community where he lived
and died, his fame has not been forgotten as it has been elsewhere. Today, while the names of Van Buren and Benton,
of Webster and Clay, of Buchanan, Calhoun, and James K.
Polk still ring with some significance to the average American,
Wright's is virtually unknown. It was not always so.

When Silas Wright died late in the summer of 1847, he
was a central figure in American politics. A leading popular
biographer of the day hastened to tell the story of his life;
and another author, whose works have better stood the test
of time and historical criticism, produced within a year a
second biography. General Zachary Taylor, fighting the Mexican War from his headquarters at Monterey, yet maintaining
a keen interest in politics at home, observed that with Wright
had died the probable Democratic candidate for President in
1848.[1] If Wright had lived, he would probably never have
been elected to that office, for unlike many politicians, he did

---

1 The early biographers were John S. Jenkins, *Life of Silas Wright*
(1847) and Jabez D. Hammond, *Life and Times of Silas Wright* (1848),
also printed as the third volume of Hammond's *History of Political Parties
in the State of New York*; Taylor to R. Ward, Oct. 5, 1847, *Taylor Letters,*
p. 139.

not want to be the nation's chief executive. But if he had made
this abundantly clear upon many occasions, it was still true
that few of his friends and none of his political opponents believed him. In any discussion of the presidential possibilities
for 1848 in either political camp, his name was bound to be
prominent, for he was one of the most important politicians
in the United States between 1844 and his death.

The evidence for this is overwhelming. As early as July,
1844, William H. Seward, former Whig governor of New
York, was seriously alarmed at the popularity of " the discreet and generous friend of Van Buren " who was then
campaigning in New York in behalf of James K. Polk. In
August, Walt Whitman, writing in the *Brooklyn Daily Eagle,*
proposed him as the Democratic standard bearer for 1848.
One of the toasts at the dinner which the New York Presidential Electors held at Albany in December, 1844, was to
the man whose " eminent worth and fidelity in the public
service, entitle him to the highest honors of the People in
1848." That man, they felt, was Silas Wright.[2] About the
same time, Senator Cave Johnson, of Tennessee, campaign
manager of the newly elected Polk, wrote that he thought
the Presidency would be " thrown upon " Wright, regardless
of his already professed objections; and a newspaper in Alabama expressed " little doubt " that he would be Polk's successor.[3]

Wright at this time was Governor of New York. He had
behind him a long and honorable record as United States
Senator, and had inherited the party leadership in his home
state from his best friend, Martin Van Buren, when the Little
Magician retired after failing to receive the Presidential nom-

2 Seward to Weed, September 24, 1844, Seward, *Autobiography,* F. W.
Seward, ed., p. 722; *Brooklyn Daily Eagle,* quoted in *Albany Argus,* Aug.
12, 1844; *Argus,* Dec. 5, 1844.

3 C. Johnson to J. Fine, Dec. 4, 1844, Flagg papers, New York Public
Library; "From a Florence Alabama paper," quoted in *Albany Atlas,* Dec.
19, 1844.

ination in the 1844 convention at Baltimore. Righteous indignation was widespread after the convention's rejection of
Van Buren, and the loyal support which the New York Democrats had given to James K. Polk seemed to insure to the
Empire State a controlling voice in the selection of the party's
next candidate. Wright's unblemished record, his utter refusal to seek political preferment, his loyal sacrifice in running
for Governor in 1844 to help carry the state for Polk, had
enhanced his already important national reputation and given
to his name a popular appeal that it had not before com-
manded outside New York. Politicians of both parties saw
this clearly. In February, 1845, Thurlow Weed, the stalwart
boss of the New York Whigs, made a futile effort to check the
Wright boom. In his newspaper, the *Albany Evening Journal,*
he accused the then Democratic state legislature of being
governed not by matters of policy but merely by a desire to
further Wright's candidacy at the next presidential canvass.[4]
His protest, however, could not stem the tide.

Even defeat could not check it. In 1846, running for reelection
as Governor, Wright was beaten and beaten badly. But his
national reputation did not suffer. Purely local issues, splitting
the New York Democracy asunder, had caused his defeat,
but this did not detract from the Wright boom, and the widespread feeling that Wright would be the Democratic choice
in 1848 continued.

Late in 1846, John C. Calhoun, who had been very important in engineering Van Buren's defeat at Baltimore two
years earlier, told his brother James that he was almost certain that Wright would be the candidate. John A. Dix, then
Senator from New York, reported repeated suggestions made
to him that Wright's name be presented to the people formally. In January, 1847, Secretary of State James Buchanan
felt that Wright was "a stronger man in the Union than he
has ever been before." Buchanan told one of his friends that

4 *Albany Evening Journal,* Feb. 8, 1845.

he would support the New Yorker for the Presidency as much
as his position as a cabinet member would permit.[5] Salmon
P. Chase, champion of the anti-slavery forces, by the summer
of that year not only looked on Wright as a strong candidate,
but was willing to promise him the support of the Liberty
party if he would publicly endorse the Wilmot Proviso.[6]

The full explanation of Silas Wright's great prominence at
this time is rooted in his career in state and national politics
over a period of twenty-five years. As the story of his career
unfolds in these pages, this should become quite clear. Why
then has he failed to retain a place in the "average man's"
history of America? Perhaps there is no answer. But the man
who has been called "a preliminary sketch for Abraham Lincoln"[7] is known today only to professional historians and
citizens of northern New York, while many lesser men of his
day are well remembered. It is true that his outstanding abilities were not those which tend to hold popular notice, but he
demonstrated great powers of growth, and when he died he
was one of the most respected and popular men of his time.
The story of his life will show that his memory deserves a
better fate.

*   *   *   *   *

The earliest Wright in America was one Samuel, who came to
Massachusetts during the Great Migration and died at Northampton in 1665. He was a man of some substance, but the
history of his descendants is one of mediocrity and obscurity
for five generations. One Wright was killed by the Indians in
1675; most of the others lived and died at Northampton without acquiring much property or popular notice. Finally the

5 J. C. Calhoun to J. E. Calhoun, Dec. 12, 1846, *Correspondence of John
C. Calhoun*, J. F. Jameson, ed., p. 714; Dix to Flagg, Nov. 9, 1846, Flagg
papers; J. E. Develin to S. J. Tilden, Jan. 17, 1847, Tilden Papers, New
York Public Library.

6 Chase to P. King, July 15, 1847, *Diary and Correspondence of Salmon
Portland Chase*, R. B. Warden, ed., pp. 120-1.

7 A. M. Schlesinger, Jr., *Age of Jackson*, p. 460.

man who was to be Silas' grandfather moved the family to the town of Hadley (now Amherst) where his son, Silas Wright, Sr., became a tanner and shoemaker. He had been apprenticed at an early age, and thus had had little regular education, but his wife, Eleanore Goodale Wright, was by the standards of the day well educated, and with her help, he did a good deal to improve on his own meagre schooling. Into this simple, hard-working family, on May 24, 1795, Silas Wright, Jr., was born.

Western Massachusetts in 1795 was less than ten years removed from Shays's Rebellion. The Berkshire area had been a stormy region then, and the economic conditions which had given birth to that unrest had not been by any means dispelled. Because of the almost impossible condition of inland transportation, it was only in regions very near seaports and river towns that anything beyond mere subsistence agriculture was possible. With no market, there was nothing to encourage the farmers of New England to abandon the wasteful and inefficient methods of their forebears. Conditions were discouraging for the artisan as well. The shoemaking craft, for example, was rapidly passing into the hands of merchant capitalists, who provided men like the elder Wright, formerly independent producers, with the raw materials of their trade, taking away the finished article and paying only for the labor involved in the task.[8]

Conditions were better than they had been to be sure, but many Massachusetts men were dissatisfied with their lot, and new land to the north and west was tempting. With his responsibilities rapidly increasing, and his prospects in postrevolutionary Massachusetts far from promising, it is not hard to understand why the Amherst shoemaker pulled up stakes which had been buried in Massachusetts soil for one

8 J. T. Adams, *New England in the Republic*, Chapter VIII; B. E. Hazard, *Organization of the Boot and Shoe Industry in Massachusetts,* p. 24 ff.

hundred fifty years and headed for the new state of Vermont.

These were the years when Vermont was growing faster than any other state in the Union except Kentucky. At the outbreak of the Revolution the Green Mountain area contained less than 40,000 people, but by the time the Wrights arrived there it boasted a population four times that figure. Nearly half of this gain came in the last decade of the eighteenth century. So it was into the midst of a stream of moving Americans that the Wright family plunged in March, 1796, when young Silas was still less than a year old.

In Vermont, the Wrights settled at Weybridge, in the shadow of Snake Mountain, across the southern end of Lake Champlain from Crown Point. Vermont in those days was in every sense of the word a young community. The country was newly settled, and the people themselves were nearly all very young. As late as 1800, two-thirds of the population were under twenty-six years of age, and only ten per cent had passed forty-five.[9]

In this new and growing country Silas spent a happy childhood. " I have enjoyed the best parents in the world," he reflected later in life. His father became a farmer, and the boy therefore lived the life of a typical youth in an agricultural society. During the farming season he worked at home, and in the winter, when chores were few, he went to school. Meanwhile the family enjoyed a moderate prosperity. Settling at Weybridge had been a happy choice. In a mountainous region like Vermont, conditions of climate and soil vary decidedly, but the Weybridge area was well favored. It was easy to develop exportable surpluses of wheat, livestock, and forest products, and nearby Lake Champlain offered an easy route to the St. Lawrence and the markets of Montreal and Quebec.[10]

9 L. Stillwell, "Migration from Vermont," Vermont Historical Society, *Proceedings*, V, # 2, p. 66.

10 Wright to Van Buren, Apr. 2, 1842, Van Buren papers, Library of Congress; Stillwell, *op. cit.*, pp. 98-101. By 1792, Stillwell estimates the export of agricultural produce from Vermont as 30,000 bushels! See also, D. Ludlum, *Social Ferment in Vermont*, pp. 9-10, 48.

The elder Silas became a solid citizen in the community and was several times elected to the State Legislature.[11] So by the time his namesake was fourteen, the family was able to send him to nearby Middlebury Academy, and three lears later, in 1811, to the College.

Middlebury had been founded as an academy in 1798 and had assumed collegiate status two years later. In 1811 it was still a one-building school, but it had over one hundred students, "probably as virtuous a collection of youth as can be found in any seminary in the world." It was a Congregationalist college and when Wright entered, it was being swept by a powerful religious revival. This movement was a reaction to the anti-Congregationalist offensive waged in Vermont by various Protestant sects, freed on the frontier from the rigid Congregationalist control which had checked them in Massachusetts and Connecticut, and by free thinkers and Deists of the school of Ethan Allen, whose famous "Reason, the Only Oracle of Man" had been published in 1784. There had already been three of these emotional upheavals at the college since its foundation, and most of the upper classmen had seen the light, but "many who had entered in 1811 with the freshman class were unsaved." The pressure on these unfortunates was tremendous. Religion dominated every aspect of the life of the school. "Confessions" of "sinners" before the assembled faculty and student body at Saturday night chapel were a regular event, and one student later recalled being summoned from his bed at two o'clock in the morning to pray for the soul of a comrade suddenly overwhelmed by his own iniquity.

Unfortunately there is no record of how young Wright reacted to all this. But he was not particularly religious at any stage and was politically opposed to the Congregationalist group—largely Federalist in its affiliations. So it is probably safe to assume that he was unaffected by the revival spirit,

11 L. Deming, ed., *Catalogue of the Principal Officers of Vermont*, pp. 23-4.

and remained " unsaved " throughout his student days.[12]

By his own accounting, Silas was never " a swift scholar."
As a young lawyer he wrote in a letter to one of his younger
brothers that in school he had " supported a kind of mediocrity
from which I hope you will rise." He had, he said, done well
enough to get by in Latin and Greek, and was rather good at
mathematics, but had suffered from acute embarrassment in
his efforts at public speaking and composition.[13]

Wright spent the winters while at Middlebury teaching at
nearby district schools to make enough money to supplement
what his father was able to provide. One winter it was the
school at Provost's Corners, and two others at Orlando, a
town in Rutland County.

Although he was already an ardent Republican and a firm
supporter of the war with England that raged while he was
at college, Wright took no active part in the hostilities. His
father, however, and his elder brother, Samuel, were both
members of the local Vermont militia. They took part in the
battle of Plattsburg, in 1814, which checked the advance of
the British General Prevost who was trying to follow the path
blazed by Burgoyne in his march down Lake Champlain to
the Hudson during the Revolution. By the time Silas had graduated from Middlebury the war was over and he, along with
most of his countrymen, turned away from European affairs
and became absorbed in the rapid development of American
life.

A young college graduate in a frontier community might
naturally turn to the law for a career, and this is what Wright
did. Shortly after graduation he entered the firm of Martindale and Wait at Sandy Hill, in Washington County, New
York. At this time the legal profession, in disrepute after the

12 S. Swift, *History of the Town of Middlebury*, pp. 376-90; W. S. Lee,
Father Went To College, pp. 70-82; Ludlum, *Social Ferment*, p. 8.

13 Wright to P. Wright, May 15, 1822, Wright papers, St. Lawrence
University.

Revolution, was beginning a revival that was to continue until the decline of standards of the 1830's. It was even possible for a prospective lawyer to receive a really thorough legal education. John C. Calhoun, for example, had already been graduated from the famous Litchfield Law School in Connecticut, which had been established in the 1780's.[14] And there were many others, though less well known. But the average young man entering the profession did so as a law clerk working in the office of an established lawyer until well enough trained to be admitted to the bar. The latter course was the one pursued by Wright.

As a means of preparation, this system had many defects. Few lawyers had very much time to give to their apprentices, and law textbooks were poor in quality and few in number. Many students got little from their training beyond a superficial knowledge of terminology and procedure. Still, a few years spent in frequenting the local courts and listening to the conversations of the judges and lawyers on the circuit were bound to teach the novice many of the tools and tricks of his future profession. At any rate, the standards of the legal gild at this time were sufficient unto the needs of the day, and they were improving all the time.[15]

Wright worked in the office of Martindale and Wait for a year and a half and then changed to that of Roger Skinner. The cause of this switch is not clear. Wright's early biographers merely guessed when they said the reasons were that Skinner, like Silas, was an old Vermont man, and that Henry C. Martindale, being strongly Federalist in his political sympathies, was upset by his young clerk's opposite views. The fact that Skinner was an important politician whose support would be of inestimable value must also have entered into the decision. At any rate, Wright became a clerk under Skinner

14 Krout and Fox, *Completion of Independence*, p. 283.
15 *Ibid.*, pp. 279-92.

and so remained until January, 1819, when he was admitted
to the bar.

The change was also a fateful one because it led to the most
important and enduring friendship of his life. One day while
travelling by steamboat to Sandy Hill, he got into a playful
altercation with a dapper, affable little man with red hair.
In the midst of the scuffling which took place, the stranger
fell (or was he pushed?) overboard, to the intense amusement of all the boat's passengers. The next day, when Wright
arrived at Skinner's office, he found the same smiling little
fellow deep in conversation with his boss, and was introduced
to him formally. The man was Martin Van Buren. The debo-
nair Van Buren was not the least ruffled or resentful and quite
frankly admitted to a previous acquaintance with his friend's
clerk. Everyone had a good laugh, and in this strange way
began a friendship that was to last until Wright died in 1847.[16]

In 1819, a young lawyer with no money and few connecting
ties might well head for the frontier. Vermont's brief heyday
as a land of opportunity was already over. The prosperous
little town of Weybridge, for example, which had jumped in
population in the twenty years after 1790 from 175 to 750,
was now leveling off its growth, and many areas in the state
were already on the decline. The Mountain State was actually
producing more lawyers than it could support,[17] but in an ex-
panding countryside there was a real demand for educated
men with some training in the law. There were all sorts of
legal matters to be handled: land titles to be established,
mortgages and deeds to be drawn up; but even more, lawyers
were needed for local leadership and office holding. Wright
was young, ambitious, and interested in politics; northern and
western New York was a fertile country, but one in which
lawyers were still scarce. In addition, he was badly run down
from close application to his studies at Sandy Hill and needed

16 R. H. Gillet, *Life and Times of Silas Wright*, I, 72.

17 Deming, *Catalogue*, p. 108; Stillwell, *op. cit.*, p. 150.

fresh air and exercise badly. What could have been more appealing than a tour of this new country on horseback for the double purpose of regaining his health and seeking a place to establish himself? So he was off. All through the summer of 1819 he rode leisurely through the beautiful forests of the New York frontier. Although the area was just beginning to be settled, he found it familiar because many of the new farmers were Vermonters (some of whom he even knew personally) who had moved on into these new and richer lands.

Finally, at Canton, a tiny town near the Canadian border where the St. Lawrence River flows northeastward toward Montreal, he found particularly congenial surroundings, for here lived the family of Captain Medad Moody, an old friend of the Wrights, who had recently migrated westward from Weybridge. Canton was a village of about thirteen hundred people. It had been settled in 1801 by a party led by Stillman Foote, of Middlebury, who later became the town inn-keeper. Though it boasted a thriving saw mill, most of the residents were farming people, and most, like Moody, were from Vermont.[18] The Moodys made the young lawyer welcome, urging him to settle in their little community. Wright had travelled far, and he must have been easy to convince. Canton was small, but it was centrally located in St. Lawrence County where the whole countryside was growing fast.[19] The nearest lawyer was ten miles away. Captain Moody even offered to build him a house if he would stay. And although there is no positive evidence to prove it, young Clarissa, Moody's fifteen-year-old daughter, was probably the most important of all the factors involved in the decision.

There was some conflict in the young lawyer's mind. For a while he considered locating at Ogdensburg, the county seat,

18 F. Hough, *History of St. Lawrence and Franklin Counties*, pp. 273-9, 571.

19 The growth of the county, and of the town of Canton, was remarkably steady all during Wright's residence. Starting in 1820, St. Lawrence grew at about the rate of 2,000 persons a year. 1820—16,037, 1830—36,351, 1840—56,706. Similarly Canton's rate of growth was approximately 100 a year. 1820—1,337, 1830—2,440, 1840—3,465, 1850—4,685. *Ibid.*, p. 571.

which was a larger town, but the combination of forces was too much for him, and Canton became his new home. Moody built him the house, a two-room affair—one room for sleeping and one for his "office"—and after a short visit with his parents at Weybridge, where he acquired some bedding from his mother and $200 from his father, he returned to Canton to start his practice.

A major problem was law books, but he managed to order some on credit from an Albany bookseller named William Gould. A letter which he wrote to Gould in February, 1820, shows how humble were his beginnings at Canton. " My business has not yet afforded me cash so that I can make you a remittance," he wrote. " I did not get the 3d. vol. of the Laws as you will see and as I am ten miles from a lawyer of any description I suffer great inconvenience for the want of it." He also desired the first and eighth volumes of " Johnson " and " Phillips Evidence if it is published... [and] if you are willing to trust me with them. . . ." [20]

Yet four years later he was a State Senator whose daily utterances were already making news in the Albany papers.

Certain local offices came his way almost automatically. This was the case with the position of surrogate of St. Lawrence County. To handle the probating of wills, the disposition of estates, and similar duties, legal training was almost essential and there were very few lawyers from whom to pick. Other local plums fell to him quickly. Within two years he was postmaster of Canton, justice of the peace, commissioner of deeds, town clerk, and inspector of highways and of common schools. In these cases, political influence came into play, and for a young man with little to offer but his talents, Wright had this aplenty. Skinner, his legal mentor, was on the all-powerful New York Council of Appointments until its dissolution under the terms of the new constitution in 1822, and thus was the dispenser of almost unlimited patronage, and his new friend, Martin Van Buren, was rapidly becoming a major figure in

---

20 Wright to W. Gould, Feb. 3, 1820, Manuscript in possession of Harry F. Landon, Watertown, New York.

New York politics. So Wright quickly became a man of influence and importance in the North Country.

And he was a happy man as well. " I am," he wrote his young brother Pliny, " as ever lazy, almost out of business, poor, merry and sad by turns and love my friends and—pity my enemies." [21] His whole personality was perfectly fitted for the community in which he was living. It was his nature to be plain spoken and direct. His own tastes, strengthened by his lack of wealth, made him perfectly willing to live frugally and unostentatiously. He was scrupulously honest, and had no more sympathy for legal complications than did the frontiersmen who were his clients.

" He was the first lawyer I ever saw whose law was all common sense," one old St. Lawrence farmer told Wright's first biographer, John S. Jenkins. " He always gave plain sensible reasons, for his opinions on any subject." Another characteristic of Wright's which was unusual in a lawyer was his eagerness to settle disputes without recourse to the courts. Once, according to North Country legend, when two litigants came to him with a boundary dispute which they wished to settle before a jury, he locked them alone in a room and refused to let them out until they had resolved their difficulties by themselves. " I don't believe in getting twelve men for a job that two can do better," was his reasoning. But what was probably more significant than anything else in explaining his success and his local popularity, he gave freely of his advice in minor legal matters, and immersed himself in the affairs of the people among whom he was living. As one local resident put it: "He was in a pre-eminent sense, a man of reality." [22]

It is therefore not surprising to find him entering state politics in 1823, as the Bucktail candidate of his district for State Senator.[23]

21 Wright to P. Wright, May 15, 1822, Wright papers, St. Lawrence University.

22 J. S. Jenkins, *Lives of the Governors of New York*, p. 732; I. Batcheller, " My North Country," *Independent*, XC, 467; Hammond, *Wright*, p. 35.

23 For biographical details, see also, Gillet, *Wright*, I, and *Democratic Review*, V, 409-18.

CHAPTER II

REGENCY POLITICIAN

"When our enemies accuse us of feeding our friends instead of them, never let them lie in telling the story."

Wright to Azariah Flagg, August 29, 1827.

IN New York as elsewhere, the Era of Good Feelings was at its height. By 1823, the Federalist-Republican line-up had just about disappeared. This, of course, did not mean that an age of political peace had settled over the nation. Although all groups claimed to be members of the party of Jefferson, local issues caused divisions, local men contended fiercely and new sectional alignments were in the making. The division in New York at this date was still amorphous. One group followed De Witt Clinton, and though generalizations about this situation are extremely dangerous, this party tended to favor liberal appropriation of state funds for the development of internal improvements like canals and roads, and easy incorporation terms for banks, insurance companies, and other corporations.

The Clintonians were opposed by the Bucktail party. The latter organization took its name from the emblem of one of its elements, the venerable and powerful Tammany Society of New York City, whose members commonly wore a buck's tail on their hats. The "Holy Alliance," an informal congeries of Albany politicians, was an even more powerful segment of the Bucktail faction. In 1821, their leader, Martin Van Buren, had been sent by the legislature to the United States Senate, and with him at Washington, the "Alliance," ruling in his absence, soon became known as the Albany Regency. Azariah Flagg, a small, intellectual-looking assemblyman from Clinton County in northern New York, who edited the *Plattsburg Republican*, William L. Marcy, the ponderous, dogged, and yet cultured State Comptroller, and Roger Skinner, the lawyer who had trained Wright, were the lead-

24

ing lights of the Regency in Van Buren's absence. In general, the Bucktails were opposed to the costly improvement policies and the wholesale corporation chartering most Clintonians espoused, but at this time their main element of cohesion was personal opposition to De Witt Clinton.

Again it must be emphasized that party ties were far from stable. The economic policy of the Clintonian group had naturally attracted most of the established and wealthy voters in New York. These groups, formerly Federalist in their sympathies, were in the main opposed to the movement for democratic reform and enlargement of the franchise which swept the state after 1818 and led to the great constitutional revision of 1821. In the debates of the Constitutional Convention of that year, these conservatives, led by James Kent, made their last stand and went down to a complete defeat. The forces of democracy controlled the Convention and wrote a new constitution providing for almost unrestricted white manhood suffrage. In the gubernatorial election of 1822, the conservatives failed even to nominate a candidate; Joseph C. Yates, the Bucktail choice, was swept into office almost unanimously; and the State Senate presented the curious appearance of a body with no minority party at all. But if the Clintonian party had been discredited by the political views of some of its more vocal adherents, its former members could still unite on its other policies. Success, however, depended on throwing off the stigma of anti-democracy. So by 1823, the Clinton men had become the People's party, ready behind a screen of democratic sentiments to advance the economic program which so many of its members favored.

Into this situation Silas Wright was rather abruptly thrust when he received the Bucktail nomination for State Senator in his district. The procedure was complicated. Senate districts consisted of several counties each, and in every district where a seat was at stake, a party caucus was held to decide which county should have the right to name the candidate. This time the choice in the fourth district had fallen to St.

Lawrence County and through it, to Wright. He was painfully conscious of his inexperience but eager to beat his opponent, Allen R. Moore, of Clinton County.

After the election, while awaiting the compilation of the returns, Wright felt very nervous and uncertain. The district was large and communication slow. As the days crept by he grew discouraged and fully expected to find that he had lost. He even had his excuses ready, declaring that he had only run to fulfill the "duty every republican owes to his party and his principles." But by November 21, about two weeks after the election, it was clear that his fears had been premature and that he was a member-elect of the Senate. The results, however, were remarkable. The fourth district, a vast but sparsely settled area, consisted of eight counties: St. Lawrence, Warren, Essex, Saratoga, Franklin, Clinton, Washington and Montgomery, and covered most of northeastern New York. Washington, Montgomery and Saratoga made up the southern section and contained a very large percentage of the people. Here Moore was strong, piling up a majority of over 1,200 votes. In Warren, Essex, Franklin and Clinton, Wright was victorious, but the electorate was smaller and the voting closer. Still, his strength in these counties did keep him in the race. But St. Lawrence produced a result that staggered the imaginations of politicians throughout the state. Of the 1,439 votes that were cast, Moore got exactly twenty! The town of Canton went for Wright 199 to 1, and an angry citizen is said to have remarked, " I wonder who that durn scoundrel was who voted ag'in Sile Wright? " [1]

Such a tremendous sweep immediately raised the new Senator to the first rank in the New York political picture. The basis of any politician's strength is his ability to carry his own bailiwick, and this he had certainly demonstrated clearly. Of course, the peculiar conditions of the day had much to do with the extent of the landslide. In St. Lawrence County, the

---

[1] Wright to Flagg, Nov. 12, 1823, Flagg papers; *Albany Argus*, Nov. 21, 28, 1823; Batcheller, " My North Country," *Independent*, XC, 467.

Clintonians had obviously backed Wright and ignored Moore. In future elections, he was not to win his own county by any such amazing margins. But the facts were there and had to be accepted. One thousand four hundred nineteen to twenty! This was the beginning of a tradition and a legend. For the rest of his life the battle cry, " St. Lawrence knows what WRIGHT is! " called the people to the polls each November. Many times hereafter St. Lawrence was the " banner county," attaining the largest Democratic majority of any county outside New York City. Strangers noticed and commented on Wright's extraordinary influence among his own neighbors. As an engineer from Pennsylvania, living in Ogdensburg while working on a canal project, said in a letter to James Buchanan: " I have taken up my residence here in the ' banner County ' of the State—where liveth or shall I say ' reigneth ' when he is at home ' the Cato of the Senate ' [Wright]. Since I have been here I have been quite astonished at the influence which that gentleman seems to possess over his friends. They wait for his nod and beck—it appears to me—with the prostration of lesser mussulmans before a pasha of three vails." [2] Even in 1846, when the party split wide open and Wright, running for reelection as Governor, suffered a smashing defeat, St. Lawrence gave him his usual heavy majority.

Carried into office in this remarkable manner, the new Senator proceeded to Albany and established himself as part of what he called a " triangular team " with Jonas Earll and James Mallory, two other Senators, in a garret at Bostwick's Hotel at 140 State Street. The town of Albany, on the west bank of the Hudson, was then a rapidly growing community of about 15,000 people. Built on the side of a very steep hill which local boosters insisted upon calling a " gentle elevation," it was the political heart of New York State.

The Capitol, at the head of State Street, was its very center. In those days it was a solid, square, three-story and base-

2 J. Morrall to Buchanan, Mar. 14, 1845, Buchanan papers, Historical Society of Pennsylvania.

ment building with an imposing façade. One observer, of limited experience, thought it "equal to the edifice which crowned Capitoline Hill in ancient Rome," but to a more sophisticated student of architecture it must have resembled nothing so much as a cross between a large cheese box and a Greek temple with chimneys. From the public square on which it stood, all the important centers of activity in the town could be observed. The Albany Female Academy, the City Hall, the State Hall (housing the Comptroller's office, the Secretary of State, and other officials), the largest hotels, banks, and business establishments, were all within sight. The city was much bigger than anything the young Senator had ever known, but it was still small enough so that an eager young man could learn to know it all and all its people. It provided an ideal transition in his rise from small town politics to national affairs.[3]

When he arrived at Albany to assume his new duties, "the Pride of St. Lawrence" was twenty-eight years of age. Of medium height, he had a broad and powerful frame which tended toward fleshiness. His hair was brown; his eyes were blue; and he had a high forehead accentuated by a tendency toward baldness. A strong chin, together with his general heavy-set appearance, gave him a very determined mien, especially when angry or pressed in debate. His complexion was florid.

How much this last was owing to nature and how much to habit, it is impossible to say. A man of otherwise unquestionable character, he had one vice—liquor. Like many men of his day, the pleasures of the table were of great importance to him, and the liquid ones even more than the solid. A hotel bill of his, for a slightly later period, is still extant. An occasional "Game dinner" hints at his fondness for food, but as to drink, no hinting is necessary. In one period of ten days,

3 *Argus*, July 5, 1830; S. Wilson, *Albany City Guide, 1844*, p. 20; J. Munsell, *Annals of Albany*, I, 305-13; H. Stanton, *Random Recollections*, p. 22.

the bill shows that he purchased six bottles of madeira, one bottle of sherry and one of gin. Plenty of madeira, with an occasional change to brandy or gin was evidently his unaltering habit, for the record covers most of two years and there is little variation. Commentators of the day all mentioned his fondness for strong drink and thought that his intemperance hindered his political progress, but this is probably incorrect. Deep drinking was common all over America—Webster and Clay, for instance, were also very heavy consumers. And no evidence of any indiscretion on Wright's part resulting from intoxication has come down to us. It is significant that he was known by friend and foe alike for his solid respectability, dependability and integrity—all characteristics lacking in anyone who is a slave to alcohol.[4]

Silas' own attitude toward his drinking is clearly illustrated in a story told by Judge Martin G. Grover, a lawyer from the western part of New York. The incident he described took place at a time when Wright was in the federal Senate, during the famous " Log Cabin and Hard Cider " campaign which preceded the presidential election of 1840. Grover was travelling by coach toward Angelica, a town in Allegany County. At one stop the coach took on another passenger, and probably as an excuse for striking up a conversation, the judge offered his new companion a drink. The stranger accepted willingly, saying that he would take it for its " medical effect."

" You take it for medicine, do you? " said Grover. " That is what we in Allegany take whiskey for. Our people take a good deal of it when they are well [also], as they have no objection to the taste, and then it may prevent sickness. In fact it is a sort of universal panacea up here."

4 Copy of hotel bill in possession of H. F. Landon, Watertown, New York; " It is amazing that a great man like Silas Wright, with pure and unselfish character and a mind clear as crystal, with a judgment almost unerring, should destroy his talents and himself by indulgence in a habit he knows to be fatal." B. F. Perry, *Reminiscences of Public Men*, II, 187.

After their drink, the two men were soon involved in a lively discussion of the coming election. They talked about the candidates, Van Buren, the Democratic choice, and William Henry Harrison, the Whig standard bearer, and about national affairs. The stranger demonstrated an unusually comprehensive knowledge of what was going on.

"May I ask where you live?" Grover finally asked, impressed by his fellow traveller's conversation.

"Well, I am at Washington a good deal," was the evasive reply.

Grover, however, was satisfied, and began to ask him about various Washington statesmen. As they talked on, he inquired if his companion knew Silas Wright.

The stranger replied that he did.

"He is an old friend of my partner Mr. Angel," said the Judge. "They were in Congress together. I have never seen Silas, but Angel has told me so much about him . . . that I feel tolerably well acquainted with him. They say he is a plain, unpretending man. Don't he sometimes put on one of those . . . senatorial airs?"

"I think he intends to pursue a pretty even course," the other answered. "He believes, I should think, that that there is not so much difference in men after all."

"Peck, [Luther C. Peck, a Congressman from western New York] says he drinks like a fish—that he punishes more good liquor than any other man in the Senate. But I feel that Peck lies about that; after all I shouldn't wonder if Silas did feel it his duty to steam up occasionally, especially as he is compelled so often to grapple with Webster, Clay, and Calhoun and those strong generals of the Whig party. But what do you think of the habits of Silas?"

"Well, I should think, perhaps, he did indulge a little too freely in the use of drinks, but I guess he can control himself," said the stranger.

Grover later discovered to his chagrin that his coach-mate had been "Silas" himself. His account may have been embellished by frequent retelling, but the incident is revealing both of Wright and what others thought of him and his drinking.[5] Very late in his life, Silas stopped drinking completely, but that is anticipating our story.

What of Wright's ideas at this time?

Generally speaking he favored the Bucktail program—keeping a close rein on banks and internal improvements. He was a democrat in the sense that he would brook no aristocracy and had a feeling of sympathy for the small farmers and frontiersmen among whom he had grown up. Mainly he was motivated by loyalty to party, friends, and the state of New York. " Love the State and let the nation save itself," he wrote after four years in the New York legislature when he was " moving up " into national politics. " It is part of my political creed always to act with my political friends, and to let the majority dictate [the] course of action." But by friends he meant not the electorate but the small clique at Albany of which he was a member. He did not consider himself a mere agent carrying out the orders of his constituents. As he had said while his election to the Senate was still in doubt, any group that sought to run him for any office, " must do it for the confidence they place in my ability and integrity . . . and not from tying me up with pledges and promises. . . ." Above all he had a deep and abiding faith in the rectitude of the spoils system. " On the subject of these appointments," he wrote to his good friend, Azariah Flagg, " you know well my mind. Give them to true and useful friends, who will enjoy the emolument if there is any, and who will use their influence to our benefit . . . . this is the long and short of the rule by which to act . . . [and] when our enemies accuse us of feeding our friends instead of them, never let them lie in telling the story." [6]

5 *Middlebury Republican*, Sept. 20, 1878, in possession of H. F. Landon, Watertown, New York.

6 Wright to Flagg, Dec. 20, 1827, Nov. 12, 1823, Aug. 29, 1827, Flagg papers.

In short, he was a hard-headed, practical politician, honest and industrious, but limited in his outlook by the small agricultural world in which he had been raised. He was intelligent but not brilliant, well meaning but not idealistic, a typical example of the new type of public official that could be seen at that time rising up in every state in the Union. In January, 1824, he was beginning a public career that was to continue uninterrupted for twenty-three years.

The new session of the state legislature began on January 6, 1824, and it soon became patent that a single subject was to dominate the meeting—the proposed modification of the method of choosing presidential electors. Under the system then in force these men were picked by the legislature, but after the revision and democratization of the constitution in 1822, this was obviously an anachronism. The vast majority of the people of New York were clearly in favor of permitting the direct choice of electors by popular vote. Under these circumstances it would seem obvious that the dominant party in the state, the Bucktails, would have been glad to adopt the change. Special factors, however, militated against such a policy on their part.

The political picture in 1824 was extremely confused throughout the nation. Monroe, the last of the line of Virginians which had held the Presidency since 1801, was completing his final term, and there was no agreement anywhere as to his successor. Four major candidates had entered the field, each with his own sectional support, but each also depending a great deal on personal popularity to garner votes in other areas. New England was strong for John Quincy Adams, who, as Monroe's Secretary of State, was the "logical" choice according to the tradition of the Era of Good Feelings. Southern support was mainly concentrated on William H. Crawford, while the new and growing West had two self-appointed champions, Henry Clay, father of the American System, and Andrew Jackson, the hero of New Orleans.

New York was torn by dissension. Settlers from New England might feel loyalty to Adams; frontiersmen might favor

Jackson or Clay; the Bucktail politicians, whatever their personal predilections, followed the line of the Congressional caucus at Washington and backed Crawford. But above everything else, these politicians wanted to preserve their own control in the state, and the state's power and influence in national affairs, by making sure *they* decided the choice, and that the vote of New York was not split among the various contestants. A solid block of thirty-six votes for a candidate approved by the Regency—this was their first objective. So they favored postponing the proposed change in the electoral system until after the 1824 struggle. If this could be done, their control of the legislature would assure a united vote for Crawford. The *idea* of the popular choice of electors did not bother them; probably most of them sincerely desired it; but the inexpediency of immediate change was to them more important than the abstract principle. "The danger to the rep[ublican] party lies in the repeal and not in the refusal." [7] So wrote Edwin Croswell, the crafty editor of the Regency's paper, the *Albany Argus,* in a very confidential letter.

But if the Regency wished to postpone action, the Clintonians, organized now as the People's party, felt differently. There was a double reason for this. The popularity of the measure was to them a perfect means of overcoming their anti-democratic reputation and regaining political power, but even more important, the confusion as to candidates, so disconcerting to the Bucktails, was exactly suited to Clintonian needs. If the choice of electors was given to the voters, the People's party could put De Witt Clinton forward as a presidential candidate! Clinton, father of the Erie Canal, had a very large personal following, and being a native New Yorker in a contest with four " foreigners " he would be sure to poll a large plurality. Thus if an electoral law could be passed, they might easily find themselves in a position to regain their lost power at the next election.

7 Croswell to Flagg, Dec. 9, 1825, Flagg papers.

In the legislature, popular pressure was so great that the measure could only be defeated by indirection. The Senate passed a resolution favoring in principle the immediate changing of the electoral law. Wright and most of his fellow Bucktails went along with this. But in order to check the Clintonians, Wright introduced a bill that would have completely destroyed the intent of the reform. If enough electors did not receive a majority of the people's ballots, this measure would allow the legislature to fill the vacancies itself. With four, and probably five candidates in the field, no one could hope to procure any electors by a majority vote. It was so clear that Wright's plan would nullify the intent of the reform that even the Bucktail Senators dared not support it, and it was defeated overwhelmingly. Finally, after a great show of deliberation and attempted compromise, the Senate decided on March 10 to postpone action until the first Monday of November. This maneuver, effectively preventing any change in the law before the election, passed by a vote of 17 to 14, and unleashed a storm of criticism on the Regency leaders, of whom Wright was already considered one. The " Seventeen " became notorious overnight. They had committed a political crime which their opponents never let them forget.[8]

Wright knew what was coming and braced himself. The day after voting for postponement he sat down and wrote a long letter of explanation to one of his Canton friends. " I am aware this result will make much noise," his story ran, " and I presume [it] will excite much hard feeling against me; but I have done all in my power to procure what I believed would be a safe law, and not being able to effect it, I voted to postpone the subject." He pointed out the ominous meaning of the Clintonian support of the electoral law and expressed his conviction that his action had been for the benefit of the

8 See, for example, the speech of N. P. Tallmadge in the Senate, June 7, 1842, *Congressional Globe*, XI, 589. The march of events can best be followed in *Argus*, January to March 1824.

party. And, as he put it, " by that party I am willing to be judged."

Explanations were certainly in order. The *Argus* rushed immediately to the defense of the embattled " Seventeen " and of the whole party. Croswell found their action wholly justifiable. When the strife of the election was over, the matter could be settled fairly and sensibly, he wrote editorially. The *Argus,* he promised, would accept any decision then made. A few days later in an article entitled, " Mr. Mallory and Mr. Wright," the inconsistency of these two stalwarts in first favoring the resolution for a change in the electoral law and then voting for postponement on the ground that they sought to preserve the electoral vote of the state intact was defended as an effort to maintain the state's great weight in national affairs. Also, ran the editorial, democrats should notice whence the attack on their leaders was coming. Party men who considered joining in the hue and cry against their own representatives should " look well upon the objects of the men with whom they are thus strangely associated. . . ." They would find, Croswell pointed out cynically, that these associates had traditionally opposed democracy, and that the object of it all was not reform but political power.

But in spite of this spirited defense, the action of the " Seventeen " was bound to weaken the Bucktails seriously. To the average man the accusation of the *New York American* that the names of the " Seventeen " would become " synonymous henceforth with everything that is versatile & unprincipled in politics " must have remained unanswered.[9]

Indeed matters were proceeding very badly for the Regency. A more honest course would probably have been better for them, even from the point of view of expediency. Unhappily their next action was even worse, both morally and politically. On April 12, the last day of the legislative session, the Regency dominated legislature (aided it is true by many malcon-

9 Wright to M. Jenisen, Mar. 11, 1824, Gillet, *Wright,* I, 65; *Argus,* Mar. 16, 19, 1824.

tents among the opposition) voted the removal of De Witt
Clinton from his position as President of the Canal Board.
Wright's part in this little drama was described years later
by Thurlow Weed, the Whig politician:

> On the last day of the session, in pursuance of a Regency
> fiat, John Bowman introduced a resolution in the Senate re-
> moving DeWitt Clinton from the office of canal commissioner.
> I had noticed a significant consultation in the Assembly
> chamber, and followed one of the gentlemen into the Senate
> chamber, who delivered a message to Senator Wright. That
> Senator immediately opened his drawer, and handed a slip of
> paper to Senator Bowman. On that slip was written the reso-
> lution to which I have referred. Mr. Bowman submitted it to
> the Senate.[10]

It is hard to see how this blunder could possibly have been
made. The politically astute men who controlled the party
knew well the popularity of Clinton's name in many areas,
especially in relation to the Erie Canal, then nearing completion. In fact they had undertaken their misguided course
on the electoral law largely in fear of his popularity. Yet they
let their personal feelings overcome their judgment, and he
was ousted. But not for long, for the People's party, already
greatly strengthened, could now openly espouse their old
leader and their old name, and in the first state nominating
convention ever held, they chose him as their candidate for
Governor. The platform was made for them by the Regency's
actions. " The only line that can be drawn in this State," ran
one of their pamphlets at this time, " is between the *Albany
Regency* (the machine of *King Caucus*) and the PEOPLE." [11]

To oppose Clinton, the Bucktails (who usually referred to
themselves as " Republicans " or " the Democracy ") had
passed over Governor Yates, and, in caucus, had settled on
Regency member Samuel Young. Wright had favored Yates,

---

10 T. Weed, *Autobiography*, H. Weed, ed., p. 109.

11 *A Short Appeal to the People*, p. 13.

but in keeping with his ideas of party loyalty, he gave Young full support. Yates, however, was understandably displeased. He evidently decided to seek popular support as an independent, and to get it he adopted the most obvious means available. He called a special session of the legislature to "consider " the electoral bill in August rather than November. This move was completely unexpected. Wright, for example, had returned to Canton to take care of his " starving business " shortly after the fateful removal of Clinton. " The *executive*," he wrote complainingly to Azariah Flagg, " has taken me completely on the wing with his *extraordinary*." [12]

Surprise did not prevent the " Democracy " from dealing summarily with this interference with normal summer activities. They swarmed into Albany with their forces " marshalled for a coup de main of the executive." The session, despite vigorous work by the People's men, lasted just five days and accomplished nothing beyond further agitation of the distressing electoral issue. Yates' move, however, was enough to finish the already staggering party of which Wright was a member. The Regency fought fiercely. Croswell, in the *Argus,* defined an Aristocrat as a " noisy, boisterous demogogue, vociferous for the interests of ' the people '—meaning his own," called bribery, " Federal fair play," and compared the Era of Good Feelings to a " box of *glass,* labelled, ' keep this side up '—contents Hartford Convention, Peacepartyism, Toryism, British Influence, Essence of Aristocracy, and Federalism." But it was hopeless. When Senator Van Buren, in his own home town, went to the polls there were shouts of " Regency! Regency! " and he was forced to go through the humiliating process of taking the prescribed oath as to his identity.[13] In as startling a reversal as can be found anywhere in American history, the Clintonians swept into office in November. St. Lawrence County, which had given Wright

12 Gillet, *Wright,* I, p. 76; Wright to Flagg, July 24, 1824, Flagg papers.

13 Wright to Flagg, July 24, 1824, Flagg papers; *Argus,* Oct. 8, 1824; Van Buren, *Autobiography,* J. C. Fitzpatrick, ed., p. 144.

such a heavy majority in 1823, now was carried by Clinton by over 600 votes. The Senate, only part of which was elected in any one year, remained in Bucktail hands, but the annually chosen Assembly went over to the Clintonians by a large margin. The Regency was completely defeated and very discouraged. As one triumphant Clintonite put it, " Van B. looks like a wilted cabbage, & poor Judge Skinner has quite lost his voice." Even their efforts for Crawford and a united electoral ticket failed. Largely through Wright's work in the party caucus, they managed to hold their own ranks firm against a strong bid by some of their members to throw part of their support to Clay, but this was a hollow victory. With Thurlow Weed, of Rochester, working effectively behind the scenes, the Clinton men united on Adams and gave him the entire New York vote and with it, as later events proved, the Presidency.[14]

All that remained to complete the picture was the passage of the electoral law which after November was supported by everyone. As finally enacted, it provided for choosing the electors by districts corresponding to the state senatorial districts. Although this encouraged the very splitting of the state's vote which Wright had all along opposed, he now gave the bill his approval. " You will think this contrary to my ground last winter," he explained to a friend. " It is, but it is more democratic, and the keeping of the vote of the State together anyway, when dishonest men try to divide it, is impracticable." [15]

14 *Argus*, Dec. 10, 1824; H. Weaton to S. Gouveneur, Nov. 21, 1824, Gouveneur papers, New York Public Library; B. Butler to J. Hoyt, Nov. 6, 9, 1824, Miscellaneous papers, New York Public Library; G. Van Deusen, *Thurlow Weed*, pp. 29-30; D. Fox, *Decline of Aristocracy in the Politics of New York*, p. 300; Weed, *Autobiography*, Ch. XIII.

15 Wright to Jenisen, Dec. 9, 1824, Gillet, *Wright*, I, p. 84. The general ticket was not adopted in New York until 1832. C. Rammelkamp, " Campaign of 1824 in New York," American Historical Association, *Report*, 1904, pp. 200-1.

This was the low point of Regency history. For one crowded year, every act had led to failure. The party had tumbled precipitously from the top of the political pile to its very base. Such times tested and cemented the friendships which made up such an important part of the Regency's strength. Attacked on all sides, the Bucktail leaders seemed a tiny group of corks tossing on the crests of a heaving sea, but in reality they did not permit themselves to become separated by billows of dissension. Wright was growing particularly attached to Azariah Flagg. The diminutive Assemblyman from Clinton County was a man after Silas' own heart. Unkempt in personal appearance, he was meticulous in his application to his job, whether it was merely preparing a report or organizing the entire state for an election. Like Wright he was plainspoken and simple, and an unwavering supporter of Bucktail ideals. After Wright moved on to the United States Senate, Flagg remained his chief contact with conditions in New York and one of his most reliable consultants on national problems. As Silas wrote after many years had passed and many political battles had further proved his friend's loyalty and ability, " Flagg . . . has long been my resort, when I was at a stand and could not make up my mind for myself." [16]

Actually the Regency's position was much stronger than it seemed to casual observers in the winter of 1824-5. The People's party had come into power on a wave of democratic enthusiasm with which many of its leaders had no real sympathy. In power, they would naturally try to press their own ideas into state policies, and this would be bound to alienate a large segment of the voting population. The Bucktails' conception of themselves as the true party of Jeffersonian Democracy had real validity, however, and they were soon to represent the Jacksonian Democracy that was just beginning to develop significant driving power. They were down, it was

16 G. Pierson, *Tocqueville and Beaumont in America*, p. 176; B. Brockway, *Fifty Years of Journalism*, p. 44; Wright to Van Buren, May 30, 1843, Van Buren papers.

true, but they still held the Senate. Their organization was
intact, and their fighting spirit was quick to revive. "Our
friends are recovering from the panic occasioned by our late
defeat, & much spirit was manifested last night at the meeting," wrote a member of the Regency caucus even in November, 1824. Wright, who tended to be pessimistic about such
matters, reported that the "political somerset" of 1824 would
be reversed in 1825, and with a dogged determination that was
already becoming characteristic, urged all loyal party men to
stand fast. "Tell them," he prompted Flagg, that "they are
safe if they fear the enemy, but that the first man we see
step to the rear, we *cut down* . . . they *must* not falter, or
they *perish.*" [17]

In this spirit the Bucktail forces went forward in January,
1825, to do battle with their enemies in the legislature. The
clash was not long in coming. On March 4, the venerable
Rufus King was to complete his term as United States Senator from New York, and according to the law his successor
was to be chosen on the first day of February. The Assembly
and the Senate, by the procedure of the day, voted separately
and then "compared" their results. If the same man had
been selected by each house, he was of course declared elected,
but if the choices of the two branches did not coincide, a
joint session was held and the senator picked by the entire
legislature voting as a unit. Under such a system it was impossible for any Bucktail to win. It seemed on the surface
that the two houses would differ, but that the joint session,
dominated by the Assembly, with over a hundred and twenty
members to the Senate's thirty odd, would declare for the
People's choice.

But the Regency was not disposed to surrender. Late in
January a party caucus was held, whereat, according to
Wright, everyone had "a glorious time." An ingenious

17 Butler to Hoyt, Nov. 9, 1824, Miscellaneous papers, New York Public
Library; Wright to Jenison, Dec. 9, 1824, Gillet, *Wright,* I, 83-4; Wright
to Flagg, Jan. 28, 1823, Flagg papers.

scheme was developed there to frustrate the majority. According to the law, the joint session was to take place if the two houses picked rival candidates. But what if one house could not agree within itself? If *no* choice was presented to the Assembly no one could tell if the two branches differed, and therefore there could be no joint session to settle this "difference." Thus, as Wright told it to Flagg, if eighteen or twenty of the Senators would agree to divide their votes among ten or twelve or even fifteen candidates, nobody could get a majority. In this plot the party was aided by dissension within the Clintonian ranks. Five of the "Seventeen" had fallen by the wayside in the sweep of 1824, but the opposition was not united in either house. The official choice of the Clinton group was Chief Justice Ambrose Spencer, but there were many People's men who could not stomach the Judge, and many others who saw in his defeat a chance to advance their own interests. "I should not suppose," wrote young Senator Wright sarcastically, that "*Senators* other than the *rascally Seventeen* would do this. But . . . . I should not be surprised if these [other] rascals should enter into some such foul combination."

This is exactly what happened. Despite many defections in the Assembly, Spencer carried that body handily, but he could only muster ten of thirty-one votes in the Senate. The other twenty-one were divided among sixteen candidates, no one of whom got more than two. Desperate efforts by the Clintonian Senators to nominate other candidates—*any* other candidate—produced similar results. Senator Cary in an angry speech declared it to be the Senate's "duty" to make some choice, and proclaimed that it " should not tamper with a great question," but Wright, who was running the show for the Bucktails, merely told him in a bantering manner to "keep cool." Cary, made furious by Wright's cavalier treatment and the frustration of his own desires, announced that he could not remain calm. He said, so the *Argus* correspondent reported, that he " could not assume the smiling countenance of his colleague at transactions which excited his

indignation." But Wright suavely rose and read to the Senate
the article of the state constitution dealing with the election
of United States Senators. Nothing could be done, so the Senate adjourned.[18]

Of course the Clintonian forces, particularly in the Assembly, were wild. Individual senators were denounced as felons
and murderers. "In all the annals of the legislature of this
state," wrote Croswell in the *Argus,* " we have never known
such epithets applied in one branch to members of another."
But a great deal of this was mere show. If the Clinton men
had been united and if they had all been friends of Spencer,
they could probably have forced the Senate to act by holding
up the rest of the legislative calendar. But they suffered from
the tendency to split under pressure which afflicted conservative parties all over the United States throughout the first
half of the nineteenth century. So nothing was done, and New
York was represented in the Federal Senate only by Martin
Van Buren until 1826, and by then the Bucktails again controlled both houses of the legislature. Their victory was
complete.[19]

With fortune once more smiling on his party, political life
for young Wright was less grim. The trials of the past months
had tested the mettle of all the Bucktails and the representative
from St. Lawrence had not been found wanting. Under the
greatest pressure he had stood his ground like a veteran; he
had exhibited loyalty to party, political acumen, skill in debate;
he had quickly won his way into the inner circle of the Regency.

He found his place a pleasant one. One of the most important reasons for the success of the Albany Bucktail leaders
was their singleness of heart. Theirs were no business friendships. They really felt strong personal attachments for one
another, and when things went badly they were not easily

18 Wright to Flagg, Jan. 28, 1825, Flagg papers; New York State Senate,
Journal, 1825, pp. 113-7; *Argus,* Feb. 4, 1825.

19 *Argus,* Apr. 5, 1825; Hammond, *History of New York,* II, 195-7.

enticed by their enemies into party-disrupting squabbles. Wright summed up this aspect of Albany politics well, when things were at their worst in April, 1824. " I must tell you," he wrote to one of his Canton followers, " that I have found some ten or twelve honest men, who are all democrats to the bone, but who would not sell their birthright . . . . [We] now stand at the brink of ruin, ready to sink, if fortune so determines, but not to say that we have forfeited our faith and conscience to serve this man or that."

The friends who had endured the tribulations of 1824 and early 1825 found time now to relax and partake of life's pleasures with greater equanimity. " I have just returned from N. York where . . . something approaching to divine honors, were lavished on the Seventeen," wrote Wright's room-mate, James Mallory. " We did not leave our good friends, while turtle soup or good madeira or champagne could be seen, tasted, or heard of. Silas enjoyed it right well. . . ." But, if his own statements can be trusted, this lush life did not turn Wright's head. Being a high and mighty state senator, he told a Canton friend, made little difference to " Old Silas." " As near as I am able to calculate, he is about the same thing yet, gets mad, and scolds and *swears* (I must say it, for it is true) about as easy as usual, and mixes about the same quantity of laugh with it." [20] Life was good.

Still, personal enjoyment had to be subordinated to the business of the day, which was the approaching election. The Bucktails said little, but while the Clintonites were celebrating the completion of the great Erie canal which their leader had done so much to create, they were getting ready for the test. Their preparation was thorough. To the obvious surprise of their antagonists, the Bucktails swept through the canvass, holding the Senate and reestablishing their control of the lower house as well.

20 Wright to Jenison, Apr. 2, 1824, Gillet, *Wright*, I, 68; Mallory to Flagg, July 19, 1825, Flagg papers; Wright to Jenison, Feb. 2, 1824, Gillet, *Wright*, I, 64.

When the result was clear Wright was exultant. Now, he wrote joyfully, " we may again *heave the Magnus* [Clinton] *down* and if . . . he does not get his *bottom scraped,* depend upon it I shall be ready to damn my friends." Then with the memory of the horrible mistake of 1824 in mind he added, " If that creature gets worried into life by us again I will quit politics." His exuberance had not left him a few days later when he wrote to Perley Keyes, one of the " Seventeen: " " The blood of the martyrs may now be truly said to be the seed of the *Church,* and the Magnus must wish the d---l had the memories of his darling people." [21]

* * * * *

The victory of November, 1825, marked the end of a phase in New York politics. The brief period since the ratification of the new constitution in 1822 had been packed with dramatic events, sudden upsets, and political alarms which had overshadowed the basic conflicts between Bucktail and Clintonian. Yet in the long run these issues were of much greater importance in settling the fate of parties and individuals. Once the Bucktails were again secure in both houses of the legislature and their adversaries had no great popular rallying point like the electoral law on which to unite, political maneuvering was less all-encompassing and elemental questions became more prominent. This meant neither that politics as such ceased to be important, nor that other matters had not been significant all along, but after the 1825 election the balance definitely was weighted in favor of affairs on which legislators differed ideologically as well as politically—matters of principle rather than expediency.

The fight raged primarily around banks and canals. On both these matters the Clintonians favored a " large " policy. Banks, said these men, were businesses in which anyone who so desired might engage. Canals were agents of prosperity which should be developed privately when possible, and publicly when individual initiative was lacking, and if this meant government borrowing and a large public debt, the state was rich and powerful, and natural expansion would take care of everything. The Bucktails had a different point of view— one that is more difficult to set forth briefly. Certainly they were not against banks as such. Many of them were stockholders in these institutions. A few, such as Erastus Corning, president of the Mechanics and Farmers Bank of Albany, were important financiers. But they could not stomach what they liked to call " overbanking " which meant expansion of banks beyond the needs of the community and the use of their facilities for speculative purposes. It may thus be said that on this subject they were the conservatives, favoring " safe and sane " financial measures against " fly by nights " and speculators. They were not categorically opposed to internal improvements like canals either, but they wished to consider each case carefully, and to give state aid only to those which would be directly and immediately practical and profitable.

In both these matters, the Bucktails were moving against the tide of the business community. The times were largely responsible for this. All during this period America was in the grip of a great speculative fever. The country was growing and speculation in the long run *had* to be profitable. Panics might come and go, but it was basically true, at least in most areas, that land inevitably increased in value as time passed, and unexploited sections were bound to be developed. In simple language it was good business to be bullish. Of course long term developments did not alleviate the unhappiness and disorder which violent cyclical depressions, aggravated by such speculation, were bound to cause in day-to-day living. But the individual business man in an age of individualism considered mainly what he thought were his own interests, and to nearly all this meant expansion, speculation, and no government interference except to help. The supporters of such policies became in New York, Clintonians. In the same way, the non-business elements—farmers, mechanics and such

—who suffered from depressions more than they profited
from speculation, tended to be pro-Bucktail. They were
joined by conservative bankers and businessmen, who were
either secure in their position and unwilling to risk their security even for the possibility of greater profits, or who were for
some reason or other unaffected by the expansionist spirit of
the times. Only a " lunatic fringe " were dissatisfied with the
working of the American economic system, and this element
was as much despised by the Regency politicians as by their
Clintonian adversaries. In a phrase, the Bucktails favored the
use but not the *ab*use of banking facilities and state aid in
internal improvements.

But if the Bucktails' opposition to banking was merely one
of degree, the practical politics of the situation frequently
called for violent tirades against banks as such, and especially
against banks in politics, for there was no doubt that the
powerful economic groups favoring " loose " banking practices did whatever they could not only to get their ideas accepted, but also to defeat the Bucktails in the great battle for
political power. " The Bank [in Chenango County]," wrote
one local leader complainingly, " has always given us more
trouble than 40 presses . . . . You can scarcely imagine the
trouble this cursed machine has given us, by getting our
friends under the hatches & applying the screws." [22] This sort
of pressure tended to blur the fine distinction in Democratic
thinking between opposition to *certain* banks, and opposition
to all banks. The final outcome, some ten years later, was the
plan of the Independent Treasury, a major purpose of which
was to remove all possible political influence from the hands
of bankers and financiers.

Toward the canal situation, the Bucktail attitude was
clearer. The big handicap was the patent success of the great
ditch between Buffalo and Albany, which gave a powerful
argument to the speculators who wished to develop all sorts
of canal projects, and who could promise with seeming logic

22 L. Clark to Flagg, Dec. 24, 1826, Flagg papers.

the same sort of success for any similar project. Proposals for canals and roads to cover the state in every imaginable direction flooded the legislature during these years, and speculators, bankers, businessmen and transport-hungry farmers, operating through lobbies at Albany, pressed for charters for private companies and even for state construction and state aid for private builders. Against these pressure groups, the Regency leaders fought constantly and in the main effectively.

It must once more be emphasized that their argument was not against internal improvements but against *uneconomic* projects. The Bucktail stand was well put forth in a report made to the Senate by Wright, as chairman of the committee on canals, in February, 1827. The report was occasioned by a petition for the construction of a spur from the Erie canal to the Allegheny River, to tap the Ohio valley. Wright quickly disposed of the special case involved, playing up the contradictory evidence supplied by various interested groups, each favoring a special route for the new waterway, and then went into a discussion of the whole theory of canal construction. He laid down three " great principles " which he felt should govern the decision in all such cases. First, was the canal practicable? Was there an available water supply at all points on the route? How many locks would have to be constructed? Were any other special engineering difficulties involved? Secondly, could the state afford to spend the money needed to build the canal? Wright believed that until the vast cost of the Erie canal had been met, further expenditures were impolitic. Thirdly, there was the question of the value of any proposed work in dollars and cents. Would the new waterway be profitable? It must, said Wright, not only be profitable for the people who would live on its banks, but for the people of the state as a whole. In summary, if a particular canal were feasible, if the state could afford the expense, and if it seemed reasonable to expect that the finished work would earn money, then, as in the cases of the Erie canal and the waterway from Lake Champlain to the Hudson, it was all right for the state to build. But the second condition made large state construction unwise until the debt of past construction had been liquidated.

Wright next directed his attention to the seductive plans of those who wished not state construction or even state loans, but who wanted to " borrow the credit " of the state. This meant that New York would guarantee the bonds of the construction companies, but would not put up any money itself. Such proposals, ran the Senator's report, were unsound. If even the Erie canal, whose productivity exceeded the hopes of its strongest adherents, could not have been built without direct state assistance, how would less fortunate ones fare?

All this seemed to add up to no more canals. The only suggestion the committee could offer was one which it did not think would be accepted. If a particular canal was practicable and if it seemed to offer future profit, it could be constructed by the state or with state aid, *provided* the people were ready to be taxed for it. That was the crucial point. No state real estate tax could be passed, Wright reminded the Senate. Popular opposition was too great. So no appropriation could be recommended by the committee, he continued, " until they are fully convinced that those for whose benefit the appropriation is asked, are fully aware of the consequences. . . ." The report concluded with a frank declaration of the Bucktail creed. Canals can be valuable assets for the whole community and should be run for the common welfare and not to enrich the treasury. Their construction, however, should be " subject always to the antecedent condition, that the treasury is able to sustain the expense, or that, if the public credit is to be pledged, the means of sustaining it . . . are morally certain." [23]

Perhaps this Regency policy dedicated to the eradication of debt and financial speculation was unimaginative. Perhaps it failed to take into account the tremendous capacity for growth which the state and nation were constantly demonstrating. But the Clintonian policy was no less extreme in the other direction. If Wright was overcautious in casting ballots for

[23] Senate *Journal*, 1827, pp. 170-82.

bank charters and for state aid for roads and canals, so the action of a man like Thurlow Weed, who voted in favor of almost any bank charter which came before the legislature while he was a member,[24] certainly gave him some reason for his caution. The Bucktails' position was at least more reasonable than that of their foes. They were almost always willing to approve charters for private road and canal construction projects, and in cases where the value of the property warranted, they were willing even to guarantee stock issues in return for mortgages upon the corporation's properties.[25] And they never came out against banks as such. The fact that the interests behind most of these chartered corporations were largely Clintonian undoubtedly added to their zeal in checking their overdevelopment, but even if these groups had been willing to keep their economic affairs out of politics, the Bucktails would probably have acted in much the same way.

This was in embryo the same struggle that the Grangers were to wage against the railroads, the Populists against monopoly, and the forces of Wilson and Franklin Roosevelt against rugged individualism. To say that politics played a rôle is only to admit that these men were practical; to admit that they were not opponents of the capitalist system, that they were often themselves interested in business and financial ventures, only emphasizes their sincerity. In New York in the 1820's the unrelenting effort of Americans to reconcile individual free enterprise with public interest was already under way. If the means and methods which were used were unlike those later called into play, this was only because circumstances were then much different than they were later to become.

24 Van Deusen, *Weed*, p. 32.

25 See, for example, the report of Wright on the petition of the Delaware and Hudson Canal Company, Senate *Journal*, 1827, pp. 117-22.

CHAPTER III
WRITING A "JUST AND LIBERAL" TARIFF

" The farmer must [now] go to the manufacturer....I would make this action reciprocal."

Wright in the House of Representatives, March, 1828.

WHILE Wright was making his important canal reports in the early months of 1827, he was already a member elect of the Twentieth Congress, which was to hold its first session the following December. There was doubt in his mind whether he could continue to occupy his seat in the State Senate until that date, so in March he resigned his old office and returned to Canton. December found him at Washington. It was understandable that he should stay pretty close to his New York friends in a strange environment. He took quarters with three other New York Representatives, Michael Hoffman, Nathaniel Garrow, and his old friend Jonas Earll, with whom he had lived at Bostwick's in Albany. The social activity of the " city of magnificent distances " fascinated the convivial Silas, but it took time for a freshman representative to get acquainted and to begin to enjoy this life. Of the little group to which Wright belonged, only Hoffman, who was not a new member of Congress, was known to Washington society. So when that worthy was invited to diplomatic dinners and other functions, his three friends were very anxious to know all about them :

> I speak of our friend, the Honable Silas Wright Jun. [wrote Hoffman to Azariah Flagg] in the brightest terms of the beauty and modesty of the Dutch Diplomatic Ladies. He is moved. Already he praises the guttural accents of the Dutch dialect and indeed dreams in Dutch. What will be his condition when he shall have seen them in splendid dresses and gay festivity & shall have inhailed most " madning drafts of beauty to the soul?" ... On my return last eve'g from a

dinner at the Palace, [the White House] your friends put me to the torture—every possible interrogatory—as to personages, beauties, ... dresses, dishes—and ... they were seriously disposed to suspect that I had taken too much of the Presidents Grape. I defended myself as well as I could, by *conditional* and *catagorical* answers, according to facts and fancy.... After this description they agreed to let me off with a gentle admonition, to eat well of *Canvass Back & Bouiller*, with no more than two full glasses of Champaigne preceeded by a little Burgundy & some old Madeira.[1]

But if "the Honable Silas Wright Jun." expressed great admiration for Washington society, the same was certainly not true of Washington politics. His apprenticeship in the New York legislature had been brief but it had also been stormy. It would be a mistake to think that he went to Washington a political novice. Any graduate of the Regency School—anyone who had taken part in New York affairs at all in those days— was sure to know the ropes pretty well, and Wright had shown greater aptitude than average. There may have been much that he could learn from old stalwarts at Washington, but he certainly did not think so himself.

"The politicians here are many of them genuine men," he conceded grudgingly to his Albany friend Flagg, "but [they] are bad managers. They dont understand these things [committee appointments] as well as the Albany Regency. . . . In N. Y. it would not be right."[2]

In justice to these "genuine men" it must be admitted that their problems were tremendous. A presidential election was approaching at a time when parties were in a state of flux that could only make for confusion and political jobbery. Then there was the ominous question of the tariff. Interests in this matter cut squarely across party lines, and something had to be done

---

1 Hoffman to Flagg, Dec. 15, 1827, Flagg papers; For Wright's letter of resignation from the New York Senate, see New York Senate *Journal*, 1827, pp. 305-6.

2 Wright to Flagg, Dec. 13, 1827, Flagg papers.

to satisfy everyone. It must have seemed to the young Congressman from Canton that he was destined always to find himself where the fighting was most severe; for judged by the criteria of confusion, manipulation, and intrigue, the situation at Washington in the winter of 1827-'8 was not unlike that at Albany four years earlier, when he had first entered the State Senate.

That the coming election was an element in determining the shape of the tariff of 1828 is probably true, but its significance has been greatly exaggerated. It has been said, for example, that the Jackson men in Congress wished to have the tariff defeated while appearing to support it, and therefore placed high duties on raw materials to make it so unpalatable to the pro-Adams New England manufacturing interests that their representatives would be forced to vote against it. According to this interpretation, Northern and Western adherents of a protective policy would be attracted to the Jacksonians as the proponents of the defeated bill, and Southerners, who were becoming increasingly opposed to high duties, could safely remain with Jackson because no high tariff would have been enacted. Possibly some Jacksonians did reason this way, but the ones who wrote the bill did not. From first to last they genuinely sought to pass it, and other matters were subordinate. As the story unfolds, this will become clear.

The movement leading to the tariff of 1828 began largely in agricultural areas. Foreign markets, which had been so important to American prosperity, disappeared after the panic and depression of 1819. At the same time came a disastrous deflation of land values. The result was a widespread demand for protection of all sorts of agricultural products, aimed, of course, at raising the domestic prices of such goods. By 1824, this demand had been answered to the extent that all four of the presidential candidates claimed to be friends of high duties. In that year a higher tariff was passed on purely sectional lines, the Western and Middle states favoring it, the South opposed, and New England divided. Besides raising duties on agricultural and mining products as desired by the Western and Middle states, this act also advanced the rates on cloth. But in the same year, the high English duty on raw wool was virtually abandoned, so that British manufacturers of woolen cloth were able to undersell American producers in the American market despite the imposts established by the law of 1824. This led to a demand by wool manufacturers for greater protection. When a bill for that purpose failed in 1827, a convention of manufacturers and other interested persons, meeting at Harrisburg, Pennsylvania, that summer, declared in favor of increased duties on both wool and wool cloth. These views, presented to Congress in a memorial drafted by the famous protectionist and editor, Hezekiah Niles, opened a barrage of publicity on both sides of the tariff question that made it inevitable that some kind of a bill would be brought before the new Congress, meeting in December. For this reason the make-up of the House Committee on Manufactures was of critical import, for to it would be entrusted the task of drawing up the new schedules.[3]

Although a freshman Congressman, Wright was given a place on this panel, probably because he was known to be so friendly with Van Buren, whose attitude could not be ignored. It was certainly not Wright's own doing, for he complained when appointed that his only serious wish regarding committee posts had been a strong desire not to be on that one. Nevertheless, on it he went, bemoaning the fact that "it is always with me as it was with Tristam Shandy's father, my important points are always defeated," and once appointed, he pitched into the work fully determined to get the kind of bill he thought best.

The Committee on Manufactures had been appointed by Andrew Stevenson, of Virginia, whom the triumphant Jacksonians had elected Speaker of the House. A Southerner, he was not personally favorable to protection, and at the start Wright was suspicious of the group he picked. First of all, the

3 Taussig, *Tariff History of the United States*, p. 68 ff.

New Yorker objected to the chairman, Rollin C. Mallary, of Vermont, who although a protectionist, was a strong Adams man and a New Englander to boot, which meant that he desired mainly prohibitive duties on woolen cloth and disapproved of tariffs on raw materials. Then he was worried by the presence of William D. Martin, because that gentleman was a Southerner, subject to anti-tariff pressure from his constituents, and his vote seemed to hold the balance. Together with Michael Hoffman, Wright collared Stevenson, and aired his objections.

As to Mallary, Stevenson convinced them that prudence was the better part of valor. There had to be some Adams man in the group, and as chairman of last year's Committee he deserved a place, no matter how objectionable his views. Mollified on this point, Wright turned to Martin:

" If Martin is on the committee," he warned, " he will either ruin himself, or he cant [*i.e.* wont] do."

Stevenson " put himself astride high Southern horse " at this, and asked Wright why Martin's motives should be suspect.

" I don't suspect," the determined New Yorker replied. " I only judge that men will act as men under certain circumstances."

The Virginian then explained (as Wright told the story a few years later to James Gordon Bennett) that Martin, although a South Carolinian, was " ultra-tariff " and an opponent of Calhoun,[4] so Wright left much relieved, finally convinced that the Committee was " safe." " There is only one anti-tariff man on it," he wrote home triumphantly to his Albany friends. " I think the committee will go as far as I would myself." [5]

4 John C. Calhoun, originally a nationalistic believer in protection, had by this time assumed the leadership of the Southern free traders.

5 Wright to Flagg, Dec. 13, 1827, Flagg papers; J. G. Bennett, " Diary," June 12, 1831, New York Public Library. Actually, Martin was anti-tariff, voting against the bill on the final vote. But he was very cooperative on the committee. See speech by Mallary, *Register of Debates*, IV, 1740. Wright to Flagg, Dec. 20, 1827, Flagg papers.

Once formed, the Committee set quickly to work. After a few meetings, the members decided that they might do better if they could question witnesses, so on the last day of the year, Chairman Mallary (although he personally opposed the idea) arose in the House and asked for the unprecedented right to " send for persons and papers," that is, to subpoena witnesses and hold hearings before drafting the bill. The purpose of this was badly misunderstood by the New England delegates who thought the Committee was merely seeking to waste time. A lively debate ensued in which it was suggested that all necessary information could be uncovered through correspondence, with the main defense of the proposal falling on Wright, as leader of the Committee majority which favored it. He stressed the inadequacy of the memorials and petitions which had been presented. There was a great need, he said, for " precise detail " which could only be procured by calling persons with such data at hand and questioning them directly. He pointed out that the Harrisburg convention had recommended increasing the duties on woolen cloth, but had not submitted any specific evidence to prove that these higher rates were needed. If witnesses could be called, then concrete information would be available, and a fair bill could be written.[6]

After much discussion, the necessary powers were voted by the House, and summonses were mailed to the desired manufacturers of woolens, iron, hemp, flax, glass, cotton goods, and rum. Twenty-eight witnesses were questioned by the Committee. Over half of them were manufacturers of woolen cloth. These men were asked pointed questions. How much cloth did they produce? How much of their wool did they import? Of what quality? How had the price of wool been behaving lately? Could they get along without foreign wool? What percentage

6 *Register of Debates*, IV, 878-9. Privately Wright wrote, "the object of the Committee is not only to procure *useful specimens* of domestic manufactures, but also the *personal attendance before the Committee* of the individual practical manufacturers themselves that they may *see* and *learn* at the same time...." Mackensie, *Van Buren*, p. 202.

of their costs was represented by the raw material? And so forth. Manufacturers of other commodities were asked similar questions. From the answers to these queries, the Committee members arrived at definite proposals which they incorporated into a bill. Increases were recommended all along the line. The duty on raw hemp was increased ten dollars a ton, that on flax, nine dollars. " Spirits " were raised ten cents a gallon, and molasses five cents a gallon. Raw wool was to bear a specific charge of seven cents a pound, plus forty per cent of its value.

All these duties, of course, would be very pleasing to the farmers of the Middle states and the West, and a general increase in the tariff on all forms of iron was viewed happily by Pennsylvania and New Jersey producers of that product. But when it came to woolen cloth the bill was not so beneficent to the manufacturer. A very complicated schedule was set up which provided some protection against the foreign product, but not as much as had been recommended by the manufacturers at Harrisburg. The agricultural bent of Wright and his colleagues is clearly reflected in the explanation which they offered for the rates they set on wool and for those on woolen cloth. The Committee, ran the report, desired " to extend every protection which the nature of the case will admit to the grower of American wool; " but with woolens, it said, the aim was to arrive " at the amount of duty which will furnish full protection, and at the same time, will not go beyond that point." [7] This was the rub as far as the wool manufacturers were concerned, for they had ideas vastly different from those of the Committee on where " that point " was located, and were horrified at the thought that raw wool would receive such high protection. Here is the basic reason for the opposition in New England to this " abominable " tariff. It had been drawn up by protectionists, but what protectionists! Their attitude was well summed up by Wright when he said in a speech at Middlebury, Ver-

[7] The full report of the committee is in American State Papers, *Finance,* V, 778 ff. For the bill, see *Register of Debates,* IV, 1727.

mont, the following winter, that his basic premise had been that in America agricultural interests were paramount and should control the settlement of the tariff question.[8]

Wright had developed an increasingly positive point of view during the time the bill was being framed. When first placed on the Committee he had no definite opinions about tariffs aside from his pro-farmer predilection described above and had appealed desperately to Flagg to learn which way the wind was blowing at Albany. But after listening to some of the testimony given before the Committee he began to have ideas of his own. Protection of manufacturers, he felt, was perfectly reasonable but it must not be granted to inefficient producers who were in financial difficulties and " want Uncle Sam to help them out." Protection for the most efficient producers against European competition was sufficient. He was sure that the only difference between success and failure in business was management. " Ordinary skill and ability " was not enough; only the very best would do well, and the tariff should protect only these. He thought these ideas were substantiated by what was said at the hearings and by the information his mail brought in. Some of the more efficient manufacturers did not want protection, he told Flagg. They were far more worried by the stimulus that high duties would give to domestic competition than they were of foreign rivals. How many manufacturers felt this way, he did not say. Probably his reasoning was only rationalization, for he drew no such subtle distinction between efficient and inefficient growers of wool. But at least he was thinking seriously about the principles involved in protection, and the results of his concentration appeared on the last day of January, 1828, in what has come to be known as the Tariff of Abominations.[9]

As Chairman, Mallary presented the bill to the House, although he was himself opposed to much of it. The opposition party leaders, especially the New England Adams men, were

8 *Middlebury Standard*, quoted in *Albany Argus*, Dec. 2, 1828.

9 Wright to Flagg, Dec. 13, 1827, Jan. 16, 1828, Flagg papers.

furious when they saw how the interests of their manufacturing constituents had been subordinated.[10] They thought the woolens duties were too low, and that all the rates on raw materials were too high. Led by Mallary they immediately began proposing amendments raising the former and lowering the latter. One of these suggested changes, lowering the specific duty on raw wool from seven to four cents a pound (a minor alteration, not affecting the prohibitive nature of the duty) was accepted by the House; every other one met with defeat. The votes, however, were very curious, and provide the basis for the theory that the entire bill was a vast plot to influence the coming presidential election, for in every case the Southern Democrats voted against the amendments. With regard to those seeking to raise the woolens tariff, this was perfectly understandable, but besides voting to reject increases on woolens, they cast their ballots against downward revision of the duties on raw materials. They seemed just as zealous as their Northern colleagues in defending the bill against all change.

Why did they do this when they were opposed to all protective duties? Obviously because they thought they could thus defeat the whole bill. If the tariff was obnoxious to New England, they reasoned, it could not pass. The thing to do was to make sure that the bill was completely distasteful to the Yankee members, and then vote with them to crush it. To this extent there was a plot to defeat the tariff of 1828, but no further. It had nothing to do with the construction of the bill in the Committee, and the Northern Democrats were not parties to it.

All politicians, in the North and South, were primarily interested in their own states. This is the reason why it was so important for the Southern representatives to squelch the tariff, but it also explains why few Northern Congressmen could agree to any " plot " that would result in such a catastrophe. It is true that Jackson's campaign managers wanted to straddle

10 " When the bill came in," said Michael Hoffman, the Adams men " were brim full of wrath & cabage." Hoffman to Flagg, Feb. 3, 1828, Flagg papers.

the issue,[11] but no politician in the North would dare to do this if it meant the failure of protection. The sentiment in favor of this principle was too powerful for even the boldest of them to flout. It is important to remember that the violent conflict over the bill in the Northern states was a struggle between rival protectionists, not between advocates of high duties and free trade disciples.

The situation in New York illustrates this clearly, and explains how it was that the bill took the final shape that it did, and why it passed in that form. The bill had been constructed primarily to help the agricultural interests in the state, mainly the wool growers. But there was also in New York a large woolen industry, and a good number of the manufacturers in this business were Democrats. When they saw the bill, they were just as angry as their New England brethren, most of whom were Adams men. Benjamin Knower, for example, the father-in-law of Marcy of the Regency, owned a woolen mill, and he did not hesitate to use his influence in favor of higher duties on cloth. For a time, the members of the Regency who thought in terms of agriculture tried to discount the importance of his complaints. " Mr. K.," wrote Flagg to Wright, " is much too interested to give an opinion on the woolen's bill or anything of the kind. In truth, his politics are tied up in a sack of wool." Flagg was firm in his belief that agricultural interests should prevail. He urged Wright not to make any concessions at all, but to press the bill as it was. " If the *political spinners* of the East go against it, it will require many *long years* to extricate them from the odium. . . . I think you have them on the hip." [12]

But Knower was no isolated case, and while it was all right to have New England " on the hip," it would not do in New York. As local discord grew more vocal, the Regency became quite alarmed. Van Buren was astounded by the commotion at

11 Marquis James, *Jackson* (1 volume ed.), p. 471.
12 Flagg to Wright, Jan. 22, Apr. 13, 1828, Flagg papers.

Albany over the proposed wool and woolens duties. He had no
real personal convictions on protection and sought mainly for
harmony. When the Woolens Bill of 1827 had been defeated in
the Senate, he had been conspicuous by his absence, and a
speech on the tariff which he had made shortly afterwards at
Albany was a masterpiece of evasion. But he wanted unity at
home. He therefore wrote hurriedly to the Regency, telling
them to " play a little deeper " in affairs at Albany, and at the
same time he communicated with Knower in an effort to keep
him in line, assuring him that " a just and liberal tariff " would
be passed.[13]

Indeed the confusion throughout the state of New York became very upsetting to all the Regency politicians then at
Washington. A few, such as Michael Hoffman, who was always
impetuous, were for a strong and determined course. Hoffman
was sure the New Yorkers who fought the bill " would be
pleased to nurse the child to kiss the mother," the " mother,"
of course, being the principle of protection. But most of Hoffman's colleagues had learned the lesson of 1824 well and were
determined to let nothing interfere with their control at home.
As early as December, 1827, Wright and the other Democrats
in the New York delegation had conferred with Van Buren.
" They all feel," wrote Wright to Flagg, " that their political
interests are identified . . . with the interests of the republican
[i.e. Bucktail] party of our State; and any of us, even Mr.
V.B. would rather jeopardize the Presidential election itself,
than risk a breaking up of our ranks at home, or of destroying
our strength and harmony in the present legislature." So when
a shrewd observer like their good friend William Marcy wrote
from Albany that there would be a " difficult and doubtful conflict at the next election " unless a tariff of some kind was
passed, they certainly were in no position to allow the bill to
fail, just to help Jackson. They had enough to do reconciling

13 Van Buren, *Autobiography*, pp. 169-71; Van Buren to Butler, Jan. 13,
1828, Knower to Van Buren, Jan. 27, 1828, Van Buren papers.

the discordant elements in New York as to *what* tariff would be passed. They could not even consider the possibility of *no* tariff; that would have been political suicide. The agricultural element in the Regency, led by Wright and Flagg, wanted the tariff as reported by the Committee, but they were realists, and when in the end they had to make certain concessions to manufacturers, they did so. Those with purely political interests in the situation, typified by Van Buren, looked for a tariff that the entire state would back, and in the end they got it.[14]

The evidence which has in the past been advanced to prove that Wright and Van Buren were really trying to defeat the bill of 1828 should be examined closely, for by showing its flimsiness, the true explanation of their behavior is made even clearer. It rises mainly from two sources, the most important of which is a speech which Calhoun made in 1837, nine years later, during a debate in the Senate on another tariff. In this oration he elaborated the story of the plot, but admitted that he personally was not in on it. " I speak not of my personal knowledge," he said, but it was " generally understood." He claimed that Wright had written the bill, and that responsibility for its passage lay with " a certain individual then a Senator, but recently elected to the highest office in the Union." This " individual," of course, was Van Buren. Wright, who was then in the Senate, immediately rose to reply, and not enough attention has been given by students of the tariff to what he said. The course of the bill in the House, he admitted, was clear to all. He for one, knew exactly what the South hoped to do, and he had tried hard to " undeceive " them as to their assumption that they could make New England vote against the bill. He tacitly admitted that he had written the bill, but denied that in doing so he had intended any deception, and stated categorically that he had known nothing of any plot.

To this Calhoun retorted, " Can any man believe that Southern men would ever have voted for such a bill as the tariff of

14 Hoffman to Flagg, Feb. 3, 1828, Wright to Flagg, Dec. 20, 1827, Flagg papers; Marcy to Van Buren, Jan. 29, 1828, Van Buren papers.

1828, unless they believed that by so voting they would insure its ultimate defeat? " There was no reply to this rhetorical question but the answer is as simple as the query. First of all, the Southerners did not vote for the bill, they only voted against amendments; and then, what else could they have done, plot or no? If they had gone with New England to amend the Committee's bill, the tariff would have been at least acceptable to all protectionists and would have been passed overwhelmingly! In short, the South had no choice. It was in a decided minority on the tariff issue, and as time was to prove, the only way it could accomplish its purpose was by threatening the Union itself.[15]

Other evidence of the great conspiracy is even flimsier. It consists of statements made by members of the opposition party at the time and later. On the horns of a dilemma which offered them a choice between a tariff they did not like and no tariff at all, they sought madly for an explanation of the Southern strategy. To them, the " plot " seemed quite logical. But actually, Henry Clay, for example, who thought that the Jacksonians as a party did not want the tariff to pass, was only guessing, and so were the others.[16]

Calhoun admitted (in fact he insisted on exposing) Wright's authorship of the tariff, but if Wright had not intended to have the bill defeated, and if he had not known of any agreement to defeat it, as his own statements in 1837 and his correspondence during the time that the bill was before Congress prove, how could there have been any plot?

It is worth taking time to examine his thoughts and acts during the critical months when the issue hung in the balance. First of all, his speeches in the House are interesting. It is im-

15 Calhoun's speech is in *Register of Debates*, XIII, 904-6, Wright's reply, *ibid.*, pp. 921-2, and Calhoun's rebuttal, *ibid.*, pp. 926-7. The debate took place on Feb. 23, 1837.

16 Clay to J. Crittenden, Feb. 14, 1828, Coleman, *Life of Crittenden*, I, 87. For other statements by Adams men see Wiltse, *John C. Calhoun, Nationalist*, pp. 369-70, and his authorities.

possible to read them and still agree with the recent writer [17] who says that the tariff was not " seriously defended " by any-one. For one thing, he upheld vigorously the high duty which had been placed on coarse wool, previously on the free list. This particular item has long been seized on by the proponents of the " plot theory " because it seemed aimed only at making the bill unacceptable to the New England wool manufacturers, for no coarse wool at all was raised in the United States. Wright was not so sure that *no* very coarse wool was produced in America, but even if none was, he said, the duty was necessary because much of the " coarse " wool imported was really of a better quality and was termed coarse to evade the duty. To prove this he referred to samples of wool in the committee room which had been brought into the country at a valuation much below their real worth. By making all wool subject to protec-tion, this subterfuge could be avoided. He quoted figures to show that since the tariff of 1824, not only had wool imports increased, but the percentage of coarse wool brought in had risen. Besides, the new duty (seven cents a pound plus forty per cent of the value) placed heavier proportional burdens not only on the poorest quality of wool, but on all the lower grades. Wright admitted bluntly that where he came from, the wool raisers were small producers, could not afford to buy blooded merino stock, and could therefore only produce a common grade of wool. These men required protection, and the bill gave it to them.

Wright also defended the duties on woolen cloth which the new schedule provided. He claimed that they equalized the cost of British and American woolens production and gave the American manufacturers the margin of the Englishmen's trans-portation costs. He cited the testimony of woolens men to prove his point. " The American Manufacturer has all the protection which he swears he needs," he proclaimed. But his main point in the debate as elsewhere was protecting the agriculturalist.

17 Wiltse, *Calhoun*, p. 370.

" The farmer," he said, " must [now] go to the manufacturer for a market for his wool. I would make this obligation reciprocal. . . . Now the manufacturer has a double advantage. He can choose between the foreign and the domestic wool, while much of the foreign wool is introduced nearly free of duty." [18]

It is hard to believe that Wright spoke these words with his tongue in his cheek. He thought, and he said in the House, that the manufacturers protested against the woolens duties mainly because of the high rate on raw wool. Perhaps he was right.

His sincerity and his freedom from all connection with any " arrangement " is further borne out by his letters. Then as always, Azariah Flagg was his friend, advisor, and confidant; what Wright said to him he really meant. During March, while the tariff was before the House and under attack from the New Englanders, he was constantly *afraid* that it would be defeated. " [I fear] the Yankees will get the better of us," he wrote late in the month. He added that the great pressure of woolens manufacturers was frightening less enthusiastic members of the party. The greed of many manufacturers, including even New York Jacksonians like Knower, crying " more, more," " will exasperate the Southorns to join the Yankees. . . . "

Could these possibly be the words of a man who had agreed with these " Southorns " to defeat the tariff?

As the debate dragged on into April, the young Representative continued to worry about his bill. The continuing complaints of manufacturers within the party were especially trying. Wright was very apprehensive lest their demands alienate the Southern wing of the party. " They [the Southerners] seem willing to sustain the shape of the bill as it is," he wrote Flagg, " but frankly say if we increase their burdens by a still further increase upon the woolens, they must go with the Eastern men. . . . " New England wants to kill the bill, " but they want to make *our friends* do it." [19]

18 Taussig, *Tariff History*, pp. 91-2; Wright's major speech was given on March 6 and 10, 1828. See *Register of Debates*, IV, 1837-70.

19 Wright to Flagg, Mar. 30, 1828, April 7, 1828, Flagg papers. This is not reflected in his 1837 statement, but that was made *after* the South had

Whose plot was this, anyway? Maybe most of the Northerners of Jacksonian persuasion felt that their Southern brothers really would vote for the bill, despite their known opposition to protection. Unlikely perhaps—but possible. There is just as much ground for this kind of deductive reasoning as for that which developed the original plot theory.

Wright was plagued by more than doubt while the bill was before Congress. The woolens interests in New York, led by Knower and Jesse Buel, who had been conspicuous at the Harrisburg convention, continued pressing for higher rates. To further the cause, Knower sent one of his wool buyers, a gentleman named Wood, to Washington. It was not a happy choice. Wood had already attempted to threaten the New York delegation by writing that he had " on hand " some 70,000 pounds of wool, and held himself " uncommitted in politics " until a more favorable woolens schedule was drawn up. This blundering threat had made Wright furious. *" I have not 70,000 lbs of wool on hand,"* he wrote self-righteously, " and therefore I shall act, as I think honest and discreet, and not from any self interest, or from any non-committal in politics."

However, when Knower (unfamiliar with Wood's letter) suggested it, the buyer went to Washington to carry on the campaign. Ensconcing himself in the reading room of a popular tavern there, where all sorts and persuasions of men were congregated, he aired his position on the tariff to anyone who cared to listen. Then he sought out members of the New York delegation. Finding Wright with his messmates, Hoffman, Earll, and Garrow, he proceeded to speak his mind. Wright tried to explain the situation to him, but the more Silas said, the more Wood made it obvious that he considered himself, and himself alone, the authority on the subject of the woolens duties. He was quite frank about it.

" I told him with equal frankness," reported Wright to his Albany friends, " that he was a fool. . . . "

---

voted against the final bill. This letter was written while the Southern delegates were still backing their Northern colleagues on every amendment.

This ended the interview for the time. Shortly afterward Wright learned about the incident in the reading room from a friend who had been there. This irritated him even more, for he knew how eagerly the Adams men would seize upon the knowledge that there was dissension within their enemy's own ranks. So it was a credit to his self-control that, when he saw Wood coming to call again a few days later, he slipped inconspicuously out of his lodgings to avoid talking to him.

Wood, however, was not to be denied, and when Wright returned, he was still there waiting. Before Silas could open his mouth, Wood began to berate him again about his " responsibility " toward his constituents. This was too much. " My powder burned quick," Wright explained later, " and for about half an hour I labored upon the *little man* in my sauciest language. He became mild and I became cool from ventilation." [20]

The whole affair passed off happily enough. Wood grew more reasonable, even acted as the messenger boy for the letter which explained the whole story to the Regency, and Knower hastened to write Van Buren that it was all a horrible mistake and that he was firm in his party loyalty. Wright was soon reporting elatedly that his strong course was keeping the " dough faces " in line, and urging that his Albany friends " strongly recommend . . . the passage of the bill in its present shape." Michael Hoffman offered the same advice.[21]

Thus the discord within the New York party was quieted. In Washington the bill passed the House despite the resistance of the South and 23 of the 39 New England representatives, and was sent to the Senate. There an identical situation developed, the South voting against all the amendments which the irate New England Senators proposed. But conditions in the Senate were different, for with all the states represented

20 Wright to Flagg, Apr. 7, 1828, Wright to Flagg and James Porter, Apr. 13, 1828, Flagg papers.

21 Knower to Van Buren, Apr. 23, 1828, Van Buren papers; Wright to Flagg, Apr. 22, 1828, Hoffman to Flagg, Apr. 28, 1828, Flagg papers.

equally, a coalition of the Southern Democrats and Northeastern supporters of President Adams would control a majority. Here Van Buren stepped into the picture. Unhampered by tariff principles, he accepted proposed increases in the woolens duties that made the bill more palatable to New England. He was joined by another Democratic Senator, Levi Woodbury, who came, significantly, from New Hampshire, and the change squeaked through the Senate by the margin of their two votes. This was enough. More than half (6 of 11) of the New England Senators voted for the modified bill and it passed comfortably. The House accepted the change without delay.

So the much maligned tariff of 1828 became law. Despite the furor, there was very little hostility to it outside of the South, where by this time all protection was anathema. The following December, when a resolution for its repeal was offered in the House of Representatives, it was rejected by a huge majority. When the general level was finally lowered a little in 1832, it was largely because of Southern pressure. Henry Clay and many other protectionists wished to retain the very law they had called " abominable " four years earlier.[22] But at that time Wright was not in Congress. In later years, his attitude toward tariffs underwent a significant change, but in 1828 he had the satisfaction of writing a bill which he felt would be for the economic benefit of his constituents, and seeing it pass almost intact.

* * * * *

Aside from the tariff, little occurred during the first session of the Twentieth Congress that was of any importance. Wright carried on the crusade against public aid in the construction of canals, but was a firm supporter of federal development of harbor facilities, and if he was influenced in this last by the fact that the harbors involved were in the state of New York— well, everyone did that sort of thing then, just as now.[23]

22 Taussig, *Tariff History*, pp. 99-103.

23 *Register of Debates*, IV, 2670-2, 2576.

He was very busy with the mechanics of his job. When not actually on the floor of the House, he told his young brother Pliny, he spent most of his time writing letters. But then Pliny was young and impressionable; it certainly would not do to distract him from his studies with tales of the convivial society which Silas unquestionably loved. Even so, there was a strong element of truth in what he did say. Congressmen in those days had no secretaries, and letter writing was the only means of communication other than personal conversation. Even for a new member the burden must have been very great. Wright wrote religiously to Flagg and to other members of the Regency at Albany, and of course his correspondence with his St. Lawrence friends had to be maintained as well. Outside New York his acquaintance was limited; probably he still had few letters to write to these " foreigners," but as time went on, as friendships were made, as he became better known throughout the nation, this burden also increased.

But as he sat at his desk, pouring over his mail, maneuvering for appointments and political plums, passing on the latest news and the most recent rumors, he was also thinking, and he was beginning to learn a few things about the United States of America. In New York, he saw everything in terms of the Regency. He *knew* that these men were, as he put it, " sound." They were honest; they did not cheat; they sincerely desired to help the common man; they fought against the forces of exploitation and corruption. So what did it matter how they achieved their ends? You had to fight fire with fire. The opposition was unprincipled, and had many potent weapons—money, influence, and all sorts of tempting schemes to lure staunch friends of the people into the paths of corruption and self-interest. So there was nothing wrong in voting against the electoral law, or in removing a canal commissioner. The end was what counted; the means were only incidental. And when the good fight had been fought, the victorious warriors were certainly entitled to " the spoils." After all, they would not misuse them. For those that did, for the corruptionist, the Regency had contempt and swift retribution. But any honest man could do most of the simple tasks involved in the job of government, and the only way to be sure you had an honest one was to pick someone you knew, or someone recommended by a " sound " friend of yours.

Washington, however, was different. It was not so easy to " distinguish between the pretender and the real friend " as it had been back at Albany. Wright began to think twice about " the political turmoil " which at home could have only one meaning. And the stakes were so much larger! Perhaps it was not as clever as it had once sounded to say, " Love the State and let the nation save itself." He began to think of something pretty big, so big that he could only call it what everyone else did, " the institutions of our Country." He was beginning to see, he wrote to brother Pliny, " the full extent to which these institutions depend upon the popular will, and . . . the necessity which exists that the body of the Community should be well informed, in order that they may distinguish between the pretender and the real friend of these institutions." [24]

Perhaps this is reading too much into his words. Perhaps he was feeling paternal and pontifical toward a college youth who he knew thought very highly of him. Certainly his attitude toward New York affairs did not change. Probably he had these thoughts, and then swept them from his mind and got down to the business of being a politician again. A man *had* to be practical or he would get nowhere, and what was worse, people would only laugh. Those were the sort of things to save for speeches on the Fourth, or just before election.

But he never used them on such occasions. Flowery oratory was not his way. He just plugged away at being a politician, enjoying the schemes and the spoils as well, taking what was his, and getting for his friends whatever he could. Somehow, the people who knew him all understood.

*   *   *   *   *

24 Wright to P. Wright, Feb. 15, 1828, Wright papers, St. Lawrence University.

With the tariff out of the way, all eyes turned toward November and the approaching election. Actually politicians of all persuasions had never had it far from their minds. Everyone wished to avoid the confusion of the previous contest, and the more sagacious leaders saw clearly that the way to do this was to stress party rather than personality. Still, any group with a candidate like Andrew Jackson could not fail to take advantage of his colorful background and wide renown. Van Buren stated the formula as early as January, 1827, when he wrote to Thomas Ritchie, of Virginia: " I have long been satisfied that we can only . . . restore a better state of things, by combining Genl. Jackson's personal popularity with the portion of old party feeling yet remaining." This was not easy to do. Political organizations were still essentially local; sectional questions were dominant; " personalities " with large groups of loyal followers could not be pressed into a simple two-party pattern. In the New York environment which attracted Silas Wright's main interest, all these centrifugal forces were at work. Strong as was his personal influence in his own North Country, he was still looked on by many of his supporters as an individual, and his party ties were of limited import. That he could swing many votes to Jackson while a New Englander was running against the Old Hero was questionable. " Our whole population are New England people and the rational prejudices are that way," he had to admit.[25]

The New York situation was also complicated at this time by the Anti-Masonic movement, which rose out of the disappearance of a man named William Morgan, who had dared to expose some of the secrets of the Order. It cut clearly across party lines, for it made membership or non-membership in the Masonic brotherhood a criterion in determining a man's vote, and there were members of the cult in both camps. Many politicians, especially non-Jacksonians (Jackson was a Mason)

25 Van Buren to Ritchie, Jan. 13, 1827, Washington, Van Buren papers; Wright to Flagg, Aug. 29, 1827, Flagg papers.

tried to profit by the enthusiasm which the Anti-Masonic crusaders had been able to generate, but they were never really successful, for they usually lost as many followers as they gained when they took a strong stand on this issue.

Then there was the persistent problem of Governor De Witt Clinton. He refused to stay put at all. Probably he thought he could some day be President himself, but whatever his reasoning, he was a Jackson man! This placed him in the same camp as the Regency! Yet his whole program in New York had been antithetical to everything the Regency stood for, and many old Bucktails thought twice about supporting any presidential candidate that the hated Magnus favored.

The Democrats (as the Bucktails were now calling themselves) sought to pick their way amid all these conflicting forces. With Anti-Masonry they tried to have as little to do as possible, attacking the movement as a divergency, but saying nothing in favor of the Order. For example, when some of his friends suggested Wright for the post of public prosecutor to investigate the disappearance of Morgan, he shied away from the job hastily. But when the supposed kidnappers of Morgan were sentenced by Judge Enos Throop, the Regency did not fail to seize the advantage thus offered; they nominated the Judge for Lieutenant Governor in hope of attracting Anti-Masonic support.[26]

Even without these vexing difficulties, it was no simple matter to develop a cohesive body of Jackson supporters in New York. Wright himself hesitated for quite some time. His main desire was that his good friend Van Buren should some day reach the coveted presidential spot, but he knew that the time was not yet ripe. Whoever was picked, Wright felt, must be a supporter of "the true principles of Jefferson and Madison." The Canton Congressman admitted to "an exalted opinion of the worth of Genl. Jackson as a soldier" but he was not so sure

---

[26] Wright to Flagg, Mar. 30, 1828, Flagg papers; Fox, *Decline of Aristocracy*, p. 548.

about his politics. Still Jackson kept better company than did Adams, whose handling of the New York patronage had antagonized the Regency leaders. So Silas finally concluded that the General was the best choice that could be made. Wright wanted New York to nominate him quickly. From Washington, when he was just getting involved in the tariff fight, he urged that a legislative caucus be held for that purpose on January 8, the anniversary of the battle of New Orleans. Hoffman also suggested this time for the choice. Their urging sprang from a desire to get the jump on the opposition, to put the name of the popular Jackson before the people officially, and to prevent an alliance of the forces of " Banks, Canals, State Roads and Rail Roads, Tunnels, Ditches, etc., etc." The name of the Old Hero would " strengthen the feeble knees of our doubtful friends," said Wright, and Hoffman feared that if the Regency forces did not put Jackson forward, the Clinton men might do so and get all the credit.[27]

Although the Magnus now professed a firm Jacksonism, the Regency men were not able to bring themselves to trust Clinton. Marcy, listing the problems before the Regency in January, 1828, gave a prominent place to " those who have joined us," and Hoffman, in the same breath in which he spoke of the Clinton-Jackson alliance, also suggested the possibility that the Father of the Canal might " unite as in 1824 federalists Clintonians Adams men Claymen and every species of Quid against the Democracy of N. Y." But fate intervened. In February, without any warning illness, Clinton suddenly died. Immediately the atmosphere was cleared. Van Buren delivered a touching and probably sincere oration in his memory, but there was no concealing the relief which the Little Magician's cohorts experienced. When Wright heard the news he wrote to Marcy that " many a strong man's scruples " would now be satisfied, and that all true Democrats could now unite behind Jackson. No longer would they be thus associating themselves with the

---

27 Wright to Flagg, Dec. 20, 1827, Hoffman to Flagg, Dec. 27, 1827, Flagg papers.

man whose name epitomized a "large" improvement policy and unrestricted banking. This was the time, he suggested, for a purification of the party. Out with all old style Federalists who had entered the party of democracy "cloaked . . . under Mr. Clinton's banner." However, penitents who wished to return to the fold should be extended "every kindness not inconsistent with full justice to those who have always remained faithful." [28]

In the meantime, the problem of the nomination had been solved and Jackson chosen by the Democratic members of the New York legislature, though not on the anniversary of his great victory.[29] By March the campaign had progressed quite far, though the state convention had not yet been held. The death of Clinton, by strengthening the solidarity of the Democrats, had done the same thing for their opponents, and a mighty struggle was making up all over the state. "We are informed from all quarters that the country [*i. e.* New York] is filled with electioneering papers in favor of the administration," wrote Marcy to Gulian C. Verplanck. "Wright's district is literally filled. . . . It is certain that the [Adams] men are directing all their efforts seconded with lavish employment of means to carry that district [and] Montgomery, Otsego, Tompkins & Tioga. . . ." The Regency could not let this challenge pass unnoticed, and soon these counties and the entire state must have been really filled (or better perhaps, littered) with campaign literature. Wright, of course, was at Washington and could not do very much to help until after Congress adjourned. Then he took an active part in the struggle. By August he felt that there was some chance in his district for the Jackson ticket,

28 Marcy to Van Buren, Jan. 29, 1828, Van Buren papers; Hoffman to Flagg, Dec. 27, 1827, Flagg papers; On Van Buren's speech, see Hammond, *History of New York*, pp. 267-8; Wright to Marcy, Feb. 18, 1828, Flagg papers.

29 Hammond, *History of New York*, II, 281. Van Buren had wanted the nomination to be made by a national convention for many reasons, not the least of which was the desire to keep Jackson in line by making him feel that this nomination was the result of party action not personal prestige. See Van Buren to Ritchie, Jan. 13, 1827, Van Buren papers.

including himself, for he was running for re-election to the House. On the twelfth of the month the St. Lawrence Democrats held a ' monster ' meeting which all of five hundred people attended. Wright found himself very busy. Flagg wanted him to prepare an address to the state convention which was to be held at Herkimer in September, but he begged off because of the press of local affairs. He did, however, attend the convention as a delegate, and was doubtless pleased when Van Buren was nominated for Governor without any difficulty.[30]

The election in November was much too close for comfort. Jackson carried the state by only 5,000 votes, and Van Buren, running against an Anti-Mason as well as a regular Adams candidate, polled less than half the votes although he won handily. St. Lawrence County, despite Wright's late-summer hopes, fulfilled his earlier predictions, and went for the Adams candidates all down the line.[31] The only exception was Wright himself, who was re-elected to the House of Representatives by a scant forty-five votes. Even that was disputed, for a few of his supporters had failed to include the " Junior " after his name, and their ballots were challenged.[32]

The Regency had won by a small margin indeed. " It seemed as if old 98 Federalism had risen from the dead," said the newly elected Governor. " Men of that school who have not been seen at the polls for years and several whom were supposed to be dead for years were in the hottest of the fight." [33] It was probably with heartfelt relief that Wright turned away from the election and headed back to Washington for the December session of Congress.

30 Marcy to Verplanck, Mar. 9, 1828, Verplanck papers, New York Historical Society; Wright to Flagg, Aug. 17, 29, 1828, Flagg papers.

31 A coalition of Adams men and the Anti-Masons was probably the reason. See Hammond, *Wright*, p. 111.

32 *Albany Argus*, Nov. 18, Dec. 13, 1828. The House, being Democratic, upheld Wright's claim.

33 Van Buren to Cambreleng, Nov. 7, 1828, Van Buren papers.

CHAPTER IV
SWAMPS, BUREAUS, DIPLOMATS, AND PATCHED TROUSERS

"The Regency at Albany have certainly some good points."

James Gordon Bennett's diary, July 28, 1831.

ON his way from Canton to Washington, Wright crossed into Vermont for a short visit with his parents. While renewing old friendships at Weybridge, he was tendered a dinner by local Democrats at nearby Middlebury. He attended with his father, who, although growing old, was still active in Vermont politics. It was a convivial affair with a multitude of toasts, and the younger Silas made a speech in which he vigorously defended his action on the tariff, stated emphatically that the newly elected President was a stout protectionist, and generally did his best to solidify party feeling.[1] Then he hurried on in order to arrive at the Capital in time for the opening of the second session of the Twentieth meeting of the Congress. But once there he found little time for legislative affairs; other business intervened.

First of all, he was concerned about Van Buren and the new administration of which the "Red Fox" was certain to be a part. It was generally assumed that the newly elected Governor of New York would be given whatever Cabinet position he desired. Wright's advice (and Van Buren's eventual choice) was to take the State Department. The Treasury, he opined, offered more valuable "internal patronage," and this he admitted Van Buren was "eminently qualified to distribute," but the first place in the Cabinet had greater prestige value.[2]

This speculation had little to do with his own prospects which were quite uncertain at the moment. Recent successes were proving profitable to loyal members of the Regency. Van Buren's seat in the Senate was now vacant and Comptroller

1 *Middlebury Standard*, quoted in *Albany Argus*, Dec. 2, 1828.
2 Wright to Van Buren, Dec. 9, 1828, Van Buren papers.

Marcy had been appointed to the State Supreme Court. This left two important posts unfilled, and Wright had been mentioned for both. Van Buren wanted him to get the senatorship and was urging this at Albany even in November, but the feeling at the State Capital was that he was more needed there. In the beginning, Wright would have been pleased to accept either position, provided that his friends were agreed that he was the proper man, but since November another factor had to be considered. He had just been reelected to the House, and this by the closest of margins against a general sweep of the district by the opposition. If he were to accept any other office, it would mean a new election with little prospect of the Democrats winning. To many people in the North Country this was very important, and Wright knew it and was very concerned. So he tried to discourage his friends from pressing his claims. To both Flagg and Van Buren he wrote urging that Jonas Earll be given the comptrollership because his seat in Congress could be more safely abandoned and because he had a large family to support. He even suggested that Flagg himself take the job. He also begged off the Senate seat, saying that his financial status would not allow him to live up to so lofty a post, and that he feared being a " political pauper." But he did not categorically refuse to accept either office. At the request of the Albany politicians Van Buren agreed not to press Silas' name for the vacant place at Washington, and late in January, the legislature appointed him Comptroller.[3] Wright accepted the situation philosophically, no doubt glad to have the higher salary which was paid the Comptroller and happy to resume Albany life. He left Washington early in February, and after a difficult trip over very heavy roads, reached his old stamping grounds on the tenth of the month.[4]

Having weathered the hard-fought battle of 1828, the Regency was entering upon the era of its greatest ascendancy, a

3 Van Buren to Butler, Nov. 17, 1828, Wright to Van Buren, Dec. 7, 1828, Van Buren papers; Wright to Flagg, Dec. 3, 19, 28, 1828, Flagg papers.

4 Wright to Flagg, Feb. 7, 1829, Flagg papers; *Argus*, Feb. 11, 1829.

period of domination that was to remain unbroken for ten years. Their popular principles, their solid organization, and the rising wave of Jacksonian Democracy on which they rode, were far too much for the opposition. But above all, they exhibited an *esprit de corps* that was of inestimable value.

" The Regency at Albany have certainly some good points—," James Gordon Bennett conceded admiringly to his diary. " They pick up young men and if they serve them faithfully they are well rewarded . . . they are true to their friends—they associate together—their families interchange civilities, their females kiss each other when they meet—their men shake each other heartily by the hand—they dine, or drink, or pray, or take snuff . . . with and in each other's company. . . . " Indeed, the Regency dominated Albany society. Once winter set in and the freezing of the Hudson put an end to easy communication with New York, everyone at Albany, great and small alike, was forced to bring his " desires, wishes and thoughts, within the limits of this ancient town." Each member of the Regency called formally at least once during the legislative session, on every member of the Assembly and Senate. All of these calls had to be returned, and a nucleus of social life was thus established. Then there were official dinner parties given by the Governor for the legislators. Every third day the Chief Executive invited a few of them to dine, choosing the names from an alphabetical list. Combined with more informal gatherings, these parties gave to life at the Capital an air of conviviality which made existence pleasant for all the politicians residing there.[5]

Into this environment, the new Comptroller entered with great gusto. His job, however, took up most of his time. " I find the duties of this office complicated and very pressing," he told a local friend, and this was no understatement. In addition to his responsibilities as the chief financial officer of the state, the Comptroller also sat on the canal board, an administrative body of great significance in the state that owned the Big

5 J. Bennett, " Diary," New York Public Library, July 28, 1831 ; Seward, *Autobiography*, pp. 166, 174, 176.

Ditch, and many other special committees. His office had to prepare for sale the deeds of all lands seized for back taxes, make an annual report on the condition of the state's finances, and provide the legislature with every imaginable sort of information about banks, insurance companies and other chartered corporations. Then there were special investigations whenever someone skipped off with the funds of any branch of the government, a frequent occurrence. As Wright put it, " the calls are so numerous, varied, and constant, as to require my utmost time and exertion to find what my duty is." [6]

To handle all these tasks, Wright had a staff of thirteen clerks, but most of the work of preparing the reports which were submitted to the legislature was his own responsibility. Of greatest importance was the annual report on the financial condition of the state, which was presented in January. The income of the state was derived mainly from two sources, land sales and canal tolls. There was also income from several special funds: one for the schools, another for the State Library, and a General Fund, a collection of assets the interest on which was supposed to pay the normal expenses of administration. But this was not what was happening when Wright became Comptroller. The government was annually operating at a considerable deficit. Though the Erie canal was fabulously profitable, its tolls had to be turned over to the canal fund to pay the great debt which its construction had entailed. The result was that the deficit, which had existed every year since 1826, had to be made up out of the capital of the General Fund, a shortsighted policy that any responsible official was bound to criticize and try to remedy. In his first report, in January, 1830, Wright recommended the establishment of a small state property tax, similar to one which had been in force for a decade before 1826. He submitted a mass of evidence to show how quickly the General Fund was disappearing and how easily a

6 Wright to C. Dayan, Apr. 17, 1829, Wright papers, New York State Library; Hammond, *Wright*, pp. 113-6; New York Senate and Assembly, *Documents*, 1830-3, *passim*.

small tax would solve the problem, but nothing was done about it, and when he made his last annual report in 1833, he was still recommending " a tax upon all the citizens and all the property of the State for the support of the government " and having to admit that doing so was " a thankless duty." [7]

Most of the work involved was mere routine, but occasionally something came up that could upset the orderly flow of business. Such an event was the affair of the Cayuga Marshes. In order to improve the navigability of the Seneca River, the state had authorized the drainage of a swampy area near Auburn, and the deepening of the river's channel. This work had been let out on contract, and three commissioners had been appointed to supervise the job and award the contracts. These commissioners were not, however, employed on a full-time basis, but were supposed to devote whatever time was necessary to the work and to charge the state two dollars a day for their services. The work had been going on over a period of years and was almost complete when, in the fall of 1829, a group of citizens from the town of Mentz, in Cayuga County, petitioned the legislature to look into certain irregularities in the commissioners' expenses. This task was referred to Wright's department. A summary investigation and a few letters of inquiry revealed that something was certainly amiss. John Buck, one of the commissioners, had issued several receipts to one of the contractors on the job, for which no work had been done, but which had nevertheless been promptly cashed. About $2,500 was involved. Wright submitted this information to the legislature and a full investigation was ordered with the Comptroller as chief inquisitor.[8]

This was in April, 1830, but Wright was so busy preparing for a big sale of lands seized for unpaid taxes that he could do little until the summer. Late in June subpoenas were issued, and early the next month he set out for Auburn. It was really

7 New York State Assembly, *Documents*, 1830, # 48; 1833,# 5.
8 *Ibid.*, 1830, # 178.

great fun. He travelled west with Azariah Flagg and several
other friends who were going that way, and was able to remind
them later, " I have never enjoyed a journey in my life as I
did ours from Albany." Soon he was " dipping into the Cayuga
marshes." First he made a brief tour of the area where the
work had been done, and then, on the twelfth of the month, he
began the interrogation of witnesses. Characteristically he did
all the work himself; he even refrained from hiring a clerk to
take down the testimony. After questioning a witness, he wrote
out a statement for him to read over and then sign. This procedure was not completed until late July.

While it was in progress the opposition press was making
merry.

> Fam'd *Silas Wright*, a first rate scout,
> Is off to " drain " thy marshy route . . . .

So wrote " Old Schoharie," the favorite poet of Thurlow
Weed's new paper, the *Albany Evening Journal,* and Weed
himself made frequent comments on the scandal.[9] The subject,
however, was completely ignored by the *Argus.*

The report which Wright submitted to the legislature, when
it met the following January, was a masterpiece of detail. The
"mistakes" which he was able to discover varied from one of
fifty-two cents to one of well over three thousand dollars, and
it was clear that the whole job had been fearfully mismanaged.
Besides the obvious frauds, Wright discovered that one of the
commissioners was still drawing his two dollars a day on
practically a full-time basis, nearly six months after the entire
project had been completed, early in 1830! It was all very, very
embarrassing for the Regency and the whole party, but it is to
their credit that they did not try to cover up the situation.
Wright's report was a frank denunciation of the whole system
under which the improvements had been undertaken.[10]

9 Wright to Flagg, July 26, 1830, Flagg papers; *Albany Evening Journal,*
July 28, Aug. 16, Sept. 11, 1830.

10 New York State Assembly, *Documents,* 1831, # 70.

It was while he was engaged in the multitudinous duties of his office that a note of personal tragedy entered his life. Pliny Wright had always been his favorite brother. Ten years younger than Silas, Pliny looked up to him and sought to follow in his footsteps. The boy had gone to college, and wanted to become a lawyer. When the new Comptroller arrived at Albany in 1829, he had arranged for his brother to serve his clerkship there, and had undertaken to pay part of his expenses. Pliny was overjoyed. He came to Albany and began his studies. All seemed well when suddenly, the following winter, he suffered a mental breakdown. It was a bitter blow to Silas, who looked upon him almost as a son and had high hopes for him. The boy was sent to the quiet atmosphere of Canton, but by May he had shown no improvement and Wright was very depressed. "On his account," he wrote to a friend at Canton, " I have experienced feelings and anxieties, during the last five months, of which I have never before known anything. . . . Room to hope is hardly left. . . . " [11]

However, Pliny improved soon after this and was able to resume his studies at Canton, although he could do very little. Wright was able to write encouragingly to his parents in midsummer, 1831. But the gain was only temporary, and after visiting with him in October of that year, Silas realized that there was little hope for permanent recovery. He felt the tragedy deeply. " I dare not trust myself," he wrote bitterly, " further than to say that if our benevolent and wise Creator delights in exhibitions of passion of any kind in His creatures. I have been mistaken in all my views of that Glorious Being. . . ."

Wright continued to care for his brother until his own death. Part of the time Pliny was kept in an asylum at Utica, but he was never dangerous and nearly always seemed happy. He lived at Canton until his death in 1890, a curious figure in old-

11 P. Wright to his parents, Mar. 6, 1829, Wright papers, St. Lawrence University; Wright to Jenison, May 24, 1830, Gillet, *Wright*, I, 140-1.

fashioned clothes, and is still remembered by the older residents there.[12]

*   *   *   *   *

Enos Throop, it will be remembered, was the new Governor of New York. He was a sincere and well-meaning person but his abilities were limited and he was far from facile with the pen. Many of his messages were very poor, leading to criticism and even ridicule. Suspecting his limitations, some of the members of the party had been hesitant to accept him as Van Buren's running mate. But they had taken him and had been agreeably surprised by his steady if not spectacular performance of his duties.[13] He was therefore renominated in 1830. The opposition party had now become the Anti-Mason group, and Francis Granger, Thurlow Weed's friend, had been named as their gubernatorial choice. But as usual, the situation was very complicated.[14] Conservatives from the eastern part of the state had little sympathy with the wild proponents of the " blessed spirit " of Anti-Masonry and were attracted to the Democratic ranks, while the newly formed Workingmen's party in New York City, drafted mainly from the ranks of the Jacksonians, was subject to all sorts of inducements by the Anti-Masonic politicians. The Regency had nothing for the " Workies," as they were called, but fear and contempt! Wright, for example, could only see the fanatical aspects of their program. He feared the land distribution schemes of Thomas Skidmore, the radical social ideas of Fanny Wright, and the educational program of Robert Dale Owen, and failed

12 Wright to Jenison, Dec. 15, 1830, Oct. 4, 1831, Gillet, *Wright*, I, 152; Wright to his parents, Aug. 24, 1831, Wright papers, St. Lawrence University; Interview with Richard C. Ellsworth, Canton, New York, July, 1946.

13 Hammond, *History of New York*, II, 308, 415; Flagg to Van Buren, May 6, 1829, Van Buren papers.

14 H. N. Cruger, a Southern friend of James Fenimore Cooper, characterized conditions felicitously when he wrote the novelist, after visiting New York during the autumn, " the politics of the State were a piece of mosaic." Cruger to Cooper, Nov. 22, 1830, *Correspondence of James Fenimore Cooper*, J. F. Cooper, ed., p. 197.

to see that the basic elements of the party were ordinary working men with no such bizarre aims. Wright was particularly incensed by the demand for what he called " republican equality " in education. He saw in it not universal free training for all but an attack on familial organization. They wanted laws, he explained excitedly to a Canton friend, " providing that all children, from infancy to maturity, shall be boarded, clothed, lodged and educated at the public expense, and that every child shall have just such board, just such clothing, just such lodging and just as much education as every other, and no more." He and most of his friends looked on the movement as " one of the most desperate devices of the old enemy " and when they saw their opponents currying the " Workies' " favor, they were only confirmed in their belief. As Governor Throop put it, " The opposition assumes a variety of shapes in the hope of breaking up our organization. . . . " [15]

To this confused situation was added the peculiar genius of Thurlow Weed, whose new paper, the *Journal,* was already the leading organ of the anti-Regency forces. Weed had been brought to Albany from Rochester where he had edited a sheet called the *Anti-Masonic Enquirer,* and he was quick to prove to the citizens of the Capital that he knew his business. He was a master of the arts of name-calling and aspersion-casting. The various members of the Regency (and he named them) were scheming politicians paltering with the " hallowed institutions " which had been established by the founding fathers, and they had " cold and heartless contempt for the great and paramount concerns of the country." He was particularly adept at holding his opponents up to ridicule. " Miss " Croswell was his particular target; " Prince Polignac " Flagg, and " Fouche " Wright [16] drew their share of his darts as well. Wright, for instance, was

15 Wright to Jenison, May 24, 1830, Gillet, *Wright,* I, 141, Van Deusen, *Weed,* pp. 56-7; Throop to Van Buren, Dec. 31, 1830, Van Buren papers.

16 After Joseph Fouche, 1759-1820, a Jacobin and Terrorist whose policy was one of expediency.

brought to task for the scandal of the Cayuga Marshes, on which he had not at that time submitted his report.[17]

But the highlight of Weed's attack, and of the whole campaign, came on October 23, when he gave over a good portion of his columns to the publication of a letter drawing aside " the curtain which has so long concealed the deformities and abominations of the Albany Regency." This epistle was from the pen of none other than Comptroller Silas Wright, Jr., and had been written four years earlier to Van Buren. It was long and involved, dealing with the politics of that day, but its publication was distressing to the Democrats for two reasons. First of all, in discussing possible Regency candidates for the governship in 1826, Wright had been embarrassingly frank in his opinions of the various prospects and their talents. This was particularly true of Judge Sanford, an important figure in the state, of whom Wright had spoken very disparagingly. Naturally there was a good chance that the Judge and his friends would be offended and that the result would be schism in the ranks of the Democrats. Of more importance, however, was one unhappy phrase in which Wright had spoken of " bringing off the spoils." This was indeed grist for Weed's mill.

Upon the publication of this letter, Wright wrote quickly to Van Buren, sending him a copy of the paper, and telling him the story in detail. The letter had supposedly been " found " in an old bureau which Van Buren had sold when he left Albany to enter Jackson's cabinet, and published by the " dishonorable individuals " who had made the purchase. The Secretary of State hastened to reply. His letter was full of his " astonishment," " indignation," and " regrets," but he assured Wright that there was not a particle of truth in the bureau story. Although he could not even remember the letter, he was sure that it had been stolen directly from his papers. It just showed, he wrote sanctimoniously, " to what a miserable & degraded state Society . . . has been reduced . . . when a reprobate like Weed,

17 *Evening Journal*, Oct. 23, 25, 29, 1830.

can with safety outrage the moral sense of the community, by publishing to the world that he has in his possession, a private letter ... which has confessedly been obtained, by an act of moral if not legal felony." [18]

The complete story of the letter will probably never be known. Judge Hammond, the historian, knew as much about it as anyone who has ever set down his information, and he was distressingly vague and even contradictory in his statements. As nearly as can now be made out, it was brought to Hammond a few days before its publication by John Van Ness Yates (a relative of the former Governor) and another man whom Hammond would never name. The Judge read the letter, saw its implications at once, and according to his story, urged that it be returned to Wright for obvious reasons of honor and because the man who had obtained it was " as it were a member of the Comptroller's family. ... " He kept it himself, intending to return it to Wright, and Yates and the mysterious stranger left. But a few minutes later, again according to Hammond, the unnamed man came back with Thurlow Weed and demanded its return. Feeling that he had to comply, Hammond surrendered the missive, and Weed then published it.[19]

At any rate, the letter was out and adding fuel to the political fires. Luckily, Judge Sanford was too much the politician to be offended. He called on Wright and assured him that he understood Weed's object and that there would be no " heartburnings " as far as he was himself concerned. So with the first shock weathered, the Regency leaders were not overly worried about the letter's effect on the election, though Weed tried to make his readers believe that " Miss Croswell cannot even hold a pen " and that " the *mind* of Wright since the publication of

18 *Ibid.*, Oct. 23, 1830. The text of the letter may be found in Weed, *Autobiography*, as well, pp. 376-8. Wright to Van Buren, Oct. 28, 1830, Van Buren to Wright, Nov. 7, 1830, Van Buren papers.

19 Hammond to A. McIntyre, Dec. 10, 1833, Van Buren papers; for a later, slightly different version by Hammond, see his *Wright*, pp. 83-4 and note.

his letter, is as ' *dry as the remainder biscuit after a long voyage.*' " [20] The confidence of the Regency was justified, for the party carried the election easily. The result demonstrated the weakness of Anti-Masonry when made a major issue, for while Granger carried the " infected " districts by a huge majority, he did very badly in the eastern strongholds of conservatism, where many normally anti-Regency men preferred Throop to fanaticism.[21]

The victory, however, merely led to further problems. The election of 1832 was approaching and to the Regency this meant above all else a chance to advance the fortunes of their affable leader, Martin Van Buren. The " Red Fox " was at this time Jackson's Secretary of State, and every loyal New Yorker hoped that he would be his successor as well. It was therefore a serious shock to his Albany cohorts when Van Buren informed them early in April, 1831, that he was resigning from the Cabinet.[22]

Despite the Regency's surprise, this was an extremely sensible move. The President's official family had become hopelessly divided, ostensibly over the petty question of Secretary of War Eaton's beautiful but socially unacceptable wife, Peggy, really over the far more serious issue of the old and seemingly feeble President's successor. Most of the Cabinet favored Calhoun, who was then Vice-President, but Van Buren rated high in the Old Hero's estimation, and the resignation, followed by his appointment as Minister to England, was merely an excuse for Jackson to form an entirely new cabinet and for " Little Van " to slip quietly away from the heat of the battle and let nature take its course.

20 Wright to Van Buren, Oct. 28, 1830, Van Buren papers; *Evening Journal*, Oct. 30, 1830.

21 Hammond, *History of New York*, II, 336; Fox, *Decline of Aristocracy*, p. 361. Weed had recognized this all along and was willing to admit it in his paper after the election. See Van Deusen, *Weed*, pp. 56-7 and *Evening Journal*, Nov. 10, 1830.

22 Van Buren to Butler, Apr. 6, 1831, Van Buren papers.

But when Benjamin Butler, to whom Van Buren's letter announcing the resignation had been addressed, broke the news to Wright, Flagg, Marcy, Croswell and a few others, they were all amazed—until they understood the Little Magician's purpose. Then everything was clear. As they discussed matters among themselves, they came to realize that it was just as well for their leader to be removed from the immediate scene for a while and that the advantage of the Cabinet revision, eliminating the anti-Van Buren elements, was very great.[23]

So the Little Magician left for England, where his necromancy proved to be both popular and successful. But back in Washington, other presidential hopefuls of both parties—Clay, Webster, and above all, Calhoun—were incensed by the clever way in which he had maneuvered matters and they sought some method of checking his good fortune. The plan upon which they hit was a vindictive one. Van Buren was a recess appointment; when the Congress reconvened in December, 1831, his name would have to come before the Senate for confirmation. Here, his enemies thought, was the perfect opportunity to smash forever his political pretensions. There was no real excuse for failing to approve his nomination, but it was not hard to manufacture any number of reasons, and as Senator Thomas Hart Benton once said, " Oh Politics! how much bamboozling is practiced in thy name! "[24] So when Van Buren's name came up, after a series of obviously political speeches, his appointment was disallowed in a carefully contrived tie vote which enabled Calhoun, as Vice-President, personally to cast the deciding ballot against him. This was late in January, 1832.

Looking back, it is almost impossible to understand how the plotters could have been as blind to the consequences of their action as they assuredly were. Certainly most of their contemporaries saw that the combination against the suave New Yorker could only bring to him the sympathy of martyrdom. Nearly two months before his repudiation, when rumors of its

---

23 Butler to Van Buren, Apr. 22, 1831, Van Buren papers.

24 T. Benton, *Thirty Years View*, I, 215.

likelihood reached Albany, Thurlow Weed proclaimed against it. It would be an act of " irreparable mischief," he wrote in the *Journal*. " Nothing could be more gratifying to Van Buren than his rejection by the Senate. It would change the complexion of his prospects from despair to hope. . . . " The only result would be his nomination for the Vice-Presidency, whence he might be " huzza'd into office at the heels of Gen. Jackson." [25] Churchill C. Cambreleng, a New York Congressman, wrote to Van Buren while the issue was before the Senate, and told him about the stir which was being made. He thought that it was all show, and that when the final vote came, Van Buren would be confirmed. He hoped his friend would be turned down, seeing at once the effect such an act would have, but he could not conceive of the opposition being so foolish. As soon as Calhoun had cast the fateful ballot, Senator Benton taunted one of his colleagues who had voted against Van Buren. " You have broken a minister, and elected a Vice-President," he told him. And even in London, when the news was known, Lord Auckland consoled Van Buren by saying, " It is an advantage to a public man to be the subject of an outrage." [26]

Van Buren's stock soared everywhere. Letters poured into London and Albany expressing sympathy and giving assurances that the reaction would be in his favor. The President, already partial to him, was now completely behind his advancement. As Senator Marcy wrote Flagg, " Jackson is rapped up in Van Buren. It would do your heart good to hear him expatiate upon his merits and reprove the injustice of his enemies."

In Albany there was a surge of indignation. A mass meeting was held at the City Hall and a committee of thirteen, of which

---

25 *Evening Journal*, Dec. 2, 1831. After the rejection, Weed took a different course, saying the act vindicated "the insulted honor" of the nation, *ibid.*, Feb. 2, 1832.

26 Cambreleng to Van Buren, Jan. 4, 1832, Van Buren papers; Benton, *Thirty Years View*, I, 215, 219. For Van Buren's account, see *Autobiography*, pp. 454-8.

Wright was one, was appointed to send letters to Jackson and Van Buren expressing the feelings of the community. Some members of the Regency were temporarily inclined to run Van Buren for Governor again, and the " Red Fox " agreed to let his Albany friends decide on the most appropriate action. " I am," he wrote to Wright, " in the hands of my Republican friends, and they will do what is best. . . . " But the great mass of opinion opposed any post for him except the Vice-Presidency. " The wrong has been done him . . . by the *Senate of the U. States,*" wrote one New York Congressman, and " it must be redressed by the *people* of all the *States,*" and an Ohioan said that Van Buren was now to be considered " the property of the nation." [27] Another reason for pushing Van Buren as Vice-President at this time was the perennial ill health of President Jackson. There must be no chance interruptions in the progress of the Pride of New York. Marcy warned Van Buren, when the question of the governorship was broached, that the chances were against the Old Hero's lasting the five years that still remained before March 4, 1837, and therefore urged him to run for Vice-President, just in case, and many others echoed the same warning and advice.[28]

So, when the first Democratic National Convention met at the Baltimore Athenaeum on May 21, the Regency was there in force ready to supervise the proceedings. John Adams Dix, Adjutant General of New York, was elected secretary of the convention, and the New York delegation included Wright, Flagg, Nathaniel P. Tallmadge (a recent convert to the party), and Ransom H. Gillet, of St. Lawrence County, a protégé of Wright's who was later to be one of his biographers. In order to demonstrate their solidarity, the Van Burenites adopted the

27 For the many letters see Flagg and Van Buren papers, Jan.-Feb. 1832. Those quoted are Marcy to Flagg, Feb. 6, 1832, Flagg papers; Van Buren to Wright, Mar. 14, 1832, Marcy to Van Buren, Feb. 12, 1832, Van Buren papers; C. Dayan to Flagg, Jan. 29, 1832, E. Haywood to Flagg, Feb. 21, 1832, Flagg papers.

28 Marcy to Van Buren, Jan. 26, 1832, F. Blair to Van Buren, Jan. 28, 1832, Van Buren papers; Dayan to Flagg, Feb. 12, 1832, Flagg papers.

fateful two-thirds rule, and then nominated Van Buren for
Vice-President on the first ballot by an overwhelming vote.
Jackson (whose nomination had been made in the old caucus
manner) was then " confirmed " as head of the ticket, and the
convention adjourned, leaving the matter of the platform to the
individual states.[29]

The New York delegation prepared a resolute document
approving uncritically all the acts of the Jackson administration[30] and returned to Albany to prepare for November. The
Jacksonian leaders felt little concern as to the outcome of the
contest, but there were some minor problems that had to be
settled. The main one was Governor Throop. In 1830, he had
been accepted despite his inadequacies, but his course since
then, although well-meaning, had not added to his stature. His
Thanksgiving Day proclamation shortly after his election, in
which he referred to the wisdom of man as " a small light "
illuminating his footsteps " while all beyond is shrouded in
darkness " did not enhance his literary reputation which was so
bad that when a few lucid passages appeared in his message to
the legislature of 1832, it was attributed to Wright's pen by
many of the Governor's critics. As James Gordon Bennett
toured the state in the summer of 1831, he found the dissatisfaction with Throop widespread. Nearly every county through
which he passed opposed the renomination. Wright was mentioned by some as a possibility, but it was already well known
that he did not want the post, and Samuel Young, a Regency
stalwart, Chancellor Walworth, and William Marcy all had
strong supporters. By the early days of 1832, even the opposition knew that Throop was finished, and tried to make political
capital of it. Wright, Flagg, and Dix had " dogged " Throop
into retiring, reported Weed. " The Regency *uses up* a Governor every two years." [31]

29 *Proceedings of the 1832 Convention*, pp. 3-8.

30 *Ibid.*, pp. 9-24.

31 On Throop, see Hammond, *History of New York*, II, 415, 406n;
Bennett, " Diary," June 21, 22, 28, Aug. 4, 12, 1831 ; *Evening Journal*, Apr.
13, 28, 1832.

The final choice of the party fell on Marcy, and at the convention at Herkimer in September, with Wright operating as party whip (as Weed carefully pointed out to his readers), the Senator received the nomination without serious opposition.[32]

In the campaign, the main issue was the rechartering of the United States Bank, with the Regency upholding Jackson's veto of the recharter bill. But the shrewder politicians among the New York supporters of Henry Clay and his National Republican party realized the unpopularity of the Bank " Monster " and tried to subordinate it as an issue. A coalition, " the Siamese Twin scheme " (Wright called it an " inconsistent " and " unprincipled " alliance, " contradictory to all honest feeling ") was forged between the Clay men and the Anti-Masons in an effort to unite all the foes of Jackson in New York, and every possible distraction was advanced. Wright's " spoils " letter of 1826 was exploited again as was a similar statement made boldly and openly in the Senate in 1831 by William L. Marcy himself. But the crowning effort came in October, when Thurlow Weed unearthed the hilarious story of Marcy's Pantaloons.

Marcy was a stickler for detail. Once, when on the circuit as a judge, he had submitted an itemized expense account which was not at all exorbitant, but which included a charge of fifty cents for " work done on my pantaloons." As Comptroller, Wright was involved, because his office had certified the account and paid out the money. How the town of Albany must have laughed with " Old Schoharie " when he went to work on this situation!

> The Party, here, ask " where was *Wright*,
> When WEED, that saucy *wicked* wight,
> Ransacked the *Books* and brought to Light
> Th' 'Axacutive's' patch'd Breeches? "

32 *Argus*, Sept. 22, 1832; *Evening Journal*, Sept. 20, 1832. Throop was not pleased with the treatment he received. Years later he blamed Wright for his failure to be renominated, and thought the reason was Wright's ambition, to which he saw himself as an obstacle. Throop to M. Throop, Apr. 23, 1868, Miscellaneous papers, New York State Library.

As the election approached, this became the main subject of the *Journal's* columns. The Regency was despondent, Weed announced. Flagg was sulking; Wright was forced to admit that everything was going wrong; and Marcy " is drawing on his Pantaloons to be in readiness for a retreat to his . . . Farm. . . . " At Rochester, the Anti-Masons erected a fifty foot pole in the middle of the main street, and suspended a huge pair of black trousers from the top. Across the seat was a large white patch, bearing the figure " 50 " in bright red paint. Poor Marcy had to suffer in silence. " I hope it will do no harm," he wrote to a New York City friend. *" I feared no danger for I knew no sin."* [33]

But the time had not yet come when such tactics could in themselves carry an election. Jackson and Van Buren gained a clearcut victory, and Marcy also won without much trouble. The area in the west " infected " by Anti-Masonry went heavily against them, but most of the rest of the state was solidly Democratic, New York City alone giving Jackson a majority of about 5,000 votes.[34] As one opponent at the Regency frankly confessed, " The result of the election has been so signally overwhelming as to leave no cause for idle or unavailing regrets." [35]

In the wake of such a complete success, Wright even found time to relax enough to act as one of the judges of an essay contest for the Albany Female Academy.[36] But while pondering over the relative merits of " The Great Principle of the Universe Is Life " and " The State of the Soul between Death and Resurrection," events were shaping up in South Carolina which were soon to involve him once more in political turmoil.

33 Wright to Niles, Sept. 24, 1832, Welles papers, Library of Congress; *Evening Journal*, Nov. 1, 2, 1832; Stanton, *Random Recollections*, p. 37; Marcy to Hoyt, Oct. 16, 1832, W. Mackensie, *Life of Van Buren*, p. 239.

34 The rivalry between the United States Bank (located at Philadelphia) and the New York banks was an important reason for this. Hammond, *History of New York*, II, 424.

35 Seward, *Autobiography*, p. 218.

36 *Argus*, Dec. 3, 1832.

CHAPTER V
RUMBLINGS OF A DISTANT DRUM

"The quarrel is to be transferred from one of taxes and imports to ...
slavery ...."

Michael Hoffman to Azariah Flagg, February 4, 1833.

THE passage of the Tariff of 1828 had been a bitter blow to all the South, and nowhere below the Mason-Dixon line was resentment more deep-seated than in South Carolina. The Palmetto State had been left behind in the economic race. The trade of Charleston, once one of the most active ports in the young nation, fell precipitously in the twenties, and the population increased only slightly when compared with the tremendous growth of most of the nation.[1] For this depression, most South Carolinians blamed the policy of protection. With an economy devoted mainly to the production of cotton, South Carolina, like most of the South, was forced to import nearly all its needs, either from other parts of the Union, or from Europe. The new tariff boosted the prices of such imports until the Carolinians felt, quite logically, that they were being taxed to support Northern manufacturers and farmers, who were largely relieved from foreign competition by the high rates of the law of 1828. Helpless against a law antithetical to their interests, the statesmen of South Carolina sought to forge a new weapon, the doctrine of nullification.

The idea that an individual state could declare void a legally enacted federal statute had been suggested in South Carolina even before 1828,[2] but it did not attract very much national attention until the anonymous presentation that year of Calhoun's *Exposition and Protest* to the South Carolina legislature. Sovereignty was indivisible, asserted that document, and

1 F. Bancroft, *Calhoun and the South Carolina Nullification Movement*, pp. 20-1.

2 *Ibid.*, p. 27 ff.

93

resided in the individual states, so that any state could declare inoperative a federal law which it considered "unconstitutional." This meant, really, that a state could ignore any national legislation that it did not want to obey. In 1828, Calhoun still had hopes that he would be President of the United States as soon as Jackson completed his term, so he let his manifesto lie fallow, but with the failure of the plot against Van Buren and the New Yorker's resultant nomination as Vice-President, the South Carolinian's immediate prospects at least, grew very dim. When Congress aggravated the situation by passing another high tariff in July, 1832, a crisis was inevitable.

It is difficult to say to what extent Calhoun was motivated by personal interest. Certainly many of his contemporaries agreed with Frank Blair, the editor of the *Washington Globe,* when he wrote confidentially, " Calhoun's whole soul is bent on producing a *thorough league* among the Southern states so as to embody them for his own object, which I sincerely believe does not stop short of Separation, if it will not avail to make him at some time Head of the whole union." [3] Whatever his purpose, Calhoun had the support of a substantial majority of the citizens of his own state when he backed the South Carolina convention which on November 24, 1832, issued an ordinance declaring the tariff acts of 1828 and 1832 null and void within the state after February 1, 1833.

The lines were quickly drawn. To Andrew Jackson, in the White House, resistance to the laws of the United States was treason, and he hurriedly issued a proclamation saying so. Outside South Carolina his determined stand evoked almost universal approval regardless of party lines. " The old man's proclamation has produced a wonderful effect here," wrote one politician from New York City. " It was read aloud in the Exchange and received with a vote of entire approval by *all parties.*" Even Philip Hone, the arch-type of New York con-

3 Blair to Van Buren, Jan. 28, 1832, Van Buren papers.

servatism, who usually hated everything the Old General stood for, commented: " Hurrah for Jackson." [4] But the answer from Charleston was defiance, and as the first of February approached the situation grew increasingly tense. " The question ' to be or not to be ' in reference to our federal union, will soon be decided," wrote William Jay to novelist James Fenimore Cooper. A new tariff bill was introduced in Congress by Gulian C. Verplanck, of New York, which reduced the rates drastically, but the South Carolinians were so incensed by Jackson's proclamation that they would take nothing that savored of his administration. The National Republicans, led by Henry Clay and Daniel Webster, joined them in a " temperate but firm " stand against the bill.[5]

For Silas Wright at Albany, these events suddenly took on special significance, for on January 5, 1833, the state legislature chose him as United States Senator. The Regency machinery was functioning smoothly. Van Buren was waiting for the fourth of March to become Vice-President. Marcy was the new Governor. Wright was to go to the Senate to replace him, with Flagg replacing Wright, and John A. Dix, the State Adjutant General, taking Flagg's old post as Secretary of State. It looked to Philip Hone as though the " little Junta called the Regency, are determined to hold all the Trumps. They make the Party shuffle the Cards and Deal, and the People—Win or Lose— pay all the Bets," but in the legislature, the party's power was so well established that the opposition hardly roused itself. Only Weed, who said that Wright was going to Washington to extend " Regency tactics over the Nation," made much of a public fuss about the entire transaction.[6]

4 M. James, *Jackson* (1 vol. ed.), p. 612; S. Swartwouth to Verplanck, Dec. 10, 1832, Verplanck papers; A. Nevins, ed., *Diary of Philip Hone*, I, p. 84, Dec. 12, 1832.

5 W. Jay to J. Cooper, Dec. 11, 1832, *Cooper Correspondence*, J. Cooper, ed., p. 301; Webster to W. Sullivan, Jan. 5, 1833, *Correspondence of Daniel Webster*, F. Webster, ed., I, 528-9.

6 *Argus*, Jan. 5, 1835; *Diary of Philip Hone*, VI, 156, New York Historical Society, Jan. 17, 1833; *Evening Journal*, Nov. 11, 1832; Seward, *Autobiography*, p. 227.

It was difficult for Wright to leave Albany with its congenial and familiar atmosphere. There must have been many reluctant farewells, and presents were exchanged. " Tell Mrs. Flagg," quipped the former Comptroller to his successor, that " if she is as successful in keeping time as I shall now be in keeping my nose clean we shall reciprocally profit by our exchanges. . . . " [7]

The new Senator sailed from Albany on the afternoon boat on January 9, arriving at New York at half-past-five the morning of the tenth. He spent that night at the United States Hotel in Philadelphia, and then proceeded to Washington, where he put up at Gadsby's famous establishment. In the early thirties, Washington well deserved the name " City of Magnificent Distances." Planned on a grand scale by Major L'Enfant, a French engineer, the Capital had grown rapidly in the forty-odd years which had passed since Maryland and Virginia had ceded their rights to the land on which it was located, but it was still for the most part a straggling village, with great areas of swamps and vacant lots. Pennsylvania Avenue, stretching from the Capitol to Georgetown, was well lined with tenements, boarding houses, and shops, and many of the other broad roads which radiated outward from the seat of Congress had occasional stores and residences at some of their intersections. But Washington as a whole was still in its architectural infancy. The Capitol, the White House, and four brick structures housing the chief departments of the government were the only really impressive structures in the city.

Gadsby's, that " vast barn or caravanserai," which was described by one visitor as " the dearest house in proportion to the amount of comfort it affords . . . where loafers assemble from all parts of the Union; where all the meats taste alike, and the bells ring from morning to night," was no place for a frugal, industrious and food-loving man like the new Senator from New York. He was unable to arrive at a satisfactory arrangement with the " unconscionable publicans " who ran it,

7 Wright to Flagg, Jan. 10, 1833, Flagg papers.

so he moved into a mess with four New York Congressmen and Austin E. Wing, the delegate from Michigan territory. Here he got " a splendid room for Washington " for twelve dollars a week. He was very pleased with his roommates. " We don't all agree on the tariff," he admitted to Flagg, " but [we] won't let that affect our relationships." [8]

But the tariff was affecting everyone's relationships in January, 1833. As soon as he arrived at the Capital, Wright hurried to see the President. Their interview took place in a crowded room at the White House, where Jackson urged Wright to communicate immediately with Van Buren and his other Albany friends to advise them of the seriousness of the situation. His own aim, he said, was to keep the rest of the South quiet while he took care of Calhoun and the other Nullifiers. The earnestness of Old Hickory made a deep impression on Wright and he hastened to get in touch with Van Buren to tell him that things were much more critical than they had thought possible. There was little chance of any tariff bill passing, he wrote, adding that the New York delegation in the House was at loggerheads. He begged Van Buren to hold a conference with the other members of the Regency to advise him as to what he should do. Though torn by doubt and hesitating to act on his own (because he knew that others would tie his acts up with Van Buren) Wright now subordinated the principle of protection. For, as he warned his friend, the Union itself was involved, and also " our most favorite political hopes and prospects." Obviously, the excitement at Washington had infected him.[9]

The next day he took his seat in the Senate and met most of his new associates. Only thirty-seven years old, he was the youngest man in the upper house, but his importance as the

8 A. Staples, ed., *Letters of John Fairfield*, p. 18; Seward, *Autobiography,* p. 277; Nevins, *Diary of Philip Hone*, II, pp. 542-5; Wright to Flagg, Jan. 10, 19, 1833, Flagg papers; J. Forney, *Anecdotes of Public Men*, I, 231.

9 Wright to Van Buren, Jan. 13, 1833, Van Buren papers.

unofficial representative of the new Vice-President was considerable. He wrote to Flagg that evening that he had been received as "the index of the feeling of our State upon the tariff and as the echo of Mr. Van Buren," and in his uncertainty of mind, this is exactly what he was, and no more. But a single day of observation and conversation lessened the panic of his first reaction. With renewed confidence he assured all who asked him that New York stood ready to back down on protection for the sake of peace. As his political craftiness returned, the remarks of some of the Southern senators especially, turned him back to his original opinion that the whole alarm was largely a matter of politics. So when Representative Wilde, of Georgia, asked him point blank how Van Buren stood on tariff reduction, he replied that he knew that the Vice-President-elect favored revision "to preserve the peace and integrity of the Union," but would not agree to this unless it was done without "apparent and palpable submission to threats and menaces." The whole crisis, he told Flagg, sprang from a plot by Calhoun, Clay and Webster, for after hearing the calm assurance of Senator King, of Alabama, that some tariff would pass he suspected that Clay and Calhoun particularly, had agreed to compromise in a manner that would separate Jackson "from all possible connection with the pacification" of South Carolina.

This prediction was remarkably accurate, but amid the boiling turbulence of Washington, Wright was unable to hold to it. Soon he felt sure once more that *no* bill would pass, and feared for the effect of this on the South as a whole. Virginia seemed ready to "go at least half way" and so did most of the other Southern states, but he thought it quite possible that the entire South would secede if duties were not lowered.[10] Nevertheless, Jackson's unrelenting preparation to enforce the federal laws had its effect, and on January 21, South Carolina suspended the operation of the Nullification Ordinance until the tariff

10 Wright to Flagg, Jan. 14, 20, 1833, Flagg papers.

issue should be settled one way or another. The tension, however, was by no means over, and the Force Bill, authorizing the use of the army of the United States in case nullification was actually tried, was still before Congress.

The New York delegation was badly split over reducing the level of duties. In Albany, the Regency was strong for compromise, but failed to offer Wright the advice he had sought as to how he should vote on Congressman Verplanck's bill. Van Buren " would sooner trust to your judgment, on a view of the whole ground, than to his own opinion," wrote Flagg to Wright. The kernel of the trouble in New York was the great agitation afoot to hold out against any change of the schedules, especially on wool and woolens. Wool speculators and " sordid manufacturers," said the Comptroller, caused all the trouble. " I have no patience with those who . . . are haggling for a few cents a yard on flannel, while the union is on the verge of dissolution."

But the wool manufacturers at Albany were stubborn. Again the leader of this pressure group was Benjamin Knower, who organized a mass meeting on January 24 in an effort to prevent any modification of the Act of 1832. Knower was deeply involved in speculation in wool, and as Van Buren said, he was " controlled by the exigencies of his pecuniary circumstances." The meeting was to be ostensibly non-partisan, but in the city of Albany, which was strongly National Republican, there was not much doubt that Knower and his friends would be able to adopt resolutions which would be embarrassing to the Administration. The forces of the Regency soon learned of what was up, and decided to turn it to their own advantage. So when the meeting was opened in the basement of the Albany City Hall, there was a packed house. The Knower group was allowed to organize the meeting without opposition. As they attempted to pass resolutions that it was " inexpedient " to modify the tariff, however, John A. Dix interrupted to submit rival resolves. A spirited debate followed, but when it became clear that the Regency forces were in the majority, the chair-

man of the meeting called for a vote on Dix's proposals and
pronounced them defeated! Complete chaos threatened. Benjamin Butler managed to get the floor and called for " those who
voted for Gen. Jackson . . . to retire to the Capitol as they were
not allowed fair play in this meeting." Just how many left the
meeting in response to this plea is uncertain. Knower said one-
third, Flagg and the *Argus* reporter said two-thirds, but at any
rate the result was two separate meetings. Butler addressed the
seceders in a speech which Flagg said " would have induced the
most sordid wool speculator to release a few cents on a pound
of wool, or to give up all claim to the inheritance of the revolutionary patriarchs," but unfortunately the " wool speculators "
remained at the other meeting.[11]

Before hearing of this schism, Wright had anticipated a
strong stand for protection at Albany and was very much irritated by the prospect. He thought that such a stand would only
keep the New York members of the House of Representatives
divided, and perhaps prevent the passage of any new tariff bill.
Also, the mercenary attitude of protectionists disgusted him.
" Patriotism, principle, concession, conciliation and party faith
seem to be forgotten or wholly overlooked, and *interest* and
consequent popularity seem to be the lords . . . which almost
wholly govern the Congressional legislation," he wrote to Van
Buren. If there is no change " we may live to see dismember-
ment and civil contention." But Flagg's account of the meeting
at Albany heartened him a great deal, and when a published
report of the proceedings reached Washington, he distributed
copies of it at the Capitol. " The effect," he reported to Albany
caustically, " has been salutary upon those who are open to
salutary influences." [12]

His own doubts had been resolved once South Carolina

11 Flagg to Wright, Jan. 21, 1833, Flagg papers; Van Buren, *Autobiography*, p. 562; Flagg to Wright, Jan. 24, 1833, Flagg papers; *Argus*,
Jan. 26, 29, 1833.

12 Wright to Van Buren, Jan. 29, 1833, Van Buren papers; Wright to
Flagg, Feb. 18, 1833, Flagg papers.

showed a willingness to back down provided the tariff was lowered. He suddenly discovered that he had all along been a low tariff man! Duties should be scaled to "the economic wants of the government," he suggested to Van Buren, though " in settling to that standard I would be as gradual and moderate as the spirit of the times and the feeling of the country would allow." The "country," of course, was South Carolina. This change of opinion was occasioned by a genuine fear of civil war. Even before South Carolina suspended the Ordinance of Nullification, Wright had written unsigned letters to the *Argus* expressing this fear in an effort to solidify the forces of compromise at Albany.[13] As time went on without any sign of a modification of the tariff and with Jackson firm in pressing the Force Bill through Congress, his fears persisted.

Interest in Congressional proceedings was intense at the Capitol. Every session of Congress was packed with spectators. This had its effect on Wright as well as on everyone else. " Every foot within the Chamber," he wrote Flagg after a session late in January, " alleys and all, was filled with ladies and there were about as many behind the President's seat as could get there and stand up. The door ways in every direction were full and a solid column of men crowded into the chamber until a firm contact with the ladies stopped them [,] and both galleries were filled to overflowing. . . . I am friendly to the ladies but I confess . . . we had a little too much of them today. . . . "

Wright thought at that time that the last chance for a peaceful adjustment of the rate problem was at hand. The Northern and Southern sections of the nation had antithetical views on the issue, he warned his friends. Unless both sides were willing to compromise it would become a matter of principle, and then " the Union must go or protection must go." He wanted it to be the latter. " People will neither cut throats nor dismember

13 Wright to Van Buren, Jan. 29, 1833, Van Buren papers; *Argus*, Jan. 23, 28, 1833; Gillet, *Wright*, I, 164-8.

the Union for protection," he wrote hopefully. " There is more patriotism and love of country than that left yet. . . . The People . . . never will balance this happy government against ten cents upon a pound of wool." [14]

His hopes were justified, for even at Albany the pressure against compromise was dying. On February 4, Van Buren wrote him that feeling was well united in favor of a bill that the South would support, and on the twenty-fourth of the month, the legislature passed resolutions disapproving of nullification, but favoring modification of the tariff.[15] But this modification was not to be accomplished through the Verplanck bill. Neither Calhoun nor Clay would swallow a measure which seemed to be the work of Jackson and Van Buren. However, when Clay advanced a compromise which would reduce the tariff gradually over a course of ten years, to a level of twenty per cent, Calhoun was willing to accept it, though it was less of a concession to the South than the Verplanck bill, because it enabled him to save face. In this way the alliance, the existence of which Wright had suspected when he first arrived at Washington, came to be. Actually it made no difference to the Administration. Jackson told Wright that he would sign any tariff which passed Congress,[16] and this was in line with the New York Senator's own feelings. If the bill took " any sufferable shape " he would vote for it, he confessed to his friend Flagg.

The main difficulty at this point came from the National Republicans, chiefly those from New England. Under a cloak

14 Wright to Flagg, Jan. 28, 1833, Feb. 2, 1833, Flagg papers.

15 Wright to Van Buren, Feb. 4, 1833, Van Buren papers; *Argus*, Feb. 26, 1833. This was nearly a month after Jackson had written to Van Buren, " why is your Legislature silent at this eventful crisis. . . . Your friends are astonished . . . and it gives rise to dark innuendoes of your enemies, that you command them. . . ." J. Bassett, ed., *Correspondence of Andrew Jackson*, V, 12.

16 " . . . the Prest. and the whole administration feel the utmost anxiety for the passage of *that* [Verplanck] bill, and a still greater anxiety for the passage of *some* bill." Wright to Flagg, Jan. 27, 1833, Wright-Butler Letters, N. Y. Public Library.

of nationalistic fervor, they spoke harsh words against compromising with the spirit of nullification. Wright had nothing but contempt for Daniel Webster, of Massachusetts, who typified this element, thinking him to be interested solely in winning debates and in personal popularity, with little concern for the Union. As Churchill C. Cambreleng expressed it, Webster was "full of fire and brimstone" in support of the Force bill, while the President's true friends were anxiously seeking an adjustment to preserve peace.[17] The situation was very delicate, for as Webster's patriotic speeches inflamed tempers that were already hot, Jackson himself was insisting on the Force Bill regardless of the outcome of the tariff struggle.

Wright was very anxious as the short month of February drew toward its close. He could not understand the Southern inclination to treat every issue as a constitutional one. The nullifiers seemed to be trying to upset their constituents by wild harangues about legal technicalities that the average man could not fathom. He felt he would like to make a speech in the Senate in an effort to bring all sides to examine the matter practically; but, pressed for time and suffering from freshman nervousness, he took no part in the debate until very near the end and then spoke only briefly. He objected to many aspects of Clay's bill. The whole idea of reducing the duties over a ten year period was unconstitutional, he thought, because it acted as a restriction on the powers of future Congresses. He spoke, too, in favor of a restoration of the duty on coarse wool, which had been removed in 1832, but without success. In the end he voted for Clay's bill as he had decided to do some time before. Webster had been anxious to know what stand he would take and he informed him, in a cold and formal note, that he felt it his "duty" to vote with Clay, and a few days later, he publicly gave the bill his support as the only measure satisfactory "to

17 Wright to Flagg, Feb. 21, 2, 1833, Flagg papers; Wright to Van Buren, Feb. 5, 1833, Van Buren papers.

all that portion of the South which believed the existing laws to be unjust and oppressive." [18]

Similar motivation lay behind the " aye " votes of most of the Northern Congressmen. The measure was carried by a comfortable margin and signed (along with the Force Bill) by the President on March second. Thirteen days later South Carolina rescinded the Nullification Ordinance. But thinking people realized that nullification had been appeased, not defeated. " On the *Tariff,*" said Congressman Michael Hoffman, " the North & South are not unreconcileably [*sic*] divided— but on *Slavery* they are. The quarrel is to be transferred from one of taxes and imports to . . . *slavery*—and this is designed to affect a more perfect *Union* at the South." [19]

*   *   *   *   *

The day after the signing of the new tariff bill Congress adjourned, and the following day Jackson and Van Buren were inaugurated. Wright returned to Canton. His object was matrimony. For fourteen years he had known Clarissa Moody, the daughter of his first Canton friend, and he had finally decided that she was the woman for him. At thirty-seven he was ready to settle down. The question was whether Clarissa would have him. There is very little evidence. When he first came to Washington as Senator, he wrote Flagg referring to Flagg's wife as " Mrs. Comptroller," and congratulating her on her husband's promotion. But, he added, " had some good lady concluded to take that title before the change in the office took place it must have been to me more gratifying to have used it." Why the lady hesitated after so many years is uncertain. She was twenty-nine years old and had known Silas just half her life. She surely must have known whether or not she liked him. Perhaps her overwhelming shyness and distaste for the public attention

---

18 Wright to Flagg, Feb. 19, 1833, Flagg papers; *Reg. Deb.*, IX, 708-9, 726, 806-7; Wright to Webster, Feb. 25, 1833, *Letters of Daniel Webster,* C. Van Tyne, ed., p. 179.

19 Hoffman to Flagg, Feb. 4, 1833, Flagg papers.

which would be hers as the wife of an important political figure was responsible. But during the summer of 1833 she finally consented and in September they were married.

This event had profound effects on Wright's career as well as on his private life. Until the time of their union he had never thought of abandoning politics; he did not seek office, but was glad to accept it when it came to him. Shortly afterward, dissatisfaction with many aspects of public life began to grow in him, and in less than ten years he was actively seeking an excuse to retire. Clarissa was a country girl who wanted to remain one. Her social timidity was astounding. On one occasion Wright invited Van Buren, the Flaggs, and another couple for a summer visit to Canton. In proffering the invitation, he told Flagg: "[Clarissa] will be greatly frightened at the meeting with persons of such standing and celebrity, but I have already had one round of argument to convince her that she has not always thought the Comptroller so frightful. . . . The V. P. will continue to have to her all the terrors of a 'Great Magician' until she sees him when I doubt not he will appear to her much more like a common man than a fearful conjurer." Another time, after Van Buren had become President, the Wrights were invited to dine at the White House. " Mrs. Wright was led to the table," her fond husband wrote her brother, " by the President himself, seated at his right hand, by a caution very proper to the occasion, did not get under the table, and went through the whole ceremony in fine style." On still another occasion, after she and Wright had stopped at Van Buren's home at Kinderhook for a visit, the " Great Magician " sent her a bunch of autumn leaves as a souvenir. Her resigned husband soon found that he had to acknowledge the little gift himself. Clarissa could not bring herself to the point of writing a letter to a man who had been President of the United States, no matter how well she knew him.[20]

20 Wright to Flagg, Jan. 19, 1833, Aug. 13, 1835, Flagg papers; Wright to L. Moody, Feb. 12, 1838, Gillet, *Wright*, I, 692; Wright to Van Buren, Oct. 25, 1841, Van Buren papers.

Combined with this bashfulness was a very delicate constitution. She was frequently ill, and since the boarding-house life of Washington did not agree with her, she did not always accompany Wright to the Capital. These separations were distressing to both for they were very fond of each other. Sometimes politics forced him to be away from home even when Congress was not in session and on such occasions the shy Clarissa showed remarkable spunk. When her husband had to attend the Democratic National Convention at Baltimore less than a month after his return from Washington in 1835 she was really put out. " For the first time the wife looks sober and threatens to turn Whig if I do not stay home more," Wright explained ruefully to Azariah Flagg.[21] As the years passed, this resistance to his devotion to politics grew, and reinforced a similar attitude of his own. The last five years of his life were characterized by constant efforts to retire, and it was the tragedy of their marriage that when he did succeed, he did not live to enjoy much of the retirement so fondly sought.

Despite his heavy drinking, Wright was a good husband. He was a home-loving man, who liked nothing better than a chance to putter around the house or work in his vegetable garden. When he was free from legislative duties he nearly always hurried straight home to Canton, stopping only, perhaps, for a short visit at Albany or with his parents in Vermont. His only bad domestic habit was his liking for small talk with his neighbors. Clarissa would call him in from the garden for dinner, and he would stop to chat with some passing friend and forget completely about the meal growing cold on the table.

Unfortunately, the Wrights were not blessed with any children. Probably for this reason, Silas took a keen interest in his many nieces and nephews, in the grandchildren of his friend Van Buren, and in all the local Canton youngsters. He was particularly fond of his brother-in-law Lucius Moody's only child, who had been named after him, and he was almost as

21 Wright to Flagg, Apr. 23, 1835, Flagg papers.

unhappy as the parents when the boy died in 1836. Whenever
he was at home, friends and neighbors were constantly in and
out of his house and their children were usually with them.
Often when he was busy with a letter or document, the house
would be crowded with small visitors who would press round
him unmercifully, but he had a smile and a few words for them
all. It was common, one local resident told Jabez Hammond,
Wright's biographer, for little boys of eight or ten to pester
their elders for days when the Senator was expected home,
demanding " When will Mr. Wright be in town? " His fondness for children was certainly not feigned, and it must have
played a part in the astounding hold which he maintained over
the whole North Country.[22]

*   *   *   *   *

In the summer of 1833, while making plans for his marriage,
a good deal of Wright's time was spent in studying the bank
situation. Jackson's veto of the recharter bill had neither destroyed the United States Bank nor removed the fears of many
Jacksonians that " Biddle's Monster " would use its great
financial power to embarrass them politically. There was even
ground for suspicion that the Bank might deliberately precipi-
tate a business panic before the election of 1836 in order to
discredit the Democrats.[23] Jackson was determined to remove
all the government funds which were deposited in it. This
would lessen its control over the money market of the nation
and curtail its political influence. During the summer the only
question that remained to be settled was *when* the federal funds
should be removed. Jackson sought Van Buren's opinion, but
the Little Magician hesitated, doubtless feeling that his own
best interests as Jackson's " heir " lay in avoiding such un-

22 Statement of "Cassie" Moody, n. d., Wright papers, St. Lawrence
University; Wright to L. Moody, June 6, 1838, Gillet, *Wright*, I, 468-9;
Hammond, *Wright*, p. 34.

23 Schlesinger, *Age of Jackson*, pp. 97-8.

settling matters as much as possible. He asked for time to consult with Wright before replying.

The Senator, too, was cautious. He probably thought of the political effects on Van Buren's future, for that was never far from his mind, but he was also worried lest " some cursed Wall Street operations . . . be developed," meaning that a decision to remove the deposits might leak out and that the information would be used by speculators. From all such "men and mousers . . . . Good Lord deliver us! " he wrote. But rather than depend upon his advice alone, Van Buren should call " a council of the Regency," he urged.[24]

" Little Van " approved of this, but wanted to see his friend personally, so Wright left Canton for a hurried visit south. On August 18, at Schenectady, he conferred with Dix and the Vice-President and then went on to Albany to see Flagg and some of the others. There was disagreement in the ranks. The majority of what Van Buren called his " most discreet " friends favored immediate removal of the deposits, while Wright thought that nothing should be done until Congress reassembled in December. Van agreed with Wright and so informed Jackson. The President replied that he considered immediate withdrawal imperative, and responding in turn early in September after Silas had returned to Canton to be married, the Red Fox said that both he and Senator Wright wished only to defer the *action* of removal; the order itself might expediently be issued at once. Besides, he continued, he had only expressed their preference; they would support wholeheartedly any action which Jackson might take.[25]

So it was done. On September 18, Jackson read his famous message to his Cabinet (Philip Hone called it a " supereroga-

24 Jackson to Van Buren, July 25, 1833, *Jackson Correspondence*, J. Bassett, ed., V, 143; Van Buren to Jackson, July 29, 1833, Van Buren papers; Wright to Flagg, Aug. 8, 1835, Flagg papers.

25 Wright to Flagg, Sept. 6, 1833, Flagg papers; *Jackson Correspondence*, J. Bassett, ed., V, 160, 179 and note, 181, 183-4.

tory act of tyranny ") ordering the removal of government funds from the Second United States Bank. Two days later the order was published, and on October 1 Secretary of the Treasury Taney began the transfer of the money to state banks in various cities. The result was an all-out battle between the Bank and the Jackson Administration.[26]

Wright's mistrust of banks was especially intense at this time. Just how he came to be so opposed to speculation and " loose " banking is obscure, but from his earliest days in politics he had always been suspicious of any but the most conservative financial houses and financial practices. His prejudices may have gone back to his youth in Vermont and to an institution called the Vermont State Bank. This had been a typical frontier corporation, backed by the state, and possessed of four branches and the confidence and cash of a good part of the people of the region. In 1811 it had collapsed and farmers throughout the state had suffered terribly.[27] Whether the Wrights were affected directly is unknown, but many of their friends must have been. An incident which occurred when Wright was a member of the New York Senate, later related by his roommates, Mallory and Earll, provides an excellent illustration of the depth of Wright's feeling. One night in 1825, after a day spent in debate on several bank charters, Wright sprang from his bed, still sound asleep and shouted: " My God! the combination is too strong—every bank will pass! " He awoke in an extremely agitated state and it was some time before he was able to relax and go back to sleep. In any event, after his experiences in New York and his observations of the United States Bank's operations during the campaign of 1832, Wright was almost violent in his opinions. " I wish in my heart," he wrote in August, 1833, while considering the ques-

26 A. Nevins, *Diary of Philip Hone*, I, 107; R. Catterall, *Second Bank of the United States*, p. 296.

27 Stillwell, "Migration from Vermont," Vermont Historical Society, *Proceedings*, II, 127.

tion of removing the deposits which Van Buren had posed to him, " there was not a moneyed incorporation in this country. They are the most irresponsible of all aristocracies and we are making them for all purposes. Where they will carry us God alone knows. . . . "

But he was really less inflexible in his opposition to business interests than this sounds. He even bought some stock in Erastus Corning's Utica and Schenectady Railroad, which was somewhat of a speculative enterprise, though when Corning, who was very friendly with all the Regency, suggested another investment, he refused. " I have been driven, while at Albany, to say much, and feel more against the interference of our friends in political situations in moneyed incorporations," he told him. " I think I was right. . . . " [28]

The Second Bank of the United States he already disliked for political reasons; now he saw it embarking on a course of credit manipulation which he abhorred. By the time he had returned to Washington for the December session of Congress he was convinced that the removal of the deposits was necessary and proper.

---

[28] Hammond, *Wright*, p. 65n.; Wright to Flagg, Aug. 10(?), 1833, Flagg papers; Wright to E. Corning, Dec. 27, 1833, Wright papers, New York State Library. Wright's real feeling seems to have been this: Banking is a necessary part of the nation's economy, but it must be " sound " banking. Speculative "wildcat" banks were to him the great evil. At this time, he and most of the members of his party attacked the United States Bank not because of its conservative banking activities, but because it used its financial power for political purposes. They did not realize, or deliberately ignored, the effect the weakening of the indirect control which the Bank exerted over most state banks would have on the nation's economy.

CHAPTER VI

BATTLE ROYAL WITH BIDDLE'S
"MONSTER."

"I am fixed in my course as firmly as the Rockey mountain.... providence
has a power over me, but frail mortals who worship Ball & the golden
calf, can have none."

Andrew Jackson to Martin Van Buren, n. d. [February, 1834.]

We have now the bank and Sir Harry [Clay] takes hold
with an appetite which affords presumption that on his northern tour he may have seen the emperor [Biddle] in his golden
costume and had his zeal quickened by the sight.[1]

THERE was much truth in this observation of Wright's, for
when Congress assembled in December, 1833, it was not the
Jacksonians but the National Republicans who assumed the
offensive. In the Senate, they and their allies held a clear
majority, for Calhoun and his followers, already wedded to
Clay as a result of the Compromise Tariff, also sided with him
in irritation at Jackson's removal of the deposits. Calhoun
was no friend of the United States Bank, but to him the removal seemed a flagrant usurpation of power by the Executive, and therefore objectionable. In the House, the Jackson
men were technically in control, but many of the representatives who made up their majority were dubious about the
removal, and might be swung into the National Republican
camp.

The strength of the Jacksonians was further taxed by the
powerful resistance of "Czar Nicholas" Biddle, the President
of the "Monster," who fought with all his wealth of resources
to influence susceptible members of Congress. Many senators
and representatives were advanced "loans" and "retainers"
with the obvious understanding that they would support the
return of the deposits and the recharter of the Bank. But the

1 Wright to Flagg, Dec. 11, 1833, Flagg papers.

most important of Biddle's allies were not his servants. The
financial distress which resulted from the contraction of credit
by the great bank at Philadelphia depressed business all over
the nation. People were thrown out of work and Congress was
flooded with memorials claiming that only a return of the deposits would bring relief. A real panic was developing, and
the Democrats were only hurting themselves when they refused to admit it. When Jackson, in his message to the new
Congress, dared say in the face of glaring conditions to the
contrary, "No public distress has followed the exertions of
the bank," the fortunes of his administration were indeed at
a low ebb.

Under these circumstances it seemed probable that a joint
resolution ordering the restoration of the deposits would pass
both houses of Congress. "This is the time to buy U. S. B.
Stock," wrote General Winfield Scott from Richmond. "If the
deposits are, in future, made in that Bank, the stock must rise
from 5 to 10 percent, & this step gained a recharter would be
almost a matter of course." But Henry Clay, "Harry of the
West," nursing a fierce hatred of Jackson and an even more
fierce ambition, was thinking primarily of politics, so he pursued a more devious course. In a powerful three-day speech,
assailing the acts of Jackson from every angle, he introduced
not a resolution returning the federal funds to Biddle, but one
censuring Jackson's action in removing them. This gave him
a wonderful opportunity to flail his enemy, but it was striking
the Administration at the one place where it was invulnerable.
Jackson men, in Congress and out, might disapprove of one
of their leader's acts, but in the main they would not stomach
a personal attack upon him. By the time enough of the true
friends of the Bank realized this, it was too late.[2]

2 Richardson, *Messages and Papers of the Presidents*, III, 31; James,
Jackson (1 vol. ed.), pp. 652-8; W. Scott to S. Gouveneur, Jan. 14, 1834,
Gouveneur papers; Catterall, *Second Bank of the United States*, p. 336. For
Clay's speech, see *Reg. Deb.*, X, 59-94.

In the Senate, Wright was placed on the Committee on Finance. The Democrats voted for him as chairman, but since they were in the minority, he was defeated.[3] Still, he was the leading Jackson man on the Committee, and a large part of the defense of the Old Hero's bank policy fell on his shoulders. Part of this work could be done behind the scenes, and this he enjoyed.

In the face of all the criticism and protest, the morale of the Administration was low and greatly in need of outside support. For this reason it was thought desirable to have the legislatures in pro-Jackson states pass resolutions favoring the President's position. Wright talked this over with Nathaniel P. Tallmadge, who had been elected as his colleague. They decided that such resolves should be proposed at Albany quickly. So after listing what they wanted in plain language, Wright sent the information on to Flagg. The Albany legislators should come out categorically against any recharter of the Bank, he wrote. They should express complete satisfaction with the removal of the deposits, approve the sense of Jackson's already famous memorandum to the Cabinet of September 18, and state " unequivocally " that they agreed with the reasons for removing the federal funds which Secretary Taney had submitted to Congress. These resolves would be the more forceful, he suggested to Flagg, if " made in the fewest possible words."

He thought that action by the legislature would have real value, but he disapproved of resorting to the enemy's technique of holding public meetings and submitting petitions. He tried, for instance, to discourage Jesse Hoyt, a New York City friend, from undertaking such an effort. Public opinion was excited enough already, he felt, and Congress was so swamped with such material that more of it would have no effect. This advice was sound, for Biddle had made credit especially tight in New York, and it would probably have been difficult to

3 *Reg. Deb.*, X, 42. The vote was 22 to 13.

evoke a very effective spirit in favor of the Administration.
But the legislature was staunchly Jacksonian and quickly
obliged with the desired resolutions.[4] They were presented in
the Senate by Wright in a speech which he delivered on January 30, 1834.

It was his first major effort in the Senate and he had been
curiously reticent about making it. All through December and
January, in the face of the most violent criticisms of Jackson's
bank policy, his entire Administration, even his character,
Wright had not once risen to the defense. Sitting silently on
the dais in the Senate Chamber, Vice-President Van Buren
noticed this and was worried. Repeated hints that Jackson
would appreciate deeply a general defense of his position by
the Senator from New York were not taken up. Finally " Little
Van " called at his friend's room at Mrs. Gooch's boarding
house on B Street and put the issue to him bluntly:

" Are you aware," he said, " that you have not, since you
have been in the Senate, realized the anticipations of your
friends? "

" I am, but I am also aware that the fault does not rest on
me."

" On whom then? "

" On my friends, for cherishing expectations which are not
authorized by any thing I have ever done."

Van Buren then gave him a thorough tongue lashing for
this " excess of modesty " which with Wright was very real.
He insisted that he and Wright's other friends were the best
judges of his abilities, and begged him to undertake a formal
defense of the Administration when he presented the resolutions of the New York legislature.

Silas was not convinced:

4 Wright to Flagg, Jan. 3, 1834, Flagg papers; Wright to Hoyt, Jan. 3,
1834, Mackensie, *Van Buren*, p. 246; Catterall, *Second Bank of the United
States*, p. 343; Hammond, *History of New York*, II, 438; *Argus*, Jan. 23,
1834.

" The administration has several friends in the Senate more competent for the task than myself."

" We do not think so," replied Van Buren, " and even if we did, we would for other reasons, prefer that what is said should come from you."

Wright interposed that he might make a mistake, and commit the government to a stand it could not support. Finally, in desperation, the Vice-President offered:

" If I reduce all we want to have said to writing, will you then undertake to say it? "

" Write and let me see it."

This was enough for the Little Magician. The next morning the desired speech was in Wright's hands and his friend had his verbal assurance that he would deliver it.[5]

Why he required such persuasion and bolstering is hard to see, for he certainly understood the issues involved and favored Jackson's policy. But self-doubt was an essential part of his make-up and characterized his every advancement. Though he soon became accustomed to his rôle as Administration spokesman in the Senate and no longer hesitated to speak his mind, when chances for further promotions were given him from time to time, his self-effacing nature always played a part in his refusals. He had other reasons, especially later on when he really wanted to retire, but in a man whose ability was so widely respected by friend and foe alike, his lack of confidence in himself was puzzling. Once he had tried a thing, he was all right, but until that time his timidity was excessive.

At any rate, the resolutions were presented and the speech made, substantially as Van Buren had prepared it. It was the first stroke in the counterattack. In the early days of the new year, Jackson had urged that his supporters abandon the defensive psychology of which his own message to Congress had been typical. This oration, prepared by the Vice-President and

5 Van Buren, *Autobiography*, pp. 728-30; for Wright's Washington residence, see *Congressional Directory*, 1834.

presented by the Senator from New York, was exactly what he wanted. It was, as Van Buren said, " The creed by which we mean to stand or fall." [6]

Wright offered the New York resolutions and then got to work. The heavy pressure on the money market, he charged, was caused by the " recent extensive and sudden curtailment, by the Bank of the United States, in the facilities for credit. . . ." He took advantage of a previous admission of Daniel Webster's that the central factor involved was not the deposits, but the very existence of the Bank. " I go against this bank, and against any and every bank to be incorporated by Congress . . .upon the broad ground, which admits no compromise, that Congress has not the power, by the Constitution, to incorporate such a bank."

While he spoke, Webster, realizing the change in tactics which this speech portended, got up from his seat and took another one closer to the speaker in order to follow what he was saying more carefully, his dark eyes watching Wright intently. Clay paced restlessly about the Chamber, sampling the different snuff boxes scattered on the tables. Calhoun fidgeted in his seat, rolling it back and forth on its castors. Other senators put aside their papers and mail.[7] The New Yorker continued:

" Still, we are told by the Senator from Massachusetts that things cannot remain as they are; that unless something. . .be done, the pressure, the distress and the agitation will continue. I have already stated the source from which. . .in my judgment, the present pressure proceeds. . . .Are we to fold our arms and obey the dictates of a moneyed power. . . .a power spoken into existence by our breath and dependent upon that breath for life and being?" His answer was a ringing

---

6 Van Buren, *Autobiography*, p. 730; *Reg. Deb.*, X, p. 397-405; Jackson to Van Buren, Jan. 3, 1834, *Jackson Correspondence*, J. Bassett, ed., V, 238-9; Van Buren to J. Van Buren, Jan. 29, 1834, Van Buren papers.

7 Van Buren, *Autobiography*, p. 730; *Argus*, Feb. 13, 1834.

negative. " I see clearly," he said, (and by this time Clay and many another Bank senator had gathered around him attentively) " that the true question is understood by the country, and that it is assuming an attitude toward the bank which the occasion calls for. . . .The Country, Mr. President, has approved of the course of the executive in his attempts to relieve us from the corrupt and corrupting power and influence of a national bank, and it will sustain him in the experiment now making. . . ."

This was the new Jacksonian line in the face of Biddle's curtailment of credit and the resultant panic. " Go to Nicholas Biddle ! " the tempestuous old President began shortly afterward to roar at the delegations which crowded into the White House to complain about the desperate state of financial affairs, and people were soon taking his advice. Wright, in spite of his reticence, found himself placed by his speech in the front rank of the counterattacking Jacksonians. " Your speech chimes in admirably with the prevalent feeling," congratulated John Dix from Albany. " It is, let me assure you, a real hit." Van Buren was particularly pleased. " The successful effort of Mr. Wright to force out the true issue has given a right direction to public sentiment," he wrote Theodore Sedgwick of Boston. The " unfaltering energy of his ' unterrified ' democracy, was the first thing to shed the gloom," a Virginia observer wrote later to Van Buren. And a New York merchant, preparing to leave for Washington with a memorial attacking the removal of the deposits, told an acquaintance, " I have only time to say that Mr. Wright's speech in the Senate seems to preclude any hopes for success from our mission. . . ." Even Webster was worried, and wrote, " We look anxiously for the effect which the recent debate in the Senate (Mr. Wright Jr) may produce at the north." For as Amos Kendall said, " Coming from one of the purest and ablest men who ever adorned the halls of Congress it could not fail to have a powerful influence on the public mind." [8]

8 Dix to Wright, Feb. 12, 1834, Flagg papers; Van Buren to T. Sedgwick, Feb. 18, 1834, Sedgwick papers, Massachusetts Historical Society; R. Parker

If his words had been forced into his mouth by Jackson and Van Buren, they were none the less an expression of his own ideas. Once he had started, he forgot his self-doubt and entered the debates with relish, battling it out with Webster and Clay on their own terms. He was not a very good speaker according to the ornate oratorical standards of the day. His voice was rather husky and not very powerful, and he seldom resorted to high-flown figures in his presentation. He had no use for what he once called " flowery, swolen, [sic] sophomoric sentences." But his speech was admirably suited to addressing a small body like the Senate. He always spoke slowly and deliberately, and depended for force upon rigid organization and logical, plain presentation. Again in his own words, he believed that " the less ornament and the more simplicity in the style of [a speech] the better." It was the opinion of one friend, Henry D. Gilpin, of Pennsylvania, that " no address was less ornamented by imagination, or even adorned by any extrinsic illustration; but in fixing the attention of his hearers, in impressing them with a conviction of the truth of his opinion, in leading them unconsciously through the train of an argument. . .no one in Congress ever surpassed him." Some of his political foes depreciated his argumentative powers. Webster, for example, said that his logic was " weak," " fallacious " and " evasive," that he was no debater, and that he " always skipped the hard places." But most commentators agreed with John Forney, a keen observer of the statesmen of that day, who thought that Wright was the " clearest logician " of his times.

One of his most valuable assets as a legislator was his complete calmness and self-control. He never grew visibly angry, no matter how far provoked, and he never resorted to personalities. Everyone, regardless of party, admitted this.

---

to Van Buren, Feb. 22, 1835, Van Buren papers; E. Anderson to Hoyt, Feb. 1, 1834, Mackensie, *Van Buren,* p. 249; Van Tyne, ed., *Letters of Daniel Webster,* p. 188; A. Kendall, *Autobiography,* W. Stickney, ed., p. 407. See also *Argus,* Feb. 5, 6, 13, 1834, and *Democratic Review,* V, 416.

" Wright. . .never deals in bluster or rant," wrote one editor
of an opposition paper when the New Yorker was at the
height of his career in the Senate. Another critic, a Democrat,
seconded this. " His self control enabled him like Humbolt,
seated on the rim of the crater, to look calmly down into the
boiling caldron below." When he spoke, the members of the
Senate usually listened with care to what he had to offer, not
only because of his intimate connection with the Administration, but also because he seldom addressed his colleagues
merely to hear his own voice. " He never speaks unless he has
something to say," wrote one admiring down-eastern Congressman, " and when he has said it, he sits down." [9]

Always in the bank debate, Wright hit at the heart of the
problem. It was not the deposits but the United States Bank
itself that was the issue.

" Does the bank need the public deposits? " he asked during
a discussion of one of the innumerable memorials that flooded
the Senate. " No sir: because the bank has more loans out
than the community can pay in four years. . . .Why does the
bank want the deposits when it has to wind up in four years
. . .? It is because its friends seek to make a pretext for the
renewal of the charter. . . ."

In this particular speech he was replying to Clay (Clay had
said, " The name of BIDDLE is patriotic, revolutionary—and
implies gallantry, and honor, and probity.") and was followed
by Webster, who attacked his position and disclaimed voci-
ferously any personal connection with the Bank. (How

9 Wright to Marcy, Jan. 15, 1837, Gratz Autograph Collection, Historical
Society of Pennsylvania; H. Gilpin, *Eulogy of Silas Wright*, pp. 16-7;
P. Harvey, *Reminiscences of Daniel Webster*, pp. 233-4; Forney, *Anecdotes
of Public Men*, I, 83; Greeley in *New York Tribune*, quoted in *St. Lawrence
Plaindealer*, 1873, Wright papers, St. Lawrence University; D. Ballou,
" Silas Wright, Governor of New York," Oneida Historical Society,
Transactions, # 5, p. 88; J. Fairfield to Mrs. Fairfield, Feb. 17, 1838 (36?),
Fairfield Letters, A. Staples, ed., p. 198. See also Brockway, *Fifty Years of
Journalism*, p. 77; Marcy to G. Newell, Feb. 2, 1841, Marcy papers, Library
of Congress; *Democratic Review*, V, 417; Gillet, *Wright*, II, 1593.

Wright would have enjoyed reading the " God-Like " Daniel's letters to Nicholas Biddle!) Soon Senator Mangum, of North Carolina, was rising from his seat to say: " The Senator from New York has so said, and we all understand that what he speaks. . .will be spoken by that party which practically controls this administration." All this within a month of his bashful refusal to open his mouth! It must have done Martin Van Buren's heart good, as he sat silently presiding over the Senate, to see the result of his persistence.[10]

Meanwhile, the Bank increased its contractions and the panic grew worse. Businessmen all over the nation were feeling the pinch, and those who had been even slightly speculative in their practices were pressed to the wall. In Albany the pressure struck close to the Regency, for Benjamin Knower, who for all his troublemaking and lobbying was still the Governor's father-in-law and a Jackson man, was forced to close his doors. The reaction of his Regency friends is interesting, for it shows that their hatred of Biddle's Bank did not lessen their horror of speculation. " Mr. Knower's failure created very little sensation here," reported John A. Dix matter of factly. " His operations were so well known that embarrassment in carrying them through was anticipated." Wright also thought that Knower was getting exactly what he deserved. " Blinded by his cupidity," wrote the Senator, he had ruined himself and his friends, and " that same blindness has led him to a dependence on his enemies." This last was true, for foresaken by his old friends, Knower turned to Henry Clay, who interceded in his behalf with Biddle in an effort to get him enough credit to squeeze through.[11]

10 *Reg. Deb.*, X, 553-4; 549, 556-7; 691. See also Van Buren, *Autobiography*, p. 730.

11 J. Dix to Wright, Feb. 11, 1834, Wright to Flagg, Feb. 7, 1834, Flagg papers; Clay to Biddle, Jan. 17, 1834, Biddle papers, Library of Congress, quoted in James, *Jackson* (1 vol. ed.), p. 658. Knower's trouble was only temporary and he was soon solvent again, without any help from Biddle. See I. Spencer, " William L. Marcy Goes Conservative," *Mississippi Valley Historical Review*, XXXI, p. 212.

If the panic hurt business in New York, it only increased the confidence of the leaders of the Regency that their own theories of sound finance were correct. "Our good friends in New York [City]," admitted Dix, " are rather prone to be carried away by excitement," but so far, " failures have been confined to those who have engaged in engrossing something or other, and I do not anticipate even among the merchants any great pressure upon the men who have done their business upon their own capital." Flagg echoed these ideas. " All men who have done a fair business are easy and safe," he wrote to Wright. " For the speculators and monopolists, the times are hard; they have nobody to blame but themselves and the U. S. Bank. If they had been discreet they would not have been within the grasp of the monster." Flagg added that he was worried about the state of affairs at Washington, and that he hoped Congress would not desert " the man whose principles they were sent there to support. . . ." Wright showed this letter to Van Buren, and he in turn, sent it on to the White House along with some letters of Dix's and Wright's and the notation that these three friends of his were " three of the finest fellows in the world." The Old General, whose fighting spirit in those days was thoroughly aroused, read the letters over and then wrote in his laborious scrawl that Van Buren should tell these friends of his not to worry about Congress. " I am as fixed in my course as the Rockey mountain; " his note said, " and. . .no human movement can change me from the course I have chalked out for myself—providence has a power over me, but frail mortals who worship Ball & the golden calf, can have none. A. J." [12]

But as the pressure of the United States Bank on the New York banks continued strong, the feeling grew at Albany that some sort of aid must be given the latter, especially since the new Safety Fund System, a form of bank insurance estab-

12 Dix to Wright, Feb. 12, 11, 1834, Flagg to Wright, Feb. 14, 1834, Jackson to Van Buren, n. d. (on back of Flagg to Wright), Flagg papers.

lished during the short governorship of Van Buren, was
threatened by the "Monster's" incessant curtailment of credit.
Finally, late in March, the legislature granted a six million
dollar loan to the Safety Fund Banks, and the crisis was
weathered. Though this measure had the support of the Regency, Wright was heartily against it. He did not see how
the failure of a few banks could hurt the state. But when he
realized that his friends, especially Van Buren, were not in
accord with his position, he agreed to keep silent. "When I
find myself differing from this sagacious man, and from my
best friends at home, I doubt myself," he admitted humbly.[13]

But the tide had already turned against Biddle. The business elements which had backed the Bank so strongly were
being hurt by its credit contractions more than anyone else.
A New York City committee of businessmen had appealed to
Biddle for relief in February, and had exerted such pressure
on him that when the state loan went through he capitulated,
promising that the contraction of credit would stop. This
really finished the "Monster," for it was a tacit admission
that the whole panic had been manufactured at Philadelphia
for political purposes. Conditions improved in New York, and
the loan to the Safety Fund Banks, which Wright had looked
upon with disfavor, and of which Philip Hone had said, "This
out-Herods Herod," never had to be used at all.[14]

In Congress too, the Jacksonians were clearly victorious.
Early in April, the House passed resolutions against either

13 Wright to Flagg, Mar. 25, 1834, Flagg papers. The fact that his own
home district did not suffer much from the panic probably explains the ex-
tremity of Wright's position. "The season in the northern part of our State
and Vermont is the best for many years," he wrote B. F. Butler. "In this
county, so far as I have yet been able to learn, we have lost nothing by
the panic...." Wright to Butler, July 25, 1834, Wright-Butler letters.

14 Catterall, *Second Bank of the United States*, pp. 343-4; Hammond,
History of New York, II, 441; A. Nevins, *Diary of Philip Hone*, I, 120.
Hone's whole statement was: "This out-Herods Herod; taxing the people
to support Mr. Van Buren's rotten banking system, taking from their
pockets the means of fastening upon their necks the yoke of their political
masters."

recharter or restoration of the deposits and ordered an investigation of Biddle's conduct. After this, though the Bank men might bluster, and though the Senate might frustrate Jackson's appointments and censure his actions, there was no chance for a Bank victory. Congress finally adjourned in June. With the defeat of his efforts Biddle ceased to check the flow of credit and the nation was soon engaged in a wild orgy of expansion and speculation.

* * * * *

That August the Wrights, accompanied by another Canton couple, Mr. and Mrs. Minet Jenison, took a trip to Michigan Territory, traveling most of the way by water. It was not as pleasant as it might have been. On the Great Lakes they ran into bad weather and suffered a good deal from seasickness, and in Michigan the Senator found himself constantly bedeviled by Western politicians. He did not think very highly of them. "Most of the men I met," he wrote Flagg, "were *to me* Jackson and Van Buren men, but the most of them wanted with it a road, a canal, a rail road, or an office. . . . While I talked freely I said nothing." [15]

Their excursion carried them fifty miles beyond Detroit, and Wright was not back at Canton until the middle of September. By then the fall elections were at hand. For Governor, the Democrats had renominated Marcy, and they were not expecting much trouble in electing him. His opponent was a red headed young unknown with a huge beak of a nose, named William Henry Seward. To Wright, Seward's nomination seemed an admission of hopelessness by the opposition. " I would rather my worthy friends should run against men approximating towards an equality with them than to run against those over whom victory brings no credit," he complained to Marcy. He was sure that Seward's followers would gladly trade him and the entire state ticket for a single Congressman. November proved his confidence well justified.

15 Wright to Flagg, Sept. 8, 1834, Flagg papers.

Marcy and the Democrats won so easily that Thurlow Weed even considered giving up the ghost and heading for the frontier, and Philip Hone, stalwart conservative that he was, took to his bed with an attack of vertigo and a headache, admitting, " we were beaten—badly beaten; worse than the least sanguine of us expected. . . ." [16]

* * * * *

The next years moved swiftly. The nation was in the grip of a mighty wave of prosperity and expansion. The national debt, an inheritance of the Revolution, was finally paid off, and a surplus began to accumulate that proved to be far more troublesome than the debt had ever been. Land purchases in the West zoomed to previously undreamed-of figures—$24,-000,000 was paid into the Treasury in 1836 alone for new lands, a sum greater than the total receipts for the entire period between 1820, when the sale of land on credit was stopped, and 1834 when the boom began. A great pyramid of credit was a-building. Speculators in the East borrowed money from local banks, purchased land with it in the West, and then borrowed more money, using the land as security. As the amount of paper in circulation skyrocketed, prices naturally rose, and as the land boom continued, property values increased tremendously. During the winter of 1834-'5 the recently defeated William H. Seward, who owned a good deal of real estate in western New York reported a " great rage " of speculation, with property values up twenty-five per cent and selling easily. This trend was not confined to the West. In February, 1835, for example, Abraham Schermerhorn, of New York, sold a 170 acre farm in the town of Gowanus, about three miles from Brooklyn, for $102,000 after having offered it four years earlier for $20,000 with no takers. Such cases were common.[17]

16 Brockway, *Fifty Years of Journalism*, p. 11; *St. Lawrence Republican*, July 22, 1834; Wright to Marcy, Sept. 20, 1834, Wright papers, New York State Library; Fox, *Decline of Aristocracy*, p. 371; A. Nevins, *Diary of Philip Hone*, I, 141, Nov. 5, 6, 1834.

17 J. McMaster, *History of the People of the United States*, VI, p. 324; Seward, *Autobiography*, p. 251; A. Nevins, *Diary of Philip Hone*, I, 148.

During the last years of Jackson's second administration, the hard money men among his followers, of whom Wright was one,[18] struggled fruitlessly to check this overexpansion and inflation. The volume of money in circulation rose nearly forty million dollars between 1834 and 1836. The system which had been created as a political weapon against the bank of Nicholas Biddle, was producing an economic situation which men like Wright feared every bit as much as the " Monster " itself.

To Wright, speculation was the great evil, because it corrupted men's hearts with thoughts of private gain and handicapped the development of any program demanding disinterested statesmanship in either state or national affairs. As he once said to Azariah Flagg, " it is not the public business but the private gambling which protracts the legislative sessions and so greatly increases their expense." But it was when speculation became tied up with banks that it grew really dangerous, he thought.

By itself, speculation was only a nuisance. If a man thought his interests would be furthered by the construction of a road past his front door, he might vote for someone who would promise to have it constructed, but if it was not, he would say, " ' I have lost nothing in fact, but have failed in a profitable bargain which I had hoped to make.' " But let him borrow a little money from a bank and invest it in a road construction company seeking a charter or government aid, and then " his living, or his speculation, depend upon the action. The loss is not contingent but positive, if he is disappointed, and he therefore, can neither be resisted in his course, nor reconciled to his defeat." The result? A desperate

18 Wright and Thomas Hart Benton were the most prominent in the Senate. It is difficult to determine how closely these two worked together, for most of the papers of both have been destroyed. They were good friends, however, and probably were indebted to each other for ideas on all financial measures. See Benton's tribute to Wright in his *Thirty Years View*, II, 700-2.

group seeking legislation with utter disregard for the general welfare. The banks were the organizing and directing forces which controlled the whole procedure. " I do not think there is much danger of profligate legislation," he told Flagg, " when banks are not behind to push on the bad measures." [19]

Still, he was no extremist. " I am not yet so entirely *loco foco* or ' Bentonian ' that I would, if I could, annihilate banking from the earth," he said. And when " Old Bullion," Thomas Hart Benton, Senator from Missouri, introduced in the spring of 1836 a measure making all paper money redeemable in specie on demand, he opposed it as a too rapid change in a nation which had gone to extremes in " paper circulation." " We must," he said, " retrace our steps gradually, and with care and caution, if we would avoid convulsion. . . ." [20]

But he did want to supply a brake to the unrestricted speculation that was in progress. He supported Jackson's Specie Circular of July, 1836, which checked the boom in land sales by requiring that new lands be paid for in coin, and he opposed Clay's scheme of " distributing " the new federal surplus among the states, which he felt would only add fuel to the fires of credit expansion.

Gradually he was becoming convinced that the government must be separated from all connection with the banks if it was to operate in a disinterested manner:

> The Banks are the most active agent . . . and if they can be disposed of in any way not fatal to the public interests the contest with the other two most prominent [agents], speculative internal improvements . . . and taxation to raise money for distribution . . . will be less powerful . . . . [Whether] public money is to be faithfully expended or wantonly squandered, they are the reservoirs which . . . take up and retain the scattered treasure . . . [and] reap the fruits of a suicidal policy to the people.[21]

19 Wright to Flagg, Jan. 15, 1837, Feb. 26, 1837, Flagg papers.

20 Wright to Flagg, Feb. 26, 1837, Flagg papers; *Reg. Deb.*, XII, 999-1004.

21 Wright to Flagg, Feb. 26, 1837, Flagg papers.

When the "way not fatal to the public interests" appeared, he followed it.

The great boom continued through 1835 and 1836. Symptomatic of its growth was the rapid increase in the number of banks. Six hundred and seventy-seven separate financial institutions existed in the United States by the end of 1836, more than twice the number in operation when Jackson had first become President.[22] Against this trend, Wright, Benton, and some of the other hard money men in the Senate, fought with all their might, but the lure of easy money was powerful, and defection developed within the ranks of the Jackson party. Wright was especially concerned with what was happening in New York. The legislature of the Empire State was firmly Democratic during these years, but it was deeply affected by the speculative trend of the times. In February, 1834, Flagg had been able to write proudly, "The last 3 days have been distinguished by the Death of 30 Bank applications. . . .We have never had a legislature. . .so sound on these matters. There seems not to be a mischievous man in the whole body." But this was at the peak of the panic caused by Biddle's contractions; when the boom began things were different. Two years later Wright had to admit with disgust that it seemed to him that as many banks would be authorized as the money interests desired. As Judge Hammond put it: " The cormorants could never be gouged." Many New York Democrats who had been ardent champions of the fight against Biddle could see no reason for altering the system their victory in that conflict had made possible. It was so easy to make huge profits by speculation. There developed at Albany a shameless scramble for bank charters, with legislators frequently supporting the requests of companies in which they were personally interested. Along with the banks went all sorts of schemes for internal improvements. The old Clintonian policy was winning out

22 McMaster, *History*, VI, p. 339.

behind the shield of Jackson.[23] This was especially disillusion-
ing to the Regency because there were defections close to home.
Edwin Croswell, whose *Argus* was an essential part of the Regency organization, was weakening. Croswell, a small man,
with a swarthy complexion, curly black hair, and the typical
printer's stoop resulting from long years spent over count-
less fonts of type, had grown rich as the recipient of valuable
patronage connected with the official State Printing, and much
of his money was invested in lands and in bank stocks. A
smooth, persuasive individual, with unusual conversational
powers, he had fitted well into the Regency pattern which controlled so thoroughly the political and social life of Albany,
and it was with genuine sorrow that his more radical friends
observed his gradually changing attitude on questions of
money and banking. " For the first time in my life," wrote
Wright sadly in the spring of 1836, " the Argus has. . .re-
mained unopened. . . . [It is filled with speeches favoring] the
most profligate projects for the accumulation of an unmanage-
able State Debt, without a single argument against these projects, and a regular statement of the progress of making banks
and trying Senators for corruption in stock matters have met
my eye. . . ." " Croswell is a most fine, honest, true hearted
man and labours to keep peace on all sides," he told Van Buren
somewhat later, " but [he] is so deeply immersed in hazzard-
ous speculations as to be too far in the power of the moneyed
institutions." The Senator made no effort to conceal his displeasure with what was going on in the state, and this caused
much irritation in certain quarters. He began to get letters
from local politicians telling him politely to keep his nose out
of state affairs, and reminding him, not very subtly, that he
was coming up for reelection in 1837, and that it would not
do to antagonize the legislature. His reaction to these warnings reflects the first signs of Clarissa's influence and the

---

23 Flagg to Wright, Feb. 14, 1834, Wright to Flagg, May 26, 1836, Flagg
papers; Hammond, *History of New York*, II, 447-8.

beginnings of a growing disgust with the sordid politics he saw all around him. As he informed Flagg, "if they had known how very little I care personally about that matter they would have spared themselves the shameless exhibition of the extent to which their log-rolling system has emboldened them to proceed openly." A little later he wrote to another friend, "I have had no cold chils about my re-election. . . .I have a most excellent wife with me who begs me to go home and remain there, and not to follow public life longer. She is right. You will say all this may be so, but that no one wants to be beaten. I agree. . . and. . .I would rather be re-elected, as I have not declined; but if I am not I shall suffer as little mortification as ever did a beaten man." [24] When the time actually arrived, he was reelected without much formal opposition, but only after the Regency leaders applied every pressure at their command against recalcitrant members of the legislature. When the party caucus met, the anti-Wright forces had forty-nine men pledged against him, according to Thurlow Weed. "Vengeance dire was threatened against every man who should vote against Wright," the Albany editor told Francis Granger. The caucus was forced to toe the mark but the "Regency have had at least half a bushel of trouble for three or four days." [25]

Despite feeling aroused over financial policies, the party lines held firm in New York and throughout the nation. There was too much at stake for schism. Eighteen thirty-six was an election year, and the Jacksonians buried their differences and backed Van Buren. For Wright, the campaign meant a great deal of hard work, most of it at his desk writing letters.

24 Brockway, *Fifty Years of Journalism*, pp. 16-7; Wright to Flagg, May 25, 1836, Flagg papers; Wright to Van Buren, May 13, 1837, Van Buren papers; Wright to N. S. Benton, Jan. 11, 1837, property of H. F. Landon, Watertown, N. Y. See also Wright to Marcy, Jan. 15, 1837, Gratz collection.

25 Weed to F. Granger, Feb. 3, 1837, T. Barnes, *Memoir of Thurlow Weed*, p. 50; Hammond, *History of New York*, II, p. 465.

Everyone seemed to want to know something about the Little
Magician. March, 1835, found him writing to Thomas Ritchie
of the *Richmond Enquirer,* explaining his friend's attitude on
slavery, and to others he wrote defending and accounting for
the Candidate's position on the War of 1812, the Missouri
Compromise, and nearly every other political event with
which he had been even remotely connected. Mr. Van Buren
favors this, Mr. Van Buren opposes that; it would seem highly
impolitic to Mr. Van Buren to do so and so,—it was a laborious task.[26] The convention was held at Baltimore, in May,
1835, a full year-and-a-half before the election and Wright
was of course present. There were many difficulties. Tennessee
had failed to send delegates, but Silas ran into a citizen of
that state whom he knew, on the street in Baltimore, and
helped persuade him to attend the meeting and cast the
state's fifteen votes for Van Buren and Richard Mentor Johnson. Johnson was another problem. An extremely colorful
Southerner who never appeared in public without a bright
red vest, his exotic habits and his mulatto mistresses (with
whom he *openly* consorted) weakened him in some quarters,
especially in the South. But he was very popular with working men in the East, and had been offered the Vice-Presidency
to check the formidable campaign he had been making for the
top spot itself. Though he was given the nomination by the
convention, the Virginia delegation refused to support him
under any circumstances. They were, as Wright put it, " sore."
" Do treat them kindly," he urged Van Buren. " They are too
astute as to their principles and too little practical in their
political course. If they are compelled to choose between evils
they seem determined, with the best of motives, to choose the
greatest." These words, so disparaging of " principles " he
would someday have to eat.[27]

26 Wright to Ritchie, March, 1835, Wright to J. Watkins, Feb. 9, 1835,
Wright to ? , Feb. 25, 1835, Van Buren papers.

27 L. Meyer, *Life and Times of Col. R. M. Johnson*, pp. 414-5; 310-11;
Wright to Van Buren, May 22, 1835, Van Buren papers.

However, the convention made the nominations with little difficulty, adhering to the two-thirds rule of 1832, and a committee was then appointed to write an *Address to the Democratic Republicans of the United States.* The group chosen consisted of Wright, former Speaker of the House of Representatives Andrew Stevenson, and four others. Wright was named chairman, but he persuaded the convention to change to Stevenson, who wrote the *Address,* the first Democratic national party platform ever drawn up.[28] As much as possible, the Democrats tried to make the election turn on the question of continuing the policies of Jackson. The opposition, abandoning the name National Republican because they wished to attract States' Rights opponents of Jackson, were beginning to be known as Whigs. A strange agglomerate, they had in common only their dislike for Old Hickory and " Little Van." [29] Minus a leader with a nationwide appeal, they sought to throw the election into the House of Representatives by nominating " favorite sons " in each section: Webster in New England, General William Henry Harrison, a hero of the Indian Wars, in the West, Hugh Lawson White in Jackson's stronghold, Tennessee, and Senator Mangum, of North Carolina, in the South. This strategy was probably sound, but was not successful. Van Buren beat them all, as the wise ones of both parties had expected.[30] The President-elect, wrote Wright after the election, " seems to feel like a man whose greatest ambition was nearly gratified, and who at the same time had been so confident of success and...of meriting it as not to

28 Meyer, *Johnson,* pp. 416-21; E. Eriksson, " Official Newspaper Organs and the Presidential Election of 1836," *Tennessee Historical Magazine,* IX, 121; Wright to Van Buren, May 22, 1835, Van Buren papers.

29 " The truth is, that we Whigs...are a very impracticable set of fellows," wrote Seward. " We all agree that the Tories are ruining the country, and that it is our duty to avert the calamity. But each man must have his own way of averting it." *Autobiography,* p. 250.

30 For Whig defeatism, see *ibid.,* pp. 257-8.

have been made delirious by the anticipated result." [31] The long years of waiting and planning were over but events were soon to demonstrate that Van Buren and his lieutenants were not to enjoy the fruits of their labor in quiet. Dark trouble loomed ahead even before the new President took office.

31 Wright to Flagg, Dec. 16, 1836, Flagg papers. The Whig strategy did succeed in preventing the direct election of Johnson, but when that issue was placed before the Senate, he was chosen anyway.

CHAPTER VII
THE "SECOND DECLARATION OF INDEPENDENCE"

"I would much sooner openly advocate a return ... to the iron money of Lycurgus than pretend to repose further confidence in Banks which made a period of peace, prosperity and plenty such as no country ever before witnessed the excuse for the worst possible kind of bank insolvency...."

Wright to William L. Marcy, June 22, 1837.

JUDGE ENOS THROOP, essentially a practical politician, was trying to do something about the unhappy condition of the Democratic party in New York. "There is a false sense of things at Albany, difficult to penetrate," he informed the President-elect, and he added that the main problem was the financial policy of the Administration. After all, *some* banks are necessary, and " safe ones such as those of our State " should not be attacked by the government, though it is true that they are " prone to abuse power." There is no question but that the government should " keep a watchful eye on them," but " I beleive [*sic*] we shall find a disposition throughout the Union to cherish them."

> We see [he went on] in all parts of the Country immense public enterprises in progress.... Rail roads & canals penetrating New Jersey ... radiating from Philadelphia to reach the western parts of our State, Ohio, Michigan and the far west, & Michigan and Ohio responding to their efforts — Virginia stretching through her State, and crossing the mountains.... South Carolina from Charleston through her own State and North Carolina and Tennessee to Knoxville ... Georgia with her branch railroad connecting all her great navigable waters, and all her important cities with the navigation of the Tenesee river.... Indiana with her congeries of rail roads and canals ... stretching from the Ohio river along the Wabash & Maumee to Lake Erie....

" When we see our Country alive with these enterprises," the Judge concluded, " it seems to me. . .that this active people

will not be satisfied without banks. They see a large field before them for the employment of money, & they will have it
by some means." [1]

This stirring appeal, penned in January, 1837, on the eve
of the great crash, was a protest against the hard money,
credit restricting program of the Jackson administration, particularly the Specie Circular, which had checked the wild
expansion in western lands. The election was over; considerations of self-interest which had held the discontented members
of the party in line were now dissipated; it was time for the
affable " Red Fox " to back down a bit and be " reasonable."
This is certainly what many experienced Whig politicians expected him to do. " I predict," one of them wrote confidently
shortly after Van Buren's inauguration, " that ' the Magician '
will speedily suspend the order."

Vocal discontent within the Democratic party had been
noticeable even before the Specie Circular had been issued,
and now Senator Tallmadge, of New York, a bolter from the
Clintonian ranks, was showing his old colors. As Governor
Marcy said, Tallmadge and Wright " did not harmonize on
all points " in the Senate during the 1836 session. Tallmadge
had criticized Wright's stand on the disposal of the new surplus, and had made an important speech favoring the credit
system and opposing the doctrines of the hard money men.
Given these opinions, he naturally was displeased with the
Specie Order, but he remained quiet until after November.
Congress reassembled in December, as the Old General neared
the end of his stormy reign. The clouds were gathering; it was
indeed time for the Magician to head for cover. But he kept
silent in the face of increasing protest from the malcontents.
While on his way to Washington from Canton for the December session of Congress, Silas Wright had a fine opportunity
to tangle with one of these protesters. [2]

1 Throop to Van Buren, Jan. 28, 1837, Van Buren papers.

2 Seward, *Autobiography*, p. 328; Marcy to Wetmore, July 20, 1836,
Marcy papers; Schlesinger, *Age of Jackson*, p. 200.

In those days travel was often very complicated. To get from New York to Philadelphia it was necessary to take a steamboat to New Brunswick, on the Raritan river, a journey of some forty-five miles, and then proceed by stage to Trenton, on the Delaware. From there another river boat made the journey to the City of Brotherly Love. Arriving in New York from Albany early in the morning to catch the New Brunswick boat, Wright discovered that his colleague, Tallmadge, and Henry Hubbard, a Democratic Senator from New Hampshire, were to be fellow voyagers, but he had little time to converse with them in the bustle of getting aboard, and soon lost track of them on the crowded boat. Suddenly, while sitting in the cabin waiting for breakfast, Wright was accosted by Sherman Paige, a Congressman from Otsego County, New York, who led him hurriedly to the after part of the cabin. Picking his way through the crowd, Wright found Hubbard in the middle of a loud and excited speech which everyone seemed to be enjoying tremendously. The New Hampshire Senator stopped when he saw Wright, greeted him, and then resumed his lecture:

" I will repeat what I was saying, that I have been unable to learn, nor do I believe there are, but three men in the Union who approved of the Specie order. I will now name the men. I mean *old* Jackson, Kendall and Blair,[3] and I would thank any man to show me another man who approves that d - - d order."

This remark produced a great guffaw from Hubbard himself, in which the crowd joined heartily. Wright looked on in stony silence, struggling to control his anger. The others quickly became aware of this and there was an awkward pause. Clearly something was expected of him.

Wright surveyed his audience briefly. He noticed Tallmadge, Daniel Wardwell, one of the New York delegation,

3 Amos Kendall, Jackson's Postmaster General, and Frank Blair, editor of the *Washington Globe*.

several other Congressmen, and Matthew Davis, a newspaper columnist who wrote under the pseudonym, "The Spy in Washington." Then he addressed himself to Hubbard:

" My good friend I am a supporter of the President, who, I suppose, is the person alluded to by you under the denomination of *old* Jackson. Being so, if I have fault to find with him, or his acts, this is not the place, the occasion or the audience, before which I should choose to prefer my charges. . . . I have sought, during my whole life, to avoid the reputation of a stage coach, steam boat, or travelling politician. I do not remember ever to have attempted to raise the laugh of a travelling crowd to the prejudice of a political opponent, much less to the prejudice of a political *friend*. I will only, therefore, do myself the pleasure to show you, Sir, and any others, if there be any others here to whom such a sight would be a curiosity, a fourth person, within the United States. . .who approves that d - - d order, as you please to characterize it."

" The screws, the screws," muttered the " Spy " as everyone stood abashed, and Tallmadge turned pale. The gathering broke up immediately; there was nothing else to say.

Hubbard, who was really a good Jackson man, sat down with Wright for a little social chat. " I was a little too fast," he admitted ruefully, " but you was d - - d severe." And so the incident passed. Yet the spirit of it was ominous.[4]

As the last weeks of the administration of Jackson sped by, the signs of the now rapidly developing panic grew more threatening and the conservative element in the Democratic party more restless. In the Senate, the leadership of this group fell to Tallmadge and William C. Rives, of Virginia. Strangely enough, each of these men owed his position in the Senate to default. Tallmadge, dark, stocky, ambitious, almost overly friendly, and by the florid standards of the day an accomplished speaker, had been chosen by the New York legislature over

4 Seward, *Autobiography*, p. 207; Wright to Flagg, Jan. 9, 1837, Flagg papers.

the opposition of Van Buren, largely because Benjamin Butler, the Magician's law partner and staunch supporter of the Regency, had refused to accept the post. Rives was indebted for his place to John Tyler's exaggerated reverence for the States' Rights doctrine, which had caused him to resign his seat when the Virginia legislature "instructed" him to vote for a measure of which he disapproved.[5] Seeking relief from the stringent restrictions of the Specie Circular, Tallmadge, Rives and their supporters in Congress voted with the Whigs to repeal it, and so great was the fear of the impending collapse that only five senators, (Wright, Benton and Lewis Linn, of Missouri, John Ruggles, of Maine, and Thomas Morris, of Ohio) voted against this new coalition. The measure got through the House as well at the end of the session, but Jackson, firm to the end, put the bill in his pocket and let it expire with the Congress which had passed it.[6]

The new President faced a very trying situation as letters continued to pour in on him calling for the repeal of the Circular. Tallmadge himself addressed a desperate appeal to Van Buren, stressing the fact that Congress had expressed its desires by a solid majority, and warning that the next Congress would be Whig controlled if no action were taken. In this crisis, Van Buren turned to Wright and asked him to stop at New York City on his way home to Canton to report on the state of opinion there. The Senator was agreeable, but he was delayed for two weeks at Washington by the illness of his wife, and did not arrive at the metropolis until March 18.[7] That was a Saturday. The next morning, right after breakfast, he was out "perambulating the city" to see what he could discover. He had expected universal displeasure with the Circu-

5 L. Beardsley, *Reminiscences*, pp. 305-11; *Argus*, Feb. 4, 1833; Seward, *Autobiography*, p. 182; McMaster, *History*, VI, 312-3.

6 James, *Jackson* (1 vol. ed.), p. 718.

7 Tallmadge to Van Buren, Mar. 15, 1837, Van Buren papers; Wright to Flagg, Mar. 19, 1837, Flagg papers.

lar among the merchants because of its restrictive effects on
credit, so he was agreeably surprised when he learned that
there was a substantial group of what he called the "more
dependable class" of businessmen who were well satisfied with
it. They approved the Order, these men told Wright, because
in preventing the flow of capital to the West for land purchase,
it left more for the business needs of New York.

Wright had been very alarmed upon his arrival by a report
that the banking house of the Joseph brothers, one of the
largest in the city, had been so hard hit by the panic that it
had closed its doors. He thought that this news would
frighten the business community, but surprisingly enough,
the reaction of many of the merchants he met was exactly the
opposite! One merchant acquaintance, Robert White, told the
Senator that he and his friends were actually pleased by the
collapse of the Josephs. This firm, White told him, had always
been unsound in its policies, and the months of tightening
credit had wreaked havoc on its operations. Unable to meet
their obligations, the Josephs had been forced to borrow money
in large amounts, and in an already tight money market, their
desperate efforts to raise funds had driven the interest rate
up as high as seven per cent. This was a ruinous price to pay
for cash, but faced with failure, the Josephs had been willing
to pay it. Other merchants and businessmen with less urgent
but still important needs were unable to borrow at profitable
rates, so many felt that the failure of the Josephs would relieve the pressure and enable them to get money on more reasonable terms.[8]

The next day, a rumor came to Wright that the Josephs
had weathered the storm. A large sum was thought to be on
its way from outside the city to enable them to resume busi-

---

8 Even Philip Hone, who was a friend of neither the Democratic party
nor the Circular, admitted to his diary that the failure of the Josephs,
"Men almost strangers amongst us and of that class or nation in whom
we have no great reason to place much confidence," was a result of their
own recklessness. Nevins, *Diary of Philip Hone*, I, 248-9, Mar. 17, 1837.

ness. He was disappointed by this news, for he could not conceal the relish with which he observed the collapse of any speculative enterprise such as theirs. He hurried down to Wall Street to see what his friends there thought of the story. They were not impressed. "The knowing ones,"[9] Wright reported later to Van Buren, "laid their fingers by the side of their nose and said, ' they cannot and will not resume.' " And they did not.

Certain men of all political faiths on the Street told Wright that it was foolish to attribute the state of affairs in the financial world to any government policy. They were no doubt right, for the depression that was developing in 1837 was world-wide. At most Jackson's Specie Circular only hastened a collapse which the wave of speculation and inflation of the past few years had made inevitable. But as Silas knew, the men who realized this represented only a minority of the business guild—those intelligent and dispassionate enough to understand the economic forces at work. "It is undoubtedly true that the mass, numerically counted, consider the order as more or less the cause of all pecuniary embarrassments under which the country is now suffering and. . .the sole cause of the present excessive prices of money and everything else," he admitted to the President when he told him of his experiences in New York. He believed that the Circular should not be rescinded, and while admitting that some modification of it might help the financial condition of the western states, he could not suggest any practical plan for doing this.[10]

While in New York, he paid a visit to Enos Throop and relayed the President's desire for the ex-Governor's continued

9 It has not been possible to identify the merchants with whom Wright conversed, but it is probable that he was correct in referring to them as members of the "more dependable class," meaning those who were conservative in their business practices because they were already rich and well established. Wright's hard money attitude made him popular with this group. Witness his strength in New York City in the gubernatorial elections of 1844 and 1846.

10 Wright to Van Buren, Mar. 21, 1837, Van Buren papers.

support. Throop was impressed and expressed deep loyalty to Van Buren and the party, but soon he was writing to Washington along the lines of his earlier letter.[11] Van Buren did nothing to relieve the pressure on the money market or to bolster the confidence of business. As conditions deteriorated, with banks failing and businesses closing their doors in larger and larger numbers, the possibility of compromise within the Democratic party grew more remote. Flagg's views delineated the stand of the hard money faction: Land, cotton and stock speculators, he suggested to Van Buren, were only " reaping the fruits of their wretched bubbling system; " any assistance from the government in the form of easing credit would merely prolong " the malignant disease which for 2 years has afflicted the body politic." The many failures were the only cure for the " demoralizing, demoniac spirit " of the day. As in 1828, when the tariff had been the big issue, Flagg was primarily an agrarian. The farmers " are generally free from debt, and have a little hard money for a cloudy day," he wrote.[12] This was the " ultraism " of which Throop had complained and about which he and many others continued to write the President.

Once again, Wright took on the rôle of investigator. Early in May, he made a hurried trip from Canton to Albany and discovered that the split there was just as serious as had been feared. Croswell he found to be well-meaning but still controlled by his speculative interests; Flagg was firm but very irritable; the legislature disunited. It was a sober letter that he wrote in passing his observations on to Van Buren. Its only good news was on Governor Marcy. Wright had been

11 Throop to Van Buren, Mar. 22, May 10, 1837, Van Buren papers.

12 Flagg to Van Buren, Apr. 10, 1837, Van Buren papers. Wright commented similarly: " I have never known the farmers of the north so well off, so lightly indebted and with so abundant means of payment." Wright to Van Buren, May 28, 1837, Levi Woodbury papers, Library of Congress. The fact that their own people were not harmed by the depression no doubt accounts for the willingness of men like Flagg and Wright to let the sufferers pay the penalty for their indiscretions in full measure.

very doubtful about Marcy's loyalty to the Specie Circular until he saw and spoke to him, but now, he informed "Little Van," he was sure the Governor was "sound and ardent and more bold than I have ever known him." [13]

As Wright left Albany on May 8, his report was very badly timed, for while he was returning home the situation changed radically. The banks of New York City, unable any longer to meet the demands for coin which the panic was causing, were forced to suspend specie payment. Within a few days the rest of the nation's financial institutions followed suit. Under the New York law establishing the Safety Fund System, non-specie paying banks automatically lost their charters, but this emergency prompted the state legislature to rush through a bill granting a year's grace to all the suspended banks. An effort was also made to repeal a law which prevented small bills from circulating, for public hoarding had driven most of the small change in the state into hiding, but the session was about to end and the hard money men were able to block such a change.

Wright was outraged by the failure of the banks to continue meeting their obligations in specie. "I will confess that my deep disappointment, mortification and vexation at the course of our Banks exceeds any thing I have ever experienced," he wrote to Governor Marcy. "I believe my searches after a remedy are impeded by the uncontrollable inclination to turn and curse them and their managers." There were a few honest banks, he admitted, but they were "few and far between."

> I have not been very celebrated for my friendship to . . . Banks, but . . . [I thought] that a large number of our banks saw and felt their duties and responsibilities to the Country as institutions in whose hands the preservation . . . of our currency was placed. I did therefore think there were some of them which would sustain themselves if the heavens should fall. . . . But no! I deceived myself. . . .

13 Wright to Van Buren, May 13, 1837, Van Buren papers.

"Had I been the fiscal officer of a Bank in this State," he went on fervently, "it should have been sustained as a specie-paying bank until relieved from that sacred obligation by law or I should have ceased to be an officer of it." Wright confessed to owning $1,200 in bank stocks (a large part of his capital) but said that if this money had been "sunk" in order to continue specie payment, he would have been grateful rather than disappointed. He did not openly complain about the extension granted by the legislature, but he wanted it definitely settled that there should be no further leniency when the year was up. If the banks knew they had to resume, they would set their affairs in order and do so, he suggested to Marcy. Otherwise they might continue in their present condition indefinitely. He admitted that forcing the banks to liquify their assets might work hardships on some of their customers, but it was not in his makeup to offer mercy to speculators. "We know well that a very large proportion of the credits of the last three years can never be wound up but in insolvencies," he said. "Twelve months is surely time enough to enable sound and solvent men to separate themselves from the excessive devotees of the credit system."

Wright was naturally opposed to the repeal of the law prohibiting the circulation of small bills. The attitude of men like Tallmadge, who published a letter favoring repeal, reminded him of the story of the "very worthy presbyterian clergyman and a very wicked paritioner [sic]." The minister had urged his wayward sheep to try to "overcome the world of the flesh and the Devil." To this suggestion the culprit replied that he had always made it a habit "to have no transactions whatsoever with the Devil" in the first place, and that he had also found the one possible way of overcoming the flesh. He offered to tell the clergyman what this method was, and the latter was of course eager to know. "Gratify it at once," the sinner said. "That is the only way to prevent its giving you trouble."[14]

14 Hammond, *History of New York*, II, 470-1; Beardsley, *Reminiscences*, p. 319; Wright to Marcy, June 22, 1837, Gratz Collection.

This, said Wright, was exactly what men like Tallmadge were doing when they yielded to demands for paper money.

Silas was thus clear-cut and positive in his mind as to what New York should do, but despite much thought during the month that followed the suspension, he was unable to suggest any practical remedy for the problem which this suspension posed for the national government.

By their refusal to convert their paper into hard money the banks of the nation had forced the issue, for the Van Buren administration had either to remove its funds from the banks or abandon the Specie Circular. The President acted quickly. As soon as the banks ceased to pay in coin he called a special session of Congress for September, and submitted a general plan to his friends. This called for removing the federal monies from all banks and depositing them in government sub-treasuries in various cities throughout the country.

Notice how this would work. The government, which received money from two main sources, import duties and land sales, would put its funds in government vaults and keep them there until needed to meet expenses. The money could not be lent out at interest by any private banker for personal profit. Also, none of the people's money could be used in private speculation. The proceeds from the sales of public lands could not be used as a basis for pyramiding bank credits and inflating values as they had been used during the boom of 1834-36. This did not mean that the banks would be controlled by the government. They would still be free to engage in any sort of speculative ventures they desired. But they could not use the government's money to do so.

Now add to this the Specie Circular, requiring that sums due the government be paid in coin, or paper money redeemable in coin. A man wishing to buy public land, for example, would have to pay for it in hard cash. But once again, no direct restriction would be placed on private banks. They would not have to redeem their bills in gold or silver on demand. But if they did not, the government would not accept their notes as money, though private persons might do so if they wished. Once again the principle of the plan is clear. The banks do as they wish, they set and maintain their own policies, and the government does likewise. The people collectively, the nation, sets its own monetary standards, the people individually do as they please.

The response to this proposal was enthusiastic among Van Buren's hard money friends. Wright, however, had his doubts about its success in Congress, and these were augmented by the depressed and querulous condition into which he had sunk after the suspension by the New York banks. Much as he tried, he could not refrain from the sort of recrimination he had expressed in his letter to Marcy. He found it almost impossible to look to the future, and when he forced himself to do so, he could see nothing but further defeat for his cherished ideals. Clarissa's illness and her complaints about the special session which would keep him away from home most of the fall intensified his low spirits.

But he liked the financial plan itself because it severed the government's connection with all banks. " I can most safely say," he wrote Van Buren, " that I had rather repose any degree of confidence connected with our monied affairs in the worst executive. . .than in the best bank. . . .In the one case there is responsibility that can be reached. In the other, as soon as interest and insolvency harmonize, there is not the least, and these two seeming contradictions will harmonize the moment it becomes inconvenient for these souless institutions to meet their liabilities." The difficulty, in his opinion, lay in the fact that a strong party had " wedded every feeling of their hearts to Banks." " It is true they would prefer a monarchy to an oligarchy as a bank government, but to be bank governed has become their passion." In his despondency he was afraid that many Democrats would go along with them in this aim.

Wright was also afraid that if the Sub-Treasury plan failed to pass, the opposition would capitalize on it by representing it as another attempt at "executive usurpation" of power. Perhaps this was a "cowardly" fear, he admitted, but he felt that a defeat would be an "immeasurable disaster." Yet he realized that there could be no compromise. If the government left its funds in the banks and accepted from them paper that could not be redeemed in hard money, the whole wave of speculation which had just collapsed would be revitalized. The thought of that possibility stirred him deeply. He fumed at the government's impotence. That the banks could refuse to make payments in coin, and that Congress could meet in special session not to make them do so, but to hear them explain that any attempt to force such payment would result in the complete loss of the Treasury's money angered him no end. In anger, he became more determined. He assured the new President that he was anxious to continue the struggle with the banks " until the great interests of our society and especially of our labouring classes are placed beyond the reach of their caprice and cupidity, and until they shall cease to be political institutions and be made faithfully to serve the wants of trade and commerce. . . ." He prayed that all Democrats would stand firm, but feared they would not.[15]

During June, Van Buren kept a steady stream of information on the new plan headed toward Canton. He sent drafts of proposed bills, letters from other politicians, requests for further suggestions, and finally the news that he had definitely decided to push the proposal at the special session. Meanwhile, Wright was travelling around his own countryside sounding out public opinion. He was much heartened by what he discovered. Everyone seemed to favor the complete separation of public funds and private banks, and more important, all seemed to think that Congress would back the new scheme. This was exactly what the Senator had needed to resolve his doubts. It was characteristic of him, when he was uncertain about a new issue, to want to talk it over with men whom he

15 Wright to Van Buren, June 4, 22, 1837, Van Buren papers.

knew and whose motives he trusted. When most of the farmers of St. Lawrence County felt one way on any question that
was enough for him, especially if they thus confirmed his own
wishes. So he told Van Buren that he favored unreservedly
the immediate prosecution of the plan, and prepared to do his
part in ensuring its success. Once he had seen the way, he had
no qualms about the rectitude of the President's course. The
country must have a currency " convertable at pleasure into
gold and silver," he told Marcy. If the banks would not supply
it, the government must supply itself. " The scarecrow terms
of *ultraism,* visionary theorizing, silly experiments, and the
like, communicate no alarm whatsoever to me, as I would
much sooner openly advocate a return. . .to the iron money of
Lycurgus than pretend to repose further confidence in Banks
which make a period of peace, prosperity and plenty such as
no country ever before witnessed the excuse for the worst possible kind of bank insolvency. . . ." [16]

Wright's particular contribution to the work of preparing
the public for the new plan was a series of eight unsigned articles on " The Times " which were printed between June 20
and August 15 in the *St. Lawrence Republican,* a local weekly
published at Ogdensburg. Picked up by big Democratic papers
like Blair's *Washington Globe,* these pieces transcended local
barriers and reached a national audience.[17] The first article
was merely introductory, laying out the plan of the series, but
in the second, *The Causes of the present deranged state of the
Commercial business of the Country,* he began to unwind his
argument.

The first cause of the trouble, he said, was " overtrading,"
buying more than was sold. He pointed out that American

16 Wright to Van Buren, June 22, 1837, Van Buren papers; Wright to
Marcy, June 22, 1837, Gratz Collection.

17 *St. Lawrence Republican,* June 20–Aug. 15, 1837; R. Gillet to
D. Manning, Aug. 29, 1874, in book of bound clippings, *The Times,* by Silas
Wright, New York Historical Society. In writing these articles, Wright
was assisted by John L. Russell, a young North Country lawyer. Wright to
Russell, Mar. 10, 1846, Gillet, *Wright,* II, p. 1728.

commodity imports had exceeded exports in 1836 by some $60,000,000. This was a debt, his reasoning ran, and was chargeable against individuals, either as merchants or stockholders in corporations.

> In either shape it is overtrading, just as much as it is overtrading for the laborer, the mechanic, or the farmer, to purchase more than the wages of his labor, the avails of his trade, or the produce of his farm will pay for.

Secondly, the crash was the result of speculation, especially in land. St. Lawrence County was an excellent example, for everyone there was affected by the " speculating mania." First the merchants became involved, then everyone possessed of a little capital joined in.

> The mad spirit of speculation, of attaching to the soil of the country ... a value bearing no reference whatsoever to convenient use, or profitable enjoyment, but merely as converting portions of our earth into commodities for sale in the market ... was preceded and has been constantly accompanied by an effort to give the same imaginary value and the same speculative character to every necessary of life.

All other causes of our troubles, Wright wrote, were only " consequences which flow from the two first. . . .And do they not prove that the origin of these evils is at home, is with ourselves, and not abroad, or with others? " He thought that they did.[18]

In the third essay he turned to why the banks had suspended specie payments. Just as commerce suffered from " overtrading " so finance suffered from " overbanking," he said. He reviewed the conditions which had resulted from the United States Bank's efforts to curtail credit in 1833 and 1834, and the unchecked expansion that had followed once the pressure was released. He stressed again the evil of using land not for what it could produce but as a commodity for gambling. Such

18 *St. Lawrence Republican*, June 27, 1837.

use, he pointed out, created a demand for capital for which there was no economic justification. As banks became weighted down with speculative loans, they reached a point where they could no longer meet the demands made upon them in hard money. Then came suspension. If suspension was not quickly terminated, he warned, it would enable the banks to resume their wild speculative practices.[19]

The New York Senator's next article weighed the effect of the Specie Circular on the crash. Here his argument was rather feeble and contradictory. He explained how the Circular had been issued by Jackson to check the speculation in western lands and extolled it for " arresting that fearful drain of capital which was so rapidly commencing from the old states. . .to seek investment in the immense public domain of the nation," but in another sentence he denied that any " real capital " had been involved in land sales before the Circular had been called into existence. In the main, this article praised the Circular without making a serious effort to clear it of any connection with the ultimate collapse.[20]

After another treatise considering the state of the banks of New York, he got to the heart of his discussion, the government's new program, in article number six. According to the Constitution, said Wright, Congress could prescribe the kind of money to be received and paid out by the federal government.

> [But] The currency of the government is the currency of the people. . . . If the governments, state and national, require a sound currency for themselves . . . by their legislation, the same legislation will provide for and secure a sound currency for the people. . . .

The government should set the standard for the banks by creating " a perfect and entire separation between the finances

19 *Ibid.*, July 4, 1837.
20 *Ibid.*, July 11, 1837.

of the nation and all the banks. . . .Let collections into the national treasury be collections of *money* or its equivalent, and not inconvertible bank notes." Then inconvertible notes would fall in value and banks issuing them would have to raise their standards and resume specie payment in order to stay in business.[21]

A general criticism of the New York banking system followed, in which he called for more rigid controls over stock issues and over loans to directors and stockholders. Then Wright concluded the series with a piece auspiciously entitled: *The duties of the People in reference to their governments, State and National, as the Constitutional power to correct abuses in either, to defend their own interests, and to secure for themselves and their posterity equal justice, public liberty and the right of private property*. The argument went like this:

In times of crisis the voters must direct their representatives; if they do not, then they themselves are to blame for abuses which may develop. Therefore, they should " see that, in. . .future legislation. . .the interests of the public and the safety of the currency are made paramount to the private interests connected with banks. . . .The interests of stockholders and managers of banks. . .are merely consequential and secondary." A "careful scrutiny" of all legislatures is necessary. It is up to the people too, to make sure that no unnecessary bank charters are issued. Each proposed charter should be examined individually. There must be no rushing them through state legislatures " in phalanx."

Popular pressure behind the standard of sound currency is essential, he continued, but above all, citizens ought to be vigilant in protecting their institutions against attacks by the money power. In 1832 the nation decided against *the* United States Bank by reelecting Jackson after his veto of the recharter bill, and in 1834 against *a* United States Bank by approving the removal of the deposits, in both cases to avoid the

21 *Ibid.*, July 25, 1837.

danger to the democratic system of government inherent in
a single bank with $35,000,000 capital. Experience since then
has shown that the smaller local banks " unite their action
upon every pressing emergency " and thus they too become
" a concentrated money power, and aristocracy of wealth."

The attack should not be directed against banks as such;
" their conduct should control their standing in the public
estimation." But they must not control the government:

> Against that the people must labor with a sleepless vigilance.
> ... If the time shall ever come when a political party shall
> rise up and be successful in our country, whose principles
> shall be found in a bank charter, or in the charter of any other
> corporate money power, then may we class our government
> with the most dangerous aristocracies upon the earth. [Then
> our people] must be content to fatten upon the humble boons
> which corporate wealth shall in mercy grant, whether those
> boons shall be presented in the mitigated form of an irredeem-
> able paper currency, or the more severe aspect of menial
> service, in a manufactory, or upon a manor.[22]

* * * * *

Wright's articles were only part of a great campaign of
education carried on by the Van Burenites all over the country.
But they were not unopposed, even within their own party.
The followers of Tallmadge and Rives, calling themselves
Conservatives because they were seeking to preserve the existing financial structure, fought hard to weaken the hard money
men's control of the Democratic organization. In Virginia,
Rives found a powerful ally in Ritchie's *Richmond Enquirer*.
In New York the Tallmadge forces were not idle. At Albany,
late in June, they grasped control of the local Democratic
machine, the Albany General Committee, and on the twenty-
ninth they issued a manifesto defending the credit system.
The depression was the result of overtrading and speculation,
ran their argument, but the situation had been aggravated by

22 *Ibid.*, Aug. 8, 1837.

the national government's accumulation of a surplus which had encouraged the people to be extravagant. The manifesto upheld the suspension of specie payments and the act of the legislature granting the banks a year to resume, said that the depression was only temporary, and claimed that prosperity was just around the next corner. Unlimited bank credit was no doubt dangerous, it concluded, but " we cannot agree with those who decry the whole credit system. . . .Prudence, industry and economy, will soon set all things right. . . ."

This analysis of the depression, so similar to conservative explanations of another, similar upheaval a century later, was slipped into the *Argus* without the knowledge of editor Croswell. Croswell still adhered to the official party position, though by now he could not have been seriously opposed to what the manifesto said. But there was no doubt that its publication was " a scurvy trick," as Flagg put it. The *Argus* made a belated attempt to repair the damage, printing what Dix called " corrections," and Tallmadge, whose friends had been responsible for the piece, was roundly denounced.[23]

The Conservatives in open opposition to the Sub-Treasury were a relatively small group, but many others, like Croswell, were not pleased with Van Buren's plan at all, and only backed it out of party loyalty. The attitude of Governor Marcy, who was above all a practical politician and a frank opportunist, perhaps typified that of a large number of New York office holders. " The cause of monopolies and exclusive privileges must suffer," he wrote to George Bancroft, the historian, " but I doubt the practicability of sustaining a party which goes at once for the entire demolition of all credit as a system and shall insist on conducting the affairs of the country with no other circulating medium but gold and silver. . . .Those who will be by any such a change injuriously affected will oppose

23 *Argus*, July 1, 6, 1837; Dix to Van Buren, July 5, 1837, Flagg to Butler (?), July 12, 1837, Cambreleng to Van Buren, July 20, 1837, Van Buren papers. Croswell was in New York City with Flagg at the time the Manifesto was published.

the hard money doctrine and the republicans [*i.e.* Democrats] of that class will consult their interests in too many instances and cooperate with the Whiggs in favor of some system of credit." [24]

The Conservative leaders made no secret of their dislike for the President's program, but they were not yet willing to defy their official chief entirely. Wright, hoping for unity, had written Tallmadge telling him when he expected to arrive at New York so that they could travel together to Washington for the special session, but Tallmadge had other plans. The result was a little incident which might have been silly but for its implications.

When Silas arrived at the metropolis, he went directly to the City Hotel. As he entered, he was spotted by a small group of what he later identified as " credit " Democrats, who were in deep consultation with Senator Tallmadge and several New York Congressmen. Unwilling to be seen by Wright under such circumstances, the " credit " men bolted out a side door. Then about ten minutes later they returned. They approached the hotel bartender (who would, they probably thought, be the person in the establishment most likely to have seen the Senator) and asked if he had arrived. They were directed to the sitting room, and there accosted Wright with a great show of cordiality. Tallmadge himself, when he talked to Wright, announced very regretfully that he had to leave immediately for Washington, and could not wait even until the next day. So the two New York senators had no opportunity to discuss the vital problem that was driving them into rival camps.

Tallmadge's purpose was easy to understand. When he left for the Capital, he had in tow a large group of New York Congressmen, including several newly elected members whom

<hr>

24 Marcy to G. Bancroft, June 17, 1837, Bancroft papers, Massachusetts Historical Society. For a fuller explanation of Marcy's position at this time see I. Spencer, " William L. Marcy Goes Conservative," *Mississippi Valley Historical Review*, XXXI, 222-3, and A. Schlesinger, *Age of Jackson*, pp. 237-8.

he was trying to inveigle into seeing things his way. One of these, John Palmer, was a friend of Wright's who had been in politics for twenty years, though he was serving his first term in the House. Palmer was no greenhorn, but he played up to Tallmadge in order to discover his game and later reported his findings to Wright. The Senator's technique was amusing. Frank Blair, he had informed the gullible new Representatives, must not be elected Printer of the House, because he was already the Senate's printer and it was not considered proper in Washington for one man to hold both offices! Tallmadge also told the new men not to vote for the Administration candidate for Speaker, James K. Polk, unless Polk agreed to keep Churchill C. Cambreleng (a very close friend of Van Buren's) off the Ways and Means Committee, and to recast that body "agreeable to the principles of the 'credit system.'" Tallmadge was seconded in all this by several "experienced" members of the New York delegation, and despite Palmer's immunity, Wright was afraid that some of the other new men who were not as familiar with procedure and the state of affairs within the party would be taken in. In Washington, Tallmadge continued his efforts to convert Congressmen. He visited Senator Linn, of Missouri, and addressed him long-windedly on the value of the existing fiscal set-up. Linn later described the scene to Wright. Tallmadge, he said, "looked pale, trembled, walked the room, rubbed his hands together, and recited...." Though Linn was not impressed, Tallmadge and his fellow conspirator, Rives, may well have influenced other more susceptible souls.[25]

But ignoring such dissidents when the special session met, the President called uncompromisingly for an independent treasury and the divorce of government and banking. The Administration presses were ecstatic in their praises (the *Globe* called Van Buren's message a "second declaration of inde-

25 Wright to Flagg, Sept. 3, 1837, Flagg papers; Niles to Welles, Sept. 3, 1837, Welles papers, Library of Congress.

pendence "), the enemy papers completely condemnatory. Special pressure was brought to bear on Croswell. Tell him Van Buren expects him to support the message " without equivocation," Wright told Flagg. " He will never find better friends than many of those who wish him now again to make the Argus what it was and what it should have continued to be." Croswell reluctantly got in line, and on September 8 the *Argus* reported favorably on the message and the plan of the Independent Treasury. Wright was particularly pleased with the frank nature of Van Buren's message, which, he wrote, " exempts our President from [any] further charge of ambiguity or non-committal." It left the Conservatives looking " like a collapse of the cholera," he told Flagg.[26]

The Van Burenites hastened to marshal their Congressional strength. In the House, after some organizational jockeying, Polk was chosen Speaker despite resistance from what Wright called " our *paper* friends in our own delegation." In the Senate, where Wright was now Chairman of the Committee on Finance, things went more smoothly. A caucus of Democratic Senators (from which Tallmadge absented himself) proved to be in Wright's estimation " firm, active and determined." The course mapped out therein was quickly put into effect. In 1836, a distribution bill, providing that the proceeds of federal land sales should be " deposited " in the separate states for " safe-keeping " had been enacted. The action of this law was now suspended. Another act was passed authorizing the issuance of $10,000,000 in interest-bearing treasury notes to tide the government over the crisis which the panic had produced in the national coffers. Then the Senate turned to the Independent Treasury or " Divorce " bill. On this the debate was short but violent. The arguments of the Whigs and Conservatives were at best rather oblique. As Wright had feared they attacked the bill as an example

---

26 *Washington Globe*, Sept. 4, 1837; *Argus*, Sept. 8, 1837; Wright to Flagg, Sept. 5, 1837, Flagg papers. For a summary of the Whig reaction, see Schlesinger, *Age of Jackson*, pp. 236-7.

of executive usurpation of power; they claimed that no government official would be able to withstand the temptations involved in handling so much money. They charged that it provided one kind of money for the government and another for the people, and they said it threatened the very existence of all banks. Tallmadge's speech, on September 22, covered all these points in detail. The defense of the banks which he offered was completely unabashed. He said he had "looked with horror upon the ruthless warfare that had been carried on against the mercantile interest."

> Capital—solid wealth—is ever essentially aristocratic. It never can be generally or widely diffused. . . . The banker with his notes has done as much for the cause of freedom as either the printer with his printing press, or the schoolmaster with his grammar.

He attacked the Divorce bill as "a mere catch-phrase" and a "new experiment," decried the "temptations" which it placed before public officers, and reminded the Administration "that whilst they are talking of a divorce, they are getting up an incestuous union between members of the same family. . . ." [27]

The Democrats leaped to the defense and extolled the virtues of the proposed scheme. Wright himself, after introducing the measure, was silent until shortly before it came to a vote, and then, on October 2, he delivered a long speech which Jackson called "the tex book of the republicans for all time to come."

First of all, he began, the new system would heighten the Treasury Department's efficiency.

> It would give the treasury direct possession and perfect knowledge of all its means. . . . It would, at all times, enable the treasury to pay the demands upon it . . . whereas [under the

---

27 McMaster, *History*, VI, 416-7, summarizes the Whig argument. Tallmadge's speech is in *Reg. Deb.*, XIV, 160-84.

old system] these moneys were liable to become unavailable in the hands of banks. . . .

In the second place, it would relieve the whole government from all sorts of bank influences, ending the banks' efforts "to make money out of the money and means and credit of the people," and discharging the government "from the eternal round of imputations" to which all its financial operations had been subject. Under the old system, if a government official in good times failed to pick a particular bank as a depository for federal funds, he was attacked; in bad times, every draft on a deposit bank was looked upon as a deliberate effort to hurt the institution involved. The Independent Treasury would eliminate all such complaints.

Next Wright took up the bill's implications for the banks. It would help them, he said, because it would put them on their own, and free them from the uncertainties of federal legislation. It was nonsense to say that they could not exist without federal deposits—had they not done just that before the deposits had been removed from the United States Bank? If banks were to survive, they must "build up for themselves a new character, based upon a perfect fulfillment of all their obligations."

But the outstanding benefit, according to Wright, was the change which would be effected in the nation's currency:

> It would give a stable and uniform value to the currency received into and paid from the public treasury . . . stimulate, if not compel, the banks to elevate their paper currency . . . and go very far to measure the public confidence in these institutions by the standard which regulates the currency received and disbursed by the government. . . . If you do not fix and maintain a proper standard of currency none can exist in the country [he told the senators]. If you adopt and adhere to the constitutional standard in your transactions, the influence of your example will be all-powerful with the banks . . .

Webster, Wright charged, had said that the scheme would give good money to the government and let the people shift for themselves.

> If we do not provide a sound standard of currency, our masters, the people, cannot enjoy a sound currency. . . . We act for them and not for ourselves, and the standard . . . we adopt for the public treasury is adopted for them and not for us.

It was growing late in the afternoon, and Wright hurried to put down some of the other less sensible criticisms raised against the bill. It increased not the Executive's power, he said, but his responsibilities; it would not keep any more money out of circulation than the state bank system did, but if a surplus in the government coffers should develop then it would be better to have it "hoarded" than used by banks to stimulate speculation. Before taking his seat he added one last word in defense of his own position. He had been charged with inconsistency because he had approved the depositing of federal funds in the state banks in 1834. Time had convinced him, he said, that his confidence in that system had been misplaced. Therefore he retracted cheerfully his former support.[28]

Two days later the bill passed the Senate by a comfortable majority, but in the House, the Conservative strength was too much for it, and it was tabled by a vote of 120 to 107. So the special session ended without accomplishing its major purpose. Yet the issue was by no means abandoned. When Congress met again in December, Wright was ready to introduce the Divorce bill all over again.

* * * * *

Meanwhile, what of the divisions in New York? Travelling northward after the special session Wright stopped at Albany for a talk with Flagg about Croswell and the *Argus*. It was difficult to pin any definite disloyalty on the glib Albany editor, but his lack of enthusiasm for the Independent Treasury

---

28 *Congressional Globe*, V, appendix, pp. 113-21; Jackson to Buchanan, Dec. 25, 1837, *Jackson Correspondence*, J. Bassett, ed., V, 522.

verged on impartiality—hardly what the Regency expected of
its chief editorial spokesman. Croswell opened his columns to
free discussion on matters which to his friends were closed
and decided. Late in September, for instance, had appeared an
article signed "Marshall" attacking the Divorce bill. It was
filled with such sentiments as "the country is not in a position
to try experiments" and its general tone was one which
called upon the people to "pause" and "reflect." Croswell remarked editorially that he thought the author overemphasized
the weaknesses of the proposed Independent Treasury, but that
his opinions deserved "full and free discussion." If Croswell
knew who "Marshall" was,[29] he did not let on to members
of the Regency, who immediately took up the cudgels against
this mysterious opponent. On September 27 he was answered
by "Jefferson" (John Dix) in a stirring defense of the Divorce bill, and the next day by "Crino," who was Samuel J.
Tilden, a young law clerk fresh from New York University.
"Marshall" of course replied, and while the citizenry got a
fine chance to read about both sides of the question, that was
not what a political journal of the 1830's was supposed to provide. Then the *Argus* printed in full the speech of Senator
Tallmadge that attacked the question of the hour so bitterly,
taking the same judicial attitude toward it editorially that it
had with "Marshall's" article. Wright's speech, as one local
Democrat put it, was withheld until "the poison had been
thoroughly diffused."[30] Then, when the Divorce bill was
tabled in the House and it became clear that it could not pass
during the special session, Croswell blamed *both* the Conservatives and the regulars, and could do no more than call for
harmony. Still he claimed to be in favor of the separation of

29 The author was Samuel Beardsley, of Utica. H. Donovan, *The Barnburners*, p. 29.

30 *Argus*, Sept. 20, and Sept.–Oct. *passim*, 1837; Flagg to Van Buren,
Nov. 5, 1837, E. Tilden to Van Buren, Nov. 23, 1837, Van Buren papers.
The *Argus* printed Rives' speech on Oct. 17, Tallmadge's on Oct. 21, and
Wright's on Oct. 26.

the government funds from private banks, and to be a firm supporter of Van Buren![31]

Croswell at least maintained a nominal allegiance, and Marcy, who had been so hesitant, gradually came to accept, if not to like, the financial policy of the party. Tallmadge and the Conservatives, however, went into outright opposition, and created their own state organization. This really meant that they had become Whigs. Even in October, 1837, Tallmadge was receiving congratulations from Luther Bradish, a North Country Whig from Franklin County, for his speech against what Bradish called " the 'untried expedient ' of my Senatorial neighbor from St. Lawrence. . . ." Tallmadge's reply to Bradish is illuminating. He had acted, he wrote, " without regard to consequences personal or political." " No intimidation from any quarter shall deter me from the expression of my opinions. I consider the present period the most alarming in the history of the country. The wild spirit of radicalism encouraged by those in high places threatens. . .to prostrate our prosperity, and. . .eventually subvert our free institutions." The line between ideas like these and orthodox Whiggery was thin indeed.[32] As Seward commented sardonically on Tallmadge's actions, " So strangely do things fall out in politics! "[33]

---

31 *Argus*, Nov. 18, 1837. Croswell had grown rich as State Printer and had invested in many speculative ventures which would be threatened by the credit restricting effects of the proposed Independent Treasury. But his very position as Printer and as editor of the Regency organ, made it necessary for him to pay at least lip service to all regular party measures. This accounts for his peculiar stand. See also, I. Spencer, " William L. Marcy Goes Conservative," *Mississippi Valley Historical Review*, XXXI, 214.

32 Fox, *Decline of Aristocracy*, pp. 399-400; L. Bradish to Tallmadge, Oct. 28, 1837, Bradish papers, Box 4, New York Historical Society; Tallmadge to Bradish, Nov. 7, 1837, Bradish papers Box 4. Compare Philip Hone's summation of Jacksonism in Nevins, *Diary of Philip Hone*, I, 244, Mar. 5, 1837.

33 Seward, *Autobiography*, p. 361.

The combination of defection and depression was too much for the Democratic party in New York. The Assembly that was elected in November was overwhelmingly anti-Regency and the party's control of the Senate was weakened. The long Regency rule was broken. Flagg compared the defeat to the debacle of 1824, Cambreleng blamed it on the depression, and Van Buren wrote sadly to Jackson, " We have felt the force of the Bank power in its greatest might...." But the hard money men made the best of their misfortune. They would now know how to deal with the situation in the future, Van Buren promised the Old General when he informed him of the New York upset. Wright, always timid and hesitant in the face of success, was aggressive and determined when things were going badly. Wright had told him there could be no retreat, the cautious Judge Throop wrote the President after the Senator had visited with him on his way to Washington for the regular session of Congress. He had said, " the war must be carried forward with them, perhaps for years." And soon after Congress had convened, Wright's friend, Senator Niles, of Connecticut, was writing to Gideon Welles that the ordinarily mild-mannered Silas was debating " with unusual severity for him." [34]

34 Flagg to Van Buren, Nov. 9, 1837, Cambreleng to Van Buren, Nov. 15, 1837, Van Buren to Jackson, Nov. 18, 1837, Throop to Van Buren, Nov. 23, 1837, Van Buren papers; Niles to Welles, Dec. 26, 1837, Welles papers, Library of Congress.

CHAPTER VIII

WASHINGTON AND ALBANY—VICTORY AND DEFEAT

But determination and even " severity " in debate were not enough. The men who met at Washington in December were the same who had left the Capital in October, and their opinions had not been altered by their short vacations. Once again the Divorce bill passed the Senate, and this time an important concession was made to the opponents of hard money. The original bill had contained an amendment, proposed by Calhoun, which provided that only the notes of specie paying banks would be accepted by the Treasury. This was a vital part of the program, but in an effort to get the Sub Treasury system established, it was abandoned. To Calhoun, this " returning to the flesh pots " was anathema,[1] but Wright supported the bill anyway (for he was primarily thinking of getting the new system formally accepted) and it passed on March 25 by the close vote of 27 to 25. But in the House it met the same fate which had greeted it at the special session; again the Conservatives voted with the Whigs.

In a practical sense the whole fight for the bill was of little import, for the Independent Treasury system had really been functioning all along. Since the suspension of specie payments, all federal funds had been placed in the coffers of the Treasury Department, not in the banks. But the struggle had to be continued as a matter of principle as well as for political reasons. Van Buren had proposed the system and it was vital that he should not be defeated in his efforts to establish it.

Wright became very depressed. Even in January he complained of " an unusual visitation of hypocondria " that he was unable to shake off, and in August, after the session had ended, he wrote: " I have experienced a sort of mental apathy. . . .I have

1 Calhoun to Bancroft, Apr. 14, 1838, Bancroft papers.

been compelled to devote myself so entirely to the questions now at issue before the country for more than a year that they have become sickening almost to disgust and I find it difficult to rouse myself up to the point of attempting to think upon them." " I have never been so overloaded with business," he complained wearily to his aged parents early in 1839.[2] And others were as tired as Wright. As James Buchanan said during the spring session, the endless debate had worn the subject " thread-bare," and most of the senators left the Chamber when the Divorce bill was being discussed.

Outside of Congress a little progress was made, notably in Virginia. There Thomas Ritchie had supported Senator Rives and his faction against the regular Democrats, and in the resultant struggle, the Van Burenites were threatening to start a new newspaper to combat Ritchie's *Enquirer*. But during the spring, Wright visited Ritchie at Richmond and persuaded the editor to swing his paper to the support of the Independent Treasury. So the proposed new journal died before it was born. While this did not bring Rives to heel, it kept him in the position of a mere bolter, for the prestige of the *Enquirer* in Virginia was similar to that of the *Argus* in the Empire State. To thousands of residents of the Old Dominion, the word of " Father " Ritchie was party gospel.

The next legislative session at Washington brought failure for the third time, and in the same manner. With Calhoun's " Specie Clause " restored, the bill was lost in the House after passing the Senate once again. After Congress adjourned at the end of this session poor Wright reported himself " so fagged out " that he felt absolutely unable to " say anything about politics, or business, for a month." [3]

2 E. Shepard, *Martin Van Buren*, p. 292; Wright to Flagg, Jan. 29, 1838, Aug. 20, 1838, Flagg papers; Wright to his parents, Feb. 8, 1839, Wright papers, St. Lawrence University.

3 Buchanan to E. Buchanan, Mar. 2, 1838, Buchanan papers; C. Ambler, *Thomas Ritchie*, pp. 197-202; Wright to Flagg, Mar. 23, 1838, Flagg papers.

But he kept on fighting. The election of 1838 finally produced a majority in the House in favor of the plan, and when the new Congress assembled in December, 1839, its passage seemed assured. The measure was rushed through the Senate in January, 1840, with Wright pushing it along anxiously and skillfully. " I was compelled to stand like a minute man against the attacks, by way of amendment, of indiscreet friends and insidious enemies," he told Flagg.[4] In the lower chamber the bill did not come up for discussion until the end of May. It passed at last, 124 to 107, after a debate that was protracted until June 29. On the Fourth of July, Van Buren signed it, complete with a specie clause that was to become effective gradually, postponing full payments in coin until 1843. The long fight had ended triumphantly, but only after three years of very hard and very dull work.

But Washington was not always so uninteresting for the Senator from New York. With Van Buren in the White House, Wright's social life, if it did not assume a larger place in his daily routine, at least was conducted on a loftier level. He must have loved the vast official dinners which the urbane President gave so frequently and which he attended as often as not. The food and drink, if not the conversation, must certainly have pleased him. John Fairfield, of Maine, has left a detailed (and staggering) account of one of "Little Van's" dinners.

The meal began with soup. This was followed by a fish course, and then, in a leisurely (and probably stupefying) succession came turkey, beef smothered in onions, beef " a la mode " (?), mutton, ham, a game bird whose name the plain-living Fairfield could not pronounce, and pheasant. The guests then polished off a series of desserts: ice cream, jelly, another concoction which Fairfield had never seen before, but which he thought was fine, almonds, raisins, apples, and oranges. There

4 Wright to Flagg, Jan. 18, 1840, Flagg papers.

was, of course, appropriate liquid refreshment for each of these solid items on the bill of fare.

Wright spent a good deal of his time at the White House. Henry Wadsworth Longfellow found him there when he dropped in to pay his respects to Van Buren in February, 1839, and referred to him as a member of the President's "Kitchen Cabinet," as indeed he was. There can be little doubt that the Senator was an unofficial adviser to his friend on most of the issues of the day, but on the occasion of Longfellow's visit, the conversation was deliberately kept on a non-political plane because of the distinguished poet's Whig predilections. "We talked about the weather, the comparative expense of wood and coal as fuel, and the probability that as the season advanced it would grow milder!" the abashed poet wrote in describing his visit. This was typical of Van Buren. As another Whig, Philip Hone, once said, "Nobody knows better than Mr. Van Buren how to do such things. His tact is admirable, and whatever may be his feelings. . .he will never afford his political opponents the triumph of letting them be known." [5]

*   *   *   *   *

Wright could mix business with pleasure as well as any man, but he was a conscientious person, and what with legislative duties and letter writing he was always well occupied while at Washington. Financial policy absorbed much of his time during these years, but other issues which were inflaming the nation touched him also. The slavery question, for one, was acting as a constant irritant between Northern and Southern members of Congress. Beginning in 1836, the House automatically rejected petitions dealing with the subject of slavery in any way under what was known as the Gag Rule, but in the Senate, efforts to apply a similar regulation were

---

5 Fairfield to Mrs. Fairfield, Jan. 24, 1836, *Fairfield Letters*, A. Staples, ed., p. 82; Longfellow to his father, Feb. 9, 1839, Longfellow, *Life of H. W. Longfellow*, I, 313-4; A. Nevins, *Diary of Philip Hone*, II, 520.

not successful. Too many of the members of the Upper House were jealous of their Senatorial prerogatives to assent to any limitation on the right of debate. The effort to pass restrictive resolutions was renewed time and time again, but was never successful. Thomas Hart Benton, the inimitable Missourian, was always a leader in the fight against the gag. " Sir," he told Van Buren's son, Smith, after one skirmish, " the country knows how much patriotism and how much talent there has been in the Senate, but it can never know the *courage* which our friends have shown upon that subject. We gave notice, Sir, that we were prepared to *fight,* yes, Sir, to fight for the freedom of debate! We held out the prospect of the pistol, Sir. Yes, Sir, the *pistol* in one hand and the freedom of debate in the other, Sir, *and the other side shrunk from the pistol,* Sir! Yes, Sir, *They could not look the pistol down Sir!* ...we all gave out that Sir, as the alternative! & the *pistol saved us,* Sir!" Benton had only contempt for the House of Representatives, where the rule was in force. "Sir, there has been no House—There has been no House this session Sir!— No House at all, Sir!" [6]

Wright's stand, which was typical of the average Northerner's at this time, was clearly brought out in a senatorial exchange with Calhoun, in January, 1836. Senator Morris, of Ohio, had presented a petition urging the abolition of slavery in the District of Columbia. Calhoun opposed even the reception of such a document, and Wright took issue with him on this point. Silas was as eager as anyone else to keep the slavery question out of the halls of Congress, and had said as much only two days earlier in a letter to Flagg, but he objected to not recognizing the petition. Receive it, he suggested, and then reject it without debate; to refuse it would only help the agitators who submitted it. He tried to show that Northern opinion was just as hostile to abolitionism as Southern, using as an example the disruption, the previous fall, of an anti-

6 S. T. Van Buren to Van Buren, Sept. 12, 1841, Van Buren papers.

slavery convention at Utica, New York, by a mob. But, he said, if the petition was not received, popular feeling would turn in favor of the petitioners.

Calhoun struck back with the assertion that the sensibilities of Northerners did not deserve more consideration than those of his constituents. Everyone knew, he continued, that the petition would be immediately denied if it were acknowledged, therefore to accept it at all amounted to " juggling." He then disputed Wright's claim that Northern opinion was anti-abolitionist, citing an abolitionist article in the *Oneida Standard and Democrat,* a Utica paper, which had carried the name of Van Buren for President on its masthead. Wright, in his turn, pointed out that the office of the sheet had been wrecked by a mob after this article's publication. Besides which, he said, he was certain that the *Standard and Democrat* was not a Democratic journal as a general rule, though neither he nor anyone else could tell the editor of any paper whom he should support for President.

In a final quip, Calhoun remarked that he had always supposed that New York politics were inexplicable, and that this proved it, and in this manner the exchange ended on a pleasant note. Wright continued to fight any gag on the reception of petitions. When the *Washington Globe* reported him as voting in favor of a gag rule in December, 1837, he hurriedly wrote Blair saying that he had been absent from the Senate when the vote in question was taken, but that if he had been there, he would have *opposed,* not favored it.[7]

Outside the Senate, he also did whatever he could to quiet the stir over slavery. The main point at issue in the 1830's was the position of slavery in the District of Columbia, because there alone the federal government seemed authorized by the constitution to do away with the peculiar institution. On his way home from Congress in the spring of 1837, Wright

---

7 Wright to Flagg, Jan. 17, 1836, Flagg papers; *Congressional Globe,* III, 121-2, 130-1; *Washington Globe,* Dec. 18, 19, 1837.

stopped over in Vermont to visit his family, and while there he was invited to a dinner by the Democrats of Burlington. He did not accept, but used the opportunity provided by his letter of refusal to express his views on the mounting anti-slavery ferment in Vermont. In his letter, which was given to the papers and widely republished, he urged the Vermont Democracy to avoid all such distracting issues as "modern abolitionism," which ignored the peace of the nation, past compromises and the constitution itself. "These fanatics [abolitionists]," he wrote, "are already attempting to agitate the public mind as to the evil of slavery in the district, as if any intelligent and unprejudiced citizen attempted to defend the principles of slavery." The point was, he continued, that ending this evil in the District of Columbia "cannot have the effect to give freedom to a single slave" while the institution existed in the surrounding states, Virginia and Maryland.[8] In general, Wright's position was this: Slavery is morally wrong, but the national government has no business interfering with it where it already exists.

* * * * *

On the Fourth of July, 1839, Wright was delivering an Independence Day address to the assembled residents of Canton. He spoke the usual platitudes about the Revolutionary Fathers and the Union, and dealt at some length with his ideas on slavery. In concluding, he referred to the recent abolition of slavery in the British Empire, and to English efforts to stimulate the ending of the institution in America as well, in the following fiery phrases:

> ... that citizens of that country which forced domestic slavery upon us ... should be willing now to disturb the harmony of our country ... is not strange. That the subjects of that monarchy, schooled to bow before an earthly throne, and to cringe and tremble and be silent in the presence of hereditary

8 *St. Lawrence Republican,* May 9, 1837; *Niles' Weekly Register,* June 6, 1837, LII, 239.

aristocracy, should visit our country to lecture us upon the
subject of liberty may not be as strange as it is ludicrous; but
that the high minded citizens of our republic should be led
away by such teachers into conflicts with their political
brethren ... is more than strange.[9]

Such bombastic and high-flown language from the mild-mannered and plain-spoken Silas Wright would under ordinary
circumstances have amazed his local friends, but in this instance they probably felt that the subject provided ample excuse for his lush language. For in 1839, anti-British feeling in
the North Country was very great.

This Anglophobia had been stirred up by the Canadian Revolution of 1837, which sprang from certain grievances har-
bored by British North America against the mother country.
Here it will suffice to dwell upon the reaction south of the St.
Lawrence. When the Revolution first broke out, opinion in
the United States was mixed, except along the immediate
frontier where approval of the uprising was almost universal.
This sympathy for the Canadian insurgents was founded on
the continual intermingling of peoples from both sides of the
mighty stream which separates the two countries. Families
migrated back and forth with little regard for national limits.
A brother-in-law of Wright's, for example, settled at Montreal. Feeling was intensified by the fact that the North Country had a poor crop in the fall of 1837, which left idle hundreds
of farm hands, easily turned to mischief. Besides the excitement of an excursion against the traditional American enemy,
Great Britain, in the interest of friendly neighbors, many
North Country men were attracted to the rebel cause by the
bait of good Canadian land which might become available with
Canadian independence.

These incitements led to frequent public meetings along the
south side of the border and to filibustering expeditions into
Canada. With the arrival in December of William Lyon Mac-

9 S. Wright, *Speech at Canton*, July 4, 1839.

kensie, one of the Canadian leaders, open recruiting was begun. Although there were large elements in the population opposed to actual military aid, by the early months of 1838, the entire border from Maine to Michigan was aroused and deeply interested in the revolt. The first open act of violence by Americans occurred as early as December, 1837, when a group of " Patriots " seized Navy Island, just south of Niagara Falls. Here they ensconced themselves comfortably. Recruits flocked to their banners and the island soon became crowded. A steamboat, the *Caroline,* was chartered to keep the carefree filibusterers supplied, but one night, shortly after it had begun to serve as a supply ship, it was captured by a group of Canadian Loyalists, towed out into the middle of the river, and burned to the water-line. When taken, the *Caroline* had been resting peaceably at an American pier, on the American side of the river. Of course, there was a mighty outcry at this violation of the neutrality of the United States. A wave of fear, rapidly replaced by indignation, swept the border country. Militia were called out, and preparations for defense against further attacks were taken. Pro-rebel Americans were eager to counterattack. But General Winfield Scott rushed to the scene and convinced the Patriot leaders that invasion was useless. Finally, on January 14, Navy Island was abandoned, and though there were occasional unsuccessful skirmishes by Americans on Canadian soil during the rest of that winter, the state of feeling on the border gradually quieted.[10]

President Van Buren's response to these exciting events was conditioned by the peculiar division of authority in the government of the United States. As President, he could use the army to surpress rebellion, but he could not call upon the state militia to stop filibustering. After the *Caroline* affair, however, he sent General Scott to the border, and issued a proclamation against all those endangering the neutrality of

10 A. Corey, *Crisis of 1830-42 in Canadian-American Relations,* pp. 28-38.

the nation. Finally, in March, 1838, Congress passed a neutrality act granting the President the power to call out state militia to prevent attacks by American nationals on friendly states.

The " Patriots " were thus driven underground, and forced to develop their plans through secret societies. Late in May they engineered the destruction of the *Sir Robert Peel,* a British steamboat berthed at Oswego. Of several other acts of violence carried out, the most serious was an attack on the town of Prescott, across the St. Lawrence from Ogdensburg, the following November. Against these outbreaks, Van Buren took as firm a stand as he possibly could. But he was hampered by the scantiness of the military force at his disposal and by the non-cooperation of the civil authorities most of whom were infected with the feeling of Anglophobia which saturated the border. Although he expressed private doubts as to the extent of his legal power to check the raids, and despite the fact that a truculent attitude toward England would have been popular in most sections of the country, the President chose a statesmanlike course, and did everything in his power to prevent the violation of British territory by American citizens.[11]

It is not hard to understand why Wright, living in the midst of an ocean of anti-British feeling, had been unable to resist the temptation to give the lion's tail a bit of a twist in his Fourth of July speech quoted above. But at the same time, he fully approved Van Buren's policy, and did whatever he could to support him, regardless of the feelings of his immediate constituents. Thus, when a quaint but very popular character named " Bill " Johnston, who had been jailed for his part in the filibustering efforts of the " Patriots," appealed to him to sign a petition to the President in his behalf, Wright said: " It will not avail you anything if I should sign it but I will be candid with you. I would rather sign a petition to have you all hung. . . as you have disturbed the peace of my most

11 *Ibid.,* pp 47-9, 54, 100-1.

friendly neighbors and you had ought to be punished." Because of his wide contacts in the frontier area, Wright was an invaluable observation post and adviser to Van Buren on the state of opinion there. For example, after the burning of the *Sir Robert Peel,* he forwarded to the President a letter from the collector of the Port of Ogdensburg, Smith Stillwell, protesting against the payment of any indemnity. The letter was "too highly spiced in feeling," Wright remarked, but it did represent local sentiment. He went on to explain that another letter from his friend Judge John Fine, of Ogdensburg, in favor of an indemnity was probably colored by the fact that a good friend of Fine's had been a part owner of the destroyed vessel. Wright further advised " Little Van " on the proper handling of the many local difficulties and divisions within the party over the Canadian troubles. He almost had a much more important job to do, for early in 1839, the President was considering sending him, along with his own son, " Prince John " Van Buren, to Canada to try to arrange for the release of some Americans who had been captured in the raid on Prescott. Wright thought that a mission should be sent to Montreal because of what he called the " morbid state of feeling upon the subject of the prisoners," but Van Buren eventually decided against it.[12]

The most important result of the Canadian crises in New York was the weakening of the Democratic party in all the border counties, where large numbers of citizens normally devoted to its banners were alienated by the impartial attitude of the Administration. It was a major, if not the chief reason for the Whig victories in the Empire State in 1838 and again in 1840.

* * * * *

12 " Bill Johnston's Scrap Book," *Watertown Times,* Nov. 24, 1931; Wright to Van Buren, June 12, 1838, Mar. 16, 1839, Van Buren papers; Van Buren to A. Stevenson (received May 10, 1839) Stevenson papers, Library of Congress.

These were dark days for the Regency. Just as in 1824, everything seemed to go badly. The revolt of the Conservative Democrats, the depression, the " Patriot " war, the refusal to repeal or suspend the law prohibiting the circulation of small bills,—all these things contributed to the termination of the long Democratic domination at Albany. After the election of 1837, times were so hard for the Regency politicians that Wright found himself appealing to George Bancroft in Boston in behalf of a worthy Democrat from Maine who needed a job. He wrote that since the New York election it had been impossible to provide offices for outsiders at all.

Nor did the approach of the next campaign promise any improvement in their fortunes. Tallmadge reported to his new Whig allies that he was finding " Conservatives in every county, who are not afraid to act, and who will cooperate to save the State. . . .From my extensive personal observation, and from letters from every part of the State," he continued, " I have entire confidence in the result." Early in the summer, Thurlow Weed wrote happily from Albany, " We are all quiet here with delightful weather and cheering political prospects."

The confident Whigs nominated Seward for Governor, though he had been so badly defeated four years earlier, while Marcy was the Regency choice for the fourth consecutive time. The election repeated the result of the previous year, a Whig sweep. " Was ever triumph so complete? " asked Weed. " Was ever a strong Party so utterly overwhelmed in a single conflict, except at Waterloo? " [13]

The following year, the rout was even more devastating, for at that time the Whigs gained control of the State Senate, ending a Democratic rule in that body which extended back to the days of Aaron Burr. So the old program of Clinton finally got a chance to be tested in action. A general banking

13 Wright to Bancroft, Mar. 10, 1838, Bancroft papers; Tallmadge to Bradish, Oct. 14, 1838, Weed to Bradish, June 29, 1838, Nov. 12, 1838, Bradish papers.

law was passed, authorizing the incorporation of new financial institutions without special legislative action, and a vast program of internal improvements was begun. Samuel B. Ruggles developed and introduced the improvements plan, which, in direct contradiction to the Jeffersonian theories of the Regency, called for public construction with borrowed funds, to be repaid out of canal revenues.[14] Immediately the state entered upon what was to be a ten year period of borrowing at the rate of $4,000,000 annually to construct canals and other "improvements." It was this " $40,000,000 debt," which started the reaction that eventually restored the Democrats to power.

But as the decade of the thirties closed, there was no sign of a revival of the fortunes of the Regency. Flagg and Dix were ousted by the Whig legislature from their positions as Comptroller and Secretary of State, the lucrative State Printing monopoly was transferred from Croswell's *Argus* to Weed's *Evening Journal,* and the double apostate, Tallmadge, whose efforts had played so large a part in the Democratic collapse, was reelected to the United States Senate by his new friends.[15] Little wonder that Wright, in returning to Canton from Washington in March, 1839, deliberately avoided passing through Albany. " I felt no ardent desire," he wrote to Flagg by way of explanation " to take off my hat and make my bow to little Billy Seward. . . ." It must be admitted in connection with this that a little later on, Seward had an op-

14 Donovan, *Barnburners,* p. 21.

15 Many of the Whig politicians were not at all pleased with this arrangement. Professional office holders like John C. Spencer and Millard Fillmore were much opposed to this " policy of discarding tried and faithful friends, and of conferring the highest and most important place in our gift upon a new recruit . . . " Weed, *Autobiography,* pp. 460-1. Their protestations went unheeded, but Tallmadge did not appreciate the honors heaped upon him by the Whigs. He later accepted an appointment as Governor of Wisconsin Territory from Tyler, and in 1845, he even tried to return to the Democratic ranks, insisting that he had always been a firm party man! J. Polk, *Diary,* M. Quaife, ed., I, 57.

portunity to demonstrate a similarly petulant attitude. In June, while visiting New York City, he refused to attend a reception for President Van Buren on the grounds that it would " afford evidence of inconsistency and insincerity." [16]

As usual, Wright and the other Regency leaders became only more determined in the face of defeat. The party must be " purged " (Wright wrote to Flagg) of all " who are not democrats in principle but merely in profession and the pocket." In truth, the movement of Tallmadge and his friends into the Whig fold did much to solidify the New York Democrats behind the ideas of their more radical wing. Even the " Loco-Focos," descendants of the Workingmen's party which had been so misunderstood by the Regency, were now accepted within the party lines, President Van Buren openly appearing at the theater in New York with Alexander Ming, one of their leaders. The *Democratic Review,* a national magazine controlled by the radical wing of the party, published, in January, 1839, a scathing denunciation of appeasers within the New York Democratic organization, throwing on them (particularly Governor Marcy) the onus of the defeat of 1838. The party, said the *Review,* should have been rebuilt from the bottom up after Tallmadge's bolt in 1837. It was foolish to try to reunite this element with the mass of true Democrats, " as if such a body as the conservatives, with all their motives, interests, and feelings, which. . .attended their secession, could possibly be brought back to a sound and healthy reunion! " [17]

However, Van Buren, Wright and the other leaders of the organization, though they might talk of " purges " and associate with radicals and feel sincerely well rid of the Conservatives, had no intention of alienating the middle-of-the-roaders and opportunists of whom Marcy was typical. When that worthy, irritated by another article in the December, 1839,

16 Wright to Flagg, Mar. 23, 1839, Flagg papers; Nevins, *Diary of Philip Hone,* I, 404.

17 *Ibid.*; *Democratic Review,* V, 5-8.

issue of the *Democratic Review,* threatened to quit politics and wrote a letter to Wright at Washington complaining bitterly of the magazine's attitude toward him, the Senator made a successful effort to patch up his hurt feelings. " I confess the article seemed to me to be most outrageous and unkind as well as unjust," he wrote soothingly to Marcy, and he was not merely trying to placate an irritated politician. He took Marcy's letter to S. D. Langtree, who along with John L. O'Sullivan, an erratic young radical, edited the *Review.* Langtree insisted that Marcy was acting "more sore than there is occasion for;" that the article was " directed rather against a System than individuals." He also explained that it had been written in New York by O'Sullivan, and sent to Washington for publication without being shown to anyone. Wright gave the young editor a thorough dressing down, ending with the admonition that it was vain to think that two young men such as he and O'Sullivan could successfully edit a national magazine without experienced advisers.[18]

In the end, Marcy was mollified, and the Regency remained intact for the coming presidential election.

---

18 Marcy to Wetmore, Jan. 7, 1840, Wright to Marcy, Feb. 4, 16, 1840, Langtree to Wright, Feb. 11, 1840, Marcy papers.

CHAPTER IX

SILAS TAKES TO THE STUMP

" There is no demagogueism so low as that of an aristocracy party which courts the suffrage of a democracy it at heart despises."

Democratic Review, 1840.

" This election will be no more a free expression of the popular will than the election of General Bonaparte to be Emperor of France."

John M. Niles to Gideon Welles, Nov. 2, 1840.

SEEKING reelection in 1840, Van Buren found himself in an unfavorable position. For twelve years the party of Jackson had dominated the national scene, and the opposition which always seems to develop against a party long in power was perhaps his main stumbling-block. Although a consummate politician and a man of great personal charm, as President " Little Van " had failed to develop the popular appeal which had been such an asset to Jackson. Furthermore, he had been uncharacteristically inept (especially in New York!) in his handling of patronage, and had certainly failed to use the spoils of office to advance his own cause.[1] To this was added the hatred of most of the business community for his hard money program, and the new political techniques being evolved by the Whigs, which utterly disregarded what had come to be the established means of conducting a Presidential canvass.

The Whigs, meeting at Harrisburg, Pennsylvania, in December, 1839, decided to pit General William Henry Harrison against the Little Magician. " Old Tippecanoe " combined in his person the popularity of a military hero and the blameless innocence of one who had devoted little of his life to politics. In settling on Harrison, the party passed over its real leader, Henry Clay, mainly because Thurlow Weed did not think that " Harry of the West " could win, and Weed controlled the New York delegation at Harrisburg. Harrison's nomination

1 Hammond, *History of New York*, II, 530-1.

provided the New York Democrats with at least a particle of revenge for their recent defeats, for the traitor Tallmadge, who had cooperated with Clay in the Senate, and who was expected to carry New York for the Kentuckian at the Whig Convention, could not loosen Weed's lusty grip on the Empire State's delegates. In Washington the Democrats had a field day trying to entice Clay into a display of resentment toward Tallmadge. "Some," reported Wright, "were talking to him jocosely of the very great difference between the influence of Mr. T. in the State exerted for himself, and exerted for his friends, while others were very soberly, simply and honestly asking him how it was possible that he could have but 12 friends out of the 42 delegates from the State, when the city openly declared for him, and he had the influence and exertions of Mr. Tallmadge in the country. . . ." [2] But Clay managed to control his mercurial temper (at least in public) and spurred on by the first real chance for a Whig victory in the party's history, he and most of the Whig chiefs gave Tippecanoe their full support.

Their main obstacle, as in 1836, was their own diversity. The party of Webster, a friend of high tariffs and a powerful central government, had nominated for Vice-President, John Tyler, of Virginia, a free trade disciple and as rigid a states' rights man as could be found anywhere in the Union. Another Whig disadvantage lay in their identification with business groups and wealth generally, for as the long struggle with the United States Bank had proved, the average man had little taste for the type of appeal such groups could offer.

The solution to the Whig dilemma was unwittingly provided by the *Baltimore Republican,* a Van Buren paper, when in March of the election year it remarked sarcastically " that upon condition of his receiving a pension of two thousand dollars and a barrel of cider, General Harrison would no doubt

2 Wright to Marcy, Dec. 22, 1839, property of H. Landon, Watertown, New York.

consent to withdraw his pretentions, and spend his days in a log cabin on the banks of the Ohio." [3] A Whig newspaper man, Richard Elliot Parker, of Harrisburg, was quick to turn this remark to his own party's profit and before long the nation redounded to the praises of the Hero of Tippecanoe, who lived in a rustic cabin (where the latch string was always out) and who always drank hard cider, the simple beverage of the humble. Soon a Pennsylvania Congressman, Charles Ogle, came up with a speech that completed the picture. Van Buren, he said, in criticising an appropriation for furniture for the White House, was an effete aristocrat, dining from golden plates, consuming the finest wines, and generally luxuriating at the expense of the people. Printed in pamphlet form under the title, " The Regal Splendor of the President's Palace," this speech was widely circulated. A few quotations will illustrate the Whig technique.

> The cash of the People [is being sent] across the wide Atlantic for the purchase of " FRENCH Comfortables " . . .

> Are AMERICAN weavers, dyers, and manufacturers too dull and too stupid to make a decent Republican carpet?

> [In the White House dining room, do we find] hog and hominy [or] *schnitz, knep and sourcrout?* No, Sir, no. All these substantial preparations are looked upon by *gourmands, French cooks,* and *locofoco Presidents* as exceedingly vulgar, and fit only to be set before " Bank Whigs " . . . [and it cost] the enormous sum of ELEVEN THOUSAND ONE HUNDRED AND NINETY-SEVEN DOLLARS AND THIRTY-TWO CENTS OF THE PEOPLE'S CASH TO BUY THE TABLE " FURNITURE."

> [Van Buren] has not only taken *twenty-five thousand dollars in gold and silver* for his annual salary, but he has compelled the people to pay for HEMMING HIS DISH-RAGS into the bargain.

3 *Baltimore Republican,* Mar. 23, 1840, quoted in O. Chitwood, *John Tyler,* p. 176.

By way of contrast, Ogle made another speech extolling the simple virtues of Harrison's way of life which was summarized in the *Congressional Globe* as follows:

> He entered into a defense of the military and civil services of General Harrison; gave a description of his furniture and cooking utensils, and presented a graphic picture of the exterior appearance of his dwelling, as well as its general interior arrangement, to show his fitness for the Presidency.[4]

The idea of turning the potent weapon of aristocrat-baiting against the Democrats was not a new one. John C. Spencer, a die-hard conservative who had fought the democratization of the New York Constitution in 1821, had suggested the technique to Weed in 1832 when he wrote, " The cry of aristocracy takes with certain folks, and there is no way to meet it but to clamor louder than our adversaries...." Indeed this cunning policy dated back at least to the old People's party which had used it with such great success in 1824. But in 1840, the Whigs made it a science and a fine art. Monster mass-meetings, parades, songs by the score characterized the Whig campaign, and conventional issues like the tariff and hard money were deliberately forgotten. Log cabins were erected everywhere. Free cider poured like water. Never before had the nation witnessed such a wild, emotional and completely irrelevant canvass, and it was never to see the like of it again.

Old line Whigs like Webster were surprised—but quick to see on which side their bread was buttered. "General Harrison's nomination runs through the country most astonishingly," wrote the " God-like " man with enthusiasm, and when Joseph Hoxie, a dignified New York merchant, became a famous singer of campaign-songs and Governor Seward

---

4 C. Ogle, *The Regal Splendor of the President's Palace*, pp. 13, 17, 18, 30; *Cong. Globe*, VIII, 333.

took to travelling in an old green wagon, it was clear that a
new day had dawned for the Whigs.[5]

Against such tactics the Democrats did their best, but it
was difficult for them to conceal their bewilderment and
chagrin. In New York, though still plagued by the various
difficulties which had resulted in three consecutive defeats, the
Regency was preparing for an all-out struggle to " redeem "
the state. Operations were under the supervision of Flagg,
assisted by Dix, Benjamin Butler, and many lesser figures.
Though busy at Washington engineering the final passage of
the Independent Treasury bill, Wright was able to help these
men in the fight to reelect his best friend.

Already, in December, 1839, he was tied up in the establishment of a new newspaper in New York, which was to be
called the *Rough Hewer*. The necessity for this special paper
was rooted in the hesitant attitude toward Van Buren's financial policy taken by Croswell's *Argus*. Even William L.
Marcy, whose ideas were not far different from those of the
editor, stated at this time that " Croswell has been for a year
or two off his editorial legs and at no time more so than now.
. . .He cannot or will not enter *con amore* into the work and
therefore could not do anything effective if he should seriously
attempt it." And it was to Croswell, among others, that Flagg
referred during the height of the struggle when he said, " Too
many of our men in high places. . . .are inert, and can hardly
be moved to action by a galvanic battery."

The *Argus* continued as an Administration paper, supporting Van Buren wholeheartedly, even lending some of its type
to the *Rough Hewer*. Yet when, after nearly three years, the
Independent Treasury Act was finally signed by the President,
the best that Croswell could muster was this prosaic comment:

> Whether this measure is to have a fair trial, or is yet to en-
> counter, on mere partisan grounds, the misrepresentation and

5 Barnes, *Weed*, p. 44; *Webster Correspondence*, F. Webster, ed., II, 80;
Fox, *Decline of Aristocracy*, pp. 413, 414.

hostility of those who, from their pursuits, are most interested in preserving a stable currency . . . remains to be seen. Whatsoever their course may be, let them remember that the great measure has been carried after full discussion before people . . .

For the Albany Regency in 1840, sentiments of this sort were insufficient, and a more enthusiastic journal was called for.[6]

Wright and Flagg were agreed that the new paper should make no effort to be a regular daily. It would thus avoid the necessity of keeping up on " current transactions." Its object should be " to discuss the great questions of the campaign fully, to give [them]. . .general circulation, and to prepare the public mind against falsehoods, shifts, and false issues. . . ." Wright also felt that the paper should be cheap, so that it could have the widest possible circulation, and should be started soon, " because," as he put it, " the winter is the reading season for our farmers and working men. . . ." Furthermore, he saw it as a new and " independent " venture rather than a mere secondary edition of some established sheet. " Its contents will then come as fresh and new to one man as another, and. . .that impression gives great value to the mass of the country subscribers." He urged that "vigorous and prompt efforts " be made by all county and town organizations to promote the sale of subscriptions at fifty cents for the entire nine month period that the weekly was to be printed.[7]

The *Rough Hewer* began to take shape during the early days of 1840, the first number appearing on February 26. It was edited by Thomas M. Burt, who had been a partner of Croswell's on the *Argus*. The prospectus, printed in this issue, stressed " the importance of testing the wisdom of measures by a recurrence to principles, and the necessity of regulating the practical conduct of the government, both State and national, by those maxims of simplicity and economy which are

6 Marcy to Wetmore, Jan. 7, 1840, Marcy papers; Flagg to Welles, Sept. 27, 1840, Welles papers, New York Public Library; *Argus*, July 9, 1840.

7 Wright to Flagg, Dec. 22, 1839, Flagg papers.

embodied in the Inaugural Address of Jefferson. . . ." To show exactly what was meant by this, the paper printed Jefferson's first inaugural complete—complete, that is, except for his famous statement on the essential similarity between all Republicans and all Federalists, which though a safe enough sentiment on March 4, was a bit embarrassing before election day. The first issue also expounded in detail the practical program of the Van Buren Democrats: an independent treasury system, no assumption by the federal government of state debts, no distribution of the proceeds of the sale of public lands, and an end to all public debt, which, it said, " whether State or National, is a blight on honest industry. . . ." Hard money tenets were expressed without qualification, the paper proposing " greater infusion of the precious metals into the circulating medium of the country." [8]

The *Rough Hewer* did not sell very well at first. In the early days of March, Wright wrote from Washington that he had received word that subscriptions were not up to expectations. But though he urged that those men working on circulation " suffer no flagging," he expressed confidence that there would be a rapid increase in sales once " the contest waxes warm." In this he proved to be correct. Before the end of the month, John A. Dix, on the scene at Albany, informed Van Buren that the success of the new paper was definitely established, and that it was having a good influence on opinion in the state. Circulation had passed the ten thousand mark, and was rising steadily.[9] Its influence extended beyond New York as well, for Thomas Ritchie, of the *Richmond Enquirer,* asked Flagg for copies of it late in February. " It is," wrote Ritchie, " a good idea nobly carried out." [10]

8 *Rough Hewer,* Feb. 20, 1840.

9 The circulation reached 23,800 by October. Flagg to Van Buren, Oct. 18, 1840, Van Buren papers.

10 Wright to Flagg, Mar. 10, 1840, Flagg papers; Dix to Van Buren, Mar. 27, 1840, Van Buren papers; Ritchie to Flagg, Feb. 29, 1840, Flagg papers.

From February to November, the *Rough Hewer* performed its mission of placing before its readers a full discussion of all major issues. On March 19 it began a series of articles defending Wright's final Independent Treasury bill, then before the House, and explaining its significance, section by section. Early in April, it published an elaborate defense of the hard money doctrine, stressing the stabilizing effect of hard money on the national economy and attempting to prove that "steady employment and uniform wages" would result. "Paper," this article explained, " which always tends to excess. . ."

> is sure to interfere by its expansions and contractions, with the regular progress of industry, and bring on periodically a stagnation in all the channels of business. This is the great evil, against which the industrious classes have to guard— an evil, which can only be cured by correcting the abuses of the banking system.[11]

Throughout the campaign the paper maintained a similar barrage of argument which had absolutely no effect on the Whig tactics. As the Hard Cider campaign developed, it was necessary to reply in kind. The main weapon used by the *Rough Hewer* on this side of the struggle was the insinuation that Harrison was a mere figurehead for evil Whig bosses. In the issue of April 30 was published a skit called a " Curious Dialogue" which illustrates this counterattack. The scene is a Log Cabin before which stand three fancily dressed men. The hero of the piece, a Hoosier Farmer of obviously Democratic proclivities, approaches, and asks to see General Harrison in order to pose him a few questions. The fancily dressed men refer him to the General's speeches, but the farmer replies nobly, " I have read them, and some seem to be on one side and some on t'other. So I thought to be certain, I'd come and ask the old General plump. Let me rap." [on the door] To this the others object. The general they say, is too busy " qualifying himself for the presidency " by drinking hard cider.

11 *Rough Hewer*, Apr. 2, 1840.

Nonplussed, the Farmer demands to know if they are authorized to speak for Harrison, and when he is assured that this is the case, he asks them outright whether or not their candidate is an abolitionist.

" My dear sir," one of them replies suavely, " you mistake. We are not put here to answer questions for the old General, but only *to prevent him from answering*. All the answer we give is, that it is not politic for him to answer. Come, come; you are a friend of Harrison; you should treat him with ' generous confidence,' and believe he will make a good president, without troubling yourself about his principles."

This is too much for the Hoosier Farmer, who goes off muttering dire warnings to the Whigs as to the outcome of any election based on such tactics, while the previous speaker stage-whispers to one of his colleagues, " this is an ugly business; but anything is better than to let the poor old fellow speak for himself." As the curtain falls, there is heard from within the voice of the Whig candidate calling for " More ' hard cider.' " [12]

But putting across the *Rough Hewer* was not the only problem before the leaders of the Van Buren forces. A second, national, one was the question of nominating a suitable candidate for Vice-President. Wright and many other politicians opposed the renomination of the red-vested Col. Johnson, whose eccentricities had not been tempered by four years spent watching over the Senate. There were so many candidates seeking the job that Wright personally felt no nomination at all should be made. He thought further that since Van Buren was " as strongly and distinctly...[the] candidate [for President] as was Genl Jackson in 1832" that there should not even be a convention. Instead, each state could vote for whomever it chose as Van Buren's running mate. This would probably mean that no one would receive a majority, and the choice would devolve upon the Senate. Wright thought

12 *Ibid.*, Apr. 30, 1840.

the matter could be settled there easily enough, and more important, it would then be too late for anyone's hurt feelings to affect the outcome of the presidential race. So he urged Flagg to delay if possible the calling of any New York convention until action by other states made a national one certain, and then to oppose any Vice-Presidential choice.

But others disagreed with Wright. It was the general opinion at Washington that a convention was needed to preserve the "integrity" of the party and that to omit it would break a valuable precedent. General party feeling also favored the nomination of a full ticket. In this Andrew Jackson, still actively interested in the political situation in spite of his supposed retirement and his painful physical condition, concurred. He wanted a fellow Tennessean, James K. Polk, to be given the second position and thought it would be a serious error to refrain from a choice at Baltimore. Van Buren also preferred Polk, but because of his position felt obliged to remain neutral.

Despite his weaknesses, Johnson remained Polk's main opponent. Even Van Buren, who did not like him, realized this. As "Little Van" wrote to Old Hickory from the nation's capital, Johnson's military record would be a powerful counteractive to Harrison's, which the Whigs were playing up so much. Also, the President said, Johnson was favored by the fact that he already held the post—he would attract much sympathy if dropped from the ticket.[13]

There was no simple answer, and none at all was found until the end of April, shortly before the convention met. Then Felix Grundy, who represented the Polk interests, agreed to accept the position advocated by Wright, and as a result of this "treaty" no Vice-Presidential selection was made when

[13] Wright to Flagg, Jan. 26, 1840, Flagg papers; Jackson to Van Buren, Apr. 3, 1840, Van Buren papers; Van Buren to Jackson, Apr. 1840, *Jackson Correspondence*, J. Bassett, ed., VI, 55-6.

the convention met at Baltimore on May 5.[14] Some Democrats felt that this policy weakened the ticket, but its effect on the result was not very great.

Wright himself was much more concerned over another problem that came up during the spring of 1840. A strong effort was made by many New York Democrats to compel him to accept the gubernatorial nomination. Four years later, when a similar movement developed under even more critical circumstances, Wright accepted, but in 1840 he was adamant. The prospect of the nomination was distasteful to him for political as well as personal reasons. In a letter to Flagg in February, he developed his position at length. He had heard that the *Oneida Democrat* was going to suggest him as a candidate. Those at Albany must keep him "indemnified from such folly," he appealed to his friend. First of all the Whig New York legislature would like nothing better than a chance to force Wright to resign so that they could appoint a member of their party to his place. The legislators might be able to do this by "instructing" him on any major issue, but they dared not try such a scheme because they were afraid that if they did force him to resign he would run for Governor. Wright did not say he would subscribe to the theory that the legislature *could* order him to act in a given way on any bill, but neither did he openly deny its power to do so, and as long as the gubernatorial question was not pressed they dared not act. But if he were to refuse publicly to run for Governor, there would be no harm in the Whigs trying to "instruct" him. Being satisfied with the situation as it was, Wright was very eager to keep the Democrats from suggesting his name and making him refuse publicly. " I do not want to say anything on the subject," he wrote privately, " and it seems to me that the Argus may keep all right by saying. . .that I do not wish to

14 " Diaries of S. H. Laughlin," St. G. Sioussat, ed., *Tennessee Historical Magazine*, II, 52. See also Benton to Jackson, Apr. 24, 1840, *Jackson Correspondence*, J. Bassett, ed., VI, 59-60.

be a candidate for Governor at all, that...I prefer my present place...."

The Senator also advanced more personal reasons for his feelings, which in the light of later developments seem to have been the more weighty with him. "I do not underrate the dignity, and just honor and elevation of the place, nor...have [I] not as much ambition as any man ought in reason to have," he wrote. But he added that he had always lived prudently, and had always had to get along on his official salary, having no outside interests. "The terror of my life has been that of becoming a political pauper." If elected Governor, just setting up a suitable house "would break my bank." Besides, "I have always lived in the country, lived as I pleased, and therefore lived in a way which will enable me to continue to live when I cease to be an office holder. Make me a Governor, and compel me to retire as such, and my obligations to friends would compel me to live differently." In addition he suggested that he would be more valuable to the party in Washington than at Albany.

Flagg's reply to this letter showed that he appreciated the situation, and in his next message, Silas expressed his gratitude and lent wholehearted approval to the proposal that the party choice should be William C. Bouck, a popular Canal Commissioner. Although Bouck was not as firm on the internal improvement question as might be desired, he said, the contest itself would settle the doubtful issues. Victory would be a matter of principle not of men. Any man "not otherwise obnoxious" who supported the Regency program would get the entire Democratic vote.[15]

In his struggle to avoid the nomination, Wright received some unsolicited and probably ineffective help from the opposition. Governor William H. Seward, because of his liberal attitude toward Catholics and foreigners, had already alienated many of the more conservative members of the Whig party,

15 Wright to Flagg, Feb. 21, Mar. 10, 1840, Flagg papers.

and he did not relish facing a foe as popular throughout the state as Wright was in his fight for reelection. When it was patent that either Bouck or Wright would be the Democratic choice, Seward invited to dinner one evening, Prosper M. Wetmore, the friend and confidant of former Governor Marcy, who favored Bouck for Governor, and told him " confidentially " that he thought Bouck would be the stronger choice. Knowing that Wetmore preferred Bouck, Seward probably thought that his hint would be swallowed whole, but his guest was not taken in. John Van Buren soon knew about the story, and passed the word on to his father in Washington. This, he wrote, " is what Seward considers cunning, but shows their fears of W."

The Senator's popularity made his nomination a powerful temptation to many Democrats as well as a thing to be feared among the Whigs. At the end of June, when Wright thought that all danger of his being picked was past, John Van Buren was still urging that he be drafted for the job. " The backwoodsmen are all for Silas," he wrote the President. But when the convention finally met at Syracuse in September, this element had been pretty well convinced that Wright would not run, and Bouck was chosen with little difficulty.[16] If Wright had been the candidate, he might have carried the state for himself, but it is unlikely that the presidential contest would have been affected. Harrison's plurality over Van Buren in New York was too great.

But in 1840 it was the fear of fraud which seems to have caused more trouble for the New York politicians than anything else. As early as March, Van Buren himself prepared a draft which he called " Thoughts on the Approaching Election in New York." This dealt primarily with the danger of Whig cheating and with measures which the Democrats should pursue in checking it. The paper was given to Wright, who passed it on to the Regency at Albany. It called upon the state con-

16 J. Van Buren to Van Buren, Apr. 11, June 30, 1840, Van Buren papers.

vention to pass resolutions, first that local organizations be developed in all the towns to discuss the issues of the campaign and distribute pamphlets, secondly that " committees of vigilance " be set up to get voters to the polls and counteract Whig propaganda, and thirdly that committees of poll-watchers be detailed all over the state to prevent illegal voting. Then, in July, Wright wrote Flagg to warn him of a possible invasion of Pennsylvanians to flood the polls on election day. He urged the former Comptroller to procure a copy of the report of the Pennsylvania legislature on fraudulent voting in their 1838 election, and to " make good use of it."

But the astute Flagg needed no advice. He had already asked Attorney General Henry Gilpin, a Pennsylvanian, for information on this subject, and through him had received from J. K. Kane, of Philadelphia, a letter describing the irregularities. First of all, wrote Kane, there had been frauds in registering voters. The registration had been done secretly, and no lists of registrants was ever published. Election officials in the towns of Spring Gardens and Northern Liberties were sworn in on a directory or a " work of fiction." " Hundreds of votes," he said, " were polled in names which had never been heard of. . . ." Then, after the polls were closed, these two districts did not declare their vote until all the Democratic districts had reported, the ballot boxes being meanwhile in the custody of " notorious partisans."

Kane soon paid a visit to Albany and saw Flagg personally. On his return to Philadelphia, he travelled some distance along the New York-Pennsylvania border, and his observations on this journey prompted him to write again:

> All that I can hear alarms me for the result in New York. The wireworkers and understrappers of Stevens [a notorious Whig election " specialist "] have all crossed over into your State. Camp of Harrisburg, who was and is now probably Stevens's partner, a reckless and ingenious scoundrel [17] [and many

17 In his letter of July 19, 1840, to Flagg, Wright had inclosed one from J. Hall to Van Buren mentioning this man, and saying that he had gone with " 20 or 30 laboring hands " into New York. Flagg papers.

others] ... have left Pennsylvania as hopeless, and are to
push their efforts at your polls. ... these men are willing
to carry out anything that fraud can devise and violence
effectuate. ... [18]

Thus warned, the State Central Committee, of which Flagg
was chairman, issued a printed circular which was sent to the
Democratic county organizations throughout the state. It
urged that " vigilance committees of from 25 to 50 in each
town " be set up to protect the polls against unqualified voters
and cautioned that New York was to be the " battleground "
of the election of 1840 as it had been in 1800.

The contest is the same in principle now as then—it is between the aristocracy and the democracy . . . Mr. VAN
BUREN, is assailed with the same rancour and bitterness,
and nearly the same language, which distinguished the warfare of the federalists against Mr. JEFFERSON in 1800,
... These efforts of the aristocracy [must be] met and counteracted now, as similar efforts were in 1800, by the firmness
and active zeal of the great mass of the democratic party.[19]

The need for wariness was reiterated throughout the late
summer by letters from various New York Congressmen to
Flagg with further local reports pointing to possible irregularities. Stevens, one letter from Philadelphia said, was busy
transporting men into New York to labor on the public works
which the Whigs had undertaken. " Our friends cannot be too
careful against *fraudulent voters* " especially " British Whigs."
This fear of treachery was not confined to New York politicians. " The *Penna*. Devil for *cheating*," as one Philadelphian
dubbed Stevens, was a bogey in his own state as well as in
New York. He was said to have " plans enough concocted "

18 Van Buren papers, March 1840; Wright to Flagg, Apr. 6, 1840,
J. Kane to Flagg, May 7, Sept. 20, 1840, Flagg papers.

19 Printed circular, August 17, 1840, Flagg papers.

to throw the entire Keystone State to the Whigs. So desperate were the Democrats made by his activity that some of them were even advocating outright violence as the only corrective. " [There is] nothing the *Fed^l. whigs* dread so much as the *huge paws* and *big fists* of our Democrats," wrote the editor of a Philadelphia paper with some feeling. In October, to take another example, John M. Niles, of Connecticut, wrote to his good friend Gideon Welles, the Postmaster of Hartford, that the situation was " shocking." He said millions of dollars were being spent by the Whigs in New York and Ohio, and the fate of those states, so important in the final result, was very doubtful. After the election was over, Van Buren laid his defeat primarily to out-and-out fraud similar to that practiced in Pennsylvania two years earlier. " All that was needed to make a system used with success in a ward or a city applicable to the Union," he complained, " was money, men and time. . . ." [20]

It is hard to say how far Van Buren was correct in attributing his defeat to illegal action. He and his fellow Democrats probably tended to overlook the fact that much of the money poured into the campaign by the Whigs was used legitimately. As the party of the rich, the Whigs had a natural advantage over their adversaries in entertaining the electorate and getting their supporters to the polls.

As the campaign progressed the Whigs continued their issue-befogging tactics. Above all they sought to keep old General Harrison from committing any political *faux pas*. When Harrison sent a letter to Gulian C. Verplanck, of New York, (Verplanck had left the Democratic party when Jackson had removed the deposits from the United States Bank) in which

---

[20] Flagg papers, Witcomb to Flagg, Hobbie to Flagg, Simpson to Hoyt; H. Simpson to H. Gilpin, Sept. 3, 1840, Gilpin Papers Historical Society of Pennsylvania; Niles to Welles, Oct. 11, 1840, Welles papers, New York Public Library; Van Buren to Bancroft, Nov. 20, 1840, Massachusetts Historical Society *Proceedings*, XLII, 388. See also Benton, *Thirty Years View*, II, 206-7.

he evidently presented his views on some of the issues of the day, it arrived enclosed in another letter, from Edward Curtis, one of the Whig candidate's " advisers." " The wisest man," Curtis had written, " in the situation of General Harrison, can not write for publication, any letter, upon public affairs, that will not accomplish *far more harm than good."* He urged Verplanck to refrain from giving the General's letter to the papers, and apparently Verplanck did not, though Harrison's wish seems to have been that it should be published.

Following the party's policy of sidestepping most of the main issues, Whig electioneering was devoted to personal attacks and the development of mass hysteria. One of the stories circulated held that Van Buren in 1813 had opposed the full prosecution of the war with Great Britain. If this had nothing to do with the election of 1840, it was nevertheless an accusation that required refutation, and the *Rough Hewer* devoted many pages to denying it. Wright himself labeled the story a " sheer fabrication " in a letter to Thomas Ritchie, in April, and included in his letter a pamphlet in which it was " proved " that Van Buren had been the spirit of patriotism itself during the war.[21]

In their assaults on Democratic statesmen and politicians, the Whigs were frequently libelous, but seldom vindictive. One of the best Whig writers was " Eustacius Swammerdam," who published in the summer of 1840 a thin volume of doggerell, interspersed with a few lines of acid prose, typical of the Whig approach. One by one " Swammerdam " held up the New York Democratic politicians before his public, and liberally daubed them with his coarse but generally entertaining strokes. John Van Buren, whose friends liked to call him " Prince John " was to " Swammerdam " merely the "son of magic," but poor Churchill C. Cambreleng was

---

21 Curtis to Verplanck, May 5, 1840, Verplanck papers; *Rough Hewer,* Apr. 30, 1840.

the most insignificant of the many sychophants who fawn at
the feet of the Executive ... so assiduous is he in his adula-
tions, and so attached is he to the political ulcer that feeds him,
that he has long been known by the name of " the premonitory
symptom." His appearance being a sure indication that the
President cannot be far off.

Marcy, according to the poet, was to say the least, a careless
dresser whose manners were not as genteel as they might have
been :

> His 'kerchief loses, claps to nose his thumb,
> Blows a loud blast, and strikes refinement dumb ...
> Mentally great, yet low from head to heel,
> A filthy scabbard to a blade of steel.

For Wright, as was frequently the case, his alcoholic habits
became the target :

> What rising sun is breaking through yon East?
> What mist dispelling thing, what man, what beast?
> 'Tis Wright: the goddess of the morn, undressed,
> Is napping caught, and stands herself confessed ;
> The sun retires in deep and sad disgrace,
> Outshone by Silas' round effulgent face.
> Like some great lamp with *spirit*-gas well fed,
> He burns the brightest when he fires his head.

Still, " Swammerdam " attributed some virtue to Wright, just
as he had to Marcy. It was within the Senator's power to

> Confound the wise, confuse the ready Clay,
> Astonish all, and Webster hold at bay.
> Prone to the world, although in visage rude,
> And habits worse,—himself a multitude.[22]

The Whig press reflected this same mixture of bitter yet
humorous attack. As a counter to the *Rough Hewer* the Whigs
established the *Log Cabin*. It was edited by Horace Greeley,

22 E. Swammerdam (pseud.) *The Lash, or Truths in Rhyme*, pp. 21-8.

who had been picked for the job while still a poverty stricken
newspaper man by Thurlow Weed. The *Log Cabin* ran weekly
from May 9 until election and sold for the same price as the
Rough Hewer, but there the resemblance ended. While Greeley
did not neglect the conventional issues completely, they assumed from the start a minor place in his sheet. The main
features were songs (complete with words *and* music), pic-
tures, and descriptions of the military career of General Harrison. And these items were phenomenally successful. By the
time the third issue was off the press circulation was only a
few dozen copies below the 50,000 mark, and by July the
young editor was able to write that he was printing 62,000
copies and selling every one.[23] Weed's own paper, the *Albany
Evening Journal,* joined in the spree. In September, for example, it offered a poetical masterpiece nearly two columns
long, which dissected every member of the Regency from Van
Buren on down. One verse raised Ogle's charge that Van
Buren had spent large sums for decorating the Executive
Mansion.

> The " Royal Wilton carpets "—
> FIVE DOLLARS FOR EACH YARD,—
> Were bought in foreign markets
> With specie, bright and " hard "—
> The People's lordly Masters
> Had cash enough—but *they*
> Could scarcely get *shinplasters*
> In North America.

Another verse lampooned the Democrats for criticizing the
" Hard Cider " campaign.

> A wondrous change in morals
> Is surely hastening on!—
> The Locos rail at " *Barrels,*"

23 *Log Cabin,* May 16, 1840; Barnes, *Weed,* p. 85. In his *Recollections of
a Busy Life* (p. 134), Greeley claimed that the circulation reached 80,000.

And CRACK the demijohn ! ! !—
When WRIGHT and Bully DUNCAN
Against deep " Swigs " inveigh,
There's *hope for all the drunken*
In North America.

The last verse summed up and issued a Whig call to arms.

Up ! Patriots, up !—Determine,
Swear that you'll never rest
Till VAN, and all his vermin,
Of power are disposess'd—
And when *this* King we smother,
Good Heaven !—we beg and pray,
Ne'er curse us with another
In North America.

Weed did not spare the prose either. He was following the
general Whig policy when he reprinted, as he had at every
election since the *Journal* first appeared in 1831, the famous
letter Wright had written to Van Buren in 1824 about " carrying off the spoils." But in this election, the fur was flying
so thick and fast that a modest attack like this was lost amid
the hysterical hurrahs for the Hero of Tippecanoe.[24]

The Whig barrage was bewildering to the Democrats. They
tried manfully to reply in kind, but were completely outdis-
tanced in this new style of politics. Amos Kendall called Harrison's refusal to answer questions on important issues an attack on " the vital principles of free government " and John
Dix even tried to prove that the Hard Cider campaign was
making Democrats of many temperance men ! The injured
attitude of the *Democratic Review* well expressed the general
reaction of the party :

There has never been a period within the history of our
politics, which has exhibited the two contending parties in a
contrast more advantageous to the Democratic side, in every

24 *Evening Journal*, Sept. 29, 1840, Oct. 6, 1840.

point of view, than the present.... Never ... has our party been
in a more pure and healthy state—never more worthy of its
noble old name—than the present moment.... We make no
attempt to excite any other popular feeling than the calm
approbation of sober reason.... How glaring, on the other
hand, the contrast of the manner in which the struggle is conducted by the Whigs! There is no demagogueism so low as
that of an aristocracy party which courts the suffrage of a
democracy it at heart despises.[25]

The vigorous campaign of the printed word continued un-
abated on both sides right into November, and once Congress
adjourned in August, and the " big guns " of the two parties
returned to their home districts, it was joined by an equally
energetic struggle of the spoken, or rather (in those days of
open air meetings without the assistance of public address
systems) the shouted word. Here was a phase of political life
which Wright had never experienced, despite his many years
in the business. His career in the Senate had not prepared
him for stump speaking, and it was generally considered that
he was at his best before a small audience, where his not particularly powerful voice, and his logical detailed manner of
argument could be followed and appreciated without difficulty.[26] But this election was so important that Wright had
decided while still at Washington to make the effort if he was
badly needed. On his way home he visited Flagg at Plattsburg,
and the former Comptroller told him that his services were
considered essential. As usual, he doubted his own ability in
this new line of work, but he entered upon the task vigorously.
His first speech was on August 13 at Ogdensburg, and a few
days later he informed both Flagg and the President that he
was fully engaged in " the stumping business." He was still

25 Kendall to Niles, Aug. 9, 1840, Welles papers, Library of Congress;
Dix to Woodbury, June 22, 1840, Woodbury papers; Democratic Review,
VIII, 196-8.

26 Gilpin, Eulogy of Silas Wright, pp. 16-7; Gillet, Wright, II, 1593;
Democratic Review, V, 417.

uncertain of his talents, but he remarked only half humorously that at least his active campaigning would act as insurance against his being nominated for Governor by the approaching Syracuse convention. He told Flagg that St. Lawrence County would be fought "desperately" and was convinced that the contest in New York would decide the national election.[27]

Throughout late August he campaigned in upper New York, but by September he was venturing further afield. Wherever he went he was the principal speaker, and along with Benjamin Butler and John A. Dix, he carried the main burden of the whirlwind speaking tour conducted by the Democracy through the length and breadth of the state. On September 10 he was in New York City. He addressed a gathering in front of the Merchant's Exchange on Wall Street which according to the *New York Evening Post* was "immensely large," filling the street and the windows of all the nearby buildings.[28] During his speech, which was an effort to convince the merchants that the new Independent Treasury would be good for their business, an attempt to interrupt him was made by "about a dozen bullies." However, the *Post's* report said, "one or two of them were immediately removed [?] and the rest slunk out of the crowd." [29]

Two days later, Wright was up river again at Plattsburg with an itinerary before him which included speeches at Saratoga, Poughkeepsie, Patchogue, on Long Island, and again in the metropolitan area. In general he was following the path of the Whig's prize stumper, Daniel Webster, who was invading New York, and the tenor of most of his speeches was aimed at refuting the charges raised by the "God Like" man against the fiscal policy of the Administration. Besides their

27 Wright to Flagg, Aug. 20, 1840, Flagg papers; Wright to Van Buren, Aug. 20, 1840, Van Buren papers.

28 Philip Hone, however, claimed that the meeting was "feeble," A. Nevins, *Diary of Philip Hone*, I, 499.

29 *New York Evening Post*, quoted in *Argus*, Sept. 19, 1840.

political enmity, the two senators entertained hearty personal dislike for each other. Webster referred to Wright as "a very small man,—a mere politician, and no statesman," and called him "the most inferior man in debate that sat in the Senate," and Wright's letters were filled with sarcastic comments on "The Apostle Daniel" and "Mr. Candidate Webster," whom he looked upon contemptuously as "the Bank's man." [30]

On the hustings, Webster was not an easy man to follow without appearing anticlimactic. At Saratoga he had created a sensation. Shortly after beginning his remarks there, the makeshift platform upon which he stood had collapsed, dumping him and all the other dignitaries who had been sitting on it some seven or eight feet to the ground. Webster, unhurt, quickly mounted to the narrow top of a peddler's wagon, and from that precarious perch, continued speaking for the better part of three hours.[31] Wright's Saratoga speech almost a month later attracted much less attention, but his next effort, at Poughkeepsie, was a Democratic triumph. This was one of the major meetings of the canvass, with delegates from Troy to New York pouring into the city by road and river boat. The crowd began to collect about ten o'clock. At one point there were twelve steamers in sight, approaching the landing at the same time. A huge crowd formed at the dock, and marched through the town to the open air meeting place on a gentle slope near the river. As they passed the Democratic Headquarters, the parading thousands were reviewed by Wright and the other speakers of the day, the Senator particularly, according to the accounts, receiving the cheers of all the delegations. There were many many banners, and flags of every description, the slogan of the New York Democracy, "New York Must Be Redeemed," being the most common inscription. All sorts of catch phrases and puns were displayed, such as this classic

30 Harvey, *Reminiscences of Daniel Webster*, pp. 233-4; Wright to Flagg, Feb. 7, 1834, May 25, Jan. 31, 1836, Flagg papers.

31 J. Hunter to Van Buren, Aug. 20, 1840, Van Buren papers; C. Fuess, *Daniel Webster*, II, 86.

from among the Greene County delegation: "WM. C. BOUCK, the Republican Farmer—He will hoe out *Weeds, Roots,*[32] and *small potatoes.*" The crowd that assembled at the field was judged by the Democratic press to approximate 25,-000 people, and one private observer estimated that at least 50,000 were present. Wright spoke for about an hour, after being introduced to the multitude by the venerable Morgan Lewis, quartermaster of Gates' army during the Revolution. Not till evening did the meeting break up. Its last stages were enlivened by the belated arrival of three boatloads from Troy and Albany which had been forced to travel very slowly because they were so badly overcrowded by the great mass of "delegates" seeking to reach Poughkeepsie.[33]

At Patchogue, Wright again followed Webster, this time by only a single day. The Massachusetts Senator had created another sensation. His speech, though not in his usual style, was in keeping with the Whig campaign. "The man," he announced to his listeners, "that calls me an aristocrat—IS A LIAR!" He spoke at some length on fishing and duck hunting on Great South Bay, aped the speech and mannerisms of Wright, who he knew was to appear the next day, and only incidentally touched on the serious issues of the contest. His speech received further notoriety through James Gordon Bennett, of the *Herald,* (then New York's scandal sheet) who made a great spread of the rapidity with which his news service, using blooded horses in relays, brought the report of the speech to the city for the *Herald's* subscribers. Announcing this event before it happened, Bennett wrote rather candidly, "our intellectual readers may prepare for a rich treat tomorrow morning." What they got was probably much better suited for the intellect of the average *Herald* reader than Ben-

32 Erastus Root, particularly obnoxious to the Democrats because of his former association with them.

33 A. Davizac to Van Buren, Sept. 16, 1840, Van Buren papers; *Argus,* Sept. 16, 1840; *Poughkeepsie Telegraph,* quoted in *Argus,* Oct. 1, 1840.

nett could have expected. When the speech arrived, it was devoured eagerly in the city. Besides publishing it in his paper, Bennett sold copies of it separately for two cents each. At this price he disposed of 65,000 copies within the next few days.

Speaking the next day, Wright presented his regular defense of the new financial policy. He did not try to imitate the tactics of his fellow senator, but though his behavior was less spectacular than Webster's "the democracy of old Suffolk [were]...confirmed by both exhibitions in their ancient faith," according to the *Rough Hewer*. The *Rough Hewer* was naturally prejudiced but this statement was confirmed when Suffolk County, in those days traditionally Democratic, returned a big majority for Van Buren in the election.[34]

Late September marked the peak of the campaign in the metropolitan area. On the twenty-fourth Webster addressed a meeting at Jamaica and Wright spoke at Colonnade Gardens, in Brooklyn. Silas was a very valuable speaker in New York, because his reputation as a sound money man had some appeal to merchant and laboring classes alike. On his previous visit to the city he had spoken to the merchants; this time most of his remarks were addressed to the workingmen. The Independent Treasury would establish a standard of currency for the people as well as for the government, he assured them. If the government deposits its funds in a bank, "forty years of experience" proves that "the bank makes the standard of the value for the country, and not the government." He went on to show that everyone would benefit from the stabilization resulting from the Democratic program and compared the state of real wages in 1836, when prices were high, with the present, when they were much lower. Wages, he admitted, were lower too, but it was still obvious that the same amount of work would produce more buying power than in 1836. All classes suffer when prices fluctuate, he said, but "when a cur-

34 *New York Commercial Advertizer*, quoted in *Argus*, Sept. 28, 1840; *New York Herald*, Sept. 22, 1840, Sept. 25, 1840; *Rough Hewer*, Oct. 8, 1840.

rency is debased the poor man suffers beyond his proportion . . . .and to him of all men in the world, a stable, fixed, true standard of value is the most essential. . . ."

Wright then went on to other matters: the reorganization of the militia, and the government's expensive Indian campaigns in Florida, which he defended largely by appealing to traditional American prejudices against the red men. Finally, his voice hoarse and cracking, he urged each listener to vote " according to the convictions of [his] conscience." Completing this effort, Wright was rushed across the river to another rally at Tammany Hall, where he addressed the assembled sachems for two hours more.[35]

From New York, the Senator proceeded west, addressing crowds of four to five hundred at Prattsville, a thousand odd at Delhi, and nearly five thousand at Oxford, in Chenango County. In all these towns, acting upon the suggestion of Flagg, Wright stressed the importance of getting out the entire electorate for this election. The little ex-Comptroller thought that many of the farmers in remote areas would be attracted to the meetings by Wright's presence, enabling the party to reach just the people at whom the appeal to come to the polls was most directly aimed. In spite of Wright's seeming unfittedness for the type of oratory and argument which had predominated throughout the contest, his hectic tour was proving him an excellent campaigner. " Mr. Wright succeeds admirably as a field preacher," Flagg wrote proudly to the President. " His voice is strong and clear, and he is heard distinctly by as many persons as can be reached by voices much louder than his."

So the Senator continued on his weary way. On October 4 he was at Oswego, having arrived over roads made heavy by rain. " I find this almost constant night travelling, being always in a crowd, and field preaching tire me beyond account,"

35 *New York Herald*, Sept. 25, 1840; *New York Standard*, quoted in *Argus*, Oct. 1, 1840.

he wrote Flagg. " Not having any peculiar attachment to the business when I entered upon it, I cannot say that my relish has in any way improved." But he added that he was going right ahead, that he would be at " Buffaloe " on the nineteenth, and at Batavia on the twenty-first, and so forth. But he had to be home before election, he said, " lest while I am missionating the church at home should be endangered."

He arrived back at Canton on October 28, more tired than he had ever been, the last few days having taxed him especially because he had contracted a bad cold. Writing to his good friend at the White House, he expressed a hope of success which he probably did not feel. " My fervent hope is," he said, " that the decision of our people may be such as a reflecting judgment would certainly pronounce." [36]

However, the judgments which were deciding this contest were not " reflecting " ones, and as the election drew near, experienced politicians among the Van Burenites read the signs of the times and were not pleased. On September 27 Flagg wrote a letter to Gideon Welles, in Connecticut, explaining the situation as he saw it. "To effect a thorough organization," he wrote in his sprawling script, " time and money are necessary. The Whigs have money, we have none. Then they have thousands of broken down speculators who can devote their whole time to organization. . . ." Banks and manufacturers, seeking in Harrison's election a more liberal financial policy and higher tariffs, supplied the money. Against this the Democrats had only an " honest hearted democracy " who, being working people, had little time to devote to electioneering. Flagg thought that the main chance for success lay in getting out all the rural vote. " Mr. Wright's efforts will be used to raise up this class as far as practicable," he told Welles.

36 Wright to Flagg, Oct. 4, 1840, Flagg papers; Flagg to Van Buren, Sept. 24, 1840, Wright to Van Buren, Oct. 29, 1840, Van Buren papers.

Welles, in an effort to boost the cause, wrote to his friend John Niles, who was at Washington, suggesting that the party raise the question of Harrison's mental and physical fitness for the Presidency, but Niles told him that it was too late. The Whigs cared not for Harrison, he said, "this is not a person contest. It is a struggle for power on one side and principle on the other." Niles was very bitter about the tactics of the Whigs. On the eve of the voting he had little hope. " This election," he wrote, " will be no more a free expression of the popular will than the election of General Bonaparte to be Emperor of France. My confidence in public opinion, is of course, *shaken.*" [37]

By the end of October what the future held was pretty obvious, and most of the Democrats were resigned to their fate. Van Buren had made up his mind that he was to be cheated out of the election, and George Bancroft, in Boston, had come to view the matter philosophically to the extent that he felt that defeat might be the best thing, though on November 2 he still expressed a weak belief that Van Buren would win. But as soon as the returns began to come in the result was only too apparent. Harrison scored a clearcut victory throughout the nation, and carried New York by over 13,000 votes. Even St. Lawrence County, usually so strongly Democratic, was lost by fifty-two votes, although it did give a small majority to Bouck in the gubernatorial race, which was a good deal closer throughout the state.[38]

When the defeat had become official, the politicians performed their post mortems. Van Buren himself said that if the Whigs had deemed it necessary to go to such lengths to get him out of office, it was a compliment to his principles

37 Flagg to Welles, Sept. 27, 1840, Niles to Welles, Oct. 1, Nov. 2, 1840, Welles papers, New York Public Library.

38 Van Buren to Buchanan, Nov. 24, 1840, Buchanan papers; Van Buren to Bancroft, Nov. 20, 1840, Massachusetts Historical Society, *Proceedings,* XLII, 387; Niles to Welles, Oct. 21, 1840, Welles papers, New York Public Library.

greater in value to him than the spoils of office would be to them. Bancroft thought the President's position in defeat to be " infinitely nobler than that of Monroe, unanimously [*sic!*] re-elected." Elam Tilden, of New Lebanon, father of Samuel J. Tilden, and a local Democrat of some import himself, blamed defeat on the falling prices of goods in the six months preceding the election. Wright, speaking as a politician, blamed the debacle (in New York at least) on the condition of the banking system, and especially on the suspension of specie payments of 1837, but he was perhaps closer to the truth in a letter which he wrote to his brother-in-law while the returns were still coming in. "The appearances to us here," he wrote, " are that the whigs have whipped us, and that old Tip, and Tyler too and log-cabbins and coon skins are to have a reign. . . ." [39]

39 Van Buren to Bancroft, Nov. 20, 1840, Massachusetts Historical Society, *Proceedings*, XLII, 388; Bancroft to W. Bryant, Nov. 30, 1840, Bryant-Godwin papers, New York Public Library; E. Tilden to Welles, Jan. 19, 1841, Welles papers, New York Public Library, Wright to E. Tilden, Mar. 13, 1841, Tilden papers; Wright to L. Moody, Nov. 8, 1840, property of H. Landon, Watertown, New York.

CHAPTER X

TYLER SAVES THE DAY

"The whigs are experiencing as well the troubles as the pleasures of power."

Wright to John Fine, July 20, 1841.

"Poor Tippecanoe! it was an evil hour that 'Tyler too' was added to make out the line. There was rhyme, but no reason to it."

Philip Hone's diary, August 17, 1841.

THE session of Congress which convened in December, 1840, was characterized chiefly by hot blood, high words and an absence of any substantial achievement. The man who best typified its spirit was the senior Senator from Kentucky, Henry Clay. Intense and fervent resentment had welled up in Clay when he had failed to gain the presidential nomination at Harrisburg. Now, taking advantage of his party's victory, he sought a release for his passion that was little short of psychopathic. On December 15, in a Senate that was still solidly Democratic, he rose from his seat, and solemnly moved the immediate repeal of the Independent Treasury Act.

Of course he did not expect to carry his resolution. Senator William Allen, of Ohio, soon disposed of it neatly by moving that all of it after the word "Resolved" be stricken out, and a series of hard money homilies substituted.[1] But it offered Clay a chance to show what he intended to do as soon as the newly elected Congress should meet.

"Clay crows too much over a fallen foe," wrote John Quincy Adams in his diary shortly afterward. Indeed the Kentuckian, "ebullient with egotism, envy and eloquence," seemed determined to irritate or enrage nearly every Democrat in Washington. Under ordinary circumstances, his scathing wit and his sense of the dramatic made him a dangerous figure in debate. Once for example, in 1835, when making a speech attacking a Democratic measure creating some new government

1 *Cong. Globe*, IX, 19-20, 23.

jobs, he called out dramatically, "Come out! Come out like men and defend your position! Let us hear from you! I call for the leaders of the party!"

The Senate in those days was very small. There were only three rows of desks before the dais. Clay's place was in the last row on the presiding officer's extreme left. As he spoke, the Kentuckian turned to his own left, looking along the sweeping curve of the back row of seats. Directly in his line of vision, several places away, sat James Buchanan, and two seats beyond, sat Wright. It was patent that he was addressing his remarks to them. Wright was busy with his mail. When Clay issued this challenge he looked up, surveyed him levelly for a moment, and then resumed his writing. Buchanan however, snapped at the bait. "I am surprised at the language of the Senator from Kentucky. He knows me well, and the Senate can bear me witness, that I am prompt and direct in expressing my opinions. . .but I choose to take my own time and to consult my own counsels."

Clay affected astonishment. Articulating each word slowly and carefully, he informed the Senate blandly: "I had no allusion to the Senator from Pennsylvania when I referred to the leaders of the administration party." When Buchanan, embarrassed and therefore angry charged that Clay had looked right at him when he had made his appeal, "Prince Hal," splendidly poised, again addressed not the irate Pennsylvanian but the whole Senate: "I assure the gentleman that I had no allusion to him whatever. I might look at him, as he looks at me sometimes; but I think at the time I spoke of the leaders of a particular party, I was looking rather at the Senator from New York than to him." [2]

But in the Congress that met in December, 1840, Henry Clay was not the master of his passions that he had been ear-

2 J. Q. Adams, *Diary*, C. Adams, ed., X, 387; John Fairfield to Mrs. Fairfield, Mar. 14, 1836, *Fairfield Letters*, A. Staples, ed., p. 115; T. Clay and E. Oberholtzer, *Henry Clay*, pp. 422-3; *Reg. Deb.*, XI, 455; *Cong. Directory* gives the seating plan of the Senate.

lier. His subtle shafts of wit had become clumsy bludgeons of
invective. On January 28, 1841, he turned and unleashed his
ire on Silas Wright.

Wright had delivered a speech the day before attacking another distribution scheme, which provided for the apportion-
ment of the proceeds of land sales among the states. It had
been a typical Wright effort, determined and unspectacular,
emphasizing a series of statistics through which he sought to
demonstrate that the expense involved in the purchase and
maintenance of the government lands had always been greater
than the income from land sales. It was not a particularly good
speech, and his interpretations of credits and debits, if not his
actual figures, were certainly questionable, but as was nearly
always the case, it was serious, to the point, and utterly devoid
of personal criticism of any of the proponents of distribution.
In fact, he had undertaken it with very little preparation at
Clay's own request, because the Senator from Kentucky
wished to have the Democratic point of view set forth succinctly in order that he might reply to it. But Clay struck back
with a bitter personal assault. The evils of distribution of
which the New Yorker had complained, he compared to wind-
mills, saying that Wright "might have spared himself the
heavy blows which like another famed hero, not less valorous
than himself, he dealt upon [them]." Wright's figures on the
expense of the public domain to the government, he said,
could only have been arrived at by including costs for which
there was no foundation in actuality, by omitting credits that
ought to be allowed, or both. "The most certain operation is
the latter [i.e., the last]," said Clay, "and the senator, who is
a pretty thorough-going gentleman, has adopted it." He accused Wright of taking "a mere counting-house view" of the
lands:

> Has he exhibited [he asked the Senate] any thing more than
> any sub-accountant or clerk might make out in any of the
> departments, as probably it was prepared, cut and dry, to the

senator's hands?...the senator, by the double process of erroneous insertion, and unjust surpression of items, has shaped an account to suit his argument.[3]

Unfortunately, Wright's reply to this insinuating thrust has not been preserved, but in a manner characteristic of him, Clay " explained " those remarks which were of a personal nature, and the matter was dropped.[4] But he had also addressed disparaging remarks in the direction of the two Ohio Senators, Tappan and Allen. " Go home, Messieurs Senators from Ohio," he had orated, " and tell your constituents of your votes [on the distribution bill]." They will, he intimated, put you where you belong.

" Go home! " the angry Senator Tappan roared in reply. " We shall obey no such orders. We submit to no such dictation. Who gave the Senator from Kentucky authority over us? Autocrat of Kentucky, let him issue his orders to his obsequious slaves; but with Ohio and her representatives he has nothing to do. Sir, I repel with scorn this matchless insolence." [5]

But after the fourth of March, Clay and his fellow Whigs were in a position to do more than obstruct, for besides the Presidency, they controlled a majority of both houses of the new Congress. Harrison quickly called a special session for May 31. Everyone had expected that Old Tippecanoe would be content to act the rôle of figurehead, and there was a spir-

3 Cong., Globe, IX, appx. pp. 128-35; Mallory, Speeches of Clay, II, p. 437 ff., esp. pp. 465, 470-1.

4 Clay was famous for his ability to apologize his way out of embarrassing situations, into which he had been placed by his own headstrongness. Once he denounced the speech of another Senator in the presence of a small group that included Edwin Forrest, the great tragedian. After running the gamut of invective, Clay summed up his opinion of the Senator: " He is nothing but an actor, sir,—a mere actor." Then, suddenly remembering where he was, he turned with a polite wave of his hand to Forrest, and said, " I mean, my dear sir, a mere French actor! " After this incident, Forrest commented with real appreciation on the acting abilities of Clay himself, Forney, Anecdotes of Public Men, I, 10.

5 Mallory, Clay Speeches, II, 459; Cong. Globe, IX, 131.

ited contest between Clay and Webster for control of the Cabinet. But they had reckoned without a thorough knowledge of the new Chief Executive, who was well aware of the general opinion of his position and determined that it should be proved incorrect. Clay he quickly put in his place and though Webster was given the portfolio of the State Department and was consulted on the other posts, even he was unable to dominate the General to any real degree. As Edward Curtis, Webster's New York henchman, explained it, " Genl. Harrison gives signs of a disposition to have some voice in the matter of making his own Cabinet. However arrogant this. . .and however foolish not to leave it to the editors and office seekers, it is well ascertained that the old man, thro. the weakness incedent of waning life, is immoveable upon this point." [6]

However, Harrison's life was really " waning." Before the date for the special session had arrived, he was dead, and John Tyler, of Virginia, was President of the United States. There was some uncertainty among Congressional leaders about his position—Harrison had been the first Chief Executive to die in office—but Tyler quickly asserted his right to full power, and when Congress met, no objection was voiced to this assumption. The immediate result was a bitter conflict between the new President and Henry Clay over the chartering of a new national bank. Tyler was a states' rights theorist of the most uncompromising stripe. As Philip Hone had written apprehensively in his diary when he heard the news of Harrison's demise, Tyler was " an amiable man and a true patriot," but there was " some danger that his opinion. . .[would] not coincide [with those of the regulars]." To him, Jefferson's precept on the unconstitutionality of a national bank was gospel. On top of this, he made a fetish of consistency in a way that is characteristic of doctrinaire minds. He had once opposed the Second Bank of the United States, and would thus

6 C. Poage, *Henry Clay and the Whig Party*, p. 15 ff.; Curtis to Verplanck, Dec. 26, 1840, Verplanck papers.

be irrevocably hostile to any mere copy of it.

Still, he was anxious to remain on good terms with the Whig Congress and sought some type of compromise bank that would be acceptable to Clay and compatible with his own ideas of Congressional power. His suggestion was that a bank be established in the District of Columbia (where national power was supreme and undivided) and that it be granted the power to establish branches in any state which might give its consent.[7]

A reasonable man might have accepted Tyler's obviously sincere stand because the Whigs could not possibly carry a bank measure over a veto, but Clay, sick in mind and body, was far from reasonable. He broke completely with the nominal head of his party and determined, through his control of the Congress, to establish himself as a Prime Minister, relegating the President to the background. On the seventh of June he introduced a series of resolutions in the Senate outlining his program, which called primarily for the repeal of the Sub-Treasury Act and the establishment of a new national bank. Two days later a repeal bill passed the Senate. Then, on July 12, a plan for a national bank to be located in the District of Columbia with the privilege of establishing branches in any state which was willing to permit it was presented to the Upper House. This was Tyler's plan, drafted by Thomas Ewing, his Secretary of the Treasury. It was referred to a nine-man select committee of which Clay was the chairman. The only Democrats in the group were Wright and William R. King, of Alabama.[8]

Wright had utilized the time between the adjournment of the old Congress and the beginning of the special session for a hurried trip home to attend to personal affairs long neglected because he had spent his last vacation on the stump. When he

7 A. Nevins, *Diary of Philip Hone*, II, 535; Apr. 4, 1841; Poage, *Clay*, p. 39.

8 *Cong Globe*, X, 22; Poage, *Clay*, pp. 42-5.

returned to Washington he found that the Democrats had expected him to bring back a detailed plan of action from Van Buren. But in the limited time at his disposal, he had been unable to pay " Little Van " even a social visit, and now he was glad of this, for he realized that Van Buren's enemies within the party would have welcomed an opportunity to charge the ex-President with attempted dictation. Already Wright was thinking of his friend's chances in 1844.[9]

In the meantime the Whigs in the New York legislature were thinking about Wright and his seat in the Senate. With the election over, and the danger of his running for Governor removed at least for two years, the question of " instructing " him was given wide consideration. But nothing was done. Since senators were then elected by the state legislatures, these bodies assumed on occasion, the right to tell their own senators how to act on various measures. The theory was that an " instructed " senator must comply or resign, but there was no way to make a man do so, and many times such " instructions " were politely ignored. Although he never said, even in private correspondence, whether or not he would respect the legislature's right to tell him what course he should pursue on any question, the Whigs felt that Wright would not " give faith to the doctrine." The subject of trying to make him resign was even discussed by the Cabinet at Washington, but Postmaster General Francis Granger (Weed's good friend) advised against pressing it at Albany. Many Whigs, he said, were opposed to the idea in principle, considering it a " southern doctrine." The fact that the Whig majority in the Senate seemed safe anyway, and that Wright's term was due to expire naturally in two years probably also influenced his opponents' decision to take no action.[10]

9 Wright to Van Buren, June 21, 1841, Van Buren papers.

10 R. Blatchford to Biddle, Jan. 21, 1841, *Correspondence of Nicholas Biddle*, R. C. McGrane, ed., p. 341; T. Ewing to Verplanck, Mar. 30, 1841, Verplanck papers.

In Congress, the Democrats were helpless. They could make speeches, but they could not change the Whig course. Their only hope lay in Tyler, whose vetoes they could uphold. It must have been a bitter blow for Wright to see the Independent Treasury Act, over which he had labored so assiduously for three years, dismissed summarily by the Senate in two days. On the ninth of June, the day the vote was taken repealing it, Wright spoke at length, not with any hope of saving the system, but to show what he thought was the unfairness of the Whigs' intention. In introducing the repeal bill, Clay had compared his act with that of an architect who pulls down an old building and clears away the rubbish before constructing a new one. Over this figure, the usually prosaic Wright waxed deeply emotional. Clay, he said,

> insists upon a speedy repeal of the independent treasury law, to give place, as he says, to a national bank, when he does not know, and no man yet knows, that a national bank can be passed. . . . Suppose he should see the head of a family in this city turn his family out upon the pavement and vigorously commence to tear down the mansion which was their only shelter from the weather and the storm, and, upon inquiry, that head of that family should tell him that the timber for his proposed new house was still growing in the forest; that the bricks which were to form its walls were yet resting in the bank of earth out of which they might be formed; and that the pecuniary means for the erection of the new edifice were yet to be earned . . . would he consider that man a provident father and husband, or believe that he was following the directions of a wise architect?

" Whence," he asked, " the necessity for razing this old and plain homely building with such hot haste, because a new edifice is to be attempted in another quarter? "

> The new edifice, I doubt not, if erected, will be more splendid in its achitecture, more glittering and showy in its appearance; but the old house is not in the way, and need not be demolished

to make room for the marble palace which is to succeed it. Will not gentlemen consent to let this plain and homely building remain, useless though it may be ... ? Will they not, in this instance, follow the example of many of the hardy yeomanry of our country, who, when industry, frugality and prosperity have enabled them to do so, erect new dwellings, enlarged and beautified, but suffer the old log cabin to remain a memento of humbler circumstances, though perhaps, not of less happy days or honest dealings?

This reference to log cabins turned his mind to something else. On what grounds, he wanted to know, did the Whigs consider their victory in the election a mandate for a national bank?

It may as well be urged and upon much stronger evidence, that the decision of the people at those elections required of the distinguished individual elected to fill the presidential chair, and of him who now fills it, that they should have declined to occupy the splendid mansion at the other end of this avenue, erected by the people for the use of their President, and should have erected for their official accommodation a hovel of slabs, or a log cabin, upon the beautiful public grounds which surround that proud dwelling ... that these high functionaries and public officials should have discarded from the President's house and table the rich and gorgeous furniture which it has pleased the people to provide ... and should have supplied the deficiencies thus produced by stools and spoons and plates of wood.

Such flights of oratory were unusual in Wright and he soon reverted to a more normal course, offering a comparison between the functioning of the Independent Treasury system and the National Bank system which was designed to demonstrate the infinite superiority of the former, as he had done many times.[11] Once the repeal bill had passed the Senate, he

11 *Cong. Globe*, X, appx. pp. 21-7. Marcy saw Wright in the evening after he had finished this speech and reported him " satisfied with his days work." The general reaction to this untypical effort, again according to

took relatively little part in the hot debates that followed, being content to offer occasional amendments and enjoy the tremendous squabble that soon developed between Tyler and the Whigs.

In the select committee to which Ewing's bank bill had been submitted, Clay was supreme, and he refused to accept the bill as it was. At his insistence a different plan was presented by the committee to the Senate which provided for a bank with unlimited power of establishing branches. Wright thought that Clay did this only to force Tyler to capitulate completely and recognize openly that he could not claim to be the head of the Whig party. The President would have to " surrender or fight " Wright surmised, and he was pretty sure the unlucky Tyler would surrender. In the Senate Clay pushed his proposal remorselessly, brooking not the slightest delay, and growing more and more furious as Democrats and recalcitrant Whigs balked at his tactics. Within a week of the measure's introduction, Wright reported hearing rumors that Tyler would not sign it, but the New Yorker himself was skeptical. " He will sign any thing that is presented to him," he wrote to " Little Van." At this point Wright could not imagine that *no* bill would pass. He was positive that if the President *should* veto Clay's bill, the party would force the angry Senator to accept Ewing's proposal, which Tyler could approve without doing violence to his precious principles.[12]

But the Kentuckian was in no mood to be coerced. He rejected coldly even the most moderate changes suggested by Tyler's supporters, the Democrats gleefully going along with him to increase the dissension within the Whig ranks and the

Marcy, was very favorable. Marcy to Wetmore, June 10, 1841, Marcy papers. Wright, however, admitted to Flagg that this oration contained more " bunkum " than he was in the habit of using. Flagg papers.

12 Wright to Van Buren, June 21, 1841, June 26, 1841, Van Buren papers. Wright was also a member of the select committee, and Clay's attitude at its meetings convinced him that the Kentuckian was going to win out over Tyler no matter what action the President might take. Wright to Niles, June 27, 1841, Welles papers, Library of Congress.

possibility of a Presidential veto.[13] Clay was repeating the blunder which had led to the failure of his plans in 1834. Just as he had then pursued a course aimed first at weakening Jackson and only secondarily at restoring to the United States Bank the deposits which the Old Hero had removed, so now he was considering primarily his own position. He no doubt thought that his policy would eventuate in a national bank, but he was more interested in discrediting Tyler and making sure that the Virginian was removed as a possible rival for the nomination in 1844. This, together with his ardent desire to revenge the ignominy of Harrisburg was largely responsible for the course he chose.

For a while it seemed that his stubbornness would lead to the defeat of his bill even before it reached the President. Tyler (according to Wright) was tempting various Whig senators (he named Preston, of South Carolina, Merrick, of Maryland, Archer, of Virginia, and Barrow, of Louisiana) by offering them tasty slices of the Presidential patronage. " The power of executive influence. . .has never been so perceptible in our body, since I have been in it, as it is now," Silas wrote in mid-July. It seemed that Clay might very well *have* to back down to prevent the complete disruption of his party. As Wright told Van Buren (who had for years been a close student of the Kentuckian's moods) " You never saw Clay so unhappy, or so desperate, and never saw him so domineering over his friends and his party. Many visibly begin to feel a soreness of which they do not speak, or speak in whispers. . . ." Wright's hopes were beginning to rise at this time. Perhaps, after all, there would not be another " Monster." Still he did not dare to appear too optimistic, lest his friends be disappointed if the bill should pass. To Judge John Fine, of Ogdensburg, he wrote, " The whigs are experiencing as well the troubles as the pleasures of power. They are far from happy, but I still think they will finally so far smooth down

13 For a vivid summary of the debates, see Poage, *Clay*, pp. 50-8.

their differences as to pass their measures in some shape." [14]

But as the month of July drew toward a torrid close, it really seemed that Clay would not give way and that some of his followers who were more interested in the bank than in his presidential possibilities would break. Hurried caucuses saved the day. On July 26, Senators Preston and Merrick (significantly) were ready to go against their leader on the showdown vote, but a caucus that evening brought them in line with a "compromise" to which Clay finally consented. [15] This gave the states the right to forbid branches being established within their borders, but failure to do so at the first session of any State legislature held after the passage of the bill was to be considered as permanent consent. In this form the measure passed both houses and was sent to Tyler.

It was then the seventh of August. For the full ten days allowed by the Constitution, the President kept it on his desk and said nothing. Washington was alive with rumors as to what he would do, but no one really knew. The very day that Tyler received the bill, William Marcy, who was in Washington, an acute and astute observer of the proceedings, wrote with great assurance, "We shall have a *veto...*," and from that point on most of the Democrats were of this opinion. As the days dragged past, more and more Whigs came to the same conclusion, and when the Presidential negative finally was made public on the sixteenth, few were surprised. But many were angry. The veto is "one of the weakest and most puerile state papers we have ever had from the executive department," wrote Philip Hone. "Poor Tippecanoe! it was an evil hour that 'Tyler too' was added to make out the line. There was rhyme, but no reason to it." [16]

---

14 Wright to Van Buren, July 10, 1841, Van Buren papers; Wright to J. Fine, July 20, 1841, Wright papers, New York State Library.

15 Poage, *Clay*, p. 64.

16 Marcy to Flagg, Aug. 7, 1841, Flagg papers; A. Nevins, *Diary of Philip Hone*, II, 552-3.

Clay immediately voiced the official Whig position in a speech treating Tyler's action as another example of executive usurpation of power. There were even rumors that a strong effort would be made to force Tyler to resign. Wright observed the goings on with a growing disgust. " The desperation of the Clay whigs is beyond anything you could imagine," he wrote Flagg a few days after the veto. They were threatening to hold up appropriations to " starve " Tyler into submission. " If he had a single finger nail of Old Hickory upon his frail system, this would delight him, but. . . the melancholy truth is he is frightened by the recoil of his own gun. . . .When his passions become aroused, he talks, as I learn, as brave as a Lyon and says his ground is taken and he will maintain it. His intimate friends hope to be able to keep him up, but they hope with great fear." In general, the Democrats sought to make the most of the conflict between Tyler and the Whigs, hoping to immobilize both without helping either. The party attitude was well expressed by young Sam Tilden when he said:

> While we render to Tyler liberal credit for every good act he does, and sustain every right measure which he proposes . . . we cannot give his administration an unqualified support, or commit ourselves in favor of his re-election. . . . I never regarded Mr. Tyler as a man of very high capacity . . . [but if the Whigs try to force him to resign] we must stand by him and his official rights to the utter most.

A little later Wright again warned against " unwise and improvident commitments " and even Calhoun (who was later to ally himself with Tyler) said in 1841, " As far as we are concerned they are all whigs alike, whether Tyler whigs or Clay whigs." [17]

After some maneuvering a new bank bill was drawn up designed to conciliate the President. It was named officially the

17 Wright to Flagg, Aug. 21, 1841, Flagg papers; S. Tilden to N. Waterbury, Sept. 11, 1841, Tilden papers; Wright to Flagg, Dec. 19, 1841, Flagg papers.

Fiscal Corporation bill. (Senator Benton called it contemptuously " the Corporosity," and James Buchanan referred to it
as the " Kiteflying Fiscality.") Actually it differed very little
from the previous bill, still permitting the bank to carry on
local discounting within the states, which was the focal point
of Tyler's constitutional objections. It was a mere concession
of form, without substance. " Can it be," wondered Wright,
" that any man's fears can induce him to stultify himself for
the sake of submitting himself to such humbug? Time I suppose will show though." He delighted in the confusion in the
Whig ranks but was at the same time disquieted by the passion
and selfishness of the party's leaders. " Never was a great and
powerful party. . .more willing to do anything which is desperate and wicked and less able to determine what to do," he informed Van Buren. " We have never seen a more perfect system of log rolling and caucusing and putting on the screws,
in our capital, than we see here every day. . . ." [18]

But Wright's prejudice against Tyler made him a poor
prophet. The President, whatever his shortcomings, had more
spunk than Silas was willing to give him credit for—he would
not " stultify himself." He broke definitely with the Whigs,
vetoed the new bill, and accepted the resignations of all the
members of his cabinet except Webster. Congress adjourned
leaving the finances under executive control, thus merging the
purse and the sword in exactly the manner condemned so vigorously by the Whigs in the thirties.

*   *   *   *   *

The long special session meant that once again Wright's
time at home would be brief. He was growing increasingly
dissatisfied with public office; Clarissa's unhappy letters from
Canton and the bitter partisan quarrels which had characterized the meeting intensified his desire to retire. But he stuck
to his job, and was back at his desk early in December when
Congress reconvened. His wife's loneliness evidently over-

18 Buchanan to Flinn, Sept. 5, 1841, Buchanan papers; Poage, *Clay*, p. 80;
Wright to Flagg, Aug. 27, 21, 1841, Flagg papers; Wright to Van Buren,
Aug. 21, 1841, Van Buren papers.

came her distaste for Washington society, for she accompanied him back to the Capital. They set up quarters at Mrs. Scott's boarding house on Pennsylvania Avenue near 3rd Street.[19]

Tyler greeted the new Congress with a financial program of his own which he called the Exchequer Plan. Wright characterized it as " monstrous " and the Clayites would have nothing to do with it because of its source. The Democrats in the Senate were mystified at their opponent's refusal to press any scheme of their own. Wright thought they wanted to trick his party into some positive action, and observed shrewdly that Clay was " made for a minority not a majority " and wanted nothing better than an opportunity to resume his old rôle as " chief fault finder and tearer down of other people's measures." The New Yorker felt that Clay should be kept out of such a position, and most of the Democrats agreed. The irrepressible Senator Benton, however, would not consent to this passive attitude; he unleashed a scathing attack on Tyler's proposal, and Wright (although he considered this poor strategy) could not help admiring his spirit.

The danger of this policy of watchful waiting was its possible bad effect at home, where good Democrats might interpret silence as apathy. " Our desire is that our leading papers should not misunderstand our silence and inaction," Silas wrote to Azariah Flagg, explaining that its purpose was to make the Whigs assume " the responsibilities they have so long and unrighteously sought. . . ." But the Clay men soon made clear their dislike of the " Exchequer " and their violent attack on Tyler relieved the minority party. As Wright put it, " the darkness which has surrounded us begins to be dispelled." [20]

Though the Whigs continued to wrangle with the President, their leader had other plans for himself. Physically

19 Wright to Mrs. E. Burke, July 6, 1841, Gillet, *Wright*, II, 1215; *Congressional Directory*, 1842.

20 Benton, *Thirty Year View*, II, 275 ff.; Wright to Flagg, Dec. 19, 1841, Flagg papers; Wright to Van Buren, Jan. 12, 1842, Wright to Flagg, Dec. 29, 1842, Van Buren papers.

wasted by the tremendous pace at which he had driven himself, realizing that the bank issue was now completely dead,
and feeling that the retired statesman's rôle would solidify his
position and assure his nomination for the next presidential
race, Clay decided to resign from the Senate. He intended at
first to do so in November, postponed the date to February,
and did not bring himself to the act until the last day of
March.[21] John Crittenden, the Kentuckian who was to replace
him, had been waiting since December for the great man to
make up his mind. ("Waiting with impatience for the shoes
which were to be cast off for his wear" was the way Wright
expressed it.) Wright thought that Clay, sick as he was,
seemed sorry at the end that he had agreed to quit his post.

When the day finally arrived, the galleries were jammed
at eleven, and by noontime even the corridors outside the Senate Chamber were packed. At half past one Clay began his
Valedictory. He reviewed his long career as a senator, and
explained his reasons for retiring. " I have long. . .desired to
seek that repose which is to be found only in the bosom of
one's family—in private life—in one's home. . . .I migrated to
the State of Kentucky nearly forty-five years ago. I went there
as an orphan. . .who had never recognized a father's smile—
poor, penniless, without the favor of the great—. . .but scarcely
had I set foot upon that generous soil, before I was caressed
with parental fondness—patronized with bountiful munificence
—and I may add to this, that her choicest honors, often unsolicited, have been freely showered upon me. . . .Sir, it is to
me an unspeakable pleasure that I am shortly to return to her
friendly limits. . . ."

Silas Wright sat listening to these remarks and trying to
understand his own feelings. Though the Democrats were all
happy to see Clay out of the Senate, Wright found himself
feeling sober rather than joyful. He tried to cast off his mood
by exchanging pleasantries with some of his friends sitting

21 Poage, *Clay*, p. 114.

nearby, but it was useless. Clay depressed him. He looked older and more tired than ever before. Yet it was what he said rather than his appearance that affected Wright most deeply. Clay talking of wanting to retire! Clay speaking of unselfish devotion to duty! Henry Clay addressing the Senate, even weeping openly, speaking of his loyal friends, his worthy opponents—all this with the memory of the past year clear in everyone's mind! Such hypocrisy was too much for the Senator from New York, who could have uttered Clay's words about retiring with real sincerity.

> My ... difficulty [he wrote later to Martin Van Buren] was the place and the manner of this farce. I could not forget that it was the Senate, and that no question whatever was before us, and I looked round upon the immense audience, and thought of the vital national questions which are now daily before us, even almost without attracting our own observations, and of the cause which had brought this audience of our Countrymen together to dignify our proceedings, and I was sick and solemn in spite of myself.

" In that state of feeling," he continued, " I heard the speaker often declare that he had never acted under a selfish impulse, or entertained a motive or wish for self promotion, and asseverate his long and ardent wish for retirement and quiet... and I could not get rid of the impression that the heaviest weight upon his feelings at the moment was his heartfelt fear that the Gods had determined to gratify him in that wish. . . ." [22]

The sight of Henry Clay weeping cut deep.

* * * * *

The retirement of Clay did not end the three-cornered struggle between the Whigs and the Democrats and the followers of the President. The controversy over the proposed National Bank was abandoned, but the rest of the Whig pro-

---

22 Benton, *Thirty Years View*, II, 399, 401; Wright to Van Buren, Apr. 2, 1842, Van Buren papers.

gram was pressed forward. Two closely related issues were dominant, distribution and the tariff.

The habit of parceling the income from land sales among the several states had become popular with the development of a surplus in the federal coffers. During the great land boom of 1834-36, a period which coincided with the final payments on the national debt, the government had rapidly accumulated a large credit. As has been pointed out, this sum was "distributed" to the states for "safe-keeping" in 1837, but with the panic of that year, government income fell off precipitously and the national surplus became a deficit. Further distribution of land income was stopped. But the partial return of prosperity after 1840, coincident with the accession of the Whigs (the great proponents of the distribution idea) brought about a renewed agitation for reviving this policy during the special session. The tariff was involved because it was the only other source of government income; if the money from land sales was to be given away, duties must be raised to meet the costs of running the federal government. This, of course, was perfectly acceptable to most Whigs, but President Tyler, although he approved of distribution, would not sanction any modification of the Compromise Tariff of 1833, which was just then reaching the twenty per cent level. As a result, a Distribution Act was passed which provided that the income from federal lands should be given to the states, but only as long as the tariff did not exceed twenty per cent on any item. At the same time a new tariff was passed raising duties on many items, but maintaining the twenty per cent top.[23]

All through his career, Wright was consistently opposed to the distribution idea. He considered the public lands a nuisance to the government rather than a source of profit. " The collisions which they are periodically threatening between the new States and the federal government, and the new States and the old, have ever been frightful to me," he wrote after

23 Chitwood, *Tyler*, pp. 294-5.

he had retired in 1847. " I have feared. . .that these collisions may, some day, come to a direct issue which shall shake our Union. The spirit of plunder which the lands keep alive, by enabling demagogues to represent them as an immense fund which Congress may legitimately apply to any profligate purpose, is an evil only second to the one I have just mentioned. The distribution policy is an offspring of this spirit." [24]

But on the tariff his ideas underwent a gradual modification. In 1828 (along with most men from his section) he had been a frank protectionist. He thought primarily in terms of agriculture, but he felt that every industry was entitled to security against European competition. In 1833, he had supported the Compromise bill, but in that case he was thinking (again with most people from the Northern states) in terms of conciliating the South rather than of free trade. By 1842, he had rejected the *principle* of protection. Speaking in the Senate in August of that year he came out clearly for a revenue tariff, with " not a cent of duty for protection itself."

He developed his theories in detail, some months later in a letter to Van Buren. A tariff, he wrote, should have one main purpose, that of producing revenue, for all duties rest upon the constitutional power of Congress to raise money. " No duty therefore should be raised to a point to impair revenue. . . ." His second principle on rates held that there should be a definite distinction between luxuries and necessities. Liquor, he said, (and this must have hurt) is a proper article upon which to place a tariff, salt is not. If by doubling the total importation of a product, a duty of only fifteen per cent will produce the same amount of money as one of thirty percent, then the deciding point in settling the schedule should be whether or not it is a luxury item. The only exceptions are materials needed for national defense, but these may be protected under the constitutional power to provide for the common defense, and thus the revenue criterion need not apply.

24 Wright to Dix, Jan. 5, 1847, Gillet, *Wright*, II, 1838.

Within these basic assumptions it should be left to the judgment of the legislature to set the actual duties, Wright continued. He admitted that there could be no recourse if
the legislators deliberately violated the " rule." " We have no
tribunal authorized to inquire into the motives with which
members of Congress vote," he said. It would be necessary to
have faith, and assume that Congressmen usually act in the
public interest.[25]

Wright's hatred of distribution had probably played a large
part in propelling him to this position on the tariff. When the
Distribution bill of August, 1841, was before the Senate, he
said, " every dollar taken from the public treasury by this
bill, must be supplied, dollar for dollar, by new taxation or by
further loans. . . ." This meant increasing duties, he continued,
and that would mean taxing the people without helping the
government, because higher rates usually mean higher prices
and higher profits for producers, not increased income for the
government.

He elaborated his argument. Distribution money will be
applied by the states to the payment of their debts. At present
these debts are a charge on the property holders of the states,
because they pay the taxes which at present discharge them.
This, Wright said, was fair, for a man with $100,000 in prop-
erty paid one hundred times as much as an individual owning
only one thousand dollars worth. Besides, the state debts had
largely been incurred in the construction of public improvements like roads and canals which operate to raise property
values. " Of what value are the canals and railroads of a State
to its day laborers who are without property? They may be
calculated to cheapen to such a man, to a very limited extent
the necessaries of life, but the probabilities are that the wages
of his labor will be made to conform to any influence of this
sort, so as to leave him exactly where he would have been

25 *Cong. Globe*, XI, 829; Wright to Van Buren, Jan. 27, 1843, Van Buren
papers.

without such improvements." If distribution passes and the
tariff is raised, the poor man is hurt and the rich benefited,
for the money will be raised not on property but on the necessities of life, " which the poor must consume equally with the
rich. . . . What equality, what justice, is there in such a measure of taxation for such an object? " [26]

The Distribution Act of 1841 was not satisfactory to
Wright, but it was better than an act with no tariff limitation
as long as distribution had to be tolerated. However, when
Congress reconvened in December pressure for jacking up the
rate ceilings was resumed. The New York Senator set himself inflexibly against this. " An effort will doubtless be made
to raise the tariff feeling again," he warned a friend, " but our
point, I think, should be to raise no more revenue in any way,
or for any purpose, until the land-distribution bill is repealed.
. . ." But the government needed money badly. Since 1837 it
had operated by borrowing, and by 1841 it was becoming increasingly difficult to float loans except at very high interest
rates. The Whigs sought to solve this problem by ignoring
the arrangement of 1841 and advancing the level of duties
without discontinuing distribution. During the summer of
1842 they passed a bill which effected this; Wright voted
against it and Tyler vetoed it. This embarrassed the Whigs
in Congress, since some sort of provision had to be made for
meeting the expenses of the government. So a new bill was
drafted which elevated most schedules to about the level of
the frankly protective duties of 1832, but which stopped the
distribution of the income from federal land sales. It was a
fair compromise, but like most such adjustments it satisfied
no one. Without distribution (and to annoy Tyler) some
Whigs who had supported the earlier bill would not approve
this one, and most of the Democrats in the Senate were still
unwilling to swallow another high tariff. The bill got through

26 *Cong. Globe*, X, 380-3. Desire to gain Southern support for Van Buren's
renomination probably also influenced Wright's tariff position at this time.

the lower House, but it was clear that in the Upper Chamber the balloting would be very close.

This situation was very difficult for Wright, for he did not know how to vote. The Democratic press was vehemently opposed to it—the *Washington Globe* called it " utterly repugnant to the view of the whole Democratic party "—but he did not want to see the country left without an adequate source of income, and the stopping of distribution was after all a very important concession. " It is a horrible bill," he wrote to Flagg on August 26. " We have amended it some and I hope may amend it some more, and yet it will be a very bad bill after all we can do with it. I am miserably perplexed to know how to vote myself. . . ." He knew that if he should approve it his action would produce a " great noise " in the South and in New York City where the mercantile interests were opposed to protection. And he knew too that his attitude would be taken as an expression of Van Buren's feelings, and might be used against the ex-President by his enemies within the party at the next Democratic national convention. " If I had you or him here to advise with it would relieve me vastly," he wrote characteristically to Flagg. Yet with a determination also typical, he added, " but it is not so and I must act according to my best judgment, and as Old Hickory would say, leave the result to Providence." [27]

The next day the measure came before the Senate for a final settlement. The session was a long one with the debate dragging on until eight o'clock in the evening. The reporter for the *Washington Globe* was sitting in the gallery when Wright rose to make his final speech and declare his position. " Well," the journalist heard other spectators whisper tensely, " his course decides the question." [28] In his first sentence the Sen-

27 Wright to E. Tilden, Dec. 5, 1841, *Letters of S. J. Tilden*, J. Bigelow, ed., I, 10; *Washington Globe*, Aug. 22, 1842; Wright to Flagg, Aug. 26, 1842, Flagg papers.

28 *Washington Globe*, Aug. 27, 1842. The position of Crittenden, of Kentucky, was also critical. When both he and Wright supported it, the tariff's passage was assured.

ator from New York announced his decision to vote for the
bill. He went on to explain his distaste for this decision, declaring himself against protection as a principle. He mentioned
his connection with the high tariff of 1828, admitted that he
had then made a " great error," and said he was now learning
the truth of the old adage "that 'men's evil deeds follow
them.'" For Van Buren's sake he emphatically asserted that
he was acting on his own responsibility. No friend, "here or
elsewhere," he said, had interfered to influence his action. He
favored the bill because it ended distribution and because it
seemed to be, under the circumstances, the only way to meet
the government's financial needs. These grounds alone led him
to vote affirmatively, he assured his listeners.

When the question was called, the measure was carried 24
to 23. Within the Democratic party, the reaction to Wright's
conduct was mixed. The *Argus* supported him heartily and the
St. Lawrence Republican naturally applauded him, stating that
when the Whigs plotted to vote against the tariff to compel
Tyler to retain distribution, Wright "came to the rescue."
The Southern Democrats were very disappointed. Governor
James Hammond, of South Carolina, wrote that he had
"thought better of Wright" and the rabid Southern nationalist, Robert Barnwell Rhett, told Calhoun that the New
Yorker was insincere, and really favored protection. Northern
free trade Democrats also commented unfavorably, and despite
Wright's explicit disavowals, there was even a faction within
the party that tried to blame Van Buren. But most Democrats
agreed with Senator William Allen, of Ohio, who, while admitting that Wright had "stumbled," added, "But he is
honest and I forgive him." [29]

29 *Cong. Globe*, XI, 953-5, 960; *Argus*, Sept. 2, 13, 1842; J. Hammond to
Calhoun, Sept. 10, 1842, *Calhoun Correspondence*, J. Jameson, ed., p. 850;
Rhett to Calhoun, Feb. 21, 1844, *Correspondence Addressed to Calhoun*,
Boucher and Brooks, ed., p. 210. See also F. Byrdsall to Calhoun, Oct. 11,
1842, *ibid.*, p. 179. On the effort to connect Wright's vote with Van Buren,
see R. Wallace to Van Buren, Sept. 12, 1842, W. Allen to Van Buren,
Jan. 18, 1843, Van Buren papers.

During the closing days of the long session of 1842 Wright was also concerned with the Webster-Ashburton Treaty, which settled the long-disputed boundary between Maine and British North America. As a citizen of the North Country, Silas Wright did not like the English, though as has been pointed out, he supported Van Buren's policy of strictly enforced neutrality during the Canadian Revolution. In Congress he sought to have large sums appropriated for strengthening American fortifications along the border, and he even tried to have the funds granted to New York by the hated Distribution Act of 1841 applied to this purpose. When Webster's treaty came before the Senate, his prejudices were all against it. Not only were the English involved, but Webster had negotiated it! He thought that its terms were grossly unfair—that too much land had been conceded. " Webster," he wrote indignantly to Van Buren while the treaty was being discussed, " has been much more English than Lord Ashburton in the matter." But reason triumphed over passion in the end, and he gave in, saying, " I must vote for it, but it is hard." [30]

*　　*　　*　　*　　*

With the adjournment of Congress the Wrights turned toward Canton. They stopped at New York, and again at Kinderhook, where Silas held a conference with the ex-President and Flagg on the local " heart burnings " which were once again stirring within the party. Though the Regency's efforts in 1840 had been unsuccessful, the Whigs were unable to maintain the hysterical pitch of that campaign in 1841, and what Van Buren liked to call " the sober second thought " of the people began to have its influence. Using the " $40,000,000 debt " with great effect, the Democrats swept the fall elections, regaining both the Assembly and the Senate. This was a great victory, and not entirely expected. Wright, for instance,

---

[30] Corey, *Crisis of 1830-42*, p. 154; G. Roach, " The Presidential Campaign of 1844 in New York State," *New York History*, XIX, p. 168n.; Wright to Van Buren, Aug. 12, 17, 1842, Van Buren papers.

would have been satisfied if the party had regained only the lower house. But it appeared to all the radical Democrats as a vindication of their principles, and as Van Buren put it, an expression of the people's " natural and strong desire to wipe off the temporary stigma affixed to their character by the apparent success of last year's buffoonery." [31]

This success stimulated the old Bucktail leaders to undertake an immediate revival of their whole program. Michael Hoffman outlined the plan succinctly in a letter to Wright early in December:

> I hope we shall soon be able to agree on the only course that can save the State; organize a new administration—reform all the useless offices—reduce all salaries ... — cease expenditures —aid the revenue by a bearable tax — ... collect the moneys set apart the Erie and Champlain [canal] debts, and honestly proceed to the work of repayment.

As Wright himself said, "We must show the people the truth as to our finances, and then act as honest men would act...."

In the new Assembly, Hoffman was Chairman of the Ways and Means Committee, and under his leadership the famous " Stop and Tax Law " was passed. This statute was based on the theories outlined in Wright's report on canals made in 1827 and in his program as Comptroller, which he now saw combined and put into operation. A small property tax was established to rehabilitate the General Fund, and all canal construction not absolutely necessary was stopped. As one student has said, " It will readily be seen that the principles and prescriptions of the law were alike radical and reformatory, and that it must have represented a large body of public sentiment, to succeed in adoption." [32]

---

31 Wright to Van Buren, Oct. 25, 1841, Van Buren papers; Van Buren to H. Horn, Nov. 26, 1841, Van Buren papers, New York State Library. For the surprise of the election, see Hammond, *History of New York*, III, p. 247.

32 Hoffman to Wright, Dec. 6, 1841, Gillet, *Wright*, II, 1225-6; Wright to E. Tilden, Dec. 6, 1841, *ibid.*, p. 1220; Donovan, *Barnburners*, p. 24.

It was this unmistakable mandate which kept the conservatives among the New York Democrats in line in 1842, and enabled the party to function as it had in the late twenties and early thirties, but once the program had been enacted, the old dissensions began to crop up once again, causing the "heart burnings" which Wright desired to discuss with Flagg and the Little Magician at Kinderhook. What the three decided upon is unknown, but the outcome was a compromise which postponed a final settlement of the conflict. William C. Bouck, who had been defeated for the Governorship by Seward in 1840, was nominated to make the run again in 1842. Bouck was a stolid, hard-working farmer of German extraction who came from Schoharie County. He was of medium height, with small grey eyes, an extremely low forehead, and a tremendous shock of iron grey hair that grew straight out from his head in all directions. Seward found him dignified and gracious, but had to admit that the prevailing opinion was quite the opposite. He had received little education, and his talents were at best mediocre. After he had been elected Governor, Jabez Hammond wrote of him in his history of New York State: "When Mr. Bouck reflected that he then was placed in a seat which had been occupied by...the most accomplished scholars, jurists, and statesmen which the country has produced... there can be no doubt he felt some embarrassment...." As another contemporary more bluntly phrased it, "he was a mighty small pattern for a man for governor of the Empire State." [33]

As a Canal Commissioner, Bouck was known to favor a moderately expansionist building program, and was therefore disliked by some of the radical element. Hoffman, for example, felt that his selection would lead to the downfall of the party, and he and his group wanted John A. Dix, or better still

---

[33] Seward, *Autobiography*, p. 639; Hammond, *History of New York*, III, 324, and picture opp. page 311; Brockway, *Fifty Years of Journalism*, p. 55.

Wright himself as their standard bearer. But Wright was still inflexible in his determination to avoid the nomination and when the state convention met in September in Syracuse, Judge Fine, of Ogdensburg, was armed with a letter from him flatly refusing to accept it. He was backed in his refusal by his personal following in the North Country, including such staunch radicals as Congressmen Preston King and Ransom H. Gillet, who were willing to accept Bouck. As a result the former Canal Commissioner was entirely unopposed at Syracuse and was elected easily in November. The radical element at Albany counted on Van Buren's influence with the new Governor to protect their program, and for a time, it did.[34]

For Wright, his " escape " from the Governorship was a hollow victory, for he was unable to avoid reelection to the Senate the following February. His desire to retire was sincere (he had even made preparations for resuming his local law practice) but his devotion to his party prevented him from carrying out his wish. He knew that if he abandoned his seat a battle royal would immediately ensue over his replacement, and he feared that with intra-party tension already so high, such a squabble might disrupt the Democratic organization completely.[35]

34 Wright to Fine, July 30, 1842, Hammond, *History of New York*, III, 307-8; King to Flagg, Aug. 18 1842, Flagg papers; Donovan, *Barnburners*, p. 34 ff.

35 Wright to Van Buren, May 30, 1843, Van Buren papers; Wright to Gillet, Feb. 16, 1842, Gillet, *Wright*, II, 1539. Wright also mentioned his fear that his resignation would involve him again as a gubernatorial candidate. The approaching presidential election must have been an additional consideration, for he knew that Van Buren's best interests would be served by his own continued presence at the Capital.

CHAPTER XI
TEXAS

"[It is] more noble, more desirable, more important more patriotic, to take boldly the side of truth and principle...than to temporize with a matter which may prove to be so vital to...our Country."

Wright to Martin Van Buren, April 8, 1844.

WRIGHT sacrificed retirement for party unity in New York, but so far as Washington was concerned no such political peace was possible. At the capital every act of every public figure was being interpreted in the light of its real or supposed effect on the coming presidential election. In the spring of 1842, Clay had left the Senate apparently certain of the Whig nomination, and Van Buren's primacy among the Democrats had not yet been generally questioned. Once again the man in the White House, John Tyler, found himself suspended in the middle. He had left the Democrats; the Whigs had left him— but he had not abandoned his desire to succeed himself in 1844.

Devoid of party support, with only a small "Corporal's Guard" of personal followers, Tyler had one potent weapon at his disposal, the great mass of federal patronage which was his to distribute. Like most presidents he did his best to take advantage of this. Actually he did not abuse his right to hire and fire hundreds of government officials, great and small, but his isolated position between the two major parties made his every action subject to attack from both sides. Only if a moral distinction can be drawn between a president using the patronage for the benefit of an already existent party and one attempting to use it to create a new organization under his own leadership, can John Tyler's record be considered worse than that of Jefferson, Jackson, Lincoln, or any other Chief Executive who has faced the problem of removing large numbers of office holders unsympathetic to his administration.

The President's efforts to build a personal organization were resented bitterly by "regular" politicians of both parties. As

232

early as February, 1842, Wright had written to his wife's brother: " The state of things here in the political world is very strange just now, and as far as I can judge nominations go a good deal by trick, and that candidate stands the best chance whose friends remember to have him say, within the last six months, the most kind things about the Capt. [Tyler]."[1] A little later Wright wrote another friend that " the object of the President and his Cabinet is to make inroads in the Democratic party...by the distribution of the patronage of the administration. The President calls himself a Democrat, as does Mr. Spencer [John C. Spencer, Secretary of War] of course, and they will appoint democrats, if they feel that they will be Tyler men, and not otherwise I think." Wright's advice to friends who wanted federal jobs was to apply without disguising their political opinions; then if a post were offered, it could be accepted with a clear conscience.[2]

Though Tyler's hopes for himself were doomed to disappointment, he was in a position to do a great deal of damage to one or the other of the major parties. Probably he disliked Van Buren more than Clay. At any rate this was the opinion of Senator Tallmadge, who told a friend that he had heard on the " highest authority " (and Tallmadge was on the most intimate terms with Tyler's closest adherents) that the President considered Clay the lesser evil. " It is now well understood here," Tallmadge said, " that the President goes all length against Van Buren—he thinks V. B. can only be defeated by Clay." But as the election grew nearer, it was not clear just how the Chief Executive would act. On New Year's Day, 1844, Wright, paying a call at the White House, found

1 Chitwood, *Tyler*, Ch. XXIII; Wright to L. Moody, Feb. 25, 1842, Wright papers, St. Lawrence University. The President had served briefly during the War of 1812 as the head of a local Virginia militia company, and during his later career he was usually referred to by his opponents as " the Captain."

2 Wright to O. Hungerford, Apr. 14, 1843, Wright papers, St. Lawrence University.

Tyler in buoyant spirits, and had to admit that he had never before seen the Mansion so crowded. However, most of the leading Whigs were conspicuous by their absence and there was no sign of a reunion of the President and the friends of Clay.[3]

Indeed the President seemed to be making a determined effort to put himself at the head of the *Democratic* party! In December, 1843, Justice Smith Thompson of the Supreme Court had died. Thompson, a New Yorker, had been an old friend of Van Buren's (the ex-President had even named one of his sons after the Judge) and it seemed likely that the vacancy would be filled by another citizen of the Empire State. Casting about for a suitable choice, Tyler evidently hit upon what must have seemed an ingenious scheme—why not offer the appointment to Van Buren himself? His acceptance, of course, would eliminate him as the possible Democratic choice for the Presidency in 1844. It is not certain just how seriously the proposal was considered at the White House, but it was broached in an extraordinary manner to Silas Wright.

It all happened on a stormy day late in December, 1843, when General Mason, the father of a former Governor of Virginia, dropped in at Wright's lodgings at Mrs. Scott's, and told him quite formally that he thought Van Buren would be an ideal choice for the vacant justiceship.

" I can usually keep my face when I try hard to do so and have any warning that the effort will be required," wrote Wright to Van Buren when he told him of the General's visit, " but this took me too much by surprise and I did not succeed at all, but met the suggestion with a most immediate fit of laughter."

His visitor, however, patently did not look upon it as a laughing matter, and Wright perceived this quickly. Then it dawned on him that this was no social call, that Mason was an emissary from someone higher up. He changed his manner

3 Tallmadge to S. Stillwell, Dec. 26, 1843, Miscellaneous papers, New York Public Library; Wright to Van Buren, Jan. 2, 1844, Van Buren papers.

at once and bade his visitor explain himself, affecting deep interest. The General remained about two hours, and the proposed appointment was fully discussed. Wright told him that he did not think Van Buren would accept such an offer, but he was careful now to treat the subject " decorously," and Mason seemed to feel that he was making an impression. He told Wright that he, Mason, was Van Buren's friend, but that he did not think the Little Magician could possibly be elected President. He even intimated that if Van Buren accepted the Judgeship, the way would be open for Wright to garner the Presidency!

Wright listened to all this and then asked Mason what he thought Tyler would say about it. Mason replied that he had not " seen or conversed " with the President, but that he " *knew* " that Van Buren's name had been suggested to him. The General asked repeatedly whether Wright and the other Van Buren men in the Senate would look upon the nomination as an unfriendly act on Tyler's part, and if they *could* vote against it. He seemed especially anxious to hear Wright's answer to these questions. Silas told him that no one could consider a nomination to the highest tribunal in the nation as a hostile act, and that no person in the country could be " degraded " by being offered so high a position. Seeming to be troubled, he added that he did not see how he, personally, could vote against such a nomination.

Mason seemed highly elated. " You are right, you are right," he laughed excitedly, " you *can't* vote against him." Then he rose to leave, but paused to ask the Senator once more just what he thought of the proposal.

Wright looked at him levelly, and said: " Tell Mr. Tyler for me that if he wants to give the whole country a broader, deeper, heartier laugh than it ever had, and at his own expense, he can effect it by making the nomination."

This naturally brought Mason up short, and he departed immediately. " I laughed myself almost sick, not entertaining a doubt...that the Capt. had sent him to me," Wright told Van Buren.[4]

There is no proof that this interview caused Tyler to change his plans, but at any rate, the name of the Red Fox of Kinderhook was not submitted to the Senate. Instead the President nominated John C. Spencer. Spencer was an old style Whig whose career in New York politics ran back to the days of the Constitutional Convention of 1821. But he was an office seeker of the most blatant type, and had been happy to head the War Department when Tyler had rebuilt his Cabinet after the bank vetoes. Now he was to reap the reward of his opportunism. When his name was proposed it was attacked by Democrats and Whigs alike. Wright found himself in a dilemma of sorts. Was it safe, he asked Van Buren, to indulge in the " bloody disposition " he would prefer? To Marcy he voiced his problem in greater detail. " If I go for Spencer and he is confirmed, I shall certainly be cursed for the vote as long as he shall live. ...If I vote against him...[and some Whig is then selected] I shall be told by many certainly that S. would have been far preferable, and I shall feel so. What shall I do then? " Fortunately the Whigs hated Spencer so thoroughly that they did not try to embarrass the Democrats by making them responsible for his rejection. Their leaders were outspoken in their criticism of him, and he was rejected. It was a " terrible but just punishment," wrote Thurlow Weed, and nearly everyone agreed.[5]

This left the Judgeship open, and one of the most eager of the candidates was William L. Marcy. To his name Wright could give full approval and he did what he could to help his cause. But Marcy's best connection in Washington was Thomas Gilmer, Tyler's Secretary of the Navy, and when he was killed on Washington's birthday by the explosion of

4 Wright to Van Buren, Jan. 2, 1844, Van Buren papers.

5 Wright to Van Buren, Jan. 8, 1844, Van Buren papers; Wright to Marcy, Jan. 25, 1844, Marcy papers. For the Whig reaction to the nomination see, Warren, *Supreme Court* (1937 ed.) II, 111-2.

a cannon on the gunboat *Princeton,* Marcy's chances were dimmed.[6] Tyler in the meantime had had another idea; this time he offered the position to Wright himself.

First he approached Wright through intermediaries. During the last days of February, several people hinted to the New York Senator that he would be offered the vacant seat. These hints he politely discouraged. Then, on the afternoon of March 5, the President's son, Robert, accosted him in the Senate Chamber, and told him that his father desired to see him. Wright called at the White House the next morning and talked with Tyler for about half an hour. Tyler admitted that he had been " sounding him out " through friends and then offered him the nomination point blank. Wright thanked him profusely, but declined flatly to consider it. Still not satisfied, Tyler asked Associate Justice Peter Daniel to urge Wright to reconsider, and Daniel wrote to Wright accordingly, but the Senator was adamant. He gave Justice Daniel two reasons for his refusal. First of all, he said that he did not feel properly qualified, because his law practice had for years been very limited, and secondly he could not give up politics at a time when he was needed so badly by the Van Burenites. His explanations give a good insight into his character.

> The consciousness of want of qualification [he wrote Daniel] would have been a very serious, if not insurmountable obstacle, if I had been left to contend with that alone; but as neither you nor any other friend can very well discuss that point frankly with me, I lay that aside.... I did think, at one time, of writing privately to some few friends at home; but reflection induced me not to do so.

Again he was reacting to a new situation with doubts as to his worthiness and an almost compulsive desire to " consult " with the Regency. But he did not do so. Why?

6 Stevenson to Marcy, Feb. 16, 22, Mar. 8, 1844, Wetmore to Marcy, Mar. 8, 1844, Marcy papers; Wright to Van Buren, Mar. 1, 1844, Van Buren papers.

They must have said, and that one [Van Buren] especially, "he wants to take the place, but desires our sanction to his leaving the Senate," and none of them would have interposed ...whatever might have been their [sic] real views of the policy of the step or its propriety. And the one friend would have been compelled to feel that even doubt or reluctance on his part might be imputed to selfishness, and he could have said nothing, or must have said "yes." For these reasons I have not consulted a mortal, and for my conclusion I am solely responsible.[7]

His rejection of Tyler's offer was probably the most difficult thing he had ever done, because he would have liked to have accepted it, and it is hard to see how even the Whig controlled Senate could have found an excuse to avoid confirming his name. But in writing to Van Buren about it, he did not even hint at his disappointment. Two things, he told his friend, had kept him from getting "befogged," the previous offer of the post to "Van" himself, and the insistent opposition of Clarissa. "I have one of the safest wives ever a politician had, and she constantly and firmly remonstrated against my taking the place...."

The Democratic press praised his unselfish behavior without qualification. The *Washington Globe* asked its readers: "Has the political history of the country furnished a nobler proof of disinterestedness than that manifested by Mr. Wright?" and the *Philadelphia Pennsylvanian* said he refused the offer in order to avoid any action that "might seem to be a desertion of Mr. Van Buren." Both the *Argus* and the *Albany Atlas,* representing the radical wing of the party in New York, approved wholeheartedly. Judge Daniel showed Wright's letter to Thomas Ritchie, and the editor was so moved by it that he wrote to Wright, "I cannot forbear offering you my heart-felt tribute of thanks for your conduct. Your example is so rare

7 Wright to Butler, May 17, 1844, Wright-Butler letters; Wright to P. Daniel, Mar. 8, 1844, Gillet, *Wright,* II, 1544-6.

in this office hunting & greedy Age, that it is as honorable to you as it is extraordinary."

The much-bandied-about vacancy on the Supreme Bench was not finally filled until after the election, when Judge Samuel Nelson, of New York, was nominated and finally confirmed by the Senate.[8]

*   *   *   *   *

Even before the Court question had arisen to complicate the already muddled political picture, Wright was planning for the coming campaign and trying to keep the entire Democratic party united behind the Little Magician. He had been deeply distressed by the Whig victory in 1840 because he considered that it had been achieved by misrepresentation if not by outright fraud. There must be no repetition of that debacle. Every step which Van Buren took, each word which he uttered, had to be weighed carefully and considered from all possible angles. In February, 1842, Wright was already worried about the ill-effects which Van Buren's trip to visit Jackson in Tennessee might have in certain quarters. The Washington scene needed watching too, because of Tyler's manipulation of the patronage, and since every Democratic politician in the Capital seemed to be out full tilt for the presidential nomination. "Aspirations of this sort are cutting our minority into cabals, and all are intent upon pushing forward their favorite. . . ." Silas was particularly anxious to get the national convention out of the way as quickly and quietly as possible, thus settling the troublesome candidate question and forcing the many factions within the party to stand together. This strategy would call for a meeting of the delegates sometime before December, 1843, so as not to conflict with the meeting of the new Congress. He suggested to his good friends William Allen and Benjamin Tappan, the senators from Ohio, that their state legislature

8 *Ibid.*, p. 1546; Wright to Van Buren, Mar. 22, 1844, Van Buren papers; *Argus*, Apr. 1, Mar. 11, 1844; *Albany Atlas*, Apr. 1, 1844; Ritchie to Wright, Mar. 20, 1844, Van Buren papers; Warren, *Supreme Court*, II, 115-8.

might get things moving by calling for a convention in September, 1843, but when an Indiana friend informed him that his state might take such action, Wright approved heartily. He felt that the initial push must not come from New York, because it ought not appear that Van Buren was pressing for a quick settlement in his own favor. This was in November, 1842.[9]

The followers of John C. Calhoun, however, did not see things the same way at all. They knew that their man lacked the strength of the ex-President and saw in delay their only hope. Even in August, 1842, a not inconsiderable Calhoun faction in New York City was trying to stir up dissatisfaction within the Van Buren forces. By the beginning of 1843, a New York friend of Marcy's was writing, " Does it not strike you that *Mr. Calhoun* is preparing for a stronger fight than was expected? " In Virginia the Calhoun element was especially troublesome. Stressing in the early months of 1843 the question of annexing Texas, upon which Van Buren had taken no stand, newspapers began to appear with the names of Calhoun and (of all people!) Silas Wright on their mastheads for President and Vice-President.[10] This sort of thing which was plainly an attempt to divide Van Buren's supporters, angered Wright more than anything else. As Joel Poinsett, a Van Buren man despite his residence in South Carolina, said, " The Devil has taken our friend M^r. Silas Wright to the summit of a lofty mountain and shown him this fair land offering him dominion over it if he would fall down and worship John C. Calhoun. . . ." Wright was not subject to temptation of this sort, but the ticket did have a wide appeal in certain areas, and

9 Wright to Gillet, Feb. 16, 1842, Gillet, *Wright*, II, 1539-40; Wright to J. Russell, June 18, 1842, *ibid.*, II, 1327-8; Wright to J. Law, Nov. 5, 1842, Personal Miscellany, Library of Congress.

10 J. Scoville to R. Hunter, *Correspondence of R. M. T. Hunter*, C. Ambler, ed., p. 40; Wetmore to Marcy, Jan. 27, 1843, Marcy papers; Benton to Van Buren, Apr. 17, 1842, Van Buren papers, inclosing clipping from the *Norfolk Chronicle and Old Dominion*; Ambler, *Ritchie*, pp. 226-8.

the Calhounites pressed it as hard as they could. At Richmond, " Father " Ritchie, whose paper had supported Van Buren faithfully in 1840, found himself " in a narrow place " regarding the presidential question, because the Calhoun faction was large and to alienate it might throw the state into the hands of the Whigs. Calhoun's Virginia friends worked assiduously, flooding the state with copies of the *Life of John C. Calhoun,* written (anonymously) by John C. Calhoun, but in the state convention in March, the Van Buren element managed to win the day. Ritchie then came out for the former President and all seemed clear for the time.[11]

Meanwhile Wright in Washington was increasingly burdened with correspondence. He told Van Buren that he was constantly being forced to commit him to various policies, and that it was useless to try to pick a politic path amid all the traps being laid for him. " I really feel," he wrote in February, " that every thing required is to meet promptly and frankly all inquiries from honest sources. . .and that time and the honest democratic spirit of the Country will do the rest." He still hoped the convention would be held before Congress met, but he now considered it useless to try to accomplish this by outsmarting the groups opposed to Van Buren. He told " Little Van " plainly that his nomination would have no value unless the whole party acquiesced in it, and that it would be better to wait until May, 1844, if the Calhoun men made an issue of that point. A little later, in a long talk with Senator Robert J. Walker, of Mississippi, (an advocate of deferring the convention until May) he suggested that Walker and Senator Tappan canvass all the Democratic Congressmen and try to arrive at a mutually satisfactory date for the meeting, and he promised that the New York delegation would accept any recommendation approved by the rest of the party. You will see, he told Van Buren in informing him of this, that " I am attempting to do a very large business here upon your Capital. . . ." [12]

11 J. Poinsett to Van Buren, June 5, 1842, W. Roane to Wright, Feb. 9, 14, 1843, Van Buren papers; Ambler, *Ritchie,* pp. 227-32.

12 Wright to Van Buren, Feb. 19, 27, 1843, Van Buren papers.

There was much of the practical about Wright's new attitude toward the nomination. Van Buren seemed pretty sure
of receiving it anyway, and any selection that was based on
out-maneuvering or tricking a large section of the Southern
element of the party would have little chance of succeeding in
November. If Van Buren was not forced forward there was
a far greater chance of maintaining a united party, and this
Wright considered more important than the choice of the
standard bearer. The wild Southern talk of a separate convention and a third candidate which was being bruited about the
Capital upset him, and he was even more worried by men like
Thomas Hart Benton, who seemed to care only for defeating
the pretensions of Calhoun. He tried to explain to Benton the
need of going along with the Calhoun men for the sake of
peace, but could not do so. Benton wanted the election to be
" the occasion for driving from the communion and killing off
C. especially, and if the consequence of that movement should
lead our Pa. friend [Buchanan, who was also flirting with the
nomination] to the same fate. . .he would not shed tears about
it," Silas wrote in May.

Amid the pre-convention intrigue, Wright thought it wise
to sidestep questions which were deliberately advanced to
cause trouble. This was what he had meant when he had recommended that Van Buren answer frankly all interrogations
from " honest " sources. He did not mean that his friend should
be rash. When William " Extra Billy " Smith, a Calhoun man
who had just failed of reelection as Governor of Virginia, sent
Van Buren a long list of queries, Wright advised that they be
treated strictly for what they were worth, without any more
candor than the occasion and the source seemed to require. By
June he was convinced that the convention could not be held before the following spring. " The only thing to do is to get to
May quickly and harmoniously," he informed Van Buren. But
he wanted the state convention which was to choose New
York's delegates to Baltimore, organized quickly. It was very
important, he thought, that the growing conflict within the
party in the Empire State be kept out of presidential politics.

The primacy of the national issues at stake and their total separation from state problems should be stressed, he said. Actually, there was little resistance to the Little Magician's candidacy within the Democratic party in New York. Marcy, who toured the state during the summer of 1843, found anti-Van Buren sentiment only in the western counties which had been resolutely Whig or Anti-Mason since the twenties. Here the local Democrats thought that a " new " name would be more likely to attract dissatisfied elements from the Whigs than would Van Buren's. When Marcy asked whom they wanted instead, they named Wright. Marcy pointed out that Wright was just as thoroughly identified with the Democratic party as was the ex-President, and added that the Senator would never consent to run in the first place. They then agreed to support the choice of the convention, whoever it might be. " I found little or no Calhounism, Cassism or Johnsonism in any other part of the state," reported Marcy. In general the conservative faction in New York did not connect Van Buren with the anti-canal faction, despite his advocacy of sound money, and they were perfectly willing to support him.[13]

For a while the movement against Van Buren was quiescent even at the national capital. Contrary to Wright's expectations, when Congress met it was organized with little difficulty, the party functioning smoothly. Wright characteristically worried about this ominous calm, but even he had hopes that it meant that the discontented segments of the party had given up trying to prevent Van Buren's nomination and were concentrating on 1848. On February 1, Calhoun formally withdrew from the contest and the desperate struggle among the Democrats of Virginia seemed to be amicably settled.[14]

13 Wright to Van Buren, May 30, June 19, Marcy to Van Buren, July 2, 1843, Van Buren papers.

14 Wright to Flagg, Dec. 6, 1843, Flagg papers. See also Wright to Van Buren, Dec. 6, 1843, Van Buren papers. Commenting on the Virginia result, Thomas Ritchie wrote in the *Enquirer* that "the Ark ... which has been agitated on the billows of the sea of liberty ... has now touched the summit of Mount Ararat ... " Ambler, *Ritchie*, pp. 233-4.

It was during this period of calm and confidence, that the Regency leaders began to plan a campaign biography of the Sage of Kinderhook. The previous spring, Benjamin Park, editor of the *New York World,* had suggested that Wright turn out such a work to offset the one on Calhoun which had just been published by Harpers. Wright was far too busy for this, but he thought that a short sketch, stressing Van Buren's humble origins and his self-propelled rise to success would be a big help in the coming campaign. Marcy reluctantly considered writing the piece, but Van Buren himself finally decided upon George Bancroft. It was a wise choice, for Bancroft was America's first great historian, and his prestige throughout the nation was considerable. The first volume of his monumental *History of the United States* had appeared just ten years earlier, and the patriotic tone of his work, demonstrating (as one critic has phrased it) that "God was visible in history, and history culminated in the United States," made it extremely popular. Anything which flowed from his pen was bound to receive attention.

The historian undertook the work in March, assisted by Marcy who brought to him at Boston a mass of material and his own intimate knowledge of the candidate's career. Bancroft agreed with Wright's opinion that the story should be brief, and tried to keep it within a hundred pages. By early April the book was in proof, and copies were sent to Flagg and Wright for editing. Poor Silas was by then so swamped with business that he had to put his aside. " I cannot lock myself up so tight here as to command half a day," he explained to Bancroft. " As every man who calls himself of our party, and wishes to make a complaint, thinks he has a right to make it of me, my interruptions are of a character, which totally disqualify me from the service you want." [15]

15 B. Park to Wright, Mar. 10, 1843, Van Buren papers; Wright to Marcy, Feb. 5, 1844, Massachusetts Historical Society, *Proceedings*, XLII, 418-9; Marcy to Van Buren, Feb., 1844, *ibid.*, p. 419; Van Buren to Bancroft, Feb. 25, 1844, *ibid.*, pp. 417-8, and 425n.; Marcy to Van Buren, Mar.

A new problem was responsible for Wright's feverish activity. In 1844, the Republic of Texas had been maintaining its independence for about eight years, ever since the battle of San Jacinto, in April, 1836, when General Sam Houston had led a band of Texans and volunteers from the United States to victory against the Mexican forces of Santa Anna. During that time there had been a constant demand for annexation to the United States both in America and in Texas. But the Texan Republic's request for annexation had been turned down by both the Jackson and Van Buren administrations, and the question languished. Of course, the crux of the matter was slavery. Texas was slave territory, and the Northern states opposed its admission on those grounds.

When Tyler (a Virginian) became President, he wanted to renew negotiations for annexation, but as long as Daniel Webster (a Massachusetts man) remained at the head of the State Department, there was no opportunity to do so. Then, in 1843, Webster resigned, and Abel Upshur, a Southerner, replaced him. By that time, however, the Texans had taken a new tack and were flirting with Great Britain, and when Upshur proposed an annexation treaty, he was rebuffed. Whether an Anglo-Texan alliance (which would probably have included the abolition of slavery in Texas) was ever seriously considered by either party is uncertain, but the fear of it in the South was very real. Tyler and Upshur pressed their proposal upon Houston, who was then President of Texas, assuring him that a treaty could be ratified by the Senate, and promising full protection against the Mexicans, who had never recognized his country's freedom. Then the dreadful explosion on the *Princeton* on Washington's birthday killed Upshur, and in the

---

20, 1844, Van Buren papers; Wright to Bancroft, Apr. 8, 1844, Bancroft papers. The biography, turned out so hurriedly, was not a very valuable contribution to historical knowledge. When Van Buren failed to receive the nomination, it was withheld, over the objections of Wright and Flagg, and was not published until 1889! Van Buren to Bancroft, July 3, 1844, Massachusetts Historical Society, *Proceedings*, XLII, 431. The quotation on Bancroft is from Van Wyck Brooks, *Flowering of New England*, p. 127.

cabinet changes which followed, John C. Calhoun became Secretary of State. Calhoun pressed for the treaty eagerly, and by April an agreement had been signed and was submitted to the Senate.

Tyler's aggressive Texas policy naturally provoked much discussion and speculation at Washington, and thus took up a great deal of Wright's time. Neither Clay nor Van Buren favored the addition of the Lone Star Republic to the Union. The Whig leader was opposed to it on three grounds which he elaborated in a confidential letter to his friend John Crittenden, in December, 1843. First, he said, "the territory of the United States is already large enough. It is more important that we should unite, harmonize, and improve what we have than attempt to acquire more...." This was Clay the nationalist, the proponent of the American System. Secondly, annexation would lead to war with Mexico, with whom the United States had no quarrel. And thirdly it would fail to do even what its enthusiasts expected; it would not give the South a preponderance in the federal government, for there was always the danger that it might unleash a spirit of conquest that would add Canada to the United States. Clay rationalized his stand with the conviction that:

> Texas is destined to be settled by our race, who will undoubtedly carry there our laws, our language, and our institutions; and that view of her destiny reconciles me much more to her independence that if it were to be peopled by an unfriendly race; we may [i. e. should] live as good neighbors, cultivating peace, commerce, and friendship.[16]

During the winter of 1843, however, the Kentuckian said nothing publicly about Texas, and Van Buren maintained a similar silence, but in the South, agitation of the issue grew steadily and great pressure was exerted to make both the leading candidates clarify their positions. In March, Thomas Ritchie sent Silas Wright a copy of a letter which he had re-

16 Clay to Crittenden, Dec. 5, 1843, Coleman, *Life of Crittenden*, I, 209-10.

ceived. " Van Buren will be elected," it ran, " but if he goes against Texas. . .all is lost." In the North too, people wanted to know how the leaders stood. Marcy, who was in Massachusetts working with Bancroft on the biography, reported to Van Buren that the people there were so aroused over Texas that some definite stand would have to be taken soon.

Washington was filled with all sorts of rumors, for no one knew exactly what Calhoun's treaty with Texas would provide. Wright, as was usual in a crisis, looked about for someone tried and true with whom he could " consult." There were too many " croakers " about, he complained to Van Buren, and not enough sound men. John Fairfield, a Democratic senator from Maine, and Representative Preston King, of St. Lawrence County, who were messmates of his at Mrs. Scott's, were his only " cabinet." [17] He was definite in his opinion that the whole idea of annexation, which was certain to be part of the treaty, was unconstitutional,[18] but he had no idea what should be done about it. He forwarded Ritchie's letter to Van Buren, saying " I am certain I have no passion upon this subject, but if. . .this matter is popped upon the Country in this form, the excitement it will produce will surpass any I have witnessed . . .all I desire is that I may enter the contest in a way that the democracy may approve when time shall have permitted passion to subside." Thus his first wish was to avoid the whole subject because it would further complicate the already tangled political situation. After " passion " had subsided would naturally mean after the election.[19]

17 T. Ritchie to Wright, Mar. 20, 1844, Marcy to Van Buren, Mar. 20, 1844, Van Buren papers; Fairfield to Mrs. Fairfield, Dec. 3, 1843, *Fairfield Letters*, A. Staples, ed., p. 311.

18 To Wright's mind there was a great distinction between annexing Texas and the annexation of a colony, such as Florida, or Louisiana. Texas was a sovereign nation, not a dependency. " She sells herself, and if her Treaty making power[s] have the right to make the Contract, then our own treaty making power has the right to sell us out." Wright to Van Buren, May 13, 1844, Van Buren papers.

19 Wright to Van Buren, Mar. 22, 1844, Van Buren papers.

But his attitude quickly changed as he came to realize the ramifications of annexation—a probable war with unoffending Mexico and increased agitation of the slavery problem. On April 1 he again wrote to Van Buren at his home in Kinderhook, once again enclosing a letter from a Virginia Democrat calling for annexation, but now his own comment was different. " This subject," he said, " begins to assume an importance beyond excitement to my mind, and to point at the Union, rather than at a presidential election." Still, the next day he had a long talk with the disaffected Virginian, William Selden, and tried hard to convince him that the Texas issue should be kept out of the canvass. The tariff question and the gag rule debates, which were constant sources of irritation, made for enough sectionalism, he said. To add Texas would be " not the pea, but the mill stone, which would sink the camel, rather than simply break his back." Selden seemed impressed, and Wright was more hopeful.[20]

In the meantime, the annexationists in the Democratic party led by the friends of Calhoun, were plunging ahead with their campaign to force Van Buren to commit himself. Late in March, Ritchie's *Enquirer* published a letter written by Jackson more than a year earlier in which he had spoken favorably of the general idea of adding Texas to the Union. Van Buren had known of this letter for some time, and it may be, as Ritchie's biographer has claimed, that in publishing it the Richmond editor was sincerely trying to bring Van Buren to the annexationist position rather than to destroy his chances for the nomination. But it remains unexplained why Jackson's letter was deliberately held back until the agitation over Texas was reaching its peak, and why the date was altered from 1843 to 1844 when Ritchie printed it, making it appear that Old Hickory was urging immediate annexation.[21]

20 Wright to Van Buren, Apr. 1, 3, 1844, Van Buren papers.

21 Ambler, *Ritchie*, pp. 236-7. The next day Ritchie published the correction, but the letter was widely copied with the 1844 dateline.

The next step came on March 27, when William H. Hammet, a Representative from Mississippi and a delegate to the coming national convention, wrote a letter to Van Buren asking him to state his views on annexation publicly. Hammet's letter was not particularly important; the prospective candidate had received and was receiving many requests of this nature; but it became prominent because it was *the* one which the Little Magician chose to answer. Wright believed Hammet to be sincere, although " rash, impetuous, and not a little influenced by...Calhoun...." He approved giving him a frank answer. The Texas question, Silas wrote Van Buren now, appeared to " put all other questions in the shade, and to involve consequences much more momentous than the result of a single election....The question *must* be met....I feel little or no sensitiveness about your position, because that is swallowed up in my deeper apprehension for the Union itself." It is, he continued, " more noble, more desirable, more important more patriotic, to take boldly the side of truth and principle, though it may be disastrous in a popular sense, than to temporize with a matter which may prove to be so vital to the perpetuity of our institutions, and to...our Country." [22]

A " more noble, more desirable, more important more patriotic " letter Wright never wrote. For nearly four years he had been working almost ceaselessly to effect his friend's reelection, to avenge the ignominy of 1840. To achieve this he had rejected a seat on the Supreme Court and passed up an opportunity to retire which he had fervently sought. He knew what refusing Texas would mean to Van Buren's chances, or better, he knew how simple the renomination and reelection of the Little Magician would be if he would only accept annexation. But there was no hesitancy in Silas Wright now, no surrendering to expediency, no consideration of any higher goals that might be attained by a Democratic victory gained through

22 See the Van Buren papers for March, 1844, for many Texas letters. Wright to Van Buren, Apr. 6, 8, 1844, Van Buren papers. See also, Wright to Bancroft, Apr. 8, 1844, Bancroft papers.

espousing annexation. He had come a long way since 1824 when he had sacrificed principle for practical advantage in the battle with the People's party. It is no exaggeration to say that in April, 1844, he ceased to be a politician and became a statesman.

*   *   *   *   *

It is clear from Wright's correspondence at this time that if Clay and Van Buren had, as is often claimed, agreed to keep Texas out of the coming contest, he and the other members of the Regency knew nothing of it. Benjamin Butler, en route from New York to Tennessee to visit Jackson, had stopped at the Capital. While there, John C. Spencer, who was still Tyler's Secretary of War, told him that Clay (saying Van Buren "will not get that whip raw upon [me]") had told him that he would not come out against annexation. Spencer suggested that he and Butler try to arrange an understanding on the Texas issue between the two leaders. Since Butler was leaving town, he proposed that Wright act in his place, promising Spencer that the New York Senator would get in touch with him. When Wright heard of this, he was very disturbed. He doubted that Spencer knew anything at all about Clay's views, and he disliked the idea of a bargain. So he wrote to Van Buren for advice. Clearly, he knew nothing of any agreement already made.[23]

Nothing came of this anyway, for Van Buren had already decided to take Wright's advice and speak out publicly against immediate annexation. He had chosen to do so by answering Hammet's letter. Wright had no definite knowledge of what " Little Van " would say, but he did get in touch with Hammet and had a long talk with him. Hammet claimed that he had no desire to embarrass Van Buren, and said that when he had written his request he had been sure that the ex-President would come out in favor of annexation—that members of the New York delegation in the House had told him he

23 Wright to Van Buren, Apr. 8, 1844, Van Buren papers.

would. Wright replied that no one in the world knew what his friend thought, and anyone who predicted his stand was only guessing. This seemed to take the Mississippian by surprise, but he went on to suggest that Van Buren state publicly that he would answer *his* letter. Wright vetoed this on the grounds that Clay would then wait to see what his rival was going to say before committing himself. As the interview ended, Wright could not help feeling that Hammet's main interest was in the notoriety which would be his if Van Buren chose to answer his missile rather than in what the Little Magician might say.[24]

Finally, at eight o'clock on the evening of April 26, Van Buren's reply to Hammet, addressed in care of Silas Wright, arrived at Washington. It was a long letter, and did not say that Van Buren was unalterably opposed to adding Texas to the Union. " Van " even agreed, if elected, to be governed by the action of Congress on the subject. But he did state flatly that annexing the Lone Star Republic would lead to war with Mexico, and that until Mexico's consent to annexation could be peaceably procured, the United States should keep out. Wright read it immediately, slept on it, read it again in the morning, and decided that it was good. Next he called in his " cabinet," King and Fairfield, along with Lemuel Stetson, a New York Congressman who was also living at Mrs. Scott's, and the four of them went over Van Buren's words again in Wright's office in the Capitol. Finally they took the fateful message to Benton, and once again perused it carefully. By this time the morning papers were out, and the Whig *National Intelligencer* contained a statement by Clay, dated from Raleigh, North Carolina, in which he committed himself against Texas in words similar to those he had addressed privately to Crittenden in December. Wright and his friends were astounded by this coincidence, but it confirmed their determination to get Van Buren's letter in print at once. They

24 Wright to Van Buren, Apr. 11, 1844, Van Buren papers.

were afraid that if this was not done, Democrats all over the country would commit themselves to annexation merely out of opposition to Clay. " We knew great efforts would be made to raise the mad dog cry upon Clay," Wright wrote to Benjamin F. Butler, " and we thought it best that the other letter should appear before that had gone far." They left Benton's office in search of Hammet, locating him about three in the afternoon. When the Mississippi Congressman read the letter he was frightened, for he knew its repercussions would be tremendous, but he behaved well and made no effort to prevent its publication. The little band hurried over to the office of the *Globe,* which was an evening paper. There John C. Rives, Blair's co-editor, was holding the press. Hammet turned the letter over to him, and it was soon on the streets.

When it was all over, Wright must have felt wonderfully relieved. He wrote to " Little Van " that he had no idea what the effect would be on the coming convention or on the election, but that at least " our principles and our character are safe." [25]

The public reaction to the Raleigh and Hammet letters was immediate. Throughout the South, large sections of the Democratic party denounced Van Buren. In Virginia, Ritchie openly repudiated him, and sent him a sampling of the mass of correspondence addressed to his journal calling for a candidate favorable to Texas' annexation. Unmoved, Van Buren returned the letters without a single comment.[26]

At Washington, the Democratic annexationists met in the Capitol on the evening of Monday, April 29. Robert J. Walker, Senator from Mississippi, presided. The majority of the meet-

25 Van Buren to Hammet, Apr. 20, 1844, *Niles' Register,* LXVI, 153; Wright to Van Buren, Apr. 21, 1844, Van Buren papers; Wright to Butler, May 17, 1844, Wright-Butler letters.

26 Ritchie to Van Buren, May 6, 1844, Van Buren papers, Ambler, *Ritchie,* p. 240. To Wright the " somerset at Richmond " was " the most astounding and unaccountable thing of all." Wright to Butler, May 17, 1844, Wright-Butler letters.

ing declared for Lewis Cass, of Michigan, but at least one calm observer thought that their real preference was Calhoun. By no means all those who favored annexation felt that Van Buren must be abandoned. As Cave Johnson, of Tennessee, put it, " most of us sit still and try to calm the excitement. . . ." He belonged to a group that placed party solidarity above Texas, and called for moderation. The sincerity of the more violent annexationists is open to question, and it is probably true that Calhoun and his personal followers were more interested in uniting the South in defense of slavery than in adding another star to the flag. Calhoun saw it this way: If the campaign was waged by Van Buren and Clay on the issues of Clay's American System and the Independent Treasury, his own states' rights ideas would be completely subordinated. On the other hand, if Texas and slavery extension could be made the main questions the Democrats could be split in the same way that Tyler had split the Whig party, into Southern and Northern wings. Then he (or any man he supported) as the leader of the entire South, would be in a more nearly equal position in a three-cornered contest with Clay and Van Buren. The election would be thrown into the House of Representatives, as it had been in 1824, with a very strong chance that the Southern man would carry off the prize.[27] So intent were the Calhoun men upon carrying out this plan that they rejected all efforts of the Northern Democrats to compromise the various issues which tended to divide the party sectionally. When a tariff bill came up in Congress in 1844 which would have lowered considerably the level established in 1842, the Southerners were strangely reticent, and at a party caucus in April, Robert Barnwell Rhett, of South Carolina, spoke against pressing it for a vote. As one Van Burenite said, the Southerners were behaving " most base and unmanly," claiming to be

27 C. Johnson to Polk, Apr. 30, 1844, Polk papers, 1st series, Library of Congress; Poage, *Clay*, pp. 129-32. Wright quoted Calhoun as saying, " I can beat Clay and Van Buren put together upon this issue." Wright to Butler, May 17, 1844, Wright-Butler letters.

" Ultra Anti-Tariff " but doing everything they could to avoid
passing a new law.[28] Silas Wright certainly understood Calhoun's motives. As long as he lived he believed that the Texas
issue had only been a pretext for abandoning Van Buren and
the party. At the time he expressed his feelings very plainly in
a letter to a Canton friend. " Mr. Calhoun's plain object," he
wrote, " is to rule or ruin, and, as he surrenders the Union,
he intends, by the shape of the Texas question, to divide it."

That Tyler and his friends, who were of course fervent annexationists, reasoned the same way is less probable, but their
only chance to win lay likewise in disrupting party lines. In
fact, it seems doubtful that any of the politicians was primarily
interested in Texas. The moderate annexationists, typified by
a man like Cave Johnson, thought first of party solidarity and
then of the Lone Star; the others thought first of *breaking*
parties. Still the fact remains that an indeterminate but unquestionably large section of the population wanted Texas in the
Union, and the more the question was agitated, the larger this
group grew. Soon it became a movement of nationalism, of
expansion, of what John L. O'Sullivan was soon to christen
" manifest destiny." Whatever the motives of the politicians
who sponsored it, the demand for the annexation of Texas
among the people was sincere.[29]

Wright felt the full force of the wave of anti-Van Buren
sentiment. On all sides he found " the state of things. . .as bad
as it can be." Tyler, he said, was trying to bribe delegates to
the Democratic convention with offers of federal jobs, and
many party men were wavering. Ritchie's attitude seemed particularly dangerous, for there was no questioning the great
influence of his paper. Many Democrats at the nation's capital

[28] Stevenson to Marcy, Apr. 21, 1844, Marcy papers. Wright also understood this situation. See Wright to Van Buren, Jan. 8, 1844, Van Buren
papers; Wright to Marcy, Jan. 28, 1844, Marcy papers.

[29] Wright to Van Buren, Apr. 14, 1847, Van Buren papers; Wright to
Russell, May 15, 1844, Gillet, *Wright*, II, 1518; J. Pratt, " O'Sullivan and
Manifest Destiny," *New York History*, XXXI, 226 ff.

were becoming panicky, but conditions like this brought out
the best that was in Wright. He warned Van Buren to stand
firm and " leave to the Convention the responsibility of dis-
banding the democratic party of the Nation, if that must
be done," and to George Bancroft he wrote:

> I regret that you think unfavorably of the Texas letter. It
> seems to me that there is a principle of national faith and
> honor ... to surrender or disregard which would have been
> to surrender all national character to a very questionable
> political impulse. . . . If there be any northern democrat who
> can sustain the present Treaty [Calhoun's, then before the
> Senate] . . . he looks at the matter, I fear, more with reference
> to the pending election than to its influence upon our Union.[30]

At his home in Kinderhook, the man whom people liked to
call the " Magician " and the " Red Fox " continued to ply
a straight and open course. He withstood soberly and calmly
the uproar raised against him. " The Whig Saturnalia of 1840
has well nigh disorganized political Society in the U. States,"
he wrote to Wright. " That our own party should have been
entirely untouched by its blighting influence was hardly to be
expected." That was his attitude toward the furor raised
against the Hammet letter. He expressed sorrow that Wright
had been forced to undergo so many " mortifications " in his
behalf, and promised that he would not falter in his faith
in the principles upon which he had based his forthright
declarations on Texas. Now that the entire subject was out in
the open, he and Wright both felt that there was much less to
worry about. Their consciences were untroubled. Should
defeat come, Wright consoled his friend, at least " your skirts
are clear and your honor and character saved, and your principles are preserved." In this spirit they awaited the twenty-
seventh of May, and the opening of the Democratic national
convention at Baltimore.[31]

30 Wright to Van Buren, May 6, 1844, Van Buren papers; Wright to
Bancroft, May 6, 1844, Bancroft papers.

31 Van Buren to Wright May 10, 1844, Wright to Van Buren, May 13,
1844, Van Buren papers.

CHAPTER XII

"WHO IS NERO?"

"I do not think I have ever witnessed such a state of utter disorder, confusion and decomposition as the Democratic party now presents."
Henry Clay to Thurlow Weed [Spring, 1844.]

"Nero fiddled while Rome burned, & probably the political Nero of this Country is exulting over the flames he has raised."
Samuel Young at the Democratic national convention, 1844.

THOUGH men like Van Buren and Wright were able to keep both their heads and their courage, there could be no doubt that the Hammet letter was unpopular and that the Little Magician's strength had been seriously depleted. For as one observer said at this time, Texas is " the question which regulates all our politics, the pivot on which party spirit moves, and the stepping stone...[for] Presidential candidates...."[1] Political " weak sisters " began scurrying for cover, and prospective candidates began to appear like sharks around the flanks of a wounded whale. Early in May, Wright heard a rumor that James Buchanan considered Van Buren " a dead cock in the pit " and was thinking of " taking his chances before the convention." " Old Buck," a large, fussy, rather pompous man, fond of immaculate cravats and huge collars, and inordinately proud of his impressive bearing and very small feet, had little liking for Van Buren. He had been hostile ever since 1840, when the Little Magician had appointed Henry Gilpin, of Philadelphia, as his Attorney General, for Buchanan and Gilpin were rivals within the Pennsylvania Democratic party. In 1842, he had written a friend that the former President " ought never have permitted himself to become a candidate " for " a *third* time." In his correspondence Buchanan repeatedly protested that he " had not raised a finger " to press his own candidacy, and insisted that events

1 A. Nevins, *Diary of Philip Hone*, II, 701, May 14, 1844.

should be allowed to "take their natural course," but when asked to suggest other names he exhibited a curious inability to do so. It must be admitted in all fairness that he did not actively seek the post for himself, and though he did not see why "Van" should have any special claim to what he called a "re-re-nomination," he was ready to back him if he did receive the call at Baltimore, and he did not try to get the pledged Van Buren men to break their promises. With the Pennsylvania delegates to the convention he sent a letter authorizing the use of his name only if Van Buren failed to be nominated and his New York friends acknowledged his failure, which was reasonable under the circumstances. Wright, however, always feared the worst where Buchanan was concerned, for he knew him to be an inveterate office seeker. " He can never know the impulses which govern the democracy of this country," he once said of the Pennsylvanian. " If he shall ever be so fortunate as to reap the benefit of those impulses as he wishes, he will know as little why he does, as what they are." [2]

But if Buchanan was more or less loyal to Van Buren there were others who were not. Wright's friend John Fairfield put it well. " Our camp is full of traitors and there is danger in letting them remain and danger in exposing them. ....The great object of these fellows now is to prevent the nomination of Mr. V. B. who is the strong man. . . ." One of the leading threats was the perennial Colonel Johnson. Once again he was ready and eager for either the first or second spot on the ticket, or whatever else he might garner. Two years earlier Buchanan (who made it his business to keep pretty close tabs on everyone's chances) had said, " Col. Johnson has as much chance of being nominated for V. P. as I have of being elected

2 Wright to Van Buren, May 6, 1844, Van Buren papers; Forney, *Anecdotes of Public Men*, I, 65; Buchanan to D. Porter, Jan. 8, 1840, to J. Foltz, Dec. 14, 1842; to W. Flinn, Sept. 5, 1841, W. King to Buchanan, May 5, 1844, Buchanan to Rhett, Sept. 25, 1843, to Pennsylvania Delegates, May 25, 1844, Buchanan papers; Wright to Van Buren, Jan. 29, 1842, Van Buren papers.

Pope by the next conclave of Cardinals," but the Colonel was
not so easily dismissed. Wright in April of the election year
thought Johnson's choice as the Vice-Presidential candidate
" quite certain " though he hated even to think about it.
Wright's sympathies had changed a great deal in the six years
since he had poked fun at those Virginians who had refused
to support the eccentric Kentuckian. " I certainly shall not lift
a straw against our friend the Col; and I believe...[in] the
importance of using his name and his disgusting popularity,"
he wrote to Van Buren. But when disinterested friends asked
him how he could reconcile such a choice with the best interests of the nation, he had to fall silent. Perhaps I am " too
fastidious," he admitted, " but I confess that non-resistance is
as much as I can promise myself." [3]

Fortunately, Wright had overestimated Johnson's prospects, and he himself realized this before the convention met.
But there were many others in the field eager to flirt with
Dame Fortune. Levi Woodbury, of New Hampshire, who had
been Van Buren's Secretary of the Treasury, sought the first
place on the ticket and so did Lewis Cass, of Michigan. Both
these men, as Azariah Flagg wittily expressed it, were seeking
" to fish for immortality in the Texas pool which Capt. Tyler
prepared exclusively for himself and his chosen household."
" No man," Wright said on the eve of the convention, " has
behaved so palpably ridiculously as Woodbury," and he
thanked God that the former Secretary had no chance.[4] Indeed it was on Cass that the opposition to Van Buren was
gradually concentrating. He had published a letter favoring
annexation, and was very popular in Virginia, which seemed

3 Fairfield to Mrs. Fairfield, May 5, 1844, *Fairfield Letters*, A. Staples,
ed., p. 336; Parmenter to Bancroft, May 1, 1844, Bancroft papers;
Buchanan to G. Lieper, May 22, 1844, Buchanan papers; Wright to Bancroft,
Apr. 8, 1844, Bancroft papers; Wright to Van Buren, Feb. 20, 1844, Van
Buren papers.

4 Wright to Bancroft, May 6, 1844, Bancroft papers; Flagg to Wright,
May 23, 1844, Wright to Van Buren, May 26, 1844, Van Buren papers.

to hold the key to the Southern vote. Cass was a peculiar man who had been Governor of Michigan Territory and Secretary of War under Jackson. He was very rich, very religious, and a confirmed teetotaller. When living in Washington he had given frequent large parties, at which the only alcoholic beverage to be seen was " Port wine " which Congressmen who tasted it found " so near to brandy that it was not worth disputing about." He had an annoying habit of inviting his guests to drink with him, raising his glass of " wine " to his lips, and then putting it down without consuming any. " This is one way to cheat the ' Old Fellow ' that I don't like," commented plain John Fairfield, of Maine.

To the section of the party which Van Buren and Wright represented, Lewis Cass was anathema, and not merely because of his odd habits. During the crisis of 1834, when Jackson had decided to remove the deposits from the United States Bank, Cass, then Secretary of War, had timorously demanded that he be cleared of any responsibility, and threatened to resign if this were not done. Jackson contemptuously consented to assume fully responsibility, and Cass remained in the cabinet. Then, after the siege had been weathered, and the popularity of the removal established, Cass made an elaborate speech at a public dinner, clearly designed to advance his own stock, in which he praised the removal as a wise and heroic act. Henceforth he was cordially disliked by hard money men, and to see him brought forth as a candidate by the friends of Calhoun, was to them proof positive of the insincerity of the Southerners.[5]

But these days, even many loyal friends of Van Buren were thinking first about themselves. Of this group James Polk, of Tennessee, was outstanding. Wright knew Polk well, and liked him. He had even messed with him at Elliot's boarding house during the session of 1836, when Polk had been Speaker

5 Ambler, *Ritchie*, pp. 241-2; Fairfield to Mrs. Fairfield, Feb. 6, 8, 1836, *Fairfield Letters*, A. Staples, ed., pp. 96-7, 99; Blair to Van Buren, Nov. 13, 1859, Van Buren, *Autobiography*, p. 608.

of the House of Representatives. By the early part of April, 1844, Wright had come to favor Polk for second place on the ticket, and in May he told Cave Johnson that the Tennessee politician was the only acceptable man for President if Van Buren failed to receive the nomination. Polk was an old Jacksonian; in fact he was more or less a protégé of the Old General, who had followed his career closely. When Speaker of the House, Polk had been an unyielding and skillful supporter of the Independent Treasury. As the convention date approached he was probably the leading candidate for the Vice-Presidential nomination, and although he had spoken clearly and firmly for the annexation of Texas, he was a sincere Van Buren man. Yet he was not immune to the presidential fever. Carefully he wrote a letter to his Washington spokesman, Representative Cave Johnson, telling him that Van Buren's nomination would mean defeat in November. Jackson, he wrote, felt this way and favored none other than James Polk as the " available " man. He, Polk, could not see it this way of course; Van Buren's friends would hold the balance of power and it was up to them to decide what was best. All this sounded well and proper until Mr. Polk wrote, the same day, another letter to Johnson, this one marked "very confidential." In it he informed his friend that the first letter was to be shown to Silas Wright. The purpose of the second letter was to instruct Johnson to seek the presidential nomination for Polk, if Van Buren should fail to get it.[6] Polk did not sabotage the Little Magician's chances, but he was ready to profit by his misfortunes.

Not everyone was looking to his own fences. Wright, of course, and the Regency at Albany were as firm as ever. Thomas Hart Benton—saying he "never felt more victorious than now "—was loyal to the bitter end, and even in Virginia

6 *Congressional Directory*, 1836; Wright to Bancroft, May 6, 1844, Bancroft papers; Johnson to Polk, May 8, 1844, Polk papers, 1st series; Polk to Johnson, May 14, 1844 (two letters), " Letters of James K. Polk to Cave Johnson," *Tennessee Historical Magazine*, I, 241-3.

an element in the party, led by Representative George Dromgoole, withstood the excitement. But many Congressmen were
panicked by what appeared to be a popular demand for annexation. " That a large number of members of Congress are impressed with the idea that some other candidate must be run
cannot be denied," wrote one member. " Whether it is so with
the people. . .they represent, is not so clear." But he was from
Massachusetts; Southern members found it difficult to maintain so magisterial an attitude, and Henry Clay, in Washington
at this time, summed up the situation well when he wrote
Thurlow Weed, " I do not think I have ever witnessed such
a state of utter disorder, confusion and decomposition as the
Democratic party now presents." [7]

As the time of the convention approached, Washington began to fill with delegates waiting until the last moment before
proceeding to Baltimore. Upon arriving they were ferreted
out by proponents of annexation and plied with tales about
the necessity of eliminating Van Buren. Bitterly Wright reflected that in the first excitement many Congressman had
gone out on a limb against his friend, and that they were now
willing to take any measures to defeat him, not because of
Texas, but to preserve their own position. He was especially
angered by the attitude of the Middle Westerners. Sidney
Breese, Senator from Illinois and a messmate of his, was supposedly a Van Buren man, but when asked by Wright for in-
troductions to some of the Illinois delegates who were in town,
Breese replied politely, " I will see that they are all straight."
Every possible intrigue was attempted. The Michigan delegates
were told that Cass could get the nomination if they would
vote for him, but that if they did not, he would fail. New
Hampshire men were informed that the convention could be
swung to Woodbury; Pennsylvanians were given the same information with Buchanan's name substituted. With the Tenn-

7 Johnson to Polk, May 12, 1844, Polk papers, 1st series; Parmenter to
Bancroft, May 6, 1844, Bancroft papers; Barnes, *Weed*, p. 120.

essee delegation, Polk was mentioned as the lucky man. Anything to stop the Little Magician.

At the same time, Tyler and Calhoun were exerting tremendous pressure on Congress, and it seemed to Wright that this also was having its effect. He wrote Bancroft that things were " shockingly bad," and to another friend he said: " You have no idea of the extent to which Capt. Tyler, by his offices, has been able to corrupt the House of Representatives. . . . every man, comparatively speaking, has been dipping in for little post-offices and other offices, and tacitly yielding his principles and his party for the little plunder. . . ." [8]

At least Wright was able to do something about the New York deputation. Early in May, he dispatched letters to all the men who were to represent his state at Baltimore, warning them of Congressional interference, and suggesting that they meet beforehand at New York to get acquainted and to organize. " Our delegation," he said, " will be looked to by all for steadiness, firmness, and order. . . ." He stressed the necessity of inflexible adherence to Van Buren's name, saying, " if we change from him, we shall be perfectly routed, no matter what other name we use. . . ." The Senator also wrote Bancroft in Boston, for the historian was himself to be a member of the convention. He told him of the proposed New York meeting and proposed a similar one for the Massachusetts representatives. It would be especially helpful, he said, if all the New England delegates could get together, perhaps with the New Yorkers, before going to Baltimore. The latter plan did not materialize, but on May 23, the members of the New York group, led by Benjamin Franklin Butler, met at the Astor House, together with the delegates from Vermont, and one or two from Middle Western states. They were perfectly agreed

8 Wright to Van Buren, May 20, 26, 1844, Van Buren papers; Wright to Flagg, May 22, 1844, Flagg papers; Wright to Bancroft, May 6, 1844, Bancroft papers; Wright to Russell, May 15, 1844, Gillet, *Wright*, II, 1517-8. See also Wright to Butler, May 18, 1844, and Wright's many letters to Butler in this period in Wright-Butler letters, N. Y. Public Library.

and the meeting produced at least one solid block of Van Buren men who were unlikely to be stricken by the Texas fever.[9]

The clamor continued at Washington until May 26, and then suddenly slackened as the delegates left the capital for Baltimore. For the first time in four weeks Wright passed a relatively quiet day. On the eve of the great contest he felt strangely calm. They had done the right thing, he assured Van Buren. "Whatever injustice rogues may do, history will tell these truths for us." If any other man should be nominated the party would be destroyed, he told his friend. Wright was always pessimistic when a crisis approached, and this was no exception. Writing to John Russell, the young Canton lawyer who had helped him with his articles on the Independent Treasury in 1837, he said:

> We are in a dilemma, as a party, and defeat appears to me to be inavoidable in any event. There will be three candidates, though who will be the third is not yet certain. The probability is Tyler; nominated by his own convention, and rumor now says, Woodbury is to be his vice-president.
>
> The true men of the convention have no resort but to adhere to Mr. Van Buren, or destroy our party. If you could see my letters daily, and read the indignant voice and feeling of the true men, coming from all parts of the country, you would see that to abandon him is to abandon principle and honor and character, and to throw off the heart and soul, and bone and sinew of the party, and to surrender to rotten rogues, under whom success would be our worst defeat.[10]

At this time, Wright also made certain last minute preparations of his own. In the mad scramble and confusion within the party, his own name had been frequently mentioned as a compromise candidate. If he had been willing to come out for

9 Wright to New York delegates, May 2, 1844, Wright to Bancroft, May 2, 1844, Bancroft papers; *Argus*, May 27, 1844.

10 Wright to Van Buren, May 26, 1844, Van Buren papers; Wright to Russell, May 22, 1844, Gillet, *Wright*, II, 1519.

Texas, he probably could have been chosen.[11] Even in the spring of 1843, a local New York politician reported being "talked to" about Wright, and after the Texas question became the only topic of discussion, references to him grew more and more frequent. His strong position on the tariff made him "available" in the South, and his great popularity in New York was supplemented by the universal approval which greeted his self-sacrificing refusal of Tyler's offer of the seat on the Supreme Court. Cave Johnson told Polk that "malcontents" were willing to take "S.W.JR." and John Stevenson, a New York politician, wrote to Marcy that he thought the convention would take Wright if it could not agree on Van Buren. "All eyes are turned to him in case of such an event," said Stevenson. The New York members of the House of Representatives were strongly in favor of Wright as a second choice if "Little Van" could not get the nomination. "We will not consent to any candidate whose friends have aided in defeating Mr. Van Buren," wrote one Congressman. "A new man must be taken and that man must be Silas Wright." This sentiment was perhaps unimportant, for it was to be expected that the New Yorkers would champion him, but as May 27 drew near and the prospects of any nomination appeared slim, a much more significant movement was developing. On the twenty-fifth, the Chamber of the House was dotted with little groups of worried Democrats seeking some way out of the approaching impasse. Soon they evolved a plan which Cave Johnson reported to the anxious Polk—swing the convention to Wright. This was the argument he presented: Wright was "right" on the tariff and he would also be correct on Texas. He was known to be against Calhoun's treaty, but would not oppose "lawful" annexation. The Northern supporters of Van Buren would accept him if the Southern wing of the party brought his name forward. "Wright will yield to no such

11 See for example, Polk to Wright, June 12, 1844, Polk Correspondence, New York Public Library.

thing but we must force him," wrote Johnson.[12] And on top of this Benjamin Butler, en route to Baltimore, was carrying in his pocket a secret letter from Van Buren. It authorized Butler to say without qualification that the Red Fox would consent to the withdrawal of his own name and would support Wright wholeheartedly if the convention should choose him.[13]

Wright knew nothing of Van Buren's letter, but he realized that his name was being mentioned, and this made him extremely uneasy. There were strong personal reasons for his abhorrence of the Presidency. He had had more than his fill of politics, and he knew enough of the duties and trials of the nation's Chief Executive to realize that the job was not for him. " My position from 1834 to 1841," he wrote a little later to William L. Marcy, " compelled me to see too much of its cares complexities and difficulties to leave a single charm about it for me."

But these personal considerations were secondary. The primary reason why he would not consider the use of his name was that it seemed part of a trick to get rid of Van Buren. He put it this way: A solid majority of the delegates at Baltimore would be pledged to Van Buren, because they had been chosen before the Texas crisis and the Hammet letter. If the two-thirds rule was adhered to, it might be possible to prevent his nomination, but in no case could anyone else be picked unless the ranks of the pledged Van Buren delegates were broken. To cry for Cass, Calhoun, Woodbury, or any other annexationist would not result in a rupture within the camp of the true Van Buren men; it would only make them more firm.

12 Flagg to Van Buren, Apr. 13, 1844, Van Buren papers; Johnson to Polk, May 8, 25, 1844, Polk papers, 1st series; Stevenson to Marcy, Apr. 21, 1844, Marcy papers; C. Hungerford to Flagg, May 6, 1844, Flagg papers.

13 Van Buren to Butler, May 20, 1844, Van Buren papers. Later Van Buren wrote to Bancroft: " My desire and hope was that the nomination might in some proper way come to Mr. Wright, and one object of the letter was to facilitate that result, if things should at any time incline in that direction." July 3, 1844, Massachusetts Historical Society, *Proceedings*, XLII, 431.

But to call for Wright, " Little Van's " friend, as a compromise might cause the Van Burenites to forget their instructions. Once they had been brought to that, Wright would be abandoned by the annexationists, for the Van Buren men would have lost their one great moral weapon, the fact that a majority of the representatives had been ordered by their constituents to vote for Martin Van Buren. " The knowing ones among [the annexationists]," Silas wrote afterward, " would rather have had V.B. than me at any time, if they must take either. . . .They knew they were safe, because they knew that I would not permit such a competition to exist in fact."

Men like Cave Johnson and some of the New Yorkers did not urge Wright's name with any such plot in mind, but the Senator was probably right in suspecting that many of his loudest supporters were reasoning just this way. He was exasperated by the fact that no matter how categorically he refused to be considered a candidate, many people would not believe that he was in earnest. As he told Marcy, " Plain and direct declarations of the groundless character of such suspicions are, as you know, never believed. . . ." [14]

So, on May 23, he wrote a letter to a man who would certainly believe him, and who would know when to give the word that would effectively check any movement in his behalf at the convention. The man was Judge John Fine, of Ogdensburg, an old friend of his and a delegate at Baltimore.

> The republicans of New York, with a unanimity never surpassed, have made it the duty of yourself and your colleagues in the convention to present for its acceptance the name of Mr. Van Buren . . . and they have given you no direction to withdraw his name and substitute any other . . . .
>
> To consent to the use of my name as a candidate, under any circumstances, would be, in my view, to invite you to compromise the express wishes and instructions of your consti-

[14] Wright to Marcy, Sept. 13, 1844, Marcy papers; Wright to Butler, June 3, 1844, Wright-Butler letters.

tuents for my personal advancement. I can never consent to place myself in a position where the suspicion of acting from such a motive can justly attach itself to me, much less to be a party to such action. . . .
I have never been vain enough to dream of the office of President . . . and were not Mr. Van Buren the candidate of our State, I should find just as little difficulty as I now do in telling you that I am not, and cannot, under any circumstances, be a candidate before your convention for that office . . . . [15]

With this letter dispatched, and with the center of action moved from Washington to Baltimore, Wright could sit back and relax, confident that whatever the outcome, he had done his best.

* * * * *

On Monday, May 27, a day " hot as Belshazzar's furnace," the delegates met in the largest hall in Baltimore, the Egyptian Saloon of the Odd Fellows on North Gay Street. The sweltering auditorium was packed when the gavel fell calling the first session to order about noontime. Hendrick B. Wright, of Pennsylvania, a large, dignified looking man, presided as temporary chairman, and after some brief formalities, the convention settled down to business.[16] The first subject to be debated was the most important of all. When R. M. Sanders, of North Carolina, rose and proposed the adoption of a rule requiring that all nominations be confirmed by a two-thirds vote everyone knew that the future of the Democratic party hung on what was to follow.

In 1832, when the first Democratic convention had met to nominate a running-mate for Jackson, it had adopted a special rule of order which made necessary a two-thirds majority before any candidate might be declared chosen. The purpose of

15 Wright to Fine, May 23, 1844, Hammond, *History of New York*, III, 456-9.

16 Dickinson to Mrs. Dickinson, May 27, 1844, *Speeches; Correspondence ...of Daniel S. Dickinson*, J. Dickinson, ed., II, 369; A. Stevenson, *Something of Men I Have Known*, p. 128.

this was to demonstrate the solidarity of the party behind Van Buren, who had no real competition for the place. In 1835, when the Little Magician had received the nomination for President, this rule was continued for the same reason. But at the next convention, before the Log Cabin campaign, a majority rule was followed, so no precedent had been established. In these three cases, the question of the two-thirds rule had really been unimportant, but now, in 1844, it was vital. It seemed fairly certain that Van Buren could command a majority of the 266 ballots which would be cast, but it was equally clear that he could not control two-thirds. Even if every delegate who was pledged to support him on the first ballot lived up to his promise, he would still fail of two-thirds by several votes,[17] and it was very unlikely that all the Southerners bound to him before the appearance of the Hammet letter would still consider themselves pledged.

The two-thirds rule of order would naturally be decided by an ordinary convention majority, and none of the members was " instructed " on it. So those committed to Van Buren who were unwilling to go against him on the first ballot could, if they did not desire his nomination, back the two-thirds rule and thus insure his ultimate defeat. If the rule was adopted, the Van Burenites would be, as George Bancroft said, " waterlogged at once." [18] They would either have to abandon " Little Van " for some candidate favoring annexation, or permit the convention to be deadlocked and disrupted, an alternative perfectly satisfactory to many Southern extremists.

The debate on Sanders' proposal was therefore acrimonious and prolonged. Benjamin Butler attacked it bitterly, and Senator Robert Walker, of Mississippi, thin, dyspeptic, one of the ugliest men ever to sit in Congress,[19] but a powerful orator,

---

17 According to *Niles' Register*, LXVI, 211-3, 171 of the delegates were so pledged; two-thirds of the Convention was 177.

18 Bancroft to Van Buren, May 23, 1844, Massachusetts Historical Society, *Proceedings*, XLII, 430.

19 W. E. Dodd, *Robert J. Walker, Imperialist*, p. 17.

defended it in an animated speech that was punctuated with loud cheers and sharp hisses. The discussion quickly degenerated into a spiteful squabble. After Sanders had spoken, Butler again took the floor in an hour-long attack. Butler was dignified and conservative in appearance, an accomplished debater and a skillful manipulator of an emotional audience. Trying his best to cement party solidarity, he criticized Sanders and Walker for merely mentioning the disgraceful defeat of 1840. How could they, he cried, even allude " to a period that had left an almost indelible stigma on the nation; a period when reason had been debauched amid log cabins, hard cider, and coon skins." As he spoke he grew terribly excited. He leaped up and down wildly, stamping on the platform as though he were crushing beneath his heels the stinging memory of those days. The already tense crowd, catching his mood, rocked the hall with their cheers, and organized discussion became impossible.

When a semblance of order was finally restored, the debate on the rule was suspended while the permanent officials of the convention were elected. Hendrick Wright was picked as President, and there were twenty-five Vice-Presidents, one from each state represented. (South Carolina did not send delegates to Baltimore.) By the time this was completed it was seven o'clock and the convention was adjourned.

On Tuesday the representatives gathered at nine, and the fight over the two-thirds rule was resumed. Walker dominated the early proceedings. He said that Butler's reason had been " blinded " by his long friendship with Van Buren, referred to his antics of the previous afternoon as the " finest specimen of tall vaulting " that he, Walker, had ever witnessed, and called for passage of the two-thirds rule. This time the crowd cheered mightily for the Mississippian. Robert Rantoul, of Massachusetts, spoke next, also supporting the rule. This was significant, for it demonstrated the effect of Tyler's use of the patronage. Rantoul had been an early and enthusiastic supporter of Van Buren and the Independent Treasury, but he had accepted the lucrative post of Collector of the Port of Boston from the President and was now an annexation man.[20] The debate continued all morning, and finally at approximately one o'clock, the ballots were cast. The result showed 148 members in favor of the rule and only 118 opposed. Of the states pledged to Van Buren, Vermont, Rhode Island, Massachusetts, Connecticut and Pennsylvania split almost evenly on the issue, giving 25 votes for the rule and 28 against it. Mississippi, Alabama, Louisiana, Illinois, Michigan and Arkansas, also sworn to "Little Van," went unanimously for it. The men pledged to Van Buren who voted "aye" combined with the uncommitted delegates who favored annexation and those instructed in behalf of various annexationist candidates, were enough to carry the measure.

The meeting was then recessed for lunch. When it was reconvened at three, the first ballot for the presidential candidate was taken. Van Buren received 146 votes—a majority, but less than 177, the required two-thirds. His pledged delegates gave him 28 more votes than they had cast against the two-thirds rule, enough to have defeated it easily. For example, the twenty-six Pennsylvania representatives espoused his cause to a man on the first ballot, where only thirteen of them had opposed the rule. Illinois' five pledged delegates all supported him after having approved the rule unanimously. But strangely enough, this duplicity was confined almost entirely to the North! The Southern states committed to Van Buren were Louisiana, Alabama, Arkansas and Mississippi. They had backed the rule unanimously. But on the first ballot for President they disregarded their instructions and only one delegate in this group named Van Buren as his choice. There was no dishonesty here; they did not want the Little Magician, they spoke openly against him, and voted that way from the very beginning. Morally, there was even some reason for ignoring the orders of their constituents, for in all these states the

20 Schlesinger, *Age of Jackson*, pp. 234, 434.

deputations had been chosen before the agitation of the Texas question had reached its peak, and many months previous to Van Buren's reply to Hammet. There was much justification for their refusal to follow an expression of popular opinion which they could be reasonably sure no longer held in their states.

It was the New Englanders, the Pennsylvanians, the Illinoisans who were tricky in their actions, not the members from below the Mason-Dixon line. The situation can best be summarized statistically:

DELEGATES PLEDGED TO VOTE FOR VAN BUREN

Area	Vote on two-thirds rule		Vote on 1st ballot for President	
	AGAINST	FOR	VAN BUREN	OTHER
New England & Middle Sts. ...	79	20	100 *	0
West, including Missouri	30	10	36	4
South	0	24	1	23

* One Pennsylvania delegate did not vote on the rule.

Why this inconsistency? In a case like Robert Rantoul's the answer is probably clear enough. Also, the tremendous excitement and pressure which had been brought to bear on the delegates who had visited Washington before the convention must have swayed many. Perhaps some of the Northerners and Westerners really thought their constituents had changed their minds, though this would not explain their voting for "Little Van" at all. Whatever their motives, there were enough delegates outside the South who did not want Van Buren but who were afraid to defy their orders, to pass the two-thirds rule and prevent his nomination.

After the failure of anyone to garner the required 177 ballots at the first test, six more efforts were made on Tuesday afternoon, all unsuccessful. Van Buren's total gradually declined as his merely nominal friends abandoned his standard, and that of Lewis Cass rose accordingly. The last trial on Tuesday, taken about six o'clock, showed Cass leading with 123 and Van Buren second with 99, of which 59 came from the solidly loyal states of New York and Ohio. Buchanan had 22 and

Colonel Johnson had 21. They favored annexation, but even if they could have been brought to yield at this point to Cass, the two-thirds rule would still have prevented his selection.

At this point, John K. Miller, of Ohio, obtained the floor and moved that in as much as Van Buren had received a majority on the first ballot, he be declared nominated. The President of the convention properly declared this out of order because of the two-thirds rule. Miller, however, leaped up on a bench and demanded a hearing. Pandemonium broke loose as the strained nerves of the tired politicians began to snap. Miller, gesticulating wildly, delivered a violent speech, but the uproar was so great that he could not be heard. John Hickman, a member from Pennsylvania, managed to attract the chair's attention and moved facetiously that Andrew Jackson be nominated. The clamor grew worse, and finally, at seven o'clock the meeting broke up in utter confusion.[21]

That evening, Benjamin Butler did some serious thinking. He knew that the remaining hundred-odd Van Buren men could be held firm for several more ballots, but he also knew that the annexationists would soon combine their forces for Cass. Johnson's supporters had told him that the Colonel would be withdrawn in favor of Cass in the morning. It would then be only a matter of time before enough Van Burenites would give way just to get the matter settled and prevent a break-up of the party. The hours of darkness were all the time he had to work against this. The moment had come to use his chief's letter offering to withdraw in favor of Wright. Butler spent the evening canvassing the various delegations to see how they would react to Wright's name. The solidly Van Buren states—Maine, New Hampshire, Ohio—and also Vermont and parts of Massachusetts and Pennsylvania were ready to back him. Butler was also pretty sure that Tennessee would support a Wright boom, and he did not think that Vir-

21 *Niles' Register*, LXVI, 211-6. The account of the convention to this point is based on *Niles'*, and Forney, *Anecdotes of Public Men*, I, 118; II, 79.

ginia would continue to support Cass once Wright entered the contest.

It was midnight by the time he had completed his investigation, and he retired to spend a sleepless night pondering his problem. He realized that Judge Fine had a letter from Wright refusing to run, and he had a general idea of the force with which the Senator had expressed himself. But he convinced himself that conditions were such that Wright's statement could now be ignored, especially in view of Van Buren's wishes, expressed in the secret letter with which only Butler and his roommate, Henry D. Gilpin, were familiar. Butler finally made up his mind to gather the New York group together in the morning before the convention reassembled, show them Van Buren's letter, and tell them that unless they advised differently, he would withdraw Van Buren's name in favor of Wright's as soon as the session began.

At daybreak, he wrote to Wright, telling him what he intended to do, and begging him not to object until he had seen Van Buren's letter, and until he, Butler, had had a chance to talk to him. Then he met with the rest of the New Yorkers and laid the whole case before them. He urged his plan with all the force at his command, but Wright had chosen his representative with care and his orders had been explicit. Fine remained obdurate—if Wright's name were suggested by Butler or anyone else he would read not only the section of his friend's letter containing his refusal to run, but all of it, including a part in which Wright stated flatly that on *all* issues his position and that of Martin Van Buren were identical. Butler persisted until five minutes to nine, but Fine was determined. Finally, unable to move him, the New Yorkers voted reluctantly but unanimously against Butler's proposal.

As the New York members entered the Odd Fellow's Hall on Wednesday morning, representatives of many of the other states crowded around Butler anxiously and asked him what had been decided. Butler told them briefly what had happened, and urged the loyal Van Buren men not to yield as long as

New York supported the Little Magician. Most of them agreed, but as the convention reconvened, the name of James Knox Polk, of Tennessee, was beginning to be heard in many places among the little knots of men in the crowded auditorium.[22]

When the meeting opened, Miller's effort to repeal the two-thirds rule was resumed, but without success. In the press section, John L. O'Sullivan sat writing a minute by minute account of the proceedings which he later sent to Van Buren. "With a deep and bitter wrath & sorrow," he wrote at this point, it was clear that " Van " must be abandoned. There was one last stand—the eighth ballot. Johnson's name was withdrawn, and Buchanan's followers also relinquished their man. Van Buren received 104 votes to Cass' 114. Polk's name appeared on the lists with 44. No decision.

The loyal Rhode Island delegates then told Butler they considered the contest useless and would turn to someone else when the roll of the states was called again. Medary, of Ohio, who had kept his state firm throughout the battle, reported that on the next ballot it would scatter its votes, and that some positive action must be taken to prevent a swing of at least some Ohioans to Cass. Butler advised them to go for Polk to avoid this, and sought to gain the floor of the convention.[23]

In the meantime, someone was making a speech in behalf of Polk, calling him the " bosom friend of Old Hickory," and the desperate politicos were getting more and more interested. The Virginia delegation asked for and received from the convention the right to retire from the auditorium to " consult." Virginia had been solid behind Cass from the first. Next Butler got the floor and requested the same privilege for New York. The crowded hall fairly vibrated with excitement. Permission was granted, but when Butler asked that no further votes be taken until his state had returned, Sanders, of North Carolina, raised an objection, and a confused debate resulted,

22 Butler to Van Buren, May 31, 1844, Van Buren papers.

23 *Ibid.*; O'Sullivan to Van Buren, May 29, 1844, Van Buren papers.

the New Yorkers remaining in their seats. Finally the venerable but passionate Samuel Young, a Regency man completely devoted to Van Buren, was recognized by the President and began to speak. He defended his delegation against the charge that they were attempting to dictate the candidate to their fellows. He pointed out that New York had not placed Van Buren's name in nomination until sixteen other states had already done so. He claimed that the excitement was false, that the Texas question was already dying out as a major issue before the people. The course being forced on the convention by the annexationists, he said, would be regretted afterward.

As he spoke, the hubbub in the auditorium grew louder and louder; tempers were straining; the convention was becoming a mob. Then Young supplied the explosive spark to the charged atmosphere.

" Nero fiddled while Rome burned," he shouted, " & probably the political Nero of this Country is exulting over the flames he has raised."

" Who is Nero? " demanded a delegate.

Young refused to commit himself, but voices from many parts of the auditorium supplied the deficiency: " John Tyler! John Tyler! " [24] The hall was in a turmoil, but Young held the floor. He moved that the two-thirds rule be rescinded and was promptly declared out of order.

" Then in God's name," he screamed above the din, " are we to be kept here for all eternity? " With that he stopped, and the New Yorkers began to leave the hall without having gained their request that voting be suspended until their return. As they filed out, Samuel Hohen, of Georgia, demanded of Young again, " Who is Nero? " But the old man would not answer. The meeting had once again degenerated into complete confusion. Cries for order, led by Hendrick Wright from the platform, had no effect. Several men in different parts of the

24 So reported the correspondent of *Niles' Register*. Young, however, was almost certainly referring to Calhoun, and this is what was inferred by his Southern listeners.

auditorium were making violent speeches which no one more than a few feet away could hear. The Georgian Hohen was still unsatisfied. He managed to gain the ear of a part of the crowd and denounced Young violently for "having thrown a firebrand into the convention, and then meanly skulking out of it." Shouts and hisses greeted this, and the enraged Southerner continued to rant threats against Young, who had by this time left the auditorium.

This was the peak of the crisis. Hohen offered to insult Young to his face, and challenge him to a duel, and this, from a young man to the venerable Colonel Young, caused a revulsion of feeling. ("What do you think of this specimen of ' Southern Chivalry '...?" scrawled O'Sullivan hastily in the detailed account he was making for Van Buren.) Henry Hubbard, of New Hampshire, one of the Vice-Presidents of the meeting, at last got things under control. He undertook a quiet speech for Polk and unity. Coming from a man whose state had been unanimous for Van Buren from the beginning, this had a very good effect on the delegates. Other speakers followed, all now praising James Polk. Finally the calling of the states for the ninth ballot was begun with Virginia and New York still out.[25]

Meanwhile, the New Yorkers had assembled in a room underneath the auditorium. It was quickly decided that Butler should announce the withdrawal of "Little Van" and give his own reasons for swinging to Polk, but that each member should reserve the right to vote in whatever way he chose. This decision had to be written out in the journal which the New Yorkers were keeping, but a messenger brought the news to some of the Van Buren men from other states, and the parade for Polk was on. When the Virginians returned to the hall, thirteen states had been polled, and the score stood, Polk 74, Cass 20. William H. Roane rose to announce the result of the Old Dominion's conference, and Hubbard invited him

25 Butler to Van Buren, May 31, 1844, O'Sullivan to Van Buren, May 29, 1844, Van Buren papers; *Niles' Register*, LXVI, 217.

to come to the platform. As Roane reached the stage, he leaned dramatically across the President's table to offer Hubbard the "right hand of fellowship."

This gesture from a strong Cass man to an equally determined Van Burenite symbolized the turn of events. Polk had two great attributes in his favor, one of which appealed to each of the hostile camps. To the Cass group he was acceptable because he had been an enthusiastic annexationist from the start. The attitude of the Van Buren forces was expressed by Butler, when he described the doings at Baltimore to the Little Magician a few days after it was all over:

> His state indeed deserved nothing from New York; but he had not been a party to the conspiracy & plots by which we had been destroyed, and his nomination, it was most obvious ... give[s] us a sound democrat by whom we can make the old issues of Bank or no Bank &c. &c. flounder with a single blow ...

It was high time to bury animosities and compromise, and Polk, although the first presidential Dark Horse, was a notillogical choice.

When Roane and Hubbard shook hands, the assembled delegates roared their approval. The Virginian then cast all his state's ballots for Polk, and proceeded to explain his change and to eulogize Van Buren! The love feast was on. As Roane was finishing, the New York members filed back into the hall. Amid further cheers, Butler explained New York's decision. In a speech full of "deep & beautiful pathos" he withdrew Van Buren's name. He spoke with feeling of the old New York-Virginia alliance which had dominated the Democratic party since the days of Thomas Jefferson. He complimented, in rapid succession, Roane, the state of Virginia, Jefferson, Van Buren and Jackson. Then he presented his own vote to James K. Polk, promising him that the Empire State would give him a majority of fifteen to twenty thousand in November. Daniel S. Dickinson, nominal head of the delegation, next announced that thirty-four of New York's remaining thirty-five representatives were also now for Polk. Only Samuel Young remained unappeased, and he cast a blank ballot. So infectious was the spirit of the convention, that while Butler was speaking, all the other New York delegates had made up their minds to support the Tennessee politician.

The rest was a mad parade. Pennsylvania voted unanimously for Polk, and then Robert J. Walker, thanking New York for saving the Union, threw Mississippi to him as well. "Immense cheering" followed. One delegate leaped to his feet and announced proudly that James K. Polk's grandfather had been a signer of the Mecklenburg Declaration of Independence; an Illinois man (starting a terrible pun that was to be a mainstay in the campaign) cried out, "Illinois will give a severe *Polk* to whiggery." The crowd was so overwrought by this time that even this remark drew forth gales of laughter. When George Bancroft cast his ballot for Polk, a Pennsylvania man called for and of course received, "three cheers for the Historian of the U.S." By now everyone was cheering for everyone. States which had already committed themselves to Cass, rose one after another to "correct" their ballots. Finally someone called for South Carolina. The presidential electors of the state of John Caldwell Calhoun were still appointed by the state legislature, so there were no official representatives present. But F. W. Pickens, a former Congressman from the Palmetto State, happened to be in the hall as an observer, and he got up and came forward. As he did so the whole audience rose as one. While Pickens spoke for unity, the crowd cheered again and again, handkerchiefs waving frantically, the hostilities of the past months forgotten. When the last vote was in and the unanimous result announced, three last cheers were given for Martin Van Buren, and in "a state of sublime enthusiasm" the convention adjourned.[26]

26 *Ibid.*

Benjamin Butler, exhausted by his labors and defeated in his main aspiration, wept unashamedly. But he found solace for his despondency in one fact. He knew that he might possibly have prevented the nomination of Polk, or anyone else, by refusing to sacrifice his chief. There would have been much justification for such action in the duplicity of the delegates who had used the two-thirds rule to avoid violating their instructions to support Van Buren. But Butler had decided against trying to create a deadlock. " Especially was I held to this course by the conviction founded on authentic evidence of declarations made by Mr. Calhoun & those at Washington that nothing would more gratify them than the dissolution of the Convention without any nomination," he wrote to Van Buren. John L. O'Sullivan, deeply disappointed himself, expressed the feelings of the true Van Buren men in a single pithy sentence. "Some of us," he said, are " weeping with one eye while we smile with the other at the overthrow of the intrigues of traitors." But it was a Whig, Philip Hone, who put the same idea most neatly, quoting in his diary these familiar lines from Goldsmith:

And now the wonder came to light
And shew'd the Rogues they lied.
The man recovered from the bite
The dog it was that died.[27]

*   *   *   *   *

The convention reassembled at three-thirty to pick Polk's running-mate. Judge Fine had held out against all Butler's urging when the New York leader had tried to get his consent to proposing Wright for the top spot on the ticket, but the excitement of the rush to Polk had worn down his judgment. He suggested to Butler that Wright's objections might not hold now that the party was again united and Van Buren had definitely lost out. Butler therefore consulted with some of the

27 Bancroft to Van Buren, June 14, 1844; Butler to Van Buren, May 31, 1844, O'Sullivan to Van Buren, May 29, 1844, Van Buren papers; *Diary of Philip Hone*, XXII, 67, May 30, 1844, New York Historical Society.

Southern leaders, especially with Roane and Walker. There seemed to be much in favor of the idea. It would demonstrate clearly the harmony of the party—the acquiescence of the Van Buren Democrats to Polk's selection—and at the same time it would constitute an acknowledgement by the party of the wrong done the Little Magician. Most of the Southerners were satisfied with Wright's name, and it met with complete approval in the North.[28]

When nominations were called for Walker named him, calling him the " Cato of the Union." [29] The delegates, weak from the emotional catharsis which they had undergone, were eager to get things settled quickly. A Kentucky delegate withdrew the persistent Colonel Johnson; George Dromgoole, of Virginia, seconded Wright, and a poll was taken. Levi Woodbury, although unnominated, received eight votes from Georgia; the rest of the convention chose Wright and he was declared the nominee. Judge Fine, taking the responsibility for violating his friend's orders, accepted for him.

The proceedings at Baltimore were known immediately at the Capital, for Samuel F. B. Morse's " MAGNETIC ELECTRIC TELEGRAPH " had just been installed between the two cities. The value of this invention was immediately recognized, especially by the press. "Intercourse assumes a new and more commanding importance. . . .Who can estimate the result?" asked Niles' Weekly Register. And at Albany, an Argus reporter got busy with his pencil and figured that a message could travel the forty odd miles from Baltimore to Washington in one second. This, he announced in open amazement, means that it travels at a speed of 150,000 miles an hour! [30]

Utilizing this latest scientific miracle, the convention requested Fine to telegraph Wright to make certain that he

28 Butler to Van Buren, May 31, 1844, Van Buren papers.

29 Cato the Elder, known for his devotion to the republican ideals of the old Romans.

30 Niles' Register, LXVI, 210; Argus, May 28, 1844.

would accept. The Senator was in the close-packed Rotunda of the Capitol reading the latest bulletins sputtering in from Baltimore when the message from Fine came in.[31] It was then about half-past six. But Wright had expected this, and had had two or three hours to think it over. Quickly his answer was flashed back to the waiting convention by Morse himself, who was handling the key at the Washington end of the line.

> WASHINGTON. IMPORTANT! MR. WRIGHT IS HERE, AND SAYS, SAY TO THE NEW YORK DELEGATION, THAT HE CANNOT ACCEPT THE NOMINATION.

The delegates read this flat refusal, but were not convinced. They could not quite trust Dr. Morse's franticly buzzing contraption. Perhaps it had made a mistake. The original message was repeated. Once again, after a brief pause, the machine at Baltimore clicked out the reply.

> AGAIN: MR. WRIGHT IS HERE, AND WILL SUPPORT MR. POLK CHEERFULLY, BUT CAN NOT ACCEPT THE NOMINATION FOR VICE-PRESIDENT.

The delegates were still not ready to accept Wright's decision. Judge Fine was instructed to try again with a more forceful presentation of their desire.

> BALTIMORE: MESSRS. PAGE, YOUNG, FINE, BALLARD AND CHURCH ARE HERE, AND HAVE RECEIVED MR. WRIGHT'S COMMUNICATION, AND HOPE HE WILL RECONSIDER IT.

But Wright's response was no different.

> WASHINGTON: UPON NO CIRCUMSTANCES CAN MR. WRIGHT ACCEPT THE NOMINATION, AND REFERS TO HIS TWO FORMER ANSWERS.

31 D. Lynch, *An Epoch and a Man*, p. 491; R. Winthrop to W. Gaston, Apr. 16, 1872, *Memorial of S. F. B. Morse from the City of Boston*, p. 9. Winthrop, a Massachusetts Congressman, witnessing the scene from the steps of the Capitol, observed shrewdly that "a new kind of *wire-pulling* had entered politics."

Despite the novelty of the new means of communication, the dialogue was beginning to get a little monotonous.

BALTIMORE: SHALL MR. FINE SAY ANYTHING TO THE CONVENTION?

WASHINGTON: YES; WHAT MR. WRIGHT HAS ALREADY SAID.

AGAIN: MR. WRIGHT HAS WELL CONSIDERED, AND BEGS HIS PREVIOUS ANSWERS MAY BE SATISFACTORY.

But the convention was unwilling to believe even this. Butler endorsed for Wright, and said that he would come around. Finally the weary politicians adjourned till morning. But it was no use. From Washington, Wright had already dispatched to Baltimore two New York Congressmen, Preston King and Orville Robinson, with letters to Butler absolutely refusing the offer. It was too late to get a train, so King and Robinson made the arduous trip during the night by wagon.[32] When they saw the words on paper, in Wright's neat, regular script, the representatives finally gave up. They resumed their deliberations, and on the second ballot, George Mifflin Dallas, of Pennsylvania, Senator Walker's brother-in-law, received the required two-thirds. At last they adjourned, *sine die*.[33]

Wright had not hesitated for a moment when called upon to make the run with Polk, for he had definite ideas on why he had been named and what the result of his acceptance would have been. He was very upset because Butler and Fine did not seem to understand their mistake in urging him on. He thought he knew why the annexationists were willing to take him. First, the "intriguers"—Calhoun, Walker, and their

32 Wright to Butler, June 3, 1844, Wright-Butler letters; Fairfield to Mrs. Fairfield, May 20, 1844, *Fairfield Letters*, A. Staples, ed., p. 339; *New York Herald*, June 4, 1844, quoted in Hudson, *Journalism in the United States,* p. 599; Wright to Butler, May 29, 1844, Wright-Butler letters; Wright to Flagg, June 8, 1844, Flagg papers; R. L. Thompson, *Wiring A Continent,* p. 25.

33 *Niles' Register,* LXVI, 218; Dodd, *Walker,* p. 9.

friends—had been beaten by the nomination of Polk, who was a good Democrat in spite of his Texas sympathies, and who was resentful of their abuse of Van Buren. To conciliate Polk, strengthen the ticket, and thus insure the annexation of Texas, it was essential that the Northern wing of the party be appeased. Secondly, for the Van Burenites to accept the Vice-Presidency would be to countenance the deceit which had deprived them of the first spot, and in this way the Southerners would be absolved of their guilt.

He could not run for the very reasons that the Southerners wanted him to. To have taken the proffered place would have made him vulnerable to the charge that he had sold out his friends for office. The whole force of the Van Burenites' righteous indignation would have been lost. Then there was the Texas question. If the rank and file in New York ever imagined that Van Buren had been rejected for any other reason than his opposition to annexation, if they discovered that there had been a plot to destroy the party and unite the South behind slavery, they would bolt. This must be prevented, for Polk was sound on all the major issues which the party had traditionally espoused, and the plotters, after supporting "a candidate notoriously rotten in democratic principles," (Cass) had been defeated. Silas hastened to write to Polk explaining his stand and assuring him that he had not refused the honor because he disapproved of the man who would have been his running-mate. But "everybody knows that my opinions upon the subject of annexation were, at least, no more favorable than his [Van Buren's]," he said, and to have run under those circumstances would have exposed the whole situation and destroyed the party in the North.[34]

34 Wright to Butler, May 29, 1844, Wright-Butler letters; Wright to Marcy, Sept. 13, 1844, Marcy papers; Wright to Polk, June 2, 1844, Polk papers, 1st series. See also Wright to Russell, June 17, 1844, Gillet, *Wright*, II, p. 1520. Wright first explained all this in a letter to Butler for the convention, but decided that his words were too strong. So he sent a second note for him to read to that body and explained at length in the longer, personal letter. The official declination note has been printed in Hammond's *History of New York*, III, 471-2.

Wright did not consider himself a martyr. When Van Buren wrote and spoke of his sacrifices he replied chidingly. None of his real friends had desired his promotion, he wrote. " My apparent modesty has been mere selfishness, and my sacrifices have been no more than *apparent*. . . .That I cannot entertain any other feeling than contempt for those who are offended at me for declining the nomination [is an understatement which affords me] richest amusement." He went on: " To see the exhibition of real spite because I have declined to be made a tool in the hands of those, who have been wantonly and deliberately trifling with our principles. . .and abusing my best friends, does not deserve even contempt. It rather excites that feeling of pity, which we cannot withhold, when we see malignity swamped in its own folly." This attitude was understood and appreciated by most of his friends, and if Fine and Butler had not been immersed in the emotional bath of those exciting hours at Baltimore, they would probably have seen it the same way. Even before the convention, Flagg had written to Van Buren that he had talked with Judge Fine and agreed with him that if "Van " failed to get the nomination, New York must not accept any place on the ticket. As Wright said, " all our delegates at Baltimore lost their judgments in the excitement. . . ." [35]

The party's acclaim of his refusal was almost unanimous. Within ten days he had received over a hundred letters on the subject, only five of which urged acceptance, and many, written before his rejection of the place was known, were bitterly critical. They " denounced me more severely than I have been denounced since 1824 '5 on the presumption that I had accepted," he wrote ruefully to Flagg. Perhaps typical of the less violent responses was the letter which James S. Wadsworth, of Geneseo, New York, wrote Van Buren.

35 Wright to Van Buren, June 10, 1844, Flagg to Van Buren, May 17, 1844, Van Buren papers, Wright to Flagg, June 8, 1844, Flagg papers.

What will Mr. Wright do? is in everybody's mouth. I shall not doubt that whatever he does will be done for the purest and most patriotic motives, but I sincerely hope he will resign. I can not bear that any one so devoted to you and so true to us should reap any share of the profits of this insult and fraud.

Such sentiment was not confined to New Yorkers. Frank Blair approved Wright's course, another Democrat, from Baltimore, spoke of the " unrivaled honor " of having been able to decline the Presidential and Vice-Presidential nominations, and Thomas Hart Benton was so pleased that he said that Wright was " the greatest man in the world." The eccentric Missouri Senator was in top form. When Wright showed him a note which Flagg had written approving the strategy of refusing to take anything from the men who had ruined Van Buren's chances, he said, " Three such letters. . .and three such men, are sufficient not merely to save a party, but an age, a generation, an era. Tell him so. Tell him so, Sir. Tell him I say so. It does not require five, as it did to save Sodom. Three are enough." [36]

Though his best friends and firmest supporters approved, and in spite of his own statements that he did not look upon his action as a personal sacrifice, his selfless stand did not fail to excite popular appreciation. At a time when Democratic politicians from all sections of the nation had been both openly and covertly seeking the presidential plum he had quietly but intransigently refused even to allow others to seek it for him, and when the Vice-Presidential nomination had been actually given to him, he had made the party take it back. Up to this point in his career he had been a respected public figure but not an especially popular one, except in his own North Country and among the professional politicians who knew him well

[36] For letters on his refusal, see Van Buren papers. Wright to Flagg, June 8, 1844, Flagg papers; J. Wadsworth to Van Buren, June 1, 1844, F. Blair to Van Buren, May 30, 1844, A. Davizac to Van Buren, May 30, 1844, Van Buren papers; Stevenson to Marcy, June 3, 1844, Marcy papers.

and appreciated his devotion to party and his willingness to give long hours to committee work, letter writing and similar tedious but necessary legislative and political duties. As a Senator, his loyalty to the administrations of Jackson and Van Buren had been unquestionable, his work in pressing the Independent Treasury plan had been appreciated, and the part which he had played in keeping the Democrats in both houses in line during the Tyler regime had been widely recognized. But like his friend Van Buren (and unlike Jackson) he had never, until 1844, done anything which had caught the public imagination. This was all changed when the news of the doings at Baltimore became known. Coming close upon his refusal of the Justiceship, and at the climax of four years of almost universal intrigue and maneuvering by politicians of both parties, his unselfish behavior made him a popular hero. People began to turn to him as a man who could be trusted, as one who acted for the right and not for the self. No longer Van Buren's right hand, he became, almost overnight, the leader of the Northern Democracy. He saw it himself, and with his characteristic self-doubt, he was frightened, but many others observed it and were pleased. "*All eyes already turn to Wright as Polk's successor,*" wrote one politician to William L. Marcy within a week of the end of the convention, and Cave Johnson, writing to the newly nominated Polk, remarked, almost in awe: " Silas Wright declined the Vice because he was fearful that he would be suspected of being connected with the intrigue to overthrow Van—what a wonderful thing, that Wright has been offered in *one month* [*sic*]. . .a seat upon the Supreme bench of the U. S. Court—the nomination with certain assurances of success of President & Vice President & *rejected them all*—and all on account of his friendship for Van Buren." [37]

37 Stevenson to Marcy, June 3, 1844, Marcy papers; Johnson to Polk, May 31, 1844, Polk papers, 1st series. See also H. Greeley, *Recollections of a Busy Life,* p. 161.

CHAPTER XIII

THE END OF WRIGHT'S "POLICY OF DECLINATION"

"[Wright] is as averse to be a candidate as I am to have him. Those who would thrust him into that position may be his friends but they are really his worst enemies."

William L. Marcy to Prosper M. Wetmore, May 9, 1844.

"I very confidentially apprehend that success will most effectually beat me...."

Wright to James Buchanan, September 23, 1844.

THE support lent by the Southern wing of the Democratic party to Cass, a man whose political honesty and party loyalty they considered open to question, had convinced the hard money Democrats that Texas was only a sham—an excuse to destroy their national organization. Though Polk favored annexation in accord with the professed sentiment of these Southerners, the Van Burenites still feared a party split. Wright wrote Polk early in June, "In my deliberate judgment our Union was never so much in danger as this moment." The Southern wing was thoroughly discredited in the eyes of sincere old-line followers of Jackson and Van Buren, not only in the North and in the anti-Texas camps, but also among many Southern annexationists. "What a painful contrast between New York and other states which I should blush to name," wrote Joel Poinsett, who had been Van Buren's Secretary of War. He was from South Carolina. And Major Andrew Jackson Donelson, of Tennessee, the Old Hero's adopted son, came to Wright in tears upon his return from the convention, saying, "There is not one grain of soundness left in the Southern democracy as a party. There are honest men, but the political leaders are all rotten....they really did not want Polk, but Cass, and this was true of the majority of the Tennessee delegation itself, but they dare not act it out." According to Wright, the "intriguers" returned from Baltimore "looking like whipped children" and all the "true" men of the South admitted that from the moment of Van Buren's defeat, " the salvation of the party, and of the honest, sound democratic principle, in this country, rested with the Northern democracy." These "true" Southerners added that if New York could support the ticket after such treatment, " she holds, from that day, the position which Virginia [the original font of Democratic principles] has so lightly thrown away." [1]

But the Southerners did not break up the party. Tyler's organization did hold a separate convention, largely attended by officeholders, but their leader thought better of it, and withdrew in favor of Polk. Perhaps to him Texas was the really important thing. As for the Calhoun forces, the nomination of Polk deflated them completely. Their pretext was gone; they had no excuse to break off and no rallying point around which to attract a united South. In a way that they had not intended, the Northern members of the party seemed to have won a real victory, for James K. Polk, on his record, was a Democrat of the old Jackson school, Texas or no. To the " sound" party men, his nomination was an unexpected boon. They had thought that the passing over of Van Buren would certainly force them to choose between Cass and schism. Instead they found themselves with an acceptable candidate and a strong moral position resulting from the deceitful defeat of the Magician. As John Dix put it, " You may imagine how much surprised I was at the result of the Baltimore Convention. If we could not have Mr. Van Buren, certainly they could not do so well as to give us Col. Polk, & accounts here from all quarters are represented by our friends to be very cheering." Wright expressed the same idea in a confidential letter to John L. Russell, his young Canton follower. " That I felt deep disappointment and regret [at Van Buren's failure], is most

1 Wright to Polk, June 2, 1844, Polk papers, 1st series; Poinsett to G. Keable, July 1, 1844, Gilpin papers, Historical Society of Pennsylvania; Wright to Marcy, Sept. 13, 1844, Marcy papers; Wright to Butler, June 3, 1844, Wright-Butler letters.

true; but my stronger and almost painful concern for the success of the democratic party, and its dearly cherished principles, so far from being diminished by the change of the party nomination from what I had hoped. . .was greatly increased; and my long acquaintance with Gov. Polk and with the uprightness of his course. . .rendered his selection most acceptable to me." [2]

* * * * *

On the eighth of June, Calhoun's annexation treaty was rejected by the Senate, only eighteen ballots being cast in its favor. Wright, of course, voted against it. Both parties now seemed ready to wait on the decision of the people in November, and Congress adjourned without any further action. The Wrights left Washington about the middle of the month. Stopping at New York, Silas was surprised to find that many Democrats there interpreted his refusal of the Vice-Presidential nomination as an indication on his part of personal hostility to Polk. So he took advantage of a rally at Castle Garden to explain his refusal. The gathering was large (the *Albany Atlas* claimed that 15,000 attended) and his appearance was received enthusiastically. After explaining his behavior, he asked the throng, "Did I do right?"

"Yes," came back the answer with a great roar.

"I did," agreed Wright emphatically, as the crowd cheered and cheered. "Yes, and my own heart responds to the answer which you have so unanimously given." He also spoke of his warm friendship for Polk and urged his audience to support the Tennesseean just as they would have Van Buren had he not been deprived of the nomination.[3]

From New York, Wright and Clarissa proceeded up the Hudson. They visited with Van Buren for two days at Kinderhook, stopped again at Albany, and then passed up the east shore of Lake Champlain to pay a call on Silas' family at Wey-

2 Dix to Flagg, June 14, 1844, Flagg papers; Wright to Russell, June 17, 1844, Gillet, *Wright*, II, 1521.

3 *Atlas*, June 21, Aug. 7, 1844. See also Hammond, *History of New York*, III, 465-8, and Wright to Marcy, Sept. 13, 1844, Marcy papers.

bridge. From there they crossed over into Canada to see some of the Moody clan who lived at Montreal. They did not arrive at Canton until July 13.[4]

Even the excitement of the past months at Washington had not driven thoughts of conditions at home completely from Wright's mind. During 1843 and 1844 he had done his best to keep abreast with the ever-present tensions within the New York Democratic party. His attitude toward the conflicts between the radicals and the conservatives was rather Jove-like. Ideologically he was allied to the former group, with its policy of sound money and no debts, but he was so preoccupied with the national aspects of political affairs, that he could not help worrying when he saw the breach between this group and the rest of the party continuously widening. " There are many good men [at Albany]," he had written to Van Buren (who was in much the same position as he) in the spring of 1843. But most of them " have come to look. . .upon their petty feuds as more important than the nation or the state." When trouble developed, he refrained from writing letters or trying to influence either side. " I could do no good and did not wish to do harm," he said on one occasion. At one time he had three hundred unanswered letters from New York, and neither the time nor the inclination to attend to them. His attitude led the conservatives of the party to connect him more closely with national issues than with their local troubles.[5]

But if they thought that his convictions on state finance or canal policy had changed, they were very much mistaken. Though he had ceased to take an active part in local problems, and though (as he himself admitted) he was " entirely behind the times " about some matters in his home state, he always knew where every important politician stood on every important question, and never doubted where he stood himself. It

4 St. Lawrence Republican, July 16, 1844.

5 Wright to Van Buren, Apr. 10, 1843, Wright to Flagg, Feb. 25, 1843, Van Buren papers. See also Wright to Van Buren July 14, 1843, Van Buren papers.

was always at the side of Flagg, Dix and Hoffman, the old Regency men, the advocates of the "stop and tax" policy of 1842. He said nothing publicly and wrote only to his closest personal friends in New York, but he never let these friends wonder where his sentiments lay. When, for example, an intra-party squabble broke out over the rich state printing monopoly between Croswell and H. H. Van Dyke, a supporter of the radical program, he kept clear of it, but wrote to Van Buren expressing disapproval of Croswell. " I can tell our friend C.," he said, " that any triumph of himself or his paper over such opponents will prove to him as bad as some of his other specu-lations. . . ." He *could* have told this to Croswell, but he did not. At another time he wrote, " I fear we have yet a great battle to fight upon our State financial questions, before we can feel sound and safe. . . ." But again, it was to *Van Buren* that he penned these words.[6]

Perhaps because he never interfered, as time went on and his national stature grew, the conservatives became more tol-erant of him than they had been in the past. If they did not feel that he was one of them, they at least were fairly sure that he was too busy with national affairs to bother with New York. His renomination by the party caucus in 1843 had been unani-mous, a great change from the bitter struggle of 1837. He had become an almost unique figure in the New York Democracy, a man satisfactory to nearly all its members.

The conditions in the state which were causing the party rift have already been described. The trouble resulted from an infiltration of the old Clintonian ideas into the regular Demo-cratic lines. The large scale internal improvement policy in-augurated so many years before by De Witt Clinton had taken an especially strong hold. The "stop and tax" law of 1842 had been a victory for the old Democratic policy, but since its passage, there had been much dissatisfaction with its operation. Many Democrats had only espoused it because it was the best

6 Wright to Flagg, Oct. 15, 1843, Flagg papers; Wright to Van Buren, Jan. 27, Oct. 2, 1843, Van Buren papers.

practical way to attack the Whigs and their "$40,000,000 debt." Once they had regained power, they sought to modify it. Governor Bouck, as a former canal commissioner, was not averse to some extension of the New York waterway network through borrowing, for many of his supporters came from areas where canal construction was popular. But he had been elected on a "stop and tax" platform. As a result, he tried to steer a middle course, paying lip service to the official party stand, but suggesting special cases and exceptions where construction might be "good economy." This kind of talk pleased the conservatives, who were beginning to be known as Hunkers, a name first applied by their enemies and probably referring to their "hunkering" after office, thought it is hard to see how this was a distinguishing characteristic of any one group.[7] These Hunkers looked upon themselves as moderates. "We steer between Scylla and Charybdis," wrote Daniel S. Dickinson, Bouck's running-mate in 1842. "The ultra speculating improvement people will want their particular work put through at any sacrifice of money, credit, or honor; and another class will probably desire to go as far the other way; but both should be avoided. . . .We are committed to the [stop and tax] policy, but we should be careful to use it as not abusing it." But a stand like this was naturally very irritating to the radicals, who wanted the "stop and tax" program to be rigidly applied. A movement developed within this faction to get rid of Bouck as soon as possible. Marcy, to whom principles were always less important than practical politics, watched this opposition to Bouck with concern. "Though the Gov. has many warm & decided friends," he wrote confidentially, "he has more opponents than he ought to have and too many are indifferent to his fate. It seems to be generally un-

---

7 Members of the other element of the party gradually came to be known as Barnburners, expressing the feeling that they were impractical idealists, willing to burn down the barn (destroy the party), to eliminate the rats (the faction that did not agree with their ideas). This name, however, did not become common until after the election of 1846. Donovan, *Barnburners*, pp. 32-3.

derstood that the state-officers—particularly Flagg & Young occupy antagonistical positions in relation to him. . . ." Marcy thought Bouck ought "to put himself right" on the anti-debt policy, and was so confirmed an opportunist himself that he could not imagine the Governor doing otherwise. Bouck no doubt tried to do so, but he could not bring himself to support a complete stoppage of further internal improvements with real warmth, and the movement against him continued.[8]

The spearhead of this drive was a new newspaper, the *Albany Evening Atlas*. The *Atlas* had been born in 1841, but not until two years later, when it came under the control of James French and William Cassidy, two young members of the radical faction, did it assume an important place in state politics. This new paper reflected the opposition to Bouck, which by the spring of 1844 was becoming very alarming.[9] Once again, as in 1840 and 1842, the man whom the radicals wanted for Governor was Wright. In March Wright complained to Van Buren about the letters he was receiving urging him to accept the nomination. He replied to these letters by refusing to consider running under any circumstances. " Of one thing I feel quite sure," he wrote confidently to Van Buren, " and that is that I shall hear no more from Albany about my being a candidate for Governor."

When Wright was brought forward, the Hunkers were placed in a difficult position. They wanted to run Bouck again, feeling that he stood for moderation and for a " sensible " attitude toward canals, but Wright was so popular, and he had been so polite and unoffending in his relations with all groups in New York, that they could not protest openly against him. So when Wright began to be mentioned, Bouck manfully of-

8 Hammond, *History of New York*, III, 323-4, 384-5; Marcy to Wetmore, Sept. 20, 1843, Marcy papers.

9 Hammond, *History of New York*, III, 348. See for example, the *Atlas*, May 27, 1844, claiming that Bouck had lobbied secretly against the Stop and Tax Law.

fered to withdraw in his favor, though he wanted another term very much.[10] This was in April, 1844.

The pressure on Wright was by this time so great that he finally wrote to Croswell asking him to publish in the *Argus* a statement that he was not a candidate for Governor, and that he disavowed all efforts made in his behalf. Croswell, who was very anxious that Bouck should be renominated, gladly complied. The Senator's forthright refusal was pleasing to the Hunkers. Once again it was Marcy, looking at the situation with his detached point of view, who saw things most clearly. " Mr. Wright is now the only man talked of [to replace Bouck]," the former Governor wrote to a friend. " He cannot be prevailed on to consent. . .and if he could, I should fear the result. He must be brought up on the ruins of Gov. B and would not be cordially supported by a portion of the Govr.'s personal friends. . . . [Wright] is as averse to be a candidate as I am to have him. Those who would thrust him into that position may be his friends but they are really his worst enemies." [11]

The radicals, who had liked using Wright's name because the Hunkers dared not criticize it, continued to press for a new Governor. They respected for the time the Senator's wish that he be kept clear of that office but they were at a loss to find anyone else who suited them. " The course of the Gov. and the Argus has done much to create division & wreck the party," wrote Joel Turrill, of Oswego, bitterly during the spring. " It would be a happy circumstance for us if we had some good man upon whom we could all unite for Gov." [12] Unfortunately he had no one to suggest. The *Atlas* faced the same problem. On May 27, the very date on which the Baltimore convention began its deliberations, it published a scathing attack on Bouck, and demanded a new candidate for November, but it named no

10 Wright to Van Buren Mar. 22, 1844, Van Buren papers ; Donovan, *Barnburners*, p. 58.

11 *Argus*, May 8, 1844 ; Marcy to Wetmore, May 9, 1844, Marcy papers.

12 J. Turrill to Flagg, May 25, 1844, Flagg papers.

one. The split in the party had proceeded so far that there seemed to be no candidate on whom all could agree. Any radical presented by the anti-Bouck men would probably be so distasteful to the Hunkers that they would bolt, just as Tallmadge and the Conservatives had done in 1837. Even the bitterest opponents of Bouck thought twice when they realized that a break might cost them the national election.

But the events at Baltimore changed the situation completely. Van Buren would not be running for President after all. Looked at in either of two ways, this encouraged the radicals to press the nomination on Wright. From one point of view, it relieved them of the fear of hurting Van Buren in case a schism should result. From another, it gave them a strong weapon with which to force Wright to accept and to make the Hunkers abandon Bouck. The state was now in grave danger of going Whig. Instead of Van Buren and a policy opposed to annexation, the party was burdened with Polk (not very well known in New York) and a platform which called for the annexation of Texas "at the earliest practical moment." Van Buren, as the popular choice of the Northern Democracy, might have been counted upon to carry the state for almost any gubernatorial candidate who received merely perfunctory party support, but with Polk leading the fight against the dynamic Clay, a strong candidate was practically essential. So the radicals had now a very strong case when they said that Wright was needed not because Bouck was "unsound" but because the national ticket needed strengthening.

Wright anticipated such an argument and decided that as soon as he arrived home from Washington he would put his name "unequivocally at rest." In his previous statement in the *Argus* he had not actually refused to run, but had only said that he was not a candidate. He had hedged to this extent because he did not want to irritate his radical friends by a public refusal as long as he thought that Van Buren would be nominated for President. He was fairly certain that with Van Buren heading the Democratic slate the radicals would accept Bouck in the end rather than smash the organization. In other words, he knew that the Hunkers had the upper hand, that there was too much at stake to risk driving them out of the party, and he wanted to let the radicals down easily. With the tables turned, it was time to come out once and for all and state his position without equivocation. This was his intention when he and Clarissa stopped off at Kinderhook on their way north in June.

Together with John A. Dix, they arrived at Lindenwald, Van Buren's country seat, on a Sunday. For the day, politics were taboo, but the next morning, after Dix had left, Wright broached the subject to the Magician, telling him that he intended to stop at Albany the next day to put his name permanently at rest with a conclusive statement in the *Argus*.

Van Buren admitted that he had expected as much, but advised careful consideration before adding anything to what he had said in the spring. Wright could see that his friend was very concerned. They left the house for a walk in the woods, talking things over as they went. Finally they sat down on a log and had it out.

" Little Van " thought Silas to be in a very difficult position. There was, he said, grave danger of carrying a " policy of declination " too far. The former President talked about the national aspects of the situation, warning Wright that people might easily interpret a refusal on his part as a lack of interest in Polk's success. Coming on top of his recent experience in New York, this hit the mark. Van Buren's arguments could not fail to influence a man like Wright whose loyalty to the party and its ideals was almost a religion. Unable to offer any rebuttal, Silas had to turn to personal matters, emphasizing his desire to keep out of the Albany squabbles, and the " utter repugnance " of Clarissa towards the idea of being the First Lady of New York.

His friend replied by saying that he, Wright, might well consider such matters, but he could not expect the public to do so. He even tried to convince Wright that the political turmoil at Washington during the coming two years would probably be even worse than at Albany! No matter what poor Silas said, the glib Van Buren had a ready answer.

Finally, Wright played his last card. " I tried to convince him," he wrote later in telling about this interview, " that I was not, and could not be, as important a man in the Nation as he seemed to assume I was, but he said that it was unimportant that he and I should discuss that point; that neither of us could see into the future, but that what was now was not matter of dispute, and I must not shut my eyes to it. . . ." There was no contradicting this, and Wright was beaten. He did make his friend agree not to urge his name on anyone, but he in turn promised to say nothing publicly, at least for the present. He no doubt hoped that by some miracle his letter to the *Argus* in the spring would protect him. The next day he left Lindenwald, and passed on to Albany, but he said nothing to any of his friends there about the governorship. Then he set out for Weybridge and Montreal, and for three weeks he lost track of political developments completely.[13]

During this hiatus events moved swiftly. On the fourth of July, a Democratic meeting was held in Columbia (Van Buren's home county) which was attended by one of the Little Magician's sons, and addressed by John Dix. At this assemblage resolutions were presented and passed naming Wright as the gubernatorial choice of Columbia Democrats. The gathering proved to be the opening gun of a determined offensive by the radicals to force the nomination upon him. The Hunkers, of course, were far from pleased. The *Argus* delayed reporting on the Columbia proceedings for two full weeks, and then criticized the movement as contrary to Wright's wishes. But Croswell was careful not to attack Wright in any way; he admitted that the Senator was worthy of any office which New York could bestow. All he could do was to refer to Wright's notice of the previous May, and squirm.[14]

13 J. C. Rives to Wright, Apr. 18, 1846, Van Buren papers; Wright to Marcy, Sept. 13, 1844, Marcy papers.

14 *Atlas*, July 5, 1844 and July and August, *passim; Argus*, July 18, 1844.

The Columbia rally brought things to a head. All over the state, radicals were asking one big question: would Wright accept the nomination if it was offered? As pressure and publicity were applied by the leaders, the rank and file began to respond. Wright had always been popular enough, but his recent self-sacrificing refusals of so many high offices for the good of the party had made him its darling. "The movement yesterday," wrote a Kinderhook Democrat after the meeting on the Fourth, "was the movement of the people. It was open canvass without an individual dissenting....the resolution nominating him was received with a great degree of enthusiasm." [15]

Wright knew nothing of all this, for he did not see a New York paper or receive any mail from the time he left Albany until July 13 when he crossed back into the United States at Ogdensburg, on the road from Montreal to Canton. No sooner had he reached Ogdensburg that his friends there, in great concern, showed him a copy of the Columbia proceedings. He was very disturbed, especially when he realized that people would connect his visit to Van Buren at Kinderhook with the meeting and with young Van Buren's appearance at it, and with Dix's speech. Then and there, despite Van Buren's convincing arguments in the woods of Lindenwald, and with the full agreement of his friends, he determined to set the use of his name definitely at rest. When he reached home later in the day, he discovered about a hundred letters waiting for him, over half of which dealt with this vexing question. They represented all varieties of opinion. Some were from close friends, asking if the Columbia resolutions meant that he had changed his mind; others stressed the importance of the national election and told him that he owed it to the party to run. Many put more emphasis on getting rid of Bouck than anything else. A letter from Dix dwelt upon the rumors which were being bruited about concerning Silas' visit to Kinderhook. There

15 J. Beekman to Flagg, July 5, 1844, Flagg papers.

were also letters from Bouck partisans and in the main, Wright believed these to be written in an honest spirit of inquiry. One was from Croswell. As soon as he could find a minute, Wright answered this one, telling the editor that his opinions and desires had not changed, and asking him to repeat the notice stating that he was not a candidate which had been published the previous May. This Croswell did on July 24.[16]

Wright had to put aside most of his correspondence and leave Canton for several days to speak at some local rallies which had been arranged while he was travelling home. With Preston King and Ransom H. Gillet he addressed gatherings at the towns of Gouveneur and Potsdam, and he spoke with King alone at Massena.[17] When he got back he found another fifty odd letters, with more arriving in every mail. His correspondence was approaching the volume it maintained when he was in Washington. These new messages were of a different tone from the earlier ones, for Bouck's friends were beginning to fear that Wright really wanted the nomination and only desired to be coaxed a little before accepting. The "Wright is public property" notes increased in number too. Since there were many more communications than he could answer individually, he decided to publish immediately a positive refusal to accept the nomination in the St. Lawrence Republican. It was then the first of August.

The notice he prepared referred to his earlier pronouncement in the Argus, and proclaimed his intention to end all doubt as to his stand. "I am not a candidate," he wrote, "and I have no right, in my judgment, to become [one]." When this flat statement reached Ogdensburg, Judge John Fine, Preston King, and some of Wright's other local disciples read it—and on their own responsibility decided to withhold it. They had changed their minds since July 13, and no longer

16 *Argus,* July 24, 1844. The account of Wright's action is based on Wright to Marcy, Sept. 13, 1844, Marcy papers and Wright to T. Burt, Aug. 6, 1844, Gillet, *Wright,* II, 1555-7.

17 Gillet to Polk, July 20, 1844, Polk papers, 2nd series.

believed he had a right to withdraw. They now considered the primary objective to be to " secure to [the] ticket the unanimous & cordial support of the democracy," and said that if this meant Wright for Governor, he should submit. King hastened to Canton and suggested as a compromise that Wright prepare a note to the *Argus* (with a copy for the *Atlas*) refusing to run, which he, King, should take to Albany to show to Bouck, Croswell and Marcy, who was by this time identified with the Hunker faction. If these men agreed that Wright's withdrawal was necessary for harmony, the letter would be published. This plan was perfectly satisfactory to Silas, and the next day he sent the required letter to King at Ogdensburg. But again his associates there demurred. Either they had changed their opinions once again, or else King had committed them to a policy they would not support. They simply urged Wright to add nothing to what he had already said.[18]

Time was passing, and to the Senator the attitude of his friends seemed merely dilatory. He wrote again for the *Republican* a definite withdrawal. Still his advisers would not relent. Judge Fine wrote suggesting a modification of the statement. It was small but important. Where Wright had said " I have no right. . .to become [a candidate]" Fine made it read like this : " I have no right. . .to become, and cannot under any circumstances, consent to be made a competitor for the nomination, either before the people, or the state convention, against any republican who is, or may become a candidate."

Wright was now really perplexed. He wanted to call on Flagg and Van Buren, his old standbys, for advice, but he refrained from doing so for the same reasons which had held his pen when he had been tempted by Tyler's offer of the seat on the Supreme Court. It was very difficult for him to disregard the strong objections of his North Country comrades, most of whom he had known and respected for years. He still wanted to go the whole way, for he realized that Fine's modification

18 Hammond, *History of New York*, III, 486-8; P. King to Marcy, Aug. 14, 1844, Marcy papers.

would destroy the whole force of what he had said, but the repeated urging of Fine and King, and the memory of his talk with Van Buren at Kinderhook probably had a cumulative effect, and he finally relented. In the August 8 issue of the *Republican,* the revised notice appeared, and was printed shortly afterward in Democratic papers all over the state.[19] Wright was relieved that it was finally decided and he wrote to Fine expressing his thanks for the help which the Judge and his other backers had given.

> This strife between personal inclination and interest and public duty, disturbs a man's judgment and makes him a very unsafe counsellor for himself. At such times it is that he requires, frank, faithful, and disinterested friends; and I really do not think there was ever a man . . . so well supplied as I have been upon this occasion.[20]

Wright really wished that his new letter would quiet the demands of the radicals, but he knew it was a hedging statement that would satisfy neither side. The varying interpretations given to it are well illustrated by the reaction of the *Argus* and that of the *Atlas.* Croswell took it as a flat refusal and criticized harshly the "*organized clique,*" acting in "*a true Iago spirit,*" which was trying to "*sow seeds of discord.*" The *Atlas* admitted that Wright should not be made to compete for the nomination. But there were, it said, divisions in the Democratic ranks which threatened the party's success, and Wright was the only man "whose position has placed him above the influence of all that was factious in these divisions." Through the rest of the summer, each journal reprinted copious reports of meetings in various parts of the state, the *Argus* featuring Bouck gatherings, the *Atlas* Wright ones. All over the state, other Hunker and radical sheets did likewise. Prob-

19 Wright to Flagg, Aug. 7, 1844, Flagg papers; Hammond, *History of New York,* III, 489n.; *St. Lawrence Republican,* Aug. 8, 1844. See also King to Marcy, Aug. 14, 1844, Marcy papers.

20 Wright to Fine, Aug. 8, 1844, Hammond, *History of New York,* III, 489n.

ably the only Democratic press in all New York which lived up to the spirit of Wright's letter was the *St. Lawrence Republican*, and St. Lawrence was the only county that tried to be impartial. Its local convention, held at Canton on August 22, passed resolutions condemning the want of harmony so noticeable in most Democratic papers and promising " hearty, zealous, and united support " to whatever candidate the state convention should select.[21]

As the date of the convention at Syracuse approached, the motives activating the various groups became clearer. To a man like Michael Hoffman, representing the extreme radical wing of the party, the defeat of the Hunkers was the main object. " Conservatism in this state is the bought slave of the Tyler Cabinet," he wrote angrily to Flagg, adding that only the candidacy of Wright could " cut [us]...loose from that tangling foreign alliance." Then he concluded ominously, " I am not unmindful of the presidential election—but I deny that the State election is subordinate to it." To other radicals Wright's nomination was merely a matter of democracy in action. Jonas Earll, Silas' old friend and former room-mate at Albany and Washington, put it this way. " A great majority of the democratic party...want some other candidate than the present executive for Governor." Wright, he said, was the people's choice. John A. Dix saw it as a matter of party harmony. Bouck's friends, he thought, would see clearly that their man could not control a majority of the coming convention. " Will not [they]...then say at once, we will go for Wright?...I feel confident...that we have nothing to fear from defection in our own ranks." [22]

On the other side, many Bouck supporters considered that Wright's great popularity was merely being used to create dissatisfaction with their man. Marcy expressed this point of

21 *Argus*, Aug. 12, 1844; *Atlas*, Aug. 10, 1844; *St. Lawrence Republican*, Aug. 27, Sept. 10, 1844.

22 Hoffman to Flagg Aug. 26, 1844, Earll to Flagg, Aug. 26, 1844, Dix to Flagg, Aug. 25, 1844, Flagg papers.

view. The anti-Bouck men, he said, were "artfully using the name of Mr. Wright...to get delegates against him [Bouck] & by this means prevent his nomination after Mr. W's name is withdrawn, as I have not the least doubt it will be." He hoped that Wright would step in and "explode the plot," for nearly all of the Governor's backers conceded that Wright himself was not interested in hurting their candidate.[23]

Governor Bouck was unable to accept the situation philosophically. After his offer to withdraw had been turned down by Wright, he had assumed that the way was clear, and he found himself in a very embarrassing position now that the opposition to him was so determined. He could not speak openly against Wright because of the Senator's obvious desire to avoid the nomination, but it was only natural for him to be jealous of his unwilling rival's popularity. Where most Van Buren men were pleased when Wright spurned the Vice-Presidential nomination, Bouck was understandably disappointed. "It is a source of regret that Mr. Wright did not consent to be a Candidate," he wrote to Polk. "Some speak of it with severity," he added almost hopefully. And later, when the campaign was over and Wright had been nominated, Bouck wrote unhappily, "Although he said that he would not be a competitor before the people...yet not a newspaper reached him which did not show him that he was my competitor...."[24]

23 Marcy to Wetmore July 20, 1844, Marcy papers; Gallup to Polk, Aug. 14, 1844, Polk papers, 2nd series.

24 Bouck to Polk, June 3, 1844, Sept. 7, 1844, Polk papers, 1st series. In justification of Bouck's attitude it must be admitted that many of the radicals utterly disregarded the spirit of Wright's letter of August 8. Preston King, for example, wrote letters during late August and early September urging that Wright be nominated, and saying that he could be brought to accept if enough pressure was applied. But Wright was ignorant of this and hostile to its intent. "Let me assure you," he wrote to a Hunker friend who was supporting the incumbent, "that, so far from taking exception against you or any of your friends for favoring the renomination of Gov. Bouck, those were the persons who were far more favoring my wishes than those who persisted in the use of my name...." Wright to Corning, Sept. 11, 1844, Gillet, *Wright*, II, 1587-9.

The reason most Democrats favored Wright lay in the national situation. New York's primary importance was apparent to all, for there was little chance that either Polk or Clay could win without New York's thirty-six electoral votes.[45] Most observers were convinced that Wright would make the difference between victory and defeat in the Empire State for the Democrats. One party man, describing himself as " a genuine son of the Emerald Isle," whose business took him frequently back and forth across the state, informed Polk that in his estimation Wright's name would be worth 20,000 votes in November. Another man with a less extensive but probably more intimate knowledge, predicted that the Senator could poll 500 more votes in his county than Bouck. A Calhoun Democrat in New York City supported Wright because he thought his nomination would mollify the die-hard Van Buren men and save the state for Polk, and Cave Johnson, who managed Polk's campaign, wrote to the candidate late in August that his ability to carry New York depended on the nomination of Wright for Governor.[26]

The Whigs too realized the effect which the candidacy of the popular Canton politician might have on the race. Horace Greeley thought that his nomination " added immensely to Mr. Polk's strength," and an observer in New York City said that the Whigs there were " aghast " at the very thought of having to buck as strong a foe as the Senator. One Democrat even quoted Daniel Webster as saying, " if Silas Wright would consent to run for Governor of the state, Mr. Clay might give up the Ship." [27]

25 See for example, Marcy to Flagg, Oct. 11, 1844, Flagg papers.

26 J. Costigan to Polk, July 15, 1844, Polk papers, 1st series; Beekman to Flagg, July 15, 1844, Flagg papers; F. Byrdsall to Polk, Aug. 10, 1844, Polk papers, 1st series, C. Johnson to Polk, Aug. 29, 1844, Polk papers, 2nd series.

27 Greeley, *Recollections of a Busy Life*, p. 161; A. Gallup to Polk, Sept. 5, 1844, Polk papers, 2nd series; Costigan to Polk, July 15, 1844, Polk papers, 1st series. But compare C. Davis to Crittenden, Sept. 7, 1844, Crittenden papers, Library of Congress.

Wright's own position did not change in the month between the publication of his letter and the meeting of the Syracuse convention early in September. He devoted his time almost entirely to stumping for Polk. But when Horace Allen and John L. Russell, the St. Lawrence County delegates, left Canton for the convention, they carried with them letters which constituted Wright's last word on the gubernatorial situation. " I entertain the confident hope that you will not, under any circumstances, feel it to be your duty. . .to place my name before the convention at all," these messages ran. If any conflict arises over the choice, " I not only authorize severally, but enjoin it upon you. . .to withdraw it wholly. . . .The only right of of our party to command the use of my name. . .is to secure. . . harmony of feeling and action. . . ." Allen also had another letter, this one confidential.

> If the nomination of Gov. Bouck can be made satisfactory to the convention and our party, I shall be most happy at such a result. . . . [I insist] that my name should not be used . . . but with the free assent of the friends of all other candidates, and most especially those of Gov. Bouck. . . .
>
> I cannot, as I have said, express more reluctance than I feel against being a candidate for this office, under any circumstances . . . [and I] hope that Mr. Russell and yourself will find it consistent with your sense of your responsible duties as members of the convention, so far from using efforts to throw this nomination upon me, to be the means of averting that result. . . .

This was his last card, played in desperation, but it was useless. A sizeable majority of the delegates were for him, and Russell and Allen ignored their specific orders and campaigned for him openly, even when it was clear that Bouck's supporters would not abandon the contest without a ballot. A vote was taken, Wright winning 95 to 30, and then Horatio Seymour, leader of the Bouck forces, acknowledged defeat by moving that the nomination be made unanimous. Addison Gardiner, a judge of the circuit court, was chosen to make the run for

Lieutenant Governor and the meeting adjourned in what appeared to be harmony.[28] Everyone seemed pleased. In New York City, a visiting Democrat from the deep South reported that the announcement of the nomination was greeted with " such an acclamation of joy [as] perhaps never was heard, the whole earth resounding with echo's [sic] for *Polk & Dallas.*" Even Charles A. Davis, a devoted Whig and the creator of " Major Jack Downing " (whose letters had lampooned Jackson so effectively) admitted that the Democrats were now using their " biggest gun," though he did comment sarcastically to John Crittenden that Wright was " but the piper thro' which Van Buren whistled." The *Atlas* extended a brotherly hand to the Hunkers, proclaiming that Wright's name offered " a point of union to the whole democratic body under which they can march, like brethren, shoulder to shoulder, in solid, unbroken array, to the victory that ever awaits their united efforts." The *Argus* was less ecstatic, but tried to accept Wright with good grace. Croswell, who attended the meeting at Syracuse personally, wrote privately that the spirit there was fine and that all groups seemed eager to "bury their differences." Marcy, even though he had thought that Bouck deserved another term, wrote ebulliently to Polk about the choice of Wright. " The current in the rank and file ran so strong for him. . .that it could not be resisted," he said, and promised the national standard bearer of the party that all would be well in the Empire State as long as the vexatious internal improvements question was kept quiet. Characteristically, Marcy hoped that Wright's position on this subject could be played down. There must be no more new questions, he said. "Minorities may safely experiment." Democrats outside New York recognized the value of the party's choice to the national ticket. Jackson commented enthusiastically when he heard the news that " that great and good man Silas Wright Jur " had

28 Wright to Russell and Allen, Aug. 31, 1844, Wright to Allen, Aug. 31, 1844, Hammond, *History of New York*, III, 746-9; *ibid.*, 492-3; Wright to Russell, March 10, 1846, Gillet, *Wright*, II, 1728; *Argus*, Sept. 7, 1844.

accepted, and Gideon Welles, from Connecticut, expressed a similar sentiment.[29]

Everybody seemed happy but poor Wright. " I cannot describe to you the want of grace, if not gratitude, with which my good wife and myself receive this proposition for further elevation," he wrote to Flagg when he heard the news from Syracuse. To George Bancroft he commented unhappily, " This is one of the fruits of the iniquity at Baltimore," and to Buchanan, he added, " Never has any incident in my public life been so much against my interests, and feelings, and judgment. . . . I do not think. . .that we shall be beaten in this State though I very confidentially apprehend that success will most effectually beat me. . . .Mrs. Wright. . .bids me to tell you she sincerely hopes the Whig governor of this State will be elected." [30]

Wright's understanding of the implications of his nomination was only too clear. He knew that the party was hopelessly divided on state policy, and he knew that he could not compromise with his own position. Up to this point, his careful refusal to become involved had enabled him to keep the friendship and respect of nearly every politician in the party, Hunker as well as radical. Daniel S. Dickinson, Bouck's Lieutenant Governor, was a good friend, and Erastus Corning, the Albany banker, another strong Hunker, managed his personal finances and maintained an active correspondence with him. As usual, the opinion of William L. Marcy was probably the most accurate summation of the party's feeling toward Wright. Marcy called Silas, in a private letter to a trusted associate, " the

29 *Atlas*, Sept. 6, 1844; Croswell to Polk, Sept. 6, 1844, Polk papers, 2nd series; A. Young to Polk, Oct. 27, 1844, Polk papers, 1st series; Davis to Crittenden, Sept. 7, 1844, Crittenden papers; Marcy to Polk, Sept. 11, 1844, Polk papers, 1st series; Jackson to Van Buren, Oct. 2, 1844, Welles to Van Buren, Nov. 3, 1844, Van Buren papers.

30 Wright to Flagg, Sept. 10, 1844, Flagg papers; Wright to Bancroft, Sept. 11, 1844, Bancroft papers; Wright to Buchanan, Sept. 23, 1844, G. Curtis, *Life of Buchanan*, I, 522.

most perfect specimen of a democrat in the nation, and one of
its ablest statesmen."

As long as he could remain *Senator* Wright, primarily a national figure, he could keep this universal approval, for the
New York Democrats were still substantially agreed on most
national problems. But once he had to take an active part in
the local troubles of the party, his popularity was doomed.
When he said in one note shortly after his nomination, " defeat would be the best thing for me," he was only demonstrating that his political sagacity had not diminished with the
years.[31] His natural pessimism in the face of the novel had
this time a solid basis in reality.

There was but one consolation—his new-found faith in the
Northern segment of the Democratic party as the guardian of
the principles in which he believed.

> The only safe hope and dependence for the republican prin-
> ciple in this country, from this time forth [he wrote to George
> Bancroft] rests upon the democracy of the North; and the
> deep conviction that the result of the pending election, and
> especially in this State, must most materially influence the
> future, as to the resting place for that hope and confidence,
> which must rest somewhere, or be lost, has forced me to sub-
> mit myself to almost any thing which should seem to promise
> security for the vote of this State.[31]

It is perhaps fortunate that he did not live to see how completely the Democratic party of the North failed to live up to
his expectations.

31 Marcy to Wetmore, May 9, 1844, Marcy papers; Wright to Dickinson,
Oct. 9, 1844, *Dickinson Correspondence*, J. Dickinson, ed., II, 371.

32 Wright to Bancroft, Sept. 11, 1844, Bancroft papers.

CHAPTER XIV

AN UNWANTED VICTORY

" Personal considerations... [make] the triumph far from joyful."
Wright to Azariah Flagg, November 12, 1844.

THE nomination of Wright settled for the time the troubles within the Democratic party. A few days later, the Whigs chose Millard Fillmore, " a vain and handsome mediocrity," as their standard bearer for the state campaign.[1] But the election in New York was to be no simple two party duel. In 1844 there were three minor groups with special interests which put forth tickets. These were the Liberty party, made up of abolitionists, the American Republican party, dedicated to anti-Catholicism and xenophobia, and the Anti-Rent party, an outgrowth of the almost feudal conditions which still existed on some of the large estates in the middle Hudson valley. None of these " one-idea " groups could be expected to carry the state—in fact only the abolitionists even drew up state and national slates—but each was important for the effect which it might have on the delicate balance of political power.

Nationally, the issues of the struggle between Polk and Clay were expressed in the slogan, " The Reannexation of Texas and the Reoccupation of Oregon," but in New York, neither of these two questions attracted much attention. The party was too closely connected with Van Buren to go heartily for Texas, and the Oregon problem, where American interests clashed with those of Great Britain, was subordinated because many New Yorkers feared that an altercation with England might mean war, and war could conceivably bring an invasion of the state from Canada. So the battle in the Empire State

1 Hammond, *History of New York*, III, 494-5; Van Deusen, *Weed*, opp. p. 150.

was conducted basically on the old lines of bank and tariff, an arrangement satisfactory to both parties.[2]

Of course an important element in the fight was the exciting but irrelevant effort made on all sides to stir up popular interest and enthusiasm. The Log Cabin campaign had taught all the politicians a lesson in psychology they were never to forget. All over the state " Clay Clubs " were formed by the Whigs and the Democrats in turn spiked the state from Buffalo to New York with hickory poles in honor of " Young Hickory " Polk, the protégé of their famous old leader. The contest had already been under way for many months when the state nominations were finally decided upon. Even in January, Wright had written worriedly to Flagg (who as usual directed Democratic operations in New York) " Everything indicates a plan of campaign similar to 1840, with the slight exception that the term ' Club House ' is to take the place of ' log cabin.' " Since 1840 Wright's fear of Whig treachery had been almost neurotic, and he now claimed to notice many signs of nefarious activity. A thief had stolen a mass of letters from the Albany Post Office and when they were recovered, a list of the addressees was published. Wright discovered that a large number of these epistles had been addressed to Horace Greeley, whose new paper, the *New York Tribune,* was already a leading Whig organ. This meant, he warned Flagg, that up-state New Yorkers and Vermonters were ordering the *Tribune.* Probably this was the work of the new Clay Clubs, for few farmers would be ordering papers on their own at that time of the year. Wright reported hearing that 1500 subscriptions to Greeley's sheet had been procured in Cayuga County, and what was infinitely more shocking, even some St. Lawrence County farmers had subscribed! Also, Wright said that he could see a great increase in the activity of enemy Congressmen at Washington. He did a little snooping around the Senate folding rooms, where documents were perpared for mailing. There he learned that most of the Whig senators were ordering "a vast quantity " of envelopes, but were sending no documents to be folded for these envelopes. He investigated a little further and discovered that in the mornings before Congress convened the Senate committee rooms were crowded with Whigs addressing these mysterious envelopes, and that huge stacks were piled about waiting for the postman. " Garbled extracts from the printed documents of Congress. . .fill these genteel envelopes," he warned Flagg. All this, Wright thought, was being financed by British investors in defunct state bonds, who believed that Clay's professed fondness for distribution offered them hope of recouping on some of the defaulted securities which they held. The explanation he dreamed up was really lurid. " The ' Club Houses ' are to collect all who can be bought, and the flags and music and coon skins and cider are to form the snake, under cover of which the British Gold is to be distributed." Wright became excited about all this very early in the political season, because he thought that Van Buren would be the Democratic candidate, and his friend's reelection was almost an obsession with him. He always looked on the defeat of 1840 as a gross fraud, and when he saw the slightest sign of a similar campaign developing, he became as panicky as a freshman Congressman about to make his first speech. Democrats complained of the way the Whigs spent money in 1840, he wrote, but " cents were not spent then, where they would spend dollars in this contest." He urged Flagg to be alert. " What can, what shall be done? Millions will be expended on our State alone. Shall we depend on our friends at home to rouse the democracy, put them on their guard against the wiles, and falsehoods and bribes of the enemy? Can our press at Albany be nerved up, and made to lead off in proclaiming the dangers? Will the members begin, at once, to urge our prominent friends in the Counties to organization, and to efforts to strengthen their country press and to extend their circulation?

...these will best distribute our printed matter, and we here shall supply them with what they want...." [3]

A little later in the year he urged Samuel J. Tilden to undertake the job of starting a new newspaper in New York City. Again the big problem was the *Argus,* which aside from local troubles, never could satisfy Wright with its attitude toward national financial policy. He suggested New York as a better place for a new paper than Albany, for there were already two Democratic journals at the Capital, and the feud between them was so severe that another sheet would be just too much for the poor town. Tilden also consulted Van Buren about the paper and got a similar reaction. A little later, the *Morning News* made its first appearance, edited by Tilden and John L. O'Sullivan, of the *Democratic Review.*

Under O'Sullivan and Tilden, the *News* injected a good deal of life into the campaign. The editors quickly demonstrated that they knew how to attack the enemy where he was most vulnerable. In an editorial entitled, " A Lesson in Grammar," on September 3, they poked fun shrewdly at Clay's " Alabama letters," in which he was trying to modify the anti-annexation stand of his letter from Raleigh. The grammar lesson consisted of a dialogue between a school teacher and a very precocious pupil:

" *Master.*—How many degrees of comparison are there? "

" *Boy.*—Three."

" *Master.*—What are they? "

" *Boy.*—Positive, Comparative, and Superlative."

" *Master.*—Give an example."

" *Boy.*—*Positive*—RALEIGH. April 17.... [Here followed liberal quotations from Clay's Raleigh letter, opposing annexation.]"

" *Comparative*—ASHLAND, July 1st ' Personally I could have no objection to the annexation of Texas.' "

3 Wright to Flagg, Jan. 23, 1844, Flagg papers.

"*Superlative*—ASHLAND, July 27th 'Far from having any personal objection to the annexation of Texas, I should be glad to see it.' " [4]

Because of its unswerving support of Polk and the radical branch of the New York Democracy, the *News* was a great help during the election year.

By the time Wright reached home in July the race was on full tilt. Partly to smother once and for all the rumor that he was not reconciled to the candidacy of Polk, and also because he thought it would help to keep him out of the Governor's chair, he had thrown himself into the distasteful task of stump speaking with great energy. Throughout August he spoke in towns and villages all over northern and western New York. Especially in the North Country, his tour assumed the nature of a triumphal procession. But he had no heart for elaborate receptions. " I have on some occasions, when attending meetings at remote places, found that committees have thought it necessary to treat me with some ceremony," he wrote to the chairman of one rally at which he had agreed to speak. " All this I entreat your committee to omit wholly. I will come to your village in time, and desire to come just as any other individual democrat does to your meeting, entirely without parade or ceremony."

In spite of his attitude, popular enthusiasm for " the Cato of the Senate " was so great that his arrival at each meeting place was a major event. The election slogans of the North Country show this spirit clearly:

POLK AND DALLAS
St. Lawrence knows what WRIGHT is.

Silas we won't trouble you
Your Wright—without the W.

4 Wright to S. Tilden, Apr. 11, 1844, *Tilden Letters*, J. Bigelow, ed., I, 21-2; J. Bigelow, *Life of Tilden*, I, 108-9; *Morning News*, Sept. 3, 1844. The first issue of the *News* appeared August 21.

Now three cheers for Polk and Dallas,
Gard'ner and our noble Silas,
Men of true Democracy.

Campaign songs were even sung to the tune of the *Star Spangled Banner*:

What is that which we hear, with its hoarse booming sound,
That rends the deep dark veil of midnight asunder!
Tis the cannon's loud roar, as it echoes around,
The patriot's response, with its loud pealing thunder!
Our standard so bright
Bears aloft in the fight
The Star of St. Lawrence, our own SILAS WRIGHT!
With him we'll defy all proud tyranny's powers,
Huzza boys! Huzza boys!—the victory's ours![5]

Probably the most important meeting of Wright's circuit was one held at Watertown, in Jefferson County. This gathering, according to friendly reports, drew some eight or ten thousand people, "all of them men who have votes." The morning of the big day at Watertown was rainy, but the weather cleared in time for the speeches. People poured into the city from all the nearby towns in wagons bearing pennants and displays, each group trying to outdo the others in enthusiasm and originality. St. Lawrence County visitors put on an especially energetic demonstration in honor of Wright. Many of their banners were somewhat incomprehensible, but they got their message across pretty well.

Peace we	War if
love best	oppressed

And,

5 Wright to W. Jewett, July 29, 1844, Gratz collection; *Argus*, July 26; Wright papers, St. Lawrence University; *St. Lawrence Republican*, Oct. 22, 1844; *Rochester Daily Advertiser*, quoted in *St. Lawrence Republican*, Oct. 8, 1844.

Polk and Dallas!
No land Plunder!
No Bank!
Veto.

The names of the principal candidates offered innumerable opportunities for some very unfortunate punning. Everything imaginable was " (W)right " and all sorts of evils were being " Polked " out of existence. One wagon, for example, contained a miniature log cabin in which was imprisoned a live coon, which the occupants of the vehicle were continually " Polking " with hickory " Polkers."

Wright's speech was a plea for a revenue tariff, and is important because it shows the full length of the swing he had taken from his ultra-protectionist stand in 1828. Then he had spoken boldly for agricultural duties, but in 1844, though addressing an audience of farmers, he opposed protection except when incidental to the revenue needs of the nation. Even on wool, he said, the duty must not be prohibitive, because that would give the farmer " a perfect monopoly of the market," and force the consumer to pay for the resultant increase in prices. He would not " raise a monopoly among our farmers any sooner than among our manufacturers....fair healthful competition in every trade and every thing."

The Senator defended his action in urging a lower wool schedule at the recent meeting of Congress on these grounds. Perhaps the most significant demonstration of his change was the stand which he took on the difference between luxuries and necessities. Where in 1828 he had favored completely prohibitive duties on coarse wool, now he called for higher duties on luxury items and lower ones on common grades of cloth. " If you favor either," he told his listeners, " you should favor those who purchase and wear the more necessary article."

Wright cut to the heart of the Whig argument that high tariffs mean high wages. Agricultural produce, he said, cannot be protected because few farm products are imported. So no tariff can enable farmers to pay their laborers higher rates. Though manufacturers may be able to *afford* to raise wages if they are protected from foreign competition, they will not *pay* any more for labor than they have to. Suppose, he said, that a factory owner enjoys a duty of forty or fifty percent on his product. He knows that the farmers in his part of the state pay their workers seven dollars a month.

> Will the manufacturer say, " Here is a farmer; he can't pay more than $7 a month; but I am protected, I can afford $15?" Is that your experience? I doubt not there are many laboring men here. Or will the manufacturer come to you and pay just as little as will hire you away from the farmers? If the farmer pays ten dollars, the manufacturer will pay eleven. But ... will he pay fifteen? My experience is not so ....

It is also misleading to argue that industry will expand so much if protected that its workers will eventually be able to consume all the agricultural products of the country, thus making it possible to raise tariff walls to protect the farmer. If this should happen, Wright claimed, there would be so many manufactured products that the farmers could not buy them all. "Your system is just as bad—only you have changed sides!"

Take England as an example, he suggested shrewdly. First manufacturing was protected and the farmers were badly off. Now, under the Corn laws, farmers are protected, "and the manufacturing labor of the country is starving to death."

You farmers do not want a monopoly, do you? he asked.

" No, no," shouted back the crowd.

" Then the manufacturing and mechanical interest should not...."

Remember, he concluded, what a tariff really is. " Strip it of its imaginary qualities, and the beauties of rhetoric in which they dress it up, and it is a system of taxation...." Taxes are necessary, but they must be fair.

> Tax lightly the necessities of life, and you relieve taxation on the poor and laboring classes. Tax heavily the luxuries,

and you reach property that should bear the heaviest portion of taxation. Where your interests conflict with foreign interests, bear taxation on the foreign article as hard as it will bear, consistent with revenue. You fill the treasury and relieve taxation from another source. What I pay for my coat.... I do not pay on anything else, while I aid an important interest. But the moment you depart from that principle ... I have shown you ... where the mistake must lead.[6]

Though the greater part of his talk was on the tariff, Wright did not ignore the Texas question. He spared nothing in his attack on Calhoun's treaty, but he did say that he was not opposed to annexation in principle. This was perfectly consistent with his own and Van Buren's stand from the beginning. He did not recommend any policy toward Texas at all. "It is a question," he said, "which public opinion should pass upon, and their [sic] servants should obey that popular will." But Wright had very definite ideas about Oregon, which was also part of Polk's program. "I have no more doubt of our right to it than I have that New York is part of this Union," he said flatly. "Let us take Oregon which is ours, and Texas if we choose, on proper and honorable terms."[7] This speech was printed by Democratic papers all over the state and also sold in pamphlet form. "Read it, digest it and *get your Whig neighbors to read it!*" urged the *St. Lawrence Republican,* and high tariff Whigs did so with a good deal of consternation. In New York, for instance, one Whig banker, while claiming sourly, "I don't see that he goes beyond *old truisms* such as any man admits," confessed grudgingly that the speech was "ingenious."[8]

Wright plugged away at his speech-making until the news of his nomination reached him. He had been through the

6 *Argus,* Aug. 23, 1844; *Wright's Speech at Watertown,* pp. 1-6; Gillet, *Wright,* II, 1843-55.

7 Gillet, *Wright,* II, 1862-3

8 C. Davis to Crittenden, Sept. 7, 1844, Crittenden papers.

western part of the state and was on his way back toward
Albany. His next major appearance was to have been at Plattsburg, on September 11. But once the fateful word came, he
cancelled all further appearances and returned to Canton. This
was in accord with the custom of the day; candidates for executive office did not usually speak in their own behalf. It was
" improper in my judgment that I should continue longer upon
the stump," he wrote Flagg. Of course there were other reasons. He never liked open-air campaigning and was glad to
pounce upon any excuse to avoid it. Besides there was a good
deal that would have to be done at home if he were by chance
forced to live for two years at Albany, for a governor's job,
unlike a senator's was a full time affair. He was afraid that
despite tradition, Fillmore might challenge him to a series of
debates. " Mr. Fillmore will be perfectly in the hands of Weed
and will say anything and write anything, which Thurlow
shall dictate," he told Flagg.[9]

He also had to decide whether or not to resign his seat in
the Senate. It had not occurred to him personally, and he cared
little one way or the other himself, but Judge Fine believed
that resignation was the proper action to take, so Silas wrote
Flagg and asked him what the State Central Committee
thought. Both Flagg and Marcy strongly recommended that
he keep his office. If he were to quit and then be defeated
there would be a double loss, for a Whig Governor would
probably mean a Whig legislature as well, and such a body
would of course pick a senator of similar sympathies. The pre-
cedents were all in favor of his keeping his place until after
the election. Both Marcy and Van Buren had been nominated
for the governorship while they were members of the Senate,
and neither had resigned. Silas went along with the advice
from Albany, though he did remark wistfully that a resignation

9 Wright to Flagg, Sept. 10, 1844, Flagg papers, Sept. 25, 1844, Van Buren
papers.

offered him an easy way to retire from politics in case he should be defeated in November.[10]

Once at home, he devoted the greater part of his time to letter writing and to deciding what stand to take on vital state problems. By the end of September, Ransom H. Gillet was writing to Polk that the Senator " goes like a book " at his mail. He was straightforward in expressing his determination to uphold the principles of the " stop and tax " law of 1842. He also favored a constitutional amendment providing that the indebtedness of the state might not be increased without a popular referendum. It was not that there must not be any further canal construction, he wrote in answer to one query, but " if I am charged with opposition to further taxation upon the whole property of the State, to meet the interest upon a new debt to be contracted to go on with these works, the charge is just. . . ." [11]

The Anti-Rent dilemma he could not dispatch in such summary fashion, because his mind was not clear on it. The rent problem was an old one and a very difficult one. Originally, most of the land in the central Hudson valley, including the counties of Columbia, Delaware, Renssalaer and Albany, was held by a few large landlords, and rented to tenant farmers. After the Revolution, some of these great holdings were broken up, but many others were not, and as late as 1848, 1,800,000 acres in this area were cultivated by tenants. These farmers occupied their plots under long term leases, some running for two and even three lifetimes, or forever! Usually the rent was established as a payment in produce, varying from about ten to twenty bushels of wheat a year. In the course of time, families holding property under such leases began to consider

10 *Ibid.*; Wright to Marcy, Sept. 13, 1844, Marcy papers. Weed called repeatedly during the fall for him to resign his seat. See *Journal, passim.*

11 Gillet to Polk, Sept. 23, 1844, Polk papers, 2nd series; Wright to R. Miller, Gillet, *Wright*, II, 1573. See also Wright to Van Buren, Oct. 8, 1844, Van Buren papers.

themselves freeholders and the annual payment to the " lord " as a forced, unjust " feudal " contribution.

Outbreaks of violence were sporadic in the region where these tenures existed all during the early history of the Republic, but this chronic condition did not come to a head until after 1839. That year marked the death of the " Old Patroon," Stephen Van Rensselaer, whose tremendous domains engulfed the better part of two counties, and contained over 3,000 farms. During his lifetime, much of the rent due from these farms went uncollected, for Van Rensselaer seemed to have a genuine feeling for his many tenants. When he died, about $400,000 in back rents was owed to his estate. But after his passing it was discovered that his will provided that these debts should be collected immediately to pay his own obligations, which amounted to about the same figure. It was the effort of his heirs to collect these dues that led to the outbreak of large scale organized violence. Bands of farmers disguised as Indians prevented the seizure of lands and drove off representatives of the owners and even sheriffs sent to post eviction notices. This was the so-called Helderberg, or Manor, War. Governor Seward acted with dispatch to enforce the law and troops were sent into the area. Resistance quickly collapsed and negotiations were undertaken to effect a peaceful settlement. But contemporaries realized that the problem had not been solved. As James Fenimore Cooper, whose interests were involved, and who therefore sided enthusiastically with the landlords, put it, " The Manor War is over for the present, but the evil lies deeper than the surface." [12]

While the parleys went on, the farmers appealed to Albany for remedial legislation to ease their burden and assist them in converting their leases into deeds of outright ownership. The

---

12 Ellis, *Landlords and Farmers in Hudson Mohawk Region*, pp. 227-8; 233-41; Cooper to Mrs. Cooper, Dec. 14, 1839, *Cooper Correspondence*, J. Cooper, ed., p. 408. For a vivid account of the Anti-Rent movement written from the point of view of the tenants, see H. Christman, *Tin Horns and Calico*.

breakdown of farmer-landlord discussions and a discouraging report from a legislative committee in April, 1844, which found the Van Rensselaer title to the lands to be perfect and deplored any forced adjustment as flagrant confiscation, resulted in a renewal of the troubles. At the same time the Anti-Renters began to organize politically, naming candidates for Assembly seats and courting the support of state leaders of both major parties. These conditions naturally made it necessary for Wright to give the whole problem close attention.

In September he received letters from Croswell and from Samuel Young (representing the two extremes within the Democratic party in New York) both warning him that he must expect to be quizzed by the Anti-Renters. The candidate was very upset by this, for he had not followed the situation very closely. He wrote to Young and to Flagg asking for advice. " I have long heard of the Helderberg War," he told the Comptroller, but " nothing which I recollect to have seen gives a statement of the facts about which the troubles arise, or... what the tenants demand, or desire, or expect to obtain, either from the landlords or from the Legislature." It was understandable for him to be in doubt, for the tenants had not been very specific except in saying that they wanted to be rid of the rents. If it were merely a question of converting the rents into a capital sum and paying it to the landlords, Wright said, their demands were reasonable enough, but that did not seem to be the case. " All I have been able to discover is a determined and organized resistance against the collection of Rent. . . ." He did not think it possible that they would dare to espouse such a revolutionary policy as this. As a lawyer he thought that position indefensible. " I am sure," he told Flagg, " these people cannot put themselves upon a ground so broad. . . . Hence I desire all the information which our friends can give me, that I may see what the grounds really are. . .and what they suppose, or expect, the Legislature can do for them."

He was very worried by the news (received from Croswell) that the Renters were organizing local tickets. Croswell was afraid that "Weed & Co." were behind it all, and that the sheriff of Rensselaer County was out to collect votes rather than rents. Wright was certain of one thing, and that was that it was not a matter for political maneuvering. "It appears to me, if called out [to say what we think], we cannot tamper with this matter, be the consequences what they may. . . ." Wright was indeed becoming a very bad politician—nearly everything was getting to be with him a matter of principle.

He struggled hard not to become prejudiced against the rioters. He considered advocating legislative action of some sort, but finally settled on the more cautious policy of calling upon the landlords to offer "reasonable compromises " to their tenants. To propose any program which the legislature might refuse to enact, might destroy any hope of a compromise settlement, he wrote Van Buren. He expressed fear that he would be " left with the anti-renters, with the whigs and our own folks on [his] back." The general position which he took foreshadowed the attitude that he displayed as Governor. No consideration should be given the tenants or their grievances until they ceased to interfere with the enforcement of the laws. This was logical enough, but to the farmers who owed back rent which they could not pay it meant the loss of home and livelihood, and most of them would not bow meekly to logic of that sort. As a result the troubles continued, and when the " Indians " forcefully resisted eviction proceedings, Wright replied with the use of state troops.[13]

* * * * *

As the election drew nearer and nearer, the tension in New York increased in inverse proportion to the time remaining before the opening of the polls. Meetings continued right up to the last few days, despite the approach of winter. The Democrats pressed every possible advantage. As has been said, Texas

13 Ellis, *Landlords and Farmers*, pp. 243-44; Roach, *New York and the Election of 1844*, Columbia University Master's Essay (typescript), p. 118; Wright to Flagg, Sept. 25, 1844, (n. d.) 1844, Flagg papers; Wright to Van Buren, Oct. 8, 1844, Van Buren papers.

was not the big issue in New York but the spirit of expansionism that it represented was exploited. Despite the fact that Wright had come out and stayed out against immediate annexation, the party found nothing inconsistent in associating his popular name with the general idea of adding the Lone Star Republic to the Union. A campaign song sung at a rally at Glen Falls presents an admirable précis of the Democratic platform:

> The Mechanic and the Farmer
> Both have buckled on their armor
> And have gathered here together,
>   Like freemen for the fight;
>
> Against Bank machination
> And high-tariff taxation—
> They will go for Annexation,
>   And Dallas, Polk, and Wright.

The Whigs were well content to fight the battle mainly on the bank and tariff issues. "Fillmore," wrote Thurlow Weed in the *Journal,* " is in favor of Protecting the Industry and of developing the Resources of our State. Under his auspices, the current which is just setting in, would swell, wave upon wave, into a full tide of prosperity. While, on the other hand, should Silas Wright be elected, all the dawning hopes of business would be blasted." Naturally Weed was not satisfied to stop with such sedate reasoning as this. He reminded his readers that Wright had voted against the popular election of presidential electors in 1824, that he had helped in the removal of Clinton as Canal Commissioner, and he printed the notorious " Roorback " story that a gang of chained slaves branded JKP had been seen being marched across the South. Of course he was not alone in this. The newspapers of both camps were filled with all sorts of tales based on a minimum of truth and a maximum of what the editors thought would help one side and hurt the other. It was a very hot campaign.[14]

14 *Argus,* Oct. 17, 1844; *Journal,* Oct. 5, 28, 29, 1844.

Nowhere was the contest carried out with greater zeal than in the North Country. On September 28, the Whigs held a great rally at Potsdam, in St. Lawrence County, which was addressed by William H. Seward and Cassius M. Clay, of Alabama, a cousin of " Harry of the West." Wright told Flagg that the Whigs had been " straining every nerve " for a full week before the meeting to insure a large turnout. As he wrote this letter he could see out the window of his house a procession of Whigs from Canton (there were a few) and some other towns passing by on their way to Potsdam. " Rather noisy but quite civil for Whigs," he conceded grudgingly to his friend.

The Democrats in the area outdid themselves in their efforts to pile up a big majority for Wright. Preston King, Ransom H. Gillet, John Russell and many other local politicians worked with all their might. " It is due to our younger friends in this county," the candidate wrote proudly, " to say that I have never seen men work as they are now working, being the whole time in the field, passing from Town to Town, and School District to School District, and House to House." The Whigs worked hard too, he admitted, but they were " paid from a purse made up in New York, *as we know,* while ours are men who find their own time, teams, and expenses, and go for themselves." [15]

Wright told an interesting story that illustrates the tremendous interest which the whole North Country took in the campaign. Late in October, a group of Vermont cattle-buyers came into St. Lawrence County looking for likely herds. They found the cattle easily enough but they could not hire men to drive them back to Vermont because of the approaching election. No one wanted to lose his vote. To meet this difficulty it was necessary to pair the drivers, Whig and Democrat, so that the absentees would cancel each other out. Wright reported a

15 Wright to Flagg, Oct. 24, 1844, Flagg papers. See also Wright to Buchanan, Sept. 23, 1844, Buchanan papers.

case where two Democrats were hired to move a herd to Vermont and then refused to go because no Whigs were to go with them. The buyer was forced by the men themselves to fire one of them and find an adherent of Clay to take his place! Even when drivers were paired off, the Democratic organization gave those of their number who were to go enough money to pay for stage fare back in case the Whig member " should fail on the way or attempt to cheat." " If we should find a real pipe layer in this Town on Tuesday next," Wright told Flagg on the eve of the election, " I think he would be in personal danger, for a resident whig has a hard enough time now." [16]

By this time, winter had set in in the St. Lawrence River country. On October 31, there was a foot of snow on the ground, but the campaign continued. Wright heard of one sled drawn by thirty yoke of oxen travelling eight miles each way just to attend a meeting. When he asked a local friend of his if he thought the snow would hurt the party on election day, he got this reply, " No, capital, we can track the coons better." And the farmer added with determination, " they may burrow, but the democrats will not."

The ever-cautious Wright did not expect to lose his home district, but he thought that Democratic enthusiasts were betting too much on the outcome and giving too many votes advantage in their wagers. As the big day drew near they were offering as many as 1500 votes in even money bets. Silas thought that 1000 was reasonable, but that 1500 was " hazardous." [17]

Most of his friends and many of his foes thought that Wright would run ahead of the ticket, as in fact he did, but he him-

---

[16] Wright to Flagg, Oct. 29, 1844, Flagg papers. The Whigs also tried hard to insure a full vote for their party. "Absent Whigs, Come Home!" pleaded Weed in the *Journal*. " We call on every WHIG in the State, who is now absent from the town or city in which he resides ... to repair to his home, *without fail*, in time to put in his ballot." *Journal*, Nov. 1, 1844.

[17] Wright to Flagg, Oct. 29, 31, 1844, Flagg papers.

self thought otherwise. " I will not pretend to believe that I am not fairly popular with the democracy of this State," he wrote to Polk, " but with the untrue portion, those whose politics hang on banks, canals and rail roads. . .I never was, and never expect to be a favorite." He told Polk that he expected to run *behind* the national ticket, because that would not be affected by local issues, and to Flagg he wrote, " I would cheerfully bet that the electoral ticket will poll more votes in the State than will be given to me."

The result proved that this wager would have been a bad one. Polk carried the state by about 5,000 ballots, but Wright outscored Fillmore by twice that amount, 241,096 to 231,057. The difference probably was the result of Wright's popularity, although he himself did not think so. He had expected his vote to be less than Polk's because of his stand on state issues, but when he saw that he had run ahead of the ticket, he still thought, with no apparent sense of contradiction, that his position on these matters was responsible for the result! He put it this way : " Many of the most worthy members of the Whig party. . .desire that the policy of 1842 should continue to govern the financial affairs of our State, and consequently do not wish a reascendancy of their own party here, for the present." This, he thought, accounted for his plurality of nearly 1500 over Polk in the City of New York. He also felt that many abolitionists voted for him for Governor while casting their ballots for James Birney for President. The Democrats as a group tried to minimize the difference between the vote for Governor and that for President, because they did not want Polk to think that the party had not supported him as wholeheartedly as it had Wright. The victory, said Croswell in the *Argus,* resulted from " the united, cordial, and untiring efforts of *all* the Democracy of the State." And he added fervently, " We trust that the spirit of the campaign may abide among us; and that we may not mar our triumph. . .by unprofitable dissension or unreasonable jealousy." [18] A vain hope.

18 Wright to Polk, Oct. 31, 1844, Polk papers, 2nd series; Wright to Flagg, Sept. 28, 1844, Flagg papers; Wright to Polk, Dec. 20, 1844, Gillet, *Wright,* II, 1638; *Argus,* Nov. 29, 1844.

So Polk carried New York and with it the nation, and thus became the eleventh President of the United States. There was much speculation at the time (and there still is) over just what enabled Polk to win the vital Empire State. He did not have a majority of all the ballots cast; Birney, the Liberty party man, polled 15,000 votes, three times Polk's lead over Clay. Just how many of these abolitionists would have gone to Clay if Birney had not been a candidate is uncertain. It is usually believed that the Liberty party drew most of its members from the ranks of the Whigs but there is really no proof. Before the election, members of both major parties expressed fear that they would be hurt by Birney—there was no contemporary agreement as to which side would profit from a large anti-slavery turnout. Clay's " Alabama letters," in which he tried to hedge on his previous stand against annexation to attract Southern support, may have induced many Northern Whig opponents of the peculiar institution to change their allegiance, but the fact remains that the Liberty party had decided to run Birney before Clay's letters appeared. At least one Democratic leader thought that the " Alabama letters " were written because Clay thought that it was hopeless to try to hold the anti-slavery Whigs to his standard in any case. Birney himself was much closer ideologically to the Democratic party than to the Whig, anti-slavery aside. During the campaign he spoke plainly against Whig distribution schemes, and called for a low tariff policy. It is certainly possible that this attracted Democrats whose consciences were bothering them because of slavery and repelled some Whigs who might otherwise have become Liberty party men.[19]

The nativist element in New York City also influenced the result, but again there is no way of telling which candidate was helped. "The Whigs nearly unanimously vote the American Republican tickets for Congressmen and Members of the

---

[19] Johnson to Polk, Aug. 29, 1844, Polk papers, 2nd series; McCormac, *Polk*, p. 281.

Legislature, and the American Republicans are generally going for Clay," reported the *New York Evening Mirror*. Many Democrats were included within the folds of the American Republican, or nativist, party, and some may have been attracted into the Clay ranks as the *Mirror* suggested, although at least 2000 voters who cast their ballots for the local nativists also went for Polk. On the other hand, the Whigs seemed to feel that the Irish connected their party exclusively with nativism, and that any gains growing out of the Whig-American Republican alliance were more than counteracted by the large Democratic vote of the "Adopted Citizens."

In general, most Democrats attributed their success to their own efforts and Wright's solidifying influence, preventing schism over local issues. The Whigs blamed the abolitionists and the Irish. Fillmore, Judge Ambrose Spencer, and Philip Hone, all wrote to Clay in these terms. The defeated candidate for Governor emphasized the Liberty party, saying, "Birney and his associates sold themselves to Locofocoism," and Hone expressed the anti-Irish attitude of a typical conservative Manhattanite. "Foreigners," he said bitterly, "have robbed us of our birthright....Ireland has reconquered the country which England lost...." Poor Clay, frustrated for the third time in his lifelong quest of the Presidency, was thoroughly disheartened, but he, at least, had no excuses. He wrote to Seward that it was useless to speculate upon the causes of the debacle, for whatever its origin, the result for him was the same.[20]

Wright felt fully as badly about the outcome of the contest as the Whigs did. "[In my house] personal considerations... [make] the triumph far from joyful," he confessed to Flagg. "I think the case may be likened to a family burned out and left houseless and homeless, with the reflection that the insur-

---

20 *New York Evening Mirror*, quoted in Roach, *Election of 1844*, p. 153; Fillmore to Clay, Nov. 11, 1844, *Clay Correspondence*, Colton, ed., pp. 497-8; Hone to Clay, Nov. 28, 1844, *ibid.*, p. 509. Clay to Seward, Nov. 20, 1844, Seward, *Autobiography*, p. 734.

ance was good and ample. We feel that we are broken up, and do not know exactly how we shall fare in another establishment. Yet I must admit that the wife, as yet, exercises more philosophy than I had expected." [21]

If he himself could have accepted his fate philosophically the course of the next two years in New York politics might have been very different.

* * * * *

Victory meant that Wright was at once faced with the problem of settling his affairs antecedent to moving to Albany. He managed to find a tenant for his Canton house without difficulty, but getting a suitable place for himself was not so easy. He wanted a furnished house, for he did not have the proper appointments for a Governor's Mansion in his own simple home. He had no love for lush surroundings, but he knew that his position would necessitate a fairly elaborate establishment. " I must have a place that will do according to the public feeling and judgment," he said. Yet the idea of buying all the necessary articles was staggering to a man of his limited means. John Dix had supplied Governor Bouck with a complete set of furniture at the modest rate of $300 a year, and he was perfectly willing to continue the arrangement with Wright, but getting a place to put the things proved difficult. Erastus Corning, who handled Wright's financial affairs, had accepted the task of seeking a house. For a while it seemed that he had one, but the owner changed his mind, and as December wore on the Wrights were still unsettled, with Clarissa " in painful suspense about her preparations." In desperation it was decided they would have to live at the Delevan House, Albany's leading hotel, and supply rooms there with furniture suitable for the residence of a Governor on their own. This would involve great expense, but there seemed no alternative. Wright had on deposit with Corning about seven hundred dollars and he hoped to be able to add a little to this, but he was afraid

21 Wright to Flagg, Nov. 12, 1844, Flagg papers.

that the cost would be so great that he would have to borrow more. He asked Flagg to help in locating furnishings, because he did not want to overload Corning any more than he already was doing. Besides, he commented shrewdly, "he and his good Lady, so accustomed to abundant means, might judge too liberally for me if they did not have the check of the comptroller."

Mrs. Corning had procured servants for the new Governor's household—a cook, a chambermaid, and a handyman, and this would add greatly to the upkeep of Wright's new establishment. He cannily decided that he would try to arrange with the proprietor of the Delevan House for a flat sum for each meal, regardless of what was served, "excluding wines of any kind." He had by this time slackened off a great deal in his consumption of alcohol. "I intend to be temperate, but not teetotal," he told Flagg, "and would desire the privilege of furnishing my own wines."

But at the last minute, Corning found a furnished place that suited the Governor's needs. It was owned by a man named Stevens and was located on Clinton Square, at the intersection of North Pearl and Orange Streets, a few blocks north of the Capitol. This was a great relief, for besides saving the Wrights a great deal, it enabled them to make the difficult winter trip from Canton unencumbered by too many personal possessions. Until the news reached them they had contemplated carrying beds, sofas, rugs, tables and many other bulky articles with them.[22]

Besides worrying over the housing problem, Wright was also occupied during these hectic days with the task of preparing his message to the legislature. He made a hasty and unpublicized trip to Albany to see Flagg and his other friends about some of the subjects with which he would have to deal.

22 Wright to Corning, Dec. 1, 1844, Gratz collection; Wright to Flagg, Nov. 12, Dec. 4, 9, 10, 14, 1844, Flagg papers; *Albany City Guide, 1844*, p. 25; Wright to Corning, Dec. 22, 1844, property of H. Landon, Watertown, New York; *Argus*, Jan. 3, 1845; Dix to Flagg, Nov. 25, 1844, Flagg papers.

He was nervous about going to Albany so soon after the election, for he thought that it might appear that he was overeager to assume his new office, but he did so anyway. There were important things that had to be straightened out, appointments to his personal staff to be decided upon, a host of offices to be filled, and it was much easier to do this beforehand than to wait until after the official beginning of his term. So he made the difficult trip to Albany, arriving at the Capital on November 21. He held five days of serious consultations, even going to Kinderhook to talk with Van Buren, and then hurried back to Canton to help Clarissa with the moving and to write his message.

The trip north from Albany was no simple jaunt. He went as far as Utica by train, but from there on it was a grueling journey of two nights and a day by wagon and sled, for there was no stage running. Wright was so anxious to get home that he travelled without sleeping, stopping only to eat and change horses. The frozen ground was very rough, and it was a great relief to reach country where there was snow, and where travel could be accomplished much more comfortably by sled. This was a very small improvement as it turned out, for at one point his sled overturned, dumping him unceremoniously in a drift. When he finally arrived at Canton he was very tired, and on top of that, he came down with a bad cold, and was, in his own words, " almost sick." [23]

So, weary, ill, and discouraged about his finances and his future living quarters, he undertook the task of preparing his message. It was not a congenial task, for every word he wrote must have reminded him of the morass of local difficulties into which he was plunging. But he worked away at it amid constant interruptions, determined to make it a firm declaration of his feelings. The one subject on which he would have liked to avoid committing himself was Anti-Rentism, but the continued

23 *Atlas*, Nov. 22, 1844; Wright to Flagg, Nov. 12, Dec. 4, 1844, Flagg papers.

outbreaks of "Indian" disorders in the Hudson valley convinced him that he had to take a stand. At Albany his friends had agreed that he might safely say nothing, but a letter describing an "Indian" attack which he found waiting on his return to Canton made him feel that this was no longer feasible. He wrote to Flagg to tell him this, and ask for his opinion. "I will make but one remark," he wrote. "Without the slightest sympathy of feeling for the landlords, I am so utterly disgusted with this mob law course, and mock Indian mummery, on the part of the tenants, that. . .it would be. . .not very wide of what I think would be both right and politic, to give them to understand that men who dare not show their own faces as a sanction of their acts should hope little from honest administration of the law." This was substantially what he said in his message, and if it offered nothing in a way of a solution, it at least was sound morally, and expressed the opinion of the vast majority of the people of the state outside the afflicted area.[24]

Silas worked hard at what was to be his first state paper as Governor, but it was almost impossible to concentrate on it amid the constant interruptions which plagued his last days at Canton, and he did not finish it until after he had arrived at Albany, the day after Christmas. For the few remaining days of the year he and Clarissa stayed at the Cornings'. His inauguration took place on New Year's morning and was followed by a reception in the Executive Chamber that lasted most of the afternoon. So began the last fateful period of Wright's public life.[25]

24 Wright to Flagg, Dec. 4, 1844, Flagg papers; Flagg to Van Buren, Dec. 23, 1844, Van Buren papers.

25 *Argus*, Dec. 27, 1844, Jan. 3, 1845.

CHAPTER XV
RENDING FACTIONS

"There is a serious division in our party which I fear Mr. W. with all his sagacity will be unable to heal."
William L. Marcy to George Bancroft, January 4, 1845.

TROUBLE within the Democratic party in New York, subordinated before the election, burst forth with renewed vigor even before the formal beginning of Wright's term. He was still a member of the United States Senate, and legally entitled to remain so until January first. The radicals in New York opposed his resigning before that date in order to prevent Bouck from filling the vacancy; some even wanted Wright to go to Washington until after Christmas. This was out of the question, for Silas had far too much to do as it was. He therefore thought that he should retire from the Senate, so that the state would not be deprived of its full representation. While at Albany late in November, he consulted with Governor Bouck about the subject and Bouck intimated that he thought Wright should either attend Congress for the few days that would elapse before his inauguration as Governor, or resign. This resolved any lingering doubts in Wright's mind.

"If you think so, Governor, I must resign," he told Bouck, "for I do not intend to go to Washington."

He therefore quit his Senatorship, thus giving Bouck an opportunity to make an interim appointment. Shortly before this Tallmadge had also resigned from the Senate to accept the position of Governor of Wisconsin Territory from Tyler. Thus Bouck had two very important posts to fill. His action in doing so unleashed once again the radical-Hunker conflict within the party, for he appointed Lieutenant Governor Dickinson to one of the vacancies, and Henry Foster to the other.

Dickinson was a Hunker, but he was a good party man and no serious objection could be raised to his appointment, but

Foster was a former Congressman who had bolted the party in 1837, voted against the Independent Treasury bill, and been influential in the deposition of Blair and Rives as printers of the House. His name was a shock to Wright and the radicals. " If I did not feel that my resignation was a duty beyond consequences, I should regret that I made it," the Governor-elect said when he learned the names of Bouck's choices, and the entire radical element was incensed by Bouck's complete disregard of their interests. It was at once clear that the meeting of the newly elected legislature would mark the start of a battle royal between the two factions.[1]

From the beginning Wright refused to be drawn into the contest, though he expressed his feelings freely in private. The first act of the drama was to take place when the Democrats sought to organize their majority in the Assembly. The Hunkers' choice for Speaker was Horatio Seymour, a determined advocate of a " reasonable " canal improvement policy, while radical support was thrown behind William C. Crain, a friend and disciple of Michael Hoffman. Both groups sought to discover where the new Governor stood, but he would not come out for either man. Even when Seymour called on him shortly before the inauguration and offered to prohibit the use of his own name if Wright so desired, Silas said he did not want to interfere in any way with the choice. His only act was to tell his young neighbor, John Russell, who had been elected to the Assembly from St. Lawrence County, to get to Albany before the opening of the session so as to be able to exert all possible effort in behalf of Crain.

Russell bungled this just as badly as he had his duty as a member of the convention that had nominated Wright. He did not arrive at Albany early, thus creating doubts about his orthodoxy in the minds of many of the radicals, and when he

1 *Atlas*, Oct. 22, 1844; Hammond, *History of New York*, III, 506-8; Wright to Polk, Jan. 21, 1845, Gillet, *Wright*, II, 1643; *Atlas*, Feb. 10, 1845; Gallup to G. Harris, Dec. 4, 1844, Polk papers, 2nd series; Wright to Flagg, Dec. 4, 1844, Flagg papers.

did get there he seemed to be overimpressed with a sense of his own importance. Instead of joining openly with the radicals, he went to Seymour privately and tried to persuade him to withdraw. Seymour was by this time irrevocably committed, so Russell's efforts were bound to be useless. In addition, the shrewd Hunker leader made it appear that Russell was seeking him out as a friend, and he intimated that Russell favored his candidacy. This was easily used by the Hunkers as a basis for rumors that Wright also supported Seymour, and Wright's non-committal attitude did not help to scotch them. The result was that Seymour carried the party caucus by a small majority and was elected Speaker.[2]

Wright's message to the legislature, which followed immediately upon the Hunker victory in the Speakership fight, demonstrated clearly that he was no Hunker, but in doing so it emphasized the schism. He dealt at some length with the financial condition of the state, and spoke plainly and uncompromisingly in favor of full application of the principle of the law of 1842. He reviewed the history of the internal improvement policy of the party, and said, " I am constrained to believe that the application of existing revenues to the existing debts, so far as the current expenses of the public service will permit, has become an imperious duty of the whole people. . . . I also believe that true friendship for our system of internal improvements and its safe extention equally require. . .the most speedy payment of the canal debt and the liberation of the present canal revenues from the wasting demands of interest now resting upon them." There was no balm for injured Hunker feelings in this flat avowal.

So, within a week of his taking office, Wright had outlined the policy which he was to follow as a statesman administering the state government, and as a politician running the Democratic party. The inconsistency of his position evidently

2 Hammond, *History of New York*, III, 514-6, 518; Wright to Russell, Mar. 10, 1846, Gillet, *Wright*, II, 1729-30.

escaped him. To him it was a matter of statesmanship versus politics. Wherever public policy was involved, he spoke his mind freely and openly with no regard for political consequences. But with intra-party conflicts themselves, even though they might be based on matters of principle, he would not deal. He had accepted his fate and become the Chief Executive of the Empire State but he would not accept the fact that he was also supposed to be head of the Democratic party in New York. For this the chief cause was his experience after 1840. The disgraceful Whig campaign of that year had had a profound effect upon him. Then Clay's struggle with Tyler for control of the Whig party, and the latter's selfish manipulation of the patronage in an effort to construct a personal following had aggravated and strengthened the distrust of politics which the hard cider battle had already stimulated. Finally the treatment afforded Van Buren had destroyed the last prop which had protected him from complete disillusionment. Even the Democratic party had proved to be dominated by the same type of self-seeking politician which had so clearly controlled the Whigs. Circumstances had forced him to accept the nomination for Governor, but when elected he was unable to bring himself to the performance of the *party* duties that were involved. In this he was of course being overly sensitive and even more, very foolish, for he was endangering the very principles which he was trying to place above the sordid political arena. The success of the sound financial policies of the radicals depended on their control of the party; if Wright had been willing to assume active leadership of the group within the New York Democracy which stood for the policies he believed in, the Hunkers could probably have been crushed, with effects on New York and even on national politics which would have been far-reaching. It would have been a job that would have required every trick in the bag of the most accomplished of politicians. As Marcy put it, " There is a serious division in our party which I fear Mr. W. with all his sagacity will be unable to heal." Still if anyone could have unravelled " the

tangled skein" of New York politics, Wright, a graduate of
the old Regency school, a veteran of so many political battles,
would have been the man. But he did not even try. Contemporaries were puzzled by this. "W. was not himself after he
came to Alby. as Gov." wrote Marcy, and the less charitable
Calhoun came to the conclusion that Wright was only "an
adroit advocate of other men's measures," who could not succeed on his own.[3] They were both partly correct. Wright was
certainly not the man whom Marcy had known in the twenties
and thirties, and he certainly failed when he essayed the rôle
of party chief. But if he was different he was not necessarily
less worthy, and if he failed it was a failure by default rather
than through lack of ability. He made no effort to lead the
party. When one local politician told him frankly that his
action on an important matter was weakening his position,
Wright retorted just as candidly that he expected it would.
As this man, George Newell, later explained it, Wright said
that he had not wanted the gubernatorial nomination, and
"when he found there was no escape from it he had deliberately
made up his mind that his service as Governor would be the
end of his political career." His inherent pessimism, which had
so often discouraged him in the past, had at last conquered
him. During the two years of his term he worked just as hard
as he always had; he did his job thoroughly and unflinchingly.
He had not grown suddenly weak or irresolute. As he watched
the desperate struggle within the Democratic ranks he was
more and more convinced of the rectitude of the radical stand—
he supported it fully in every *official* act—but he could not
bring himself to play the politician. He recognized his own deficiency plainly, and it worried him a great deal, not for himself,
but for his friends, who were insisting on booming him for re-

3 Lincoln, *Messages from the Governors of New York*, IV, 87-111. Quoted
section is on pp. 110-1. Marcy to Bancroft, Jan. 4, 1845, Bancroft papers;
endorsement on back of Newell to Marcy, Mar. 29, 1845, made in 1849,
Marcy papers; T. Parmelee, "Recollections of an old Stager," *Harpers*,
XLVII, 758.

election in 1846 and for the Presidency in 1848. Shortly after his inauguration he wrote a letter to President Polk begging him to disregard any talk he might hear in Washington that he, Wright, was seeking the highest office in the land. " I think the labor and care much greater than the honor and emolument, as is the fact, in my estimation, with the office I now hold," he wrote.

> I freely admit [he continued] that both are well worthy [of] the ambition of those who feel sure they can administer them well for the Country, and satisfactorily for the people; but I cannot bring myself up to a moderate degree of confidence that I can reach either of these points.... I was pleased with my place in the Senate, and while I was not very anxious to continue in it longer, I was not willing to exchange it for any other place than my private and quiet home. Circumstances which I could not control ... forced me to exchange it for my present place. I do not desire to remain in it beyond my present term.... [4]

Does this not make his behavior as Governor a little less enigmatical than it appears on the surface? There was certainly more to his peculiar position than mere childish petulance, and yet, after a hundred odd years it is impossible to study his deportment without disapproving. Whatever his motivation, Wright should not have acted as he did. He did not like the position he had been forced into, but he certainly should have accepted it entirely if at all. He knew what being Governor of New York meant, and when he acquiesced in the nomination, he should have been willing to take on *all* the duties involved. He was unwilling to recognize the completeness of his surrender of August, 1844, when he had finally acceded to Judge Fine's modification of his notice in the *St. Lawrence Republican*. As Governor he behaved honorably but not sensibly; in

4 Newell to Marcy, Mar. 29, 1844, Marcy papers; Wright to Polk, Mar. 3, 1845, Polk papers, 2nd series. See also Wright to Bancroft, Sept. 11, 1844, Bancroft papers.

office he was unable to shake off the pessimism which enveloped him. It is impossible to avoid the conclusion that he was in no small way responsible for the smashing of the Democrats' control of the state in 1846 and the destruction and reorganization of party lines which then took place.

* * * * *

The election of Seymour as Speaker of the Assembly and Wright's determined message set the stage for the battle. In the legislature, the two factions were very evenly divided, and as Wright refused to take part in the struggle the result was pretty much of a draw. In the election of state officers, the radicals managed to keep in Flagg as Comptroller, and procured the Attorney-Generalship for " Prince John " Van Buren, but Samuel Young, their candidate for Secretary of State, was defeated by a Hunker, and Benjamin Enos, another Hunker, was chosen State Treasurer. Similarly, in the caucus held in February to nominate the new senators, John A. Dix was chosen to fill Wright's seat succeeding the hated Foster, but Dickinson was picked to retain Tallmadge's place which Bouck had given him temporarily.[5] This balance of power might have prevented the disruption of the party if it could have been maintained, but it was upset by pressure from an unexpected direction—Washington.

" Who is James K. Polk? " the Whig orators had asked derisively during the campaign, and the slender Tennesseean was determined to show them. No figure-head President he, despite his " dark horse " origin. He stated even before the election that he would be a one-term President, so he had no worries about being renominated, and he planned to make the four years of his term truly the Administration of James K. Polk. He committed his cabinet plans to no one. " The Prest. keeps prudently close and so far as I can learn no man knows his view," wrote a man who was himself to be offered a seat in the new official family, and even Cave Johnson was in the

5 Hammond, *History of New York*, III, 524-5, 527-30.

dark. "My opinion is," Johnson said in December, 1844, "that *he* [Polk] *will* make his own cabinet & be the head of it."

When he arrived in Washington in February, Polk had made only one offer of a cabinet position, and that was to Silas Wright. It is impossible to determine if he was sincere in offering Wright the Treasury Department. He had heard from at least one source that Wright was committed to remain as Governor and therefore could not accept a cabinet post if one were offered, and while he was in the act of penning the offer, another letter, from Cave Johnson, was en route to him from Washington saying that it was "hardly probable" that the New Yorker would accept a seat if one were tendered him. At any rate, make the offer the President-elect did, in a letter dated December 7, from his home at Columbia, Tennessee. He also asked Wright to give his opinion "freely and unreservedly" on other possibilities for the cabinet.[6]

Wright was very favorably impressed by the frankness of Polk's letter, whatever later observers may think of it. Though Polk had not told anyone that he was tendering the Treasury Department to Wright, there had been rumors that he might. Only a few days before he received the offer, the Governor had sent on to Flagg another communication which he had seen and which mentioned him as a probable appointee with the notation, "from this letter, I more suspect, what I have all along feared, that I should get the offer, and that my declination will be misconstrued." So he was well prepared for Polk's proposition. In his answer he explained in great detail why he considered himself bound to remain on as Governor. He sketched a brief survey of the state of the party in New York, and told the President-elect that he had been forced to state unequivocally during the campaign that he would not

6 Marcy to Bancroft, Jan. 4, 1845, Bancroft papers; Johnson to Fine, Dec. 4, 1844, Flagg papers; Pickens to Polk, Nov. 5, 1844, Polk papers, 2nd series; Johnson to Polk, Dec. 6, 1844, Polk papers, 1st series; Polk to Wright, Dec. 7, 1844, Gillet, *Wright*, II, 1631-2.

accept any position in the national administration to allay
Hunker fears that he was merely running to get rid of Bouck.
The situation was much different than it had been in 1828,
when Van Buren had left the Executive chair at Albany to
head Jackson's cabinet, for then everyone had known beforehand that this was to be and had accepted the situation.

Wright spared nothing in attempting to convince Polk that
his refusal was not a personal matter, and to avow his full
support of the Washington government. " If I was ever your
friend," he wrote, " I was never more sincerely so than at this
moment," and he offered to do anything that he could to help
Polk or advise him on appointments.[7]

Polk promptly accepted Wright's proffer of advice, and
wrote that he would appreciate suggestions for the State and
Treasury Departments, as he intended to select a New Yorker
for one of these positions. At the same time he addressed a
similar request for suggestions to Van Buren. Both Silas and
" Van " agreed substantially in their recommendations. Both
suggested Benjamin Butler for the State Department and
Azariah Flagg for the Treasury, though Van Buren mentioned his friend C. C. Cambreleng as another possibility for
the latter office. Ransom H. Gillet, who knew Polk well from
the days when they had been colleagues in the House of Representatives, also suggested Butler and Flagg; and Cave Johnson told the President-elect that if he wanted a New Yorker
for the Treasury Department, Flagg was a man with financial
talents "of the Silas Wright order," and would make a fine
choice.

7 Wright to Van Buren, Jan. 17, 1845, Van Buren papers; Wright to
Flagg, Dec. 11, 1844, with Johnson to Fine, Dec. 4, 1844, Flagg papers;
Wright to Polk, Dec. 20, 1844, Gillet, *Wright*, II, 1632-9.

8 Polk to Wright, Jan. 4, 1845, Gillet, *Wright*, II, 1641-2; Polk to
Van Buren, Jan. 4, 1845, Polk Correspondence, New York Public Library;
Wright to Polk, Jan. 21, 1845, Gillet, *Wright*, II, 1642-5; Van Buren to
Polk, Jan. 18, 1845, Polk Correspondence, New York Public Library;
Gillet to Polk, Jan. 9, 1845, Polk papers, 2nd series; Johnson to Polk, Dec.
12, 1844, Polk papers, 1st series.

Up to this point, Polk had been almost over-solicitous of the interests of the Van Burenites in New York, but this soon changed. Other factors began to influence him. His obligation to New York was after all not as great as many citizens of the Empire State liked to think. True enough, the New York delegates at Baltimore might have been able to prevent his nomination, but if they had done so they would have had to take someone much less satisfactory from their own point of view. In one sense Polk was obligated to Wright personally for his help in carrying the state in the election, but here also there were two sides to the story. If the New York party had not been so badly divided on local issues, Wright's sacrifice would not have been necessary. Then there was the Texas question. Though it had been minimized in New York, Texas had been the focal point of the struggle with Clay in most parts of the Union. Polk was fully committed to quick annexation, but Wright, Van Buren and their closest followers (including the men they had suggested for the cabinet) were opposed to annexation without Mexico's consent. Many members of the New York delegation in Congress had to be listed among the doubtful voters when this vital question was under discussion. "What need New York politicians expect," one commentator observed, "on the votes of whose senators in Congress even, no certain calculation can be made until they are actually recorded in the journals." It was inevitable (and probably with good reason) that the behavior of the New Yorkers in Congress should be considered to reflect the feelings of Van Buren and Wright. Their luke-warm position irritated zealous annexationist Democrats. "So silent and so wise the place refusing Silas. But his silence scorched him a little this time. . . the age of non-committalism is gone." Such a comment was typical.[9]

The Hunker faction in New York played cleverly on these factors in order to advance their own stock. In Washington,

9 J. Morrall to Buchanan, Mar. 14, 1845, Buchanan papers.

Senator Foster had not yet been superseded by Dix, and he did his best to hurt the radicals. He openly advocated immediate annexation of Texas, throwing his support to the Southern wing of the party, whose leaders, Calhoun and Walker, were hostile to Wright. The New York Congressmen of radical persuasion were incensed by what they saw happening. Foster had gone " hook & line for Calhoun," complained Lemuel Stetson, Wright's former mess-mate. " Send such men back here and you rebuke Mr. Wright," he warned Flagg. " You will have a Member of the Cabinet from the State of N. Y. hostile to [him] ; & all the patronage of the administration will flow into similar channels. Your State administration will be placed in an attitude hostile to Mr. Polk, or if not, before one year is over democracy will have so strong a smell of niggers that ¼ of our friends will be drawn to the abolition ranks...." Another New York Representative, Orville Robinson, expressed similar sentiments. To Flagg he wrote that the selection of Foster and Dickinson by the legislature would be interpreted as a repudiation of Wright, and would throw the Administration into the hands of Calhoun. " All its patronage and power will be thrown against Mr. Wright for the succession," he warned. In the state legislature, the Hunkers introduced resolutions instructing the senators to vote in favor of annexation. They did this in order to stir the radicals to object, knowing that this would prejudice them in the eyes of the Polk administration.

Though the legislature picked Dix to replace Foster the Hunker offensive did not end. Flagg had permitted Robinson's letter to pass around among his friends, and in some way, Foster got a copy of it. He sent it to the *Richmond Enquirer* with an angry letter accusing Wright of interfering in the caucus which had deposed him in order to improve his own presidential chances in 1848. Ritchie printed both Robinson's letter and Foster's, protesting against the use of the Texas issue by any politician for his personal benefit. No man, said Ritchie

editorially, " is. . .worthy of supplanting the cause of Texas.
. . ." 10

The use of the Texas problem to discredit the radical wing
of the New York Democracy was no monopoly of the Hunkers.
Polk must have known from Wright's letters that he had no
intention of running for President, but many other Democrats
did not; even those who had seen some of Wright's statements
did not always believe them. To the average politician it was
difficult to conceive of a man who really did not want the
highest office in the land. So for selfish reasons, many politicians at Washington desired to weaken Wright in the eyes of
the Polk administration. When annexation resolutions passed
the House of Representatives, for example, one Southerner
was quick to point out to Polk that " *the distinct friends* of
Mr. Wright stood out to the last. . . ." Wright's friend, Senator Niles, of Connecticut, wrote that there was a " crusade "
at Washington " directed against all the prominent friends of
Mr. Van Buren." Niles thought that Walker, Calhoun and
Buchanan had control of Polk and were responsible for his
cabinet choices. Van Burenites were not to be proscribed, he
said, but they were no longer favorites. Buchanan and Walker
were at best cool toward Van Buren's group, " and with Calhoun & his friends there is an object lying beyond the present
possession of office; it is to injure and throw into the background New York & Silas Wright." Niles also reported that
John Pettit, a member of the House from Indiana, had heard
Walker and George Mifflin Dallas, the Vice President-elect,
making remarks " derogatory to Mr. W." Just how much influence men like Buchanan and Walker had with Polk cannot
be accurately determined of course, but in the final decisions
on the cabinet, they got the top two posts, the State and Treasury Departments.[11]

10 Stetson to Flagg, Dec. 31, 1844, Robinson to Flagg, Dec. 31, 1844,
Flagg papers; Robinson to Marcy, Jan. 1, 12, 1845, Marcy papers; *Richmond Enquirer*, Jan. 31, 1845, quoted in *New York Tribune*, Dec. 6, 8, 1845.

11 A. Brown to Polk, Jan. 24, 1845, Polk correspondence, New York
Public Library; Niles to Welles, Feb. 22, 1845, Welles papers, New York
Public Library.

Whatever his motivation, Polk did not act upon the suggestions of Van Buren and Wright. That this was to be was portended as early as January, when Aaron V. Brown, one of Polk's Tennessee friends, approached Lemuel Stetson at Washington, and asked him whether he thought New York would be satisfied if Marcy was put in the cabinet and Flagg given the job of Collector of the Port of New York. Stetson refused to commit himself, for he knew that Marcy was not in the good graces of the radicals at Albany, but he did say that in his own opinion Flagg deserved something more important than the Collectorship. After Polk arrived at the Capital early in February his attitude became clearer. He decided to offer the War Department to Butler, intending if he declined to give it to Marcy. To Butler this was unacceptable. His wife did not like Washington life, and would agree to make the sacrifice which living there entailed only if her husband were given the State Department. So Butler declined.[12]

From then on, Polk did not bother to consult with the New Yorkers about his official family, aside from informing Van Buren of his final decision after it was made. When Dix arrived in Washington, Polk made no effort to discover how the New York Senator felt about the appointment which it was generally conceded must go to New York.

The names of the new department heads were finally announced early in March. They were a great shock to all Van Buren's friends. The New Yorker in the group was Marcy, as Secretary of War, but even more distasteful to them were Buchanan and Walker. Buchanan had done nothing to help Van Buren at Baltimore, and Walker, of course, had been the guiding genius of the open opponents of "Little Van" from the start. "The Treasury arrangement. . .tells the whole story

12 Polk to Van Buren, Feb. 22, 1845, Butler to Polk, Feb. 27, 1845, Van Buren papers. In explaining to Van Buren why she objected to her husband's appointment, Harriet Butler said that her distaste might be overcome when the next President was elected, " provided he is the *Wright* man..." H. Butler to Van Buren, Feb. [27] 1845, Van Buren papers.

for New York," wrote Smith Van Buren to his father when the news broke. Senator Dix was both angry and despondent. " New York is, I fear, betrayed," he wrote Flagg. " I only desire to say that the President elect acts with *full* knowledge of the probable consequences. . . .I felt it my duty to tell him plainly & strongly. . . ." His conduct was " unwarrantable." [13]

The strong resentment of Polk's choices which was thus evidenced, was no mere chagrin over the new President's failure to distribute the plums at his disposal in a manner favorable to the friends of Van Buren and Wright. The announcement of the cabinet was an event of great significance in American history, for it marked the triumph of the Southern wing of the party of Jackson over the Northern. The nomination of Polk had seemed a reprieve, but these appointments showed that he had succumbed to those to whom Texas and slavery were more important than the old issues of bank and tariff. It is true that the Polk administration restored the Independent Treasury and lowered import duties considerably, but this was done mainly because the South favored sound money and low tariffs. The driving force of the party was directed toward expansion and the protection of slavery, and more and more, members of the Northern branch were forced to be apologists for the peculiar institution. Those who would not did what Lemuel Stetson had said they would—they became abolitionists or free soilers.

But aside from their disappointment with the general aspects of the new government, many of the radicals in New York were very upset by the honors bestowed upon William L. Marcy. During the intra-party conflict over the gubernatorial nomination, Marcy had inclined toward Bouck, and the more outspoken opponents of the " Agricultural Governor " therefore disliked him. Marcy was very discouraged after the elec-

13 Polk to Van Buren, Mar. 1, 1845, Van Buren papers; Niles to Welles, Feb. 22, 1845, Welles papers, New York Public Library; S. Van Buren to Van Buren, Mar. 3, 1845, Van Buren papers; Dix to Flagg, Mar. 3, 1845, Flagg papers.

tion. He thought that he had been abandoned by both sides because of his detached attitude toward the bitter struggles that were going on within the ranks and he seriously considered abandoning politics and accepting a job which had been offered him by a New York trust company. He would have been glad to take any one of a number of political appointments that were open. Judge Thompson's seat on the Court was still unfilled, and the two senatorships were also attractive. He had thought too, of the cabinet, but when, as was his habit, he coldly analyzed his chances for any of these offices he decided that they were negligible. As time passed his name was mentioned more and more frequently in connection with the War Department, but as late as March 2 he had no hope and had even written a letter of acceptance to the president of the trust company. Then the lightning struck, and the delighted Marcy accepted the War Department with alacrity.

In New York, the radical Democratic papers were nearly all well-disposed or at least non-committal on the cabinet appointments when they were announced. They were not pleased, but they did not want to express open dissatisfaction with the President. William Cullen Bryant, for example, in the *New York Evening Post,* said the cabinet was " an able one," and commented favorably (although it must be admitted coolly) on Marcy personally. But Croswell approved the new body enthusiastically and was almost fulsome in his praise of the new chief of the War Department, calling him a man of " practical sagacity, sound intelligence, and long-tried integrity." This was too much for the editors of the *Atlas,* who had smothered their resentment at first. When the *Argus* spoke " with warm approval " of the President's advisors, the *Atlas* lashed back:

We believe we speak the general sentiment of the democracy in saying that neither the place assigned to the State nor the person designated for that place has been very acceptable to New York, and that the . . . nomination of Mr. MARCY caused a wider and deeper feeling of disappointment than the accredited rumor that no place had been assigned to New York.... [14]

Naturally this did not help matters either in New York or at Washington.

There is no doubt that Marcy's appointment was a signal victory for the Hunkers. Members of this faction had been strong supporters of his name. John C. Wright, a Hunker State Senator, and A. C. Niven, Bouck's Adjutant General, had both written to Polk urging Marcy's nomination in the strongest terms. Van Buren described the radicals' displeasure plainly in a letter to George Bancroft, who was Polk's choice as Secretary of the Navy. " The injury done to Mr. Wright and the Democracy of the State by the decision of Mr. Polk consists in its influence to infuse new life into a faction bent upon his overthrow, which was fast dwindling away, and which but for this windfall, could not have kept itself on foot six months." The radicals' criticism of Marcy widened still further the breach within the party, and once again, Wright refused to try to heal it. When George Newell, a good friend of Marcy's, called on the Governor to warn him of the danger inherent in the growing *Atlas-Argus* row, Wright replied that he was resigned to the complete disruption of the Democratic organization. But he did express personal regard for Marcy, and said that he did not resent his appointment.[15]

While the choice of Marcy may not have been as unreasonable as some of the radicals tried to make it out to be, many of Polk's other acts in dealing with New York patronage seemed to be more openly hostile to them. Probably the most important of the second-rank jobs which the President had at his disposal in the Empire State was the post of Collector

14 Marcy to Wetmore, Nov. 10, 18, 1844, Mar. 2, 1845, Marcy papers; *Post*, Mar. 7, 1845, *Argus*, Mar. 13, 1845; *Atlas*, Mar. 12, 1845.

15 Niven to Polk, Feb. 14, 1845, J. Wright to Polk, Feb. 18, 1845, Polk papers, 2nd series; Van Buren to Bancroft, Mar. 7, 1845, Massachusetts Historical Society, *Proceedings*, XLII, 440; Newell to Marcy, Mar. 29, 1845, Marcy papers.

of the Port of New York. The incumbent, a Tyler appointee, was C. P. Van Ness and both the Hunkers and the radicals sought the right to pick his successor. Van Ness, a typical grasping office seeker, made a determined but futile effort to keep the place for himself. He wrote a harsh note to Polk, claiming that Polk's election was largely the result of his efforts and money in New York City, and at the same time subserviently telling Polk that if removed anyway, he would be happy to accept "any other honorable situation. . .either at home or abroad." For a time there was some doubt whether Polk would eject him, but many critical letters from good Democrats sealed the Collector's fate. Flagg could have had the job, but he did not want it. Though the Comptroller had refused, the radicals still believed that Polk would give the position to one of their number—if he were recommended by Wright. The leaders of the radicals in New York City were Benjamin Butler, Van Buren's law-partner, and John L. O'Sullivan. Their choice was one John Coddington. O'Sullivan went to Washington to see what he could do at that end of the line, and Butler hastened to Albany to work on Wright. The Governor refused to have anything to do with the subject, beyond admitting that Coddington would be a good choice. Here was a perfect example of the blanket of political lethargy which had settled over him. Butler and his other friends were unable to get him to agree even to write a letter of recommendation for Coddington. He just would not mix in the political-office-seeking conflict that was raging about him, regardless of his own sentiments for or against any candidate. Finally Butler wrote out what Wright had said, that is, that he, Wright, considered Coddington a good man for the place. This was then read to Wright, and he agreed that it expressed his feelings. Then the radicals had it certified as the Governor's opinion. The same procedure was followed with respect to the position of Naval Officer of New York Port. Here the man suggested was Michael Hoffman, but even for this old friend Wright would not actively intervene! In the end, Butler recommended Coddington and Hoffman to the President with no mention of Wright at all, probably considering that the peculiar form of the statements he had extracted from the Governor would do more harm than good.[16]

The radicals brought so much pressure to bear on Polk that they overplayed their cards. They accused the President of intending to keep Van Ness in office. The unstable O'Sullivan wrote Samuel J. Tilden that he was "enraged" at the President's "disavowal of his promises." He even considered starting a new newspaper at Washington to act as a "curb-rein" on Polk. All the papers at the Capital then, he wrote with some justification, were "wholly *Southern*—Southern and rotten." In the face of such behavior, there can be little wonder that Polk was soon reported as having "a feeling akin to irritation" for the supporters of Coddington. There was even a rumor that he was considering William C. Bouck for Collector! To O'Sullivan this seemed just a little too much. "There *may be* another man in the State who would be more distasteful to the Democracy of the City than Bouck," he commented acidly, "but if there is, I do not know him—." Polk did not appoint Bouck, but from the radical point of view his choice was almost as bad. Cornelius Lawrence, bank president, former Mayor of New York, and a stalwart Hunker, received the coveted plum. The key to an understanding of Lawrence's sentiments can be gained by the comment of Croswell, who called the new Collector "a democrat of liberal and elevated views." When Croswell testified to the soundness of a member of the party, it is not hard to imagine what the radical reaction to him would be. But Lawrence was doubly galling to the radicals because they could not speak openly against him. The ex-Mayor had always been, as Croswell was careful to point out, "an unwavering democrat" and was well qualified for the job.

16 Van Ness to Polk, Apr. 15, Mar. 17, 1845, Gillet to Polk, May 3, 1845, Butler to Polk, May 6, 1845, Riell to Polk, Mar. 20, 1845, Butler to Polk, Apr. 8, 1845, Polk papers, 2nd series; R. Morris to Marcy, Apr. 29, 1845, Marcy papers.

Marcy was in New York on June 14 when the announcement was made, and he reported gleefully to his colleague, Robert J. Walker, of its effect. " It takes like a charm—every body speaks well of it," he said, " even those who took such extraordinary means to force Coddington upon the President. They dare not show how they feel." [17] This was indeed the case. Even O'Sullivan had to express full approval of Lawrence in his paper, and the *New York Post* also commended him, praising a little later his wholesale removal of Tylerites from minor positions under his control.[18]

The selection of Lawrence was a blow to Wright, for if he would not take part in the internecine strife that was taking place, he still was hurt deeply when he saw the Hunkers triumph on any important point. Then, early in July, he received a letter from the President.

Polk evidently realized that his choice of Lawrence would not make Wright happy. He had named Hoffman Naval Officer, but he must have felt that Wright deserved a further explanation. " In my appointments to office," he wrote, " I resolved from the beginning to recognize & to know no divisions of the democratic party as the only means of keeping it *united* & preserving its *strength*. . . .Our party runs great hazards of being overthrown at the close of my term, unless they [*sic*] head their dissentions & continue united." [19]

17 O'Sullivan to Tilden, June 1, 1845, June 3, 1845, Tilden papers; *Argus,* June 17, 19, 1845; Marcy to Walker, June 15, 1845, Miscellaneous papers, New York Historical Society.

18 *Morning News,* June 10, 1845; *Post,* quoted in *Morning News,* Aug. 27, 1845.

19 Polk to Wright, July 8, 1845, Polk correspondence, New York Public Library. It should be mentioned that there was probably an additional reason for the selection of Lawrence. The Collectorship was one of the most responsible positions at the President's disposal, for tremendous amounts of money passed through the Collector's hands. The party had suffered much criticism when Samuel Swartwout, a Jackson appointee to the position, had absconded with over a million dollars of government money, and Polk was no doubt determined to make sure that this did not happen again. Lawrence

This letter stirred Wright from the political doldrums in which he seemed to be wallowing. He sent Polk a long letter explaining the New York situation and expressing what may be considered his final opinion on the business, science and art that made up the politics of mid-nineteenth century America. "There is, as you and I have had the strongest occasion to know, a pervading thirst for office among our population," he said. "It prevails alike with each political party, and is constantly increasing."

> This . . . is a mere passion for office, and a wish to live out of public patronage, very much regardless of principles or measures. The men who make up their minds to join this class, very soon make office seeking a business, and enter into it . . . with the same spirit with which the broker commences to gamble in stocks.

The comparison he chose is indicative of his attitude.

> They become the "bulls and bears" of the political parties, and care not who loses if they win. Of course, they are the men who make the most noise; who assume to lead and to hold influence; who praise the most freely and condemn the most positively, and who change men and parties and measures according to the prospects of the political stock market. These men are injurious to all parties . . . and all magistrates charged with the dispensation of public patronage. We have our full share of them in this State . . . .

The influence of such men, he wrote, varied with the times; when the country was not torn by any big issues they had more power than when the people were moved by a matter of principle. Fortunately, the latter condition had come to control politics in New York.

Wright went on to explain the basic questions with which the people of his state were dealing. First, should they ex-

was a wealthy man, and eminently respectable, and this must have been an important reason for his appointment.

tinguish the public debt and establish " sound " financial policies, and secondly, should they inaugurate strict control of
corporations? Wright hoped they would answer both of these
queries in the affirmative. He told Polk that he thought the
control of corporations could best be effected by abolishing the
principle of limited liability, and making every stockholder individually responsible for the whole debt of any business with
which he might be connected. His argument showed clearly
how completely his ideology was identified with that of the
radicals. A portion of the party, he said, " not formidable in
numbers, but truly powerful in wealth " was unalterably opposed to the reforms which could solve the debt and corporation
problems in New York.

> Our bankers are the strength of this interest ... but they have
> auxiliaries in the most of those whose business it is to make
> profit from the increase of the public debt.
>
> Our ... banking system ... has almost necessarily connected
> these two questions, because it requires public stock to consti-
> tute bank capital, and now admits none but the stocks of this
> State. If we pay our debt this system of banking must sub-
> stantially cease. . . . The bankers, too, must lose their business
> if public debt goes out of fashion, and banking will cease to be
> the attractive business it is, when every stockholder ... shall
> be made liable ... for [all] the notes and liabilities of the bank.

When this was done, he added, " all the charm which formerly
surrounded banking, and indeed the belief that it was a business
of that patriotic character which made it just that the public
should take all the risks; and that bankers should derive all the
profits, is forever broken in this State. . . ."

At present, Wright continued, every man in New York must
be judged by what stand he took on these vital issues. Whatever his other qualifications for any office, a candidate should
not be given any post if he were not " sound upon these questions." This was the reason for the dissatisfaction with the

appointment of Lawrence. When he was selected, Wright told the President plainly,

> you took a man identified with the bank interest, and not considered sound upon these great questions, and therefore your selection was not popular, although Mr. Lawrence is a worthy, honest, clever man, and personally, I doubt not, has as many friends as Mr. Coddington.

" It is considered as indicating your preference upon these great questions and as ranging you on the side of the bank interest," he concluded.[20]

This letter had no noticeable effect on Polk's policy toward New York patronage. He answered it politely, expressed full accord with the views which Wright had expressed on state policy, saying that in his own state, Tennessee, he had always fought for a similar program. But he defended Lawrence, whom he called " a good and true Democrat." He continued to deal what he considered even-handed justice to both factions. For this he cannot be entirely blamed, for the radicals in New York, aside from their views on their local problems, were also interested in the game of power politics as it was being played in the forties. " The truth is," wrote the President in his diary a few months later, " they are looking to the next Presidential election, and nothing could satisfy them unless I were to identify myself with them, and proscribe all other branches of the Democratic party. I will do, as I have done, Mr. Martin Van Buren's friends full justice in the bestowal of public patronage, but I cannot proscribe all others. . .in order to gain their good will." As Polk evidently realized, the situation within New York was not as clearcut a division of black and white, of right and wrong, as Wright thought it was. As time went on and the President continued to bestow his favors on Hunkers as well as radicals, Wright came to believe that Polk was being misled by members of his administration, notably Marcy. This may

20 Wright to Polk, July 21, 1845, Gillet, *Wright*, II, 1648-53.

well have been the case. At any rate, the Hunkers were able to circulate with some success the rumor that the national administration was hostile to Wright and the New York radicals. Polk characterized this rumor as " absurd," but the fact does remain that the Hunker element received a large share of the federal patronage in New York.[21]

Besides the nourishment which they got from Washington, the Hunkers also drew upon the Whig party for support. On such questions as the election of the Speaker of the Assembly, and the choosing of the state officers and United States Senators, the Democratic party still followed its caucus decisions, but in matters of policy, especially canal policy, this was not so. On May 13, one day before the adjournment of the legislature, a bill was passed by a combination of Hunker and Whig votes which provided for a resumption of canal construction on a limited scale, despite the law of 1842.

Because the session was about to terminate, Wright could have prevented the enactment of the bill by pocketing it. But he was reasonably sure that it could not command a two-thirds majority of both houses, so he vetoed it at once. Thus he was able to state once more his position on this vexing question. There was, he said, no middle ground upon which this matter could be compromised. " Payments of the debt at the day. . . must guide and control our legislation, or open expenditure, irrespective of the redemption of the debt, will control it." He pointed out that a constitutional convention had been suggested and that at the next election the people would vote on whether or not they desired one to be called. If they acted favorably, as it was generally expected they would, the whole question of the state's financial policy would be reexamined and determined by that convention. Until this was done, a change in the policy of 1842 would be unwise.[22]

21 Polk to Wright, Aug. 4, 1845, Polk correspondence, New York Public Library; Polk, *Diary*, M. Quaife, ed., I, 104, Nov. 27, 1845; Wright to Polk, Oct. 18, 30, 1846, Gillet, *Wright*, II, 1657-9, 1666-7; Polk to Wright, Oct. 26, 1846, *ibid.*, II, 1661-2. See also Polk, *Diary*, M. Quaife, ed., I, 280; Wright to Johnson, Oct. 12, 1846, Gillet, *Wright*, II, 1697-1706.

22 Lincoln, *Messages from the Governors*, IV, 194-230.

Wright's veto was upheld by the Assembly, but the combination of Hunkers and Whigs was portentous.

*   *   *   *   *

Aside from problems of patronage and finance, only one other matter of any great importance rose to trouble Wright during his administration, the Anti-Rent disturbances. Strangely enough, this was an issue on which radicals, Hunkers and Whigs were in substantial agreement, and yet it caused Wright much anguish and seriously weakened his strength in the state.

In his message to the legislature he had condemned the use of violence by the tenants, saying that any improvement of their condition must be preceded by a complete cessation of the " Indian " outrages which had been taking place. He suggested that a law be passed making the mere wearing of Indian disguises illegal, and stressed his determination to insure the enforcement of the law in every part of the state. Outside the Anti-Rent districts, this part of Wright's message was universally applauded. Even the *Evening Journal* gave its full approval, and the legislature quickly passed a statute forbidding the wearing of disguises and another authorizing state assistance in cases where county authorities were unable to maintain order. Wright also sent Adjutant General A. C. Niven into the disaffected area on what was supposedly a " mere visit of inspection " but in reality to see if there were more state troops in the area than the occasion required, and if the expense of maintaining them seemed more substantial than the legislature might reasonably be expected to provide. He also told Niven that he was to consult with the local authorities. " You cannot urge too strongly the necessity for great caution in all their proceedings. Firmness and an unalterable determination to maintain and execute the law is indispensible, but the execution of that determination should be without passion, without rashness, and without any appearance of a revengeful or retaliatory feeling." [23]

---

23 *Ibid.*, IV, 139-50; *Evening Journal*, Jan. 10, 1845; Ellis, *Landlords and Farmers*, pp. 271-2; Wright to Niven, Jan. 3, 1845, Wright papers, New York State Library.

But if Wright's stand was popular and well-intentioned, it was nonetheless shortsighted. Threatened with the loss of their farms, the tenants would not submit peacefully. It was all very well for the Governor righteously to refuse to deal with " men who will not show their faces " but there was still a practical problem to be faced. The Anti-Renters were no small clique of agitators; the whole countryside was aroused. They were convinced of the rectitude of their course. Whatever the legal nature of the question, it would have been far more humane and far wiser to have pursued a more imaginative policy. Perhaps it is hindsight to say this, but concessions had to be made in the end and much money and blood could have been saved if they had been made in January, 1845, instead of a year later. But it was not to be.

Despite the unyielding tone of Wright's message, and the new laws so speedily enacted at Albany, the Renters were uncowed, and trouble continued. The " Indian " leader, " Big Thunder," Dr. Smith Boughton, had been captured late in 1844, but the tenants fought on. During the spring, while attempting to serve warrants, Sheriff Brown, of Schoharie County, was captured by the " Indians " and his papers destroyed, and in August a deputy sheriff of Delaware County, Osman Steele, was shot and killed by calico-clad farmers while he was trying to round up the cattle of a defaulting tenant for public sale. At the time that this happened, Wright was not in Albany. He had, indeed, spent a good part of his time since the adjournment of the legislature in May in travelling. He had been to Vermont to see his mother late in that month, and in June, the death of Andrew Jackson made it necessary for him to go to New York to attend memorial services there. Then in July he had gone to Schenectady to participate in the semi-centennial of Union College, of which he was a trustee. He had no sooner returned from this ceremony when he was called to Canton by the illness of brother Pliny. The news of the death of Sheriff Steele reached him at Canton on August 12. He returned at once to the Capital, and on August 20 issued a proclamation offering five hundred dollars reward for the capture of the killer. Then on August 27, he declared Delaware County to be in a state of insurrection and sent General Niven to take command of the situation.[24]

The death of Steele intensified popular feeling against the "Indians" and though Philip Hone (who seldom found anything praiseworthy about any Democratic act) characterized Wright's proclamation as being in "a compromising spirit" and charged him with "courting...vulgar prejudices," the general attitude of men of all parties toward this declaration of martial law was favorable. The *Atlas* criticized the Anti-Renters as "misguided" and said that the Governor had "no other alternative but the vindication of the law by force," and the *Journal* also supported Wright wholeheartedly.

State troops quickly put down the violence in Delaware and dozens of arrests were made. "Big Thunder" had been brought to the bar of justice in March but the jury had disagreed. Now he was again prosecuted. After a wild trial, featuring a fist fight in the court room between "Big Thunder's" lawyer and "Prince John" Van Buren (who as Attorney General had charge of the prosecution) the prisoner was found guilty and sentenced to life imprisonment. Two "Indians" were convicted of the murder of Steele and sentenced to death, but Wright wisely commuted their sentences to life, and by December conditions were quiet enough to warrant the revocation of the Proclamation of August 27.[25]

In the meantime, the fall elections had taken place, and the great strength of the Anti-Renters in the disturbed areas had its influence on the attitude of politicians. The ending of the

24 Ellis, *Landlords and Farmers*, pp. 264-6; Christman, *Tin Horns and Calico*, pp. 187-9; 175-82; *Atlas*, May 30, June 24, July 22, 1845; Wright to H. Moody, Aug. 12, 1845, Wright papers, St. Lawrence University; Lincoln, *Messages from the Governors*, IV, 297-308.

25 A. Nevins, *Diary of Philip Hone*, II, 744, Aug. 29, 1845; *Atlas*, Aug. 28, 1845; *Journal*, Aug. 28, 1845; Christman, *Tin Horns and Calico*, pp. 151-2, 204-15, 249; Ellis, *Landlords and Farmers*, p. 267.

disturbances offered Wright an opportunity for suggesting a compromise. In his message of January, 1846, he offered a plan of action. This program consisted of three parts. First of all distress for rent was to be abolished. The right of distress, or distrain, the power to seize a man's personal property in payment of a debt, was one of the main grievances of the tenants, and Wright felt that it was reasonable to grant their demand that it should not be allowed in future contracts.

The second element in his proposed solution of the difficulties called for placing a tax on the income which the landlords received from rents. The tenants wanted such a law because they believed they were being discriminated against in the payment of local taxes. The system employed was to levy rates on the occupants of the land, tenant or owner. Thus the large landlords did not have to bear much of the local tax burden, for most of their property was occupied by small tenant farmers. The farmers argued that their rents were really interest payments on capital (their farms) " borrowed " from the landlords. In other words they felt that they were freeholders— that the landlords merely held perpetual mortgages that were never paid off. If this interpretation was accepted, the landlords would have to pay a tax on the " interest " on these " mortgages " just as any mortgage holder did.

The trouble with this was that the legal basis of land ownership in the disturbed area was very complicated. The key to the situation was the " durable " or perpetual lease. Most of the leases on the Van Rensselaers' property, and some of the ones on most of the large owners' lands were of this type. There was much justification for claiming that a man who held land under such a lease was in reality a freeholder, because subject to certain payments he and his heirs held the land " for Ever." His rights were certainly as basic as those of any holder of mortgaged land.

But not all the leases were perpetual. Many ran for long but definite terms of years, others for a stated number of lifetimes. Legally there was no difference between a lease for one year and one for ninety-nine years. As long as a definite provision for expiration of the arrangement was made, the payment provided for was rent, not interest on invested capital. The tenants considered this a foolish and arbitrary distinction. To two farmers, living in the same valley and each paying, say, thirty bushels of wheat and two fat hens a year to General Van Rensselaer, the fact that one had a perpetual lease and the other only one for ninety-nine years, was hardly a vital issue. Their grievances against their landlords were based on concrete conditions that were the same for permanent and limited tenants, and they acted together against what they considered injustices, not against any legal formality. This part of Wright's plan could not be justified logically when applied to non-perpetual leases, and he knew it. But he suggested that as a matter of pure expediency it might be advisable for the legislature to take such action.

Finally, his plan called for a limitation on the time of future leases. Aside from the legal question, he said, the long term leases common in the troubled region " are not in accordance with the spirit of our institutions," and should not be renewed.[26]

Wright's Anti-Rent program was received favorably by most Democrats and Whigs, but some of his strongest supporters were not favorably disposed to one of his suggestions. The idea of ending a landlord's power to attach the personal property of a defaulting tenant was repugnant to many Democratic city dwellers, especially in the metropolis. Aaron Vanderpoel, for example, a sound radical, claimed that this right of distress provided security which encouraged many men of moderate means to invest their savings in tenements and small houses in the city. The interests of this class, Vanderpoel said with what seemed more solicitude than the occasion warranted, would be injured by abolishing remedy by distress,

26 I. Mark, *Agrarian Conflicts in Colonial New York*, p. 63; Lincoln, *Messages from the Governors*, IV, 238-45.

which after all " is of but little value to Mr. Astor." What
worth it was to Mr. Vanderpoel, he did not say.
Another exasperated Democrat was even more emphatic:

[There is] but one impression in the view of this apparent
submission of the *strong man* of our party to the fashion of
Anti-Rentism—that of fear that the deed will be done mingled
with a sense of the great injustice that would be done to rights
that in this City have never been questioned ... The Democratic
party will be faithless to their own principles, if they suffer
this Anti-Rent laws culloterie to ride over the rights of *all*
landlords ... particularly those ... in this City. ... [Those
who advised the Governor] had better study the alphabet of
Political Economy, and learn that the three links which bind
Society together are Labor, Capital, & Real Estate—that these
are principles as distinct as the natural elements Earth Fire
& Air. . . . Our good Govr. has been caught by a mere
gossamer. ...

But the man who got to the heart of the situation and who
voiced the objection most baldly was a Whig, Gulian C. Verplanck. " I respectfully suggest," he wrote to Samuel J. Tilden,
of the Assembly, that "you. . .bear in mind that your legislation upon this subject does not bear only upon the large estates
held in great bodies, but on property scattered throughout the
state, and owned by numerous individuals, under conditions
which have never been made the cause of any complaint." [27]
In spite of this objection, a select committee of the legislature, headed by Tilden, made a report which approved
Wright's plan. Laws abolishing distress for rent and providing
for the taxation of rents were passed and received Wright's
signature, though nothing was done about limiting the time
of future leases. These concessions did not satisfy the Anti-
Renters, and their hostility to Wright did not slacken. When
November came around he was remembered as the man who
sent the militia into Delaware County, not as the formulator
of the concessions.

27 A. Vanderpoel to Tilden, Jan. 8, 1846, A. Conger to Tilden, Feb. 5,
1846, Verplanck to Tilden, Apr. 2, 1846, Tilden papers.

CHAPTER XVI

THE GREAT DEBACLE: CONFUSION
TWICE CONFOUNDED

"I can say to you with perfect truth, that I feel no shock of disappointment.
I really feel . . . as though my shoulders were relieved from a heavy burden."
Wright to Martin Van Buren, November 10, 1846.

THE New York election of 1845 had been a triumph for the
radical Democrats. It is impossible to say, of course, exactly
which members of the legislature were Hunkers and which
were radicals, for those divisions were matters of opinion and
of personal loyalty rather than organization. But of the sev-
enty-four Democratic members of the new Assembly, a large
majority were friends of Wright and of the anti-debt policy.
Wright, indeed, claimed that there were not more than a dozen
Hunkers in the Assembly, and he must have known. When
the new legislature met, the radical candidate for Speaker carried the caucus and was elected.[1]

But this was almost the last time that the two segments of
the party were able to work together. The Hunkers soon
showed that they were unwilling to be governed by caucus decisions any longer. When a party meeting voted to replace
Croswell as State Printer with William Cassidy of the *Atlas,*
the Hunkers cleverly retaliated by proposing a bill abolishing
the office itself, and providing that the official state printing
be let on contract to the lowest bidder. The radicals, placed in
a position very similar to that of the Regency in 1824, when
the People's party had advocated popular election of presidential electors, fought the bill tooth and nail. Croswell and the
Argus fought back without regard for party allegiance. When
Samuel Young, now a state senator, criticized Croswell in the

---

1 Wright to Johnson, Oct. 12, 1846, Gillet, *Wright,* II, 1702. See also
Hammond, *History of New York,* III, 578, and *Morning News,* Nov. 10,
1845.

upper house, the *Argus* called his speech "the ebullitions of a jaundiced and prejudiced mind," and labeled his supporters "Conservatives" (a name reminiscent of Tallmadge and 1837) because they wished to maintain the *status quo*.

After a hot debate, this bill was passed by a combination of Hunkers and Whigs and was signed by Wright. The new system was an admirable reform, but the spiteful nature of the Hunkers' action was highlighted when Croswell submitted a bid to do the printing for nothing! He was that determined that the radicals should not depose him from the position he had so long held.[2]

At Albany, the Hunkers also continued their campaign to drive a wedge between the radicals and the Polk administration. In this they were aided by the strategic location of Marcy in the President's cabinet. They tried to widen the split by ardently endorsing the annexation of Texas, an essential part of Polk's policy over which the radicals could never wax enthusiastic. On the first day of the session of 1846, the following trouble-seeking resolution was offered in the Senate, along with others of a less controversial nature:

> Resolved, (if the assembly concur,) That this legislature approve of the course of those of their senators and representatives in the congress of the United States, who have been the firm and consistent supporters of the great measure of the age, the annexation of Texas to the territory of this Union, and who, by their timely and energetic action, have helped to bring it to an honorable consummation.

The radicals immediately introduced another series of resolutions which made no mention of Texas at all and an acrimonious debate ensued which continued off and on for nearly three months and ended with the tabling of the whole matter. But the effect at Washington could not have been helpful to

2 *Argus*, Jan. 23, Feb. 3, 1846; Hammond, *History of New York*, III, 596-600; *Atlas*, Feb. 1-3, 25, 1846.

the Administration, now on the verge of war with Mexico because of Texas.

The rift was so bad that the Hunkers even joined hands with the Whigs to prevent the election of a radical as temporary Speaker of the Assembly when the regular Speaker was absent for a few days. Men of both groups now recognized that the party had been rent completely asunder. " The match appears to have been touched that will blow up and tear in fragments the whole democratic party of the State," wrote one of Wright's backers in New York City, and on the other side, Marcy's comment was, " I think the sword is drawn and the scabard [*sic*] thrown away." [3] Such admissions were not confined to the confidential correspondence of politicians; the newspapers were just as bold in proclaiming the open warfare between the factions. " The time has come when the vindication and defence of the Argus . . . shall no longer be postponed to the vain hope, that denunciation would cease," wrote Croswell in his paper. O'Sullivan, of the *Morning News,* set the tone for the radical press in an editorial early in February. The *Argus* and the *Atlas* represent, he said, " two conflicting, and we now believe irreconcilable elements in our politics, Conservatism [*i. e.* Hunkerism] and Radical Democracy."

Marcy was horrified at the state of affairs, for he realized that an irreparable rupture between the radicals and Hunkers could only mean Whig victories. He was constitutionally incapable of understanding Wright's refusal to take any part in the struggle. " The Govr. sees the trouble and can not be blind to the consequences but from all I can learn acts as if he was *paralised,*" he wrote to a New York friend. " Our noble party . . . is on the brink of ruin—with scarcely a hope of escaping the fatal plunge." So deeply moved was Marcy by the utter disregard for practical politics which both sides were demonstrating by this time that he resorted to Latin to find words

---

3 Hammond, *History of New York,* III, 587-95, 601; J. Kellog to Tilden, Jan. 26, 1846, Tilden papers; Marcy to Wetmore, Feb. 1, 1846, Marcy papers.

to express his amazement at such madness. " Quem Deus vult perdere prius dementat," he pontificated.[4]

*   *   *   *   *

Events now moved swiftly toward November, 1846. During the summer, a New York Constitutional Convention, the calling of which had been approved by an overwhelming vote at the previous election, met at Albany and drafted a new frame of government which represented the final triumph of the radical program. The constitution was generally more democratic than its predecessor; appointive state offices like those of the Comptroller and the Secretary of State were made elective posts. Even all judges were in the future to be chosen by popular vote. But the signal success from the radical viewpoint was the article which forbade increasing the state's debt without a popular referendum. Guided by the militant Michael Hoffman, a " towering monument " carefully courteous and respectful, but confusing his opponents with " mazes of figures and statistics which are as familiar to him as household goods," this clause was accepted by the convention after a hard fight. This was the ultimate victory of the Bucktail ideal over the Clintonian.[5]

But the outlook for November was ominous. Defeat had made the Hunkers reckless. As one of them said, " Our friends are in this delimma [sic] they must fight or die—and may as well die after fighting as before." Despite his refusal to take steps to put the Hunkers down, Wright had shown by his veto of the canal bill of 1845 and by his personal associations that he was in complete sympathy with the radicals. By February, 1846, even Weed, who had liked pretending that Wright was pursuing an equivocating course, " sitting on a rail " and " in a state of ' betweenity ' " admitted that the Governor was thor-

4 *Argus*, Feb. 3, 1846; *Morning News*, Feb. 3, 1846; Marcy to Wetmore, Jan. 21, 1846, Marcy to Newell, Feb. 26, 1846, Marcy papers.

5 Hammond, *History of New York*, III, 641 ff., esp. pp. 652-3; R. Earll to his brother, Sept. 17, 1846, *Papers of Herkimer Historical Society*, II, 420.

oughly committed to the anti-Hunker faction. Croswell voiced the general Hunker opinion of Wright in a private letter during the summer. " He has not consulted the interests or the wishes of the *entire* party," he complained. " He has chosen his confidential friends from a clique, & has surrendered his administration to their keeping—he has failed, with all the elements on his hands, to unite the dem. party—& he cannot command its united vote." [6] More and more, the Hunkers were outspoken in their opposition to Wright. They seemed unwilling to accept the fact that the Governor was acting on personal convictions; indeed most of them evidently believed he was being led astray by " the Atlas clique," meaning Flagg, Dix, Samuel Young, Hoffman, and their friends. The correspondence of leading Hunkers illustrates their fear and hatred of the " central power at Albany." " A more proscriptive, intollerant and illiberal set of men, never congregated together before. The whole power of the Government is in the hands of Mr. Flagg; and a greater tyrant does not exist." So wrote William C. Bouck, the former Governor. Bouck could find " little charity " for Wright, whom he considered partly responsible for his own defeat at the 1844 convention. Croswell also spoke of an " odious Power " at Albany ruling with an " imperious & insolent dominion," which had " brought within its grasp Governors & public men from time immemorial." It is clear that men like Bouck and Croswell could no longer look on Wright as a moderator or be expected to support him. " Gov. W. will not be a candidate," Croswell predicted in the spring of 1846. " It w'd be hasardous to his position to say the least." So strong was this feeling that Thurlow Weed too commented on it. It was beginning to look as though the Democrats might have " to look up another ' Cato ' for the November races! " he remarked slyly.[7]

6 *Evening Journal*, Feb. 9, 1846; Croswell to Seaver, Aug. 15, 1846, Miscellaneous papers, New York State Library; Marcy to Wetmore, Feb. 14, 1846, Marcy papers.

7 Bouck to Seymour, Mar. 21, 1846, Seymour papers, New York Historical Society; Croswell to Seaver, Mar. 2, 1846, Miscellaneous papers, New York State Library; *Evening Journal*, Apr. 17, 1846.

The radicals, however, were determined that Wright should run again. During the summer they waged a great battle with the Hunkers in the county meetings which elected delegates to the state convention, and when that body met at Syracuse on October first, they had a solid majority and controlled the doings there completely. Wright naturally wanted no more of the Governor's chair, and his best friends outside the state urged him to refuse. " Do not *suffer* yourself to be run even if Mr. Van Buren should persuade you to do so for *two* days on a log in the woods," warned John C. Rives from Washington. Wright passed this comment on to Van Buren with a fervent hope that he might be allowed to take Rives' advice, but he made no effort to avoid being nominated. It was not in his nature to shrink from defeat. " I am not, in any event," he told " Little Van," " to flee a sinking ship. . . ." So he kept silent and when the radical-dominated convention offered him the nomination, he accepted.[8]

Meanwhile, the race was already under way. In New York City the party was very much upset by the condition of the *Morning News*, the radical organ which John L. O'Sullivan and Samuel J. Tilden had started in 1844. During the campaign of that year it had performed yeoman service, but since then it had languished badly. Tilden was primarily a politician, and soon lost interest in the sheet, and O'Sullivan, though a brilliant newspaper man, was far too erratic to run a daily paper well. In order to succeed, a cheap daily like the *News* had to be out on the streets early in the morning, while the laboring people of the city were on their way to work. This meant that the editor had to have his editorials prepared at least a day in advance, so that they could be set up early, before the last minute rush to crowd in late news. O'Sullivan was not capable of meeting a schedule as rigorous as this. He often wandered into his office about midnight and began to

8 Hammond, *History of New York*, III, 677-9; Rives to Wright, Apr. 18, 1846, Wright to Van Buren, May 17, 1846, Van Buren papers; *Atlas*, Oct. 2, 4, 1846.

prepare the leader for the paper of the coming day. By the time he was ready to go to press, rival papers were already tucked under the arms of the city's workers, and when the *News* did reach the streets, the market for it had disappeared. Even if this did not happen every day, it occurred frequently enough to discourage the development of a *News* "habit" among working New Yorkers. As Nelson J. Waterbury, who had a financial interest in the paper, expressed it, "O'S could not be relied on for any thing." In the fall of 1845, the care-free Irishman decided that he would like to visit the Continent. He told Waterbury, who naively considered himself a silent partner in the venture, that John Bigelow, the literary editor of the *News,* had agreed to take over the whole paper while he was gone. After O'Sullivan had departed, Waterbury went to see Bigelow about the paper and discovered to his chagrin that he had heard absolutely nothing about O'Sullivan's "ar-rangement." Poor Waterbury, who knew little about running a newspaper, found himself editor-in-chief! By the summer of 1846, the paper was being edited by four different men, each responsible for writing the editorials and getting it out one or two days a week. When such a haphazard venture had to compete with the *New York Tribune,* edited by a journalistic wizard like Horace Greeley, there can be little wonder that it was not very successful. During the summer desperate efforts were made to raise money to continue publication at least until after election, but they failed, and on September 7, the *News* appeared for the last time.[9]

But it must not be imagined that Wright and his party were without the support of good journalism in the metropolis. William Cullen Bryant's *Post* was a powerful ally, and Walt Whitman, who edited the *Eagle,* across the East River in the town of Brooklyn, lent his pen eagerly to the Wright campaign.[10]

9 N. Waterbury to Wright, Aug. 27, 30, 1846, Waterbury to Tilden, Aug. 10, 1846, Tilden papers.

10 It is interesting to note that the *Eagle*, owned by Isaac Van Auden, was a Hunker paper! O'Sullivan, of the *News*, called it the "Conservative

The election, Whitman wrote editorially,

> *will involve the principles of economy in government, of rigid caution in outlays, of prompt payment of state dues, of a high-toned sustaining of credit, of no borrowing money, or lending it to special purposes.* These assumptions are justified by facts which any man can see for himself. The well known repugnance of Governor Wright to run the State in debt for any thing, is one fact. He is almost the only man we have ever had for Governor, who was not willing to swim with a temporary and local wish for an " improvement "—even at the expense of saddling it directly on the people. We need such a man most especially at this time.[11]

As time passed, rumors of the intra-party strife reached Washington in ever greater frequency. President Polk was disturbed. His policy of refusing to recognize local squabbles had been used by the Hunkers to create the impression that they and they alone had access to the Presidential ear. As word reached him that this faction was likely to oppose Wright's renomination, and even vote against him in the election, Polk's uneasiness increased. But during the summer, the President himself had aggravated the situation by offering the position of Minister to Great Britain to Senator Dix. Dix personally had been pleased and flattered by the offer but his friends at Albany had advised against it, and in the end he had turned it down. Flagg, for example, pointed out to Dix that the vacation of the senatorship would be a serious blow to the New York radicals. In the deranged state of the party they could not control the legislature's selection of Dix's successor against the combined efforts of the Hunkers and the Whigs, and they would lose their only strong voice at Washington. Dix's refusal only increased the misunderstanding between the Admin-

---

organ of Kings County." Whitman, however, resolutely supported Wright, and later the Wilmot Proviso, in his editorials. He was finally removed by Van Auden in January, 1848. *Morning News*, Feb. 2, 1846; Whitman, *Gathering of the Forces*, I, xxii-xxiii and *passim*.

11 *Eagle*, Sept. 28, 1846, Whitman, *Gathering of the Forces*, II, 26.

istration and the New York radicals, for Polk interpreted it as a personal rebuff, and the New Yorkers as a diabolical plot to weaken them by getting Dix out of the Senate.

Another move of Polk's had an even worse effect. This was the appointment of ex-Governor and arch-Hunker William C. Bouck as receiver of the public money for New York City, an act doubly offensive to the radicals because the job had been created by the passage of the new Independent Treasury Act, dear to their hearts. " The government at Washington," one radical later told Jabez Hammond, " *crowned Gov. Bouck king of the sub-treasury.* I have always considered this as the grossest insult to Gov. Wright. . . .This action was the significant indication of the guillotine prepared for Gov. Wright in November." [12]

But the radical's fear of Polk's intentions was unfounded. It is true that he overestimated the numerical strength of the Hunker element, and gave them a larger share of the patronage than they deserved, but he had no intention of causing or even countenancing the defeat of Wright. As the summer ended he began to realize that something was wrong.

The first step in clarifying the picture came from an unexpected source. Secretary of State James Buchanan, " Old Buck," for many years had not been overly friendly toward Van Buren, but neither had he acted with open hostility at Baltimore, nor, since his elevation to the State Department, had he used the patronage at his disposal against the radicals. Now, though he was still mistrusted by them, he chose the radical *Albany Atlas* to print the United States Laws in New York, rather than the *Argus*. Shortly after this he undertook to visit Albany on his way to Saratoga Springs for a short vacation.

In spite of this act of friendship on his part, the radicals remained cold. The Constitutional convention was still in session

12 Polk, *Diary*, M. Quaife, ed., II, 19; Flagg to Dix, July 19, 1846, Flagg papers; Hammond, *History of New York*, III, 686.

when the Secretary arrived at the Capital early in September, and most of the important radicals were in town, but with the exception of John Tracy, the president of the convention, and Gouverneur Kemble, they ignored him completely. The Hunkers, on the other hand, paid him every possible attention. He did see Wright, but it was a formal call and they were unable to converse privately. The Governor only managed to tell him that he would try to get up to Saratoga Springs some day the following week for a confidential visit. The vain Buchanan was hurt by the treatment afforded him by the radicals, and he wrote Polk a letter which showed much sympathy for the Hunker point of view. " The Albany Regency is odious," he said. But he did notice that the appointment of Bouck was responsible for much of the radical sulking. They see the appointment, he told Polk, " as conclusive [evidence] that your administration has taken sides against Gov. Wright & his friends."

Buchanan then moved on to Saratoga. The press of duties made it impossible for Wright to carry out his intention of visiting him there. Instead he wrote a letter thanking him for giving the federal printing to the *Atlas* and explaining why the Administration was held in suspicion by his own friends. " I am aware how selfish I must appear to you in writing this frank letter, but I do not feel that I am," he added.

> I am sure you know that I did not wish the office I now hold, and I am as little anxious to retain it as I was to take it; and nothing would so much rejoice me as to have my friends consent that I should retire. . . . If the war had not been opened upon me, I might have been able to bring about that result, but now I do not suppose that there is any hope of it. . . . Entertaining as I do these expectations, I freely admit that I would rather not be beaten, and much more strongly that our party . . . should not be beaten; and hence my strong thankfulness for your course.

This message had a profound effect upon Buchanan. His conversations with various Hunkers had convinced him that they

realized the certainty of Wright's renomination by the Syracuse convention. " Why then does the Argus keep up such a
bitter war against the Governor? " he wrote to Polk suspici-
ously. He knew Wright well, and was sure that he was sincere
in believing that the Hunkers were out to defeat him even if
he received the call at Syracuse. " Should that party cause his
defeat," Buchanan warned the President, " this will prostrate
them & in the end do the Governor no harm." [13]

Viewing the situation in a new light, he determined to tell
Wright candidly the whole story of the Administration's handling of the patronage as he saw it. He said that Polk had approved the naming of the *Atlas* for the federal printing, that
the President was actively interested in Wright's reelection.
He mentioned all the radicals that Polk had appointed, and
said that the selection of Bouck " did not justify by any in-
ference the impression which it seems [to] have created." He
spoke honestly of his own disappointment over his reception
at Albany and warned Wright that conduct of this sort had a
bad effect at the national capital. The comment there, he said
in words that shed a good deal of light on his own nature,
" will most probably be: See the thanks which Buchanan has
received for his uniform & steady friendship for Gov. Wright."

At Washington, Buchanan's sudden change of heart did not
escape Polk's notice. The President had a talk with George
Bancroft, who was on his way to Boston, and persuaded him
to stop at New York and Albany to report his impression of
conditions. Bancroft saw Benjamin Butler in New York, and
visited Wright at the Capital and Van Buren at Kinderhook.
To them and to everyone else he met, he spoke for himself
only, but he expressed what he knew were the views of the
President. His report confirmed Buchanan's, and even more
showed that the Hunker faction was not in sympathy with

13 Buchanan to Polk, Sept. 5, 1846, Polk correspondence, New York
Public Library; Wright to Buchanan, Sept. 8, 1846, Buchanan papers;
Buchanan to Polk, Sept. 10, 1846, Polk correspondence, New York Public
Library.

Polk's whole program. Texas did not becloud the issue for Bancroft; he stated frankly that the Hunkers were opposed to the new low tariff. On the other hand he was able to tell Polk that " Mr. Wright said to me emphatically, and authorized me to repeat, that he considers the New Tariff [the Walker Tariff of 1846] a great democratic measure, that he adopts and sustains it . . . . I was most confidently assured, that there would be no opposition to it, but from the very men, who had given Mr. Wright & his friends so much trouble . . . ." Bancroft also explained to Polk the resentment which some of his appointments had aroused, and told him how the Hunkers had used these plums to create the impression that the Administration opposed the radicals. He was fully convinced, however, that all the radicals would support the Washington administration in its traditional Democratic policies.[14]

By now the President was almost convinced. He had noted a growing coolness between Buchanan and Marcy as a result of the former's kindness to the *Atlas*. A letter from Albert H. Tracy, of Buffalo, with whom he had served in Congress, probably provided the final impetus which converted him to an openly pro-radical position. Tracy, who was no longer actively engaged in politics, and who could be counted upon for a dispassionate appraisal, wrote that the radicals were substantially in the right in claiming that Hunker office holders were using their power to make it seem that Polk, the font of their authority, was opposed to the Governor.

This was enough. Polk called a cabinet meeting and informed his advisers that he wished the whole power of the national organization thrown behind Wright. He told them that he expected each of them to do everything possible to correct the false impression that there was hostility to Wright at Washington. All of them assured him that they would do their

14 Buchanan to Wright, Sept. 9, 1846, Buchanan papers; Polk, *Diary*, M. Quaife, ed., II, 143-4; Bancroft to Polk, Oct. 4, 1846, Polk correspondence, New York Public Library.

best. Polk also called in Wright's friend, Ransom H. Gillet, who held a position in the Treasury Department, acquainted him with the facts, and assured him of his own deep regret that federal patronage had been used to hurt Wright and the New York radicals.

Some of the members of the cabinet made serious efforts to carry out the President's request. Wright received letters from Cave Johnson and even from Robert J. Walker, in " a language and spirit of the most friendly character." These kind words, together with the assurances he had received from Buchanan and Bancroft, convinced the Governor that Polk had been misrepresented by many of his appointees. At Bancroft's suggestion, he wrote Polk a long letter to this effect. He assured him that the " sound democracy " would support his administration, but that in the long run the Hunkers would " prefer to exchange you for a whig " to get rid of such sound democratic measures as the low tariff and the independent treasury.[15]

Polk's reply throws a good deal of light on the tangled and complicated state of New York politics. He explained again how he had tried to treat all real Democrats fairly and said that he was sorry if some offices had fallen to men who were not true supporters of the party. It had been, he said, very difficult for him to determine just where each individual stood in the intra-party strife in New York. " You would . . . be surprised, if you could see the recommendations which were made to me, of some of the persons I have appointed in New York, whose appointment yourself and the true democracy of the State regard as unfortunate," his letter ran. This was indeed the case. Men would often write letters commending a candidate for a place to the President's attention and then send other notes telling the President to disregard their previous advice,

15 Polk, *Diary*, M. Quaife, ed., II, 176-7; Gillet, *Wright*, II, 1670-1; Wright to Buchanan, Oct. 30, 1846, Buchanan papers; Wright to Polk, Oct. 18, 1846, Gillet, *Wright*, II, 1656-60.

that local pressures had forced them to write words they did not mean. Needless to say, if Wright had been willing to take a more direct part in recommending candidates for office, much misunderstanding might have been avoided. It was only in October, 1846, that the Hunker's utter disregard of the party's welfare and the letters of Polk, Buchanan, Johnson, and Walker finally stirred Wright into offering some concrete suggestions on patronage. This combined with Polk's new understanding of the situation helped a little, but it was too late to prevent the disruption of the Democratic party in New York. An earlier *rapprochement* might have produced a different result in the election. Wright maintained that federal jobs alone had sustained the Hunkers, and that if they had not received so many, they would have become so weak and so few that even in alliance with the Whigs they would not have been able to influence the outcome in any significant fashion. There is no way of determining whether or not he was correct. It can only be said that as things worked out the Hunker office holders worked diligently against Wright.[16]

To the very end, Wright refused to exert pressure against any Democrat who was opposed to him. When one of his friends wrote in October criticizing Orville Hungerford, a Hunker member of the House of Representatives, the Governor reiterated his stand. He would not interfere in any Congressional election. Hungerford, he acknowledged, was unfriendly to him, but that was Hungerford's business, not his. Wright also admitted that the Congressman was a high tariff man, but said that that was a matter between him and his constituents. The question of his renomination must be settled by the people actually concerned, Wright concluded. If Hungerford received the regular Democratic nomination, he should be supported, regardless of personal feelings.[17]

16 Gillet, *Wright*, II, 1662n.; Wright to Johnson, Oct. 30, 1846, *ibid.*, II, 1707-12; Wright to Dix, Apr. 29, 1846, *ibid.*, II, 1716.

17 Wright to A. Walton, Oct. 26, 1846, Wright papers, St. Lawrence University.

As November drew nearer, Silas kept up a confident front for friends outside New York. To Polk he wrote expressing hope for success despite his fears of the influence of federal office holders, and he said just about the same thing in letters to Cave Johnson. But even to them he confessed that the instability of the party made it hard to be sure of anything, and to John A. Dix he said ominously, " The manner in which The Argus manages ... satisfies me that the ticket is to be opposed to the extent of the ability of these men ...." [18]

The Whigs, meanwhile, settled on John Young and Hamilton Fish as their candidates for Governor and Lieutenant Governor. Young, the Whig leader in the Assembly, and a consumate politician, was a strong choice, for he had consistently supported the calling of the popular Constitutional convention, and was well disposed toward the Anti-Renters. When this group held its own convention on October 6, Young was accepted as the gubernatorial candidate. Wright was in disfavor with the Anti-Renters, in spite of his willingness to support means of alleviating their difficulties, because they thought that he had been overly severe in putting down the riots of 1845. Young on the other hand, while not countenancing violence, was a firm friend of Ira Harris, one of the Anti-Rent politicians, and had promised the angry tenants that he would pardon the men who had been convicted of disturbing the peace during the troubles and who were still languishing in jail. This Wright had refused to do on principle, though it would have been an easy way of gaining support among the tenants.

Wright was aware of the import of the Anti-Rent vote and he suggested to Van Buren that Democrats friendly to the Anti-Renters be sent into the aroused area to attempt to win over some of them by promises of concessions, for, as he wrote, " all honest and proper measures " should be taken to divide

18 Wright to Polk, Oct. 30, 1846, Gillet, *Wright*, II, 1667; Wright to Johnson, Oct. 12, 30, 1846, *ibid.*, II, 1704, 1712; Wright to Dix, Nov. 2, 1846, *ibid.*, II, 1722.

the vote of this region in order to conteract the expected loss
of Hunker support elsewhere. The Renters, indeed, were torn
by internal dissension. There were two Anti-Rent papers, the
Freeholder and the *Anti-Renter,* which hated each other even
more than the landlords. They were both handicapped by the
fact that there was no real Anti-Rent candidate for Governor.
The *Freeholder* backed Young, but only because he was less
objectionable than Wright, and the *Anti-Renter* came out for
a third candidate, Lewis Masquerier, who ran on a Free Soil
ticket. Actually Thomas Devyr, editor of the *Anti-Renter,* was
so hostile to the *Freeholder* faction that he did his best to help
Wright! Adopting Croswell's technique, he printed letters condemning Young and speaking almost with praise of the incumbent, at the same time that he adhered formally to Masquerier.

The nomination of Young by the Anti-Rent party also distressed many Whigs! The more conservative segment of that
organization was tepid toward Young because he had supported the new constitution, and his pledge to free the convicted
rioters was as salt in their wounds. As Horace Greeley, who
liked the Anti-Renters, but feared the loss of conservative
votes, put it, " The Anti-Rent nomination of Young is an act
of the most amazing stupidity...." [19] Such complications
make it extremely difficult to assay accurately the various influences which affected the outcome at the polls. The support
of " one idea " groups is usually as much a hindrance as a help
to a major party. Just as Anti-Masonic backing deprived the
old Clintonians of the votes of eastern conservatives in the
thirties, so Young's large Anti-Rent vote cost him many normally Whig ballots in the conservative wards of New York

19 Wright to Van Buren, Oct. 16, 1846, Van Buren papers; *Freeholder,*
Oct. 14, 1846; *Anti-Renter,* Oct. 31, 1846; Christman, *Tin Horns and Calico,*
pp. 273-4; Greeley to Weed, Oct. 8, 1846, Greeley-Weed letters, New York
Historical Society. See also A. Johnson to Fish, Oct. 22, 1846, Fish papers,
Library of Congress; but *cf. Weekly Tribune,* Nov. 11, 1846, quoted in
Ellis, *Landlords and Farmers,* p. 281.

City. Another example of this double reaction was brought out
by Greeley in discussing his party's effort to curry the favor
of both the nativists and the Irish-born in the metropolis. " We
might make a heavy inroad into the Adopted Citizens this
Fall," he wrote to Thurlow Weed, " if we were not obliged to
coax the Natives to vote with us. It is very difficult to gain
both ways."

Nevertheless, once Young received the Renters' formal blessing, Weed, Greeley and the rest of the Whig politicians did
their level best to make the most of it. Young was not in favor
of rioters or violence of any kind, they insisted, but he did
feel that the Anti-Renters had legitimate grievances which
should be alleviated.[20]

The Whigs worked industriously to widen the breach between the Hunkers and the radicals, and it was even later
charged that Weed and Croswell were working together to
engineer the defeat of Wright. It was difficult to make the
Governor appear as a corrupt or self-seeking politician, but his
enemies did whatever they could. " The political character of
SILAS WRIGHT is entirely indefensible. He is destitute of
stability; and an unstable man is not often an honest politician," Weed wrote in the *Evening Journal,* but aside from
Wright's now ancient " spoils letter " to Van Buren, he could
not offer any specific evidence to prove his charge. Naturally
the Whigs also criticized the Governor's stand on internal improvements, especially his veto of the canal bill of 1845. Workingmen should oppose Wright, the editor of the *Journal* wrote,
because by vetoing the bill he deprived them of an opportunity
to gain profitable employment. " What care he that this policy
at once kept Wealth from the State and Bread from the mouths
of the hungry . . . . He could see the people taxed to pay *him*
his ELEVEN DOLLARS a-day, while he could veto a bill
which would secure work and SIX SHILLINGS a-day to the in-

20 Greeley to Weed, Oct. 8, 1846, Greeley-Weed letters; *Evening Journal,*
Oct. 8, 1846.

dustrious!" The *Argus* continued to carry Wright's name at its masthead and to afford him nominal support, but in his last editorial before the election, Croswell managed to write half a column in favor of the ticket without once mentioning the party's gubernatorial choice. And he even admitted with surprising candor, that popular interest in the coming election was slight! [21]

Election day, wet and chilly, proved the accuracy of all the prophets of doom. Where he had carried the state by over ten thousand votes in 1844, Wright now lost it by an even larger margin in a contest in which the total vote declined considerably. Strangely enough, Lieutenant Governor Addison Gardiner, running for reelection, beat Fish by an even larger majority than Young piled up over Wright! But the Whigs carried the legislature, and elected a majority of the members of the House of Representatives from New York.[22]

When Wright went home to bed on election night he knew only that he had lost the city of Albany, an event more or less expected. The next morning he arose at his usual time and went to his office between seven and eight o'clock, before the morning papers were out. When his messenger came in from the post and telegraph offices with the latest news, the result was at once obvious. Later, he and Clarissa went over to the Flaggs. During the afternoon, as the returns continued to pour in from outlying counties confirming the magnitude of his defeat, he was perfectly calm and natural. He spoke frankly with Flagg and other friends who dropped in from time to time, made no effort to steer the conversation away from the all-engrossing subject of the moment, and without attempting to appear indifferent spoke of the various technicalities of the balloting in different parts of the state and considered the possibilities

21 Gillet, *Wright*, II, 1809; *Evening Journal*, Oct. 21, 8, 24, 1846; *Argus*, Oct. 31, 1846.

22 Hammond, *History of New York*, III, 689-90. For the official returns, see *Argus*, Dec. 7, 1846.

of the counties yet unheard from with a serenity that appeared to one observer almost sublime. He had earned his right to retire the hard way, but he knew that it was his at last. " I can say to you with perfect truth, that I feel no shock of disappointment," he wrote simply to Van Buren. " I really feel ... as though my shoulders were relieved from a heavy burden . . . ."

The reaction of other Democrats was not so dispassionate. Wright's " high character & talents " wrote John A. Dix, were " not sufficient to shield him from treachery, proscription, and popular neglect." There must be " a full and marked retribution," he warned darkly. George Bancroft, who had left the cabinet to take the position of Minister to England which Dix had refused, was "astonished " at the news from New York. " The hour of adversity is the hour of dignity," he wrote Polk rather pompously, but with evident sincerity. The President himself, having seen the error of his ways, now understood even more clearly the extent to which his distribution of federal patronage had been used against Wright. Speaking of the Hunkers, he confided to his diary, " This faction shall hereafter receive no favors at my hands . . . ." Shortly afterward in a conversation with John E. Develin, a member of the radical group, he expressed regret at Wright's defeat and promised not only to remove any office holders who had used their influence against the Governor, but also to be more careful in the future about New York appointments.[23]

Even Marcy expressed disappointment at the result, for as usual, the practical situation (defeat for the party) loomed larger in his mind than the personal motives which had made him a Hunker. The Whigs had had high hopes of winning

---

23 G. Little to Hammond, Dec. 21, 1847, Hammond, *Wright*, pp. 701-2; Wright to Van Buren, Nov. 10, 1846, Van Buren papers. For Wright's routine as Governor see *Atlas*, Apr. 21, 1845. Dix to Flagg, Nov. 9, 1846, Flagg papers; Bancroft to Polk, Dec. 3, 1846, Bancroft papers; Polk, *Diary*, M. Quaife, ed., II, 218; Develin to Tilden, Jan. 17, 1846, Tilden papers. See also Donovan, *Barnburners*, pp. 80-1.

the election, but they had not expected to do nearly as well
as they did. " I can scarcely believe my eyes," wrote Philip
Hone, dazed but happy at the result.[24]

All these men and many others thought they knew exactly
what had caused the great reversal, and today their explanations can be modified and qualified but not contradicted.
Wright himself placed the major responsibility on the shoulders of the Hunkers. " Anti-Rentism became an instrument, but
the conservatism of 1837 '8 was the agent, armed as it has
been . . . with the patronage of the federal government. I
doubt whether the President designed the result, but it matters not in the effect, as those who have influenced him did."
In Washington, the Van Burenites tended to emphasize the
Polk administration as the cause of the defeat. "With proper
appointments in our Custom-Houses and Post-offices," wrote
Churchill C. Cambreleng, " we should have had a more united
party, better nominations and Gov. Wright would have triumphed over anti-rentism and every other faction." D. W.
Broderick, a defeated candidate for Congress from New York
City, also placed the responsibility for his own failure and that
of the Governor on " the Custom House." [25]

The Hunkers generally attributed the defeat of Wright to
the Anti-Rent disturbances, or, when they admitted that intra-
party strife had been a factor, blamed this on the radicals.
" The unholy alliance between the Whigs & Anti-renters and
more than all the unfortunate want of harmony in the Democratic ranks arising from the proscriptive course pursued by
our leading friends at Albany . . . to brethren of the same principle have produced an alienation that has most probably
caused [the] defeat," wrote one Hunker to the President. A

24 Marcy to Wetmore, Nov. 4, 1846, Marcy papers; *Diary of Philip
Hone*, XXIV, 272, Nov. 6, 1846, New York Historical Society.

25 Wright to Niles, Nov. 6, 1846, Miscellaneous papers, New York Public
Library; Cambreleng to Van Buren, Nov. 30, 1846, Van Buren papers;
Broderick to R. Walker, Nov. 14, 1846, Miscellaneous papers, New York
Historical Society. See also B. Wood to Buchanan, Nov. 9, 1846, Nov. 28,
1846, Buchanan papers.

"new candidate for Governor could have been elected," this man said, thus silently admitting that the Hunkers had cut Wright.

The best exposition of the radical attitude was provided by the *Albany Atlas* in a series of articles early in December. Appearing between December 4 and 10, under the title, "The Result of the Election—its Causes and Consequences," these pieces studied the election exhaustively from every angle. Their author is unknown, and though one student has suggested that they came from Wright's pen, the Governor himself never admitted writing them. But it is clear that someone in the radicals' inner circle produced the pieces and that they reflected accurately the views of that group and of Wright.[26]

There were, according to these essays, several causes of the debacle. Anti-Rentism was one, Wright's veto of the canal bill another, fraud a third. But individually or collectively, none of these was *the* reason why Wright lost. Behind them all was the Hunker faction, dubbed by the author, the "Conservatives." According to "the highest authority," the argument ran, Croswell had been responsible for the Anti-Rent nominations of Young and Gardiner. At the Anti-Rent convention he had lobbied strenuously for this ticket at a time when many Democratic tenants were willing to keep the vexing rent issue out of the gubernatorial contest. When questioned as to his motives for doing so, the editor had maintained a meaningful silence.

Similarly, in the canal counties, certain Hunker politicians had organized and led the opposition to Wright, merely using his canal veto as a convenient reason for going against him. These men were named, and election statistics were advanced to show how the result had been accomplished. On the question of fraud, the author of the "Causes and Consequences" was even more specific. It was the custom of the major parties in those days, to print advance ballots for the faithful, to make

---

26 C. White to Polk, Nov. 4, 1846, Polk papers, 2nd series; Donovan, *Barnburners*, p. 78. Gillet, in printing selections, does not claim that Wright wrote them.

certain that they voted straight tickets and to avoid losing
votes through improperly marked ballots. Regulations were
very strict. A ballot marked " Wright," or even " S. Wright,"
was not counted, and with many offices to be filled, it was well
worth the trouble and expense to print the candidates' names
accurately and distribute them to the electorate. No one, of
course, was required to use such a ballot, but many did so. In
Albany County, the Hunkers had printed and distributed a
ticket in the following form:

For Senator
SILAS WRIGHT.

For Lieutenant Governor,
ADDISON GARDINER.

For Canal Commissioners,
CHARLES COOK,
THOMAS CLOWES.

For Congress,
JOHN I. SLINGERLAND.

For Sheriff,
ANDREW VANDERHEYDEN.

For Clerk,
LAWRENCE VAN DUZEN.

For Assembly,
BARENT P. STAATS,
ROBERT D. WATSON,
JOHN J. GALLUP,
JOHN FULLER.

For Coroners,
JOHN OSBORNE,
WILLIAM H. KEARNEY,
FOR GOVERNOR,
JOHN YOUNG.

Naturally, many unsuspecting Democrats, looking casually at the ballot (or not at all), would unwittingly vote for Young for Governor and Wright for State Senator. This ticket also substituted the Whig candidates for Canal Commissioners for the Democrats, John Hudson and Cornelius Allen. There is no question that this dupe was actually employed, for the official returns in Albany County (which Young carried handily) show 110 votes for Wright for State Senator. According to the author of the " Causes and Consequences " these ballots were prepared and distributed by " a man intimate with and almost exclusively under the influence, politically, of Mr. Croswell."

Thus, reasoned the author, in every way, the Hunkers were responsible for the result.

> We have said that anti-rentism was *a* cause, and that the local canal feeling was *a* cause, but the conservative defection was *the* cause.... We have shown that it was the strongest element in the combination of causes, and that it was the agent which combined and marshaled and moved other influences. It was *the* cause.[27]

* * * * *

Today, it is a very confusing task to unravel the 1846 version of the tangled skein which made up the political alignments in New York. At the time, each thread of opinion differed in its understanding of the election's significance from all others and they were all partially correct. Probably no election, state or national, before or since, shows as widespread a disregard of party loyalty on all sides.

It has already been said that the Anti-Rent element played a rôle in the breaking up of both parties. Wright's majority in New York City was at least in part the result of conservative Whig backing, and the fact that the Governor's course with regard to the manor war was almost universally popular (except in the actually disturbed areas) probably garnered many

27 *Argus*, Dec. 7, 1846; *Atlas*, Dec. 10, 1846.

scattered votes for him. Thus, while it is easy to show that he lost many many votes in the Anti-Rent counties, this is by no means proof that these counties were decisive.

But on the other side, there is much evidence to contradict, or at least qualify, the radical charge that the Hunkers' sabotaging of Wright was the cause of the Democratic defeat. A thorough examination of the returns shows that the radicals cut Hunker candidates quite as much as the reverse. The balloting for members of the House of Representatives is very interesting in connection with this point. The counties which showed majorities for Wright for Governor elected at the same time twenty-seven Congressmen. These counties were certainly radical strongholds, especially if the radical charges of Hunker infidelity are true. Surely, if the radicals were loyal to the *party* in these counties, the Democratic candidates for Congress should have been successful, regardless of their stand in the Hunker-radical quarrel. But of these twenty-seven candidates, eleven were defeated! In Jefferson County, for example, Wright defeated Young, 5295 to 4728, and the Democratic candidates for the state legislature were all elected. But Hunker Orville Hungerford, who was running for reelection to Congress, was beaten by Joseph Mullin, the Whig choice. Obviously in this case the *radicals* failed to support the party nominee. The same thing happened in Chemung County, where William T. Lawrence, a Whig, was chosen as Congressman at the same time that the rest of the Democratic slate was swept into office.

This was not confined to the Congressional contest. In Queens County, strongly radical, the entire Democratic ticket was elected except for the member of the State Assembly, and in Broome County it was the candidate for State Senator who fell by the wayside.

But it is equally true that the Hunkers voted against Wright in large numbers. Here Oneida County is an excellent example of what happened. In 1844, Wright had received a majority of 800 in this county; in 1846 he lost by 1,337. At the same time Oneida chose a Democratic Congressman and four Demo-

cratic Assemblymen, all Hunkers, but picked Nelson Beach, a
Whig, as State Senator rather than radical George C. Sherman. Onondaga County, did very much the same thing, electing Young, a Whig Congressman, a Democratic (Hunker)
State Senator, and three out of four Democratic Assemblymen.

Clearly the Democratic party in New York was completely
broken up. Party nomination meant next to nothing; normally
Democratic citizens supported or rejected the party nominees
according to each man's Hunker or radical connections. If a
man was radical his ballot went to a radical or a Whig; if a
Hunker to a Hunker or a Whig. There were for each office
three parties but only two candidates! Some Democrats of
course took no part and no interest in the intra-party conflict
and they probably turned in straight tickets, but their influence
was not decisive. Enough did consider the schism important to
destroy the effectiveness of the party. Where the Governorship was concerned, the non-radicals deserted the party, for
Wright was considered a radical, but the same rule held true
for all the other posts that were at stake. So great had the differences between the two factions become, that it is a complete
fiction to speak of the segments as members of the same party.
As one newspaper summed up the situation:

> It cannot be denied that the landmarks of party have been
> entirely lost sight of. . . . Where the " Hunkers " had the as-
> cendancy in the [county] nominating convention, the opposite
> section of the party cast their votes against the candidates,
> and where the " Barnburners " [this name was becoming
> common by 1846] had the control, the opposite faction turned
> against the whole ticket.[28]

The Whigs were also divided in this contest, but not so
badly. Young was disliked by many of the more conservative
members of his organization and his promise to pardon the
convicted Anti-Renters unquestionably cost him many votes,
especially in New York City. As Hone wrote in his diary,

28 *Ulster Republican*, quoted in Donovan, *Barnburners*, p. 62.

many Whigs refused " to do their duty " in the election.[29] But the Democratic breakup was complete, and the result was a general Whig victory. The relative stability of the two parties can best be demonstrated by comparing the number of counties which elected solid tickets. Of the twenty-four counties that gave majorities to Wright, only eleven elected complete Democratic slates. Of Young's thirty-three counties (one county, Ulster, produced a tie vote in the gubernatorial race) nineteen were solidly Whig and two more cut only Hamilton Fish.

The defeat of Fish by Gardiner seems paradoxical, but it really helps to clarify the picture of the election, and gives an insight into the real strength of the parties. Gardiner escaped the fate of the rest of the politicians of his party. Probably because of his harmless and inconsequential position as presiding officer of the State Senate, he was not especially connected with either group within the Democratic organization, and was therefore supported by both. Thus he carried every district where Wright was successful, and all but four of the counties which had voted for Young and then split their tickets in various ways. These were the areas where the Hunkers had combined with the Whigs in support of Young. Gardiner's showing in such areas shows that he had Hunker as well as radical friends. Fish attracted no outside help, and thus could only win in the counties where the Whig party had a majority by itself. The contest between Fish and Gardiner presents a picture that approximates closely the general pattern of the election of 1844, and it demonstrates what probably would have happened in 1846 if the Democrats had not split. Wright, with only half a party, polled about as many votes as did Fish, who was sustained by nearly all the " regular " Whigs.[30]

29 *Diary of Philip Hone*, XXIV, 262, Oct. 29, 1846, New York Historical Society.

30 It is interesting that in Wright strongholds, Fish ran ahead of Young! Though he trailed the head of the ticket by some 11,000 votes throughout the state, in the metropolitan area (New York, Kings, Queens, Suffolk, Westchester) and in the North Country (Clinton, Franklin, St. Lawrence)

It is apparent that the break-up of the Democratic party explains the peculiar outcome of the New York election of 1846. The Anti-Rent movement certainly hurt Wright, but not enough to produce the result which followed. Similarly, Wright's veto of the canal bill must have cost him some votes in areas where there was strong feeling for such improvements. But both of these sentiments were local, and in a state-wide election, were bound to be at least partially compensated for. In the end it is necessary to agree with the author of the " Causes and Consequences " that " defection was *the* cause," with the one very important modification that radical as well as Hunker irregularity was involved.

*　　*　　*　　*　　*

The Democratic party that was to rise from this ruin was a different organization from the one that Wright had known, but so also was Silas' own life different. At last he was in a position where he could make good his repeated threats to retire, and he did not hesitate to take advantage of the chance. " You do not know how well I feel at the prospect of a discharge from these official cares and responsibilities," he wrote to Senator Dix in December. " I intend to enjoy the leisure of a private citizen very much. I shall think of you at Washington very often, and sympathize with your cares, but I shall not look upon any of you with envy." [31] He and Clarissa did not even wait upon the formal ending of his term before they left their " mansion " on Clinton Square for more congenial quarters with the Flaggs. They also found time for a visit with Van Buren, which had been planned before the election but postponed because of the press of business. When the new year arrived, and John Young took over Wright's gubernatorial duties, there can be little question who was the happier of the two men. For the first time since 1823 Wright was no longer an office holder, and he loved it.

his vote was considerably larger than Young's. This seems to demonstrate Wright's popularity in his home region and in New York City, for obviously, many Whigs in those areas voted for Wright and Fish.

31 Wright to Dix, Dec. 1846, Gillet, *Wright*, II, 1725.

CHAPTER XVII

BACK TO THE SOIL

"I labor steadily and enjoy my food as no politician can."

Wright to John Fairfield, August 11, 1847.

"We confess that we loved Silas Wright as a true democratic friend of the people. . . . He was a perfectly upright, honest politician. He never betrayed either his friends or his own conscience . . ."

Walt Whitman, in the *Brooklyn Eagle*, August, 1847.

THE Wrights remained at the Capital throughout January visiting with friends and being "truly lazy" for the first time in many a day. They did not want to undertake the arduous trip home until the roads were well covered with snow. Finally, on the morning of February 1, they set out. The trip to Utica by rail was relatively simple, and they arrived at that city at one o'clock in the afternoon. Silas deposited his wife at Bagg's Hotel, and went to visit his brother Pliny, who was at that time an inmate of the State Asylum outside Utica. He found him as well as he ever was and seemingly very happy. When he returned to the city, Wright discovered that a group of his friends there wanted him to stay on awhile, but he insisted on pressing forward immediately. So a young German farmer named Neger, whose "politics had been endorsed," was hired to drive the Wrights to Canton on a lumber sled.

It must have been a curious sight—the ex-Governor of New York and his wife perched atop a ponderous old sled, crowded in by all their baggage. Some of his Albany associates had presented Wright with a few farming tools, and these too were piled on. Clarissa carried in her lap a well wrapped cage containing "Tommy," a bird, probably a canary, which had been given her by the Flaggs as a going away present. They set out at about five o'clock in the afternoon.

That night they stopped at their driver's farm outside Utica. Wright was touched to discover that a large delegation of young Neger's friends and neighbors had gathered to see him. These people, Neger told Wright, " had never had the honor to shake hands with a Governor " and would like very much to do so. Silas remarked that he was not a Governor any longer, but he was glad to meet and talk to the farmers. During the course of the evening three more groups appeared and were introduced. " All the men I saw," he wrote later, " seemed plain, sensible laboring men, perfectly sound politically and very much gratified with their visit." Among such men, Wright always felt at home.

The next day was perfect for travelling, and they covered over forty miles, to the town of Houseville, in Lewis County. The following day was stormy, " the wind being so strong it was impossible to carry an umbrella," and it was not until about four in the afternoon that they managed to move on. But they only got a few miles before it began to rain, so they stopped for the night at Martinsburg.

It was late when they got to bed, but Silas was up at five the next morning, waking his driver in order to get an early start. It was bitter cold, with a strong gale blowing out of the northwest. By the time they had gone as far as Lowville, the next town, one of Wright's ears was frozen, and they had to stop to warm up. But despite the fearful cold they made forty more miles and spent the night at Somerville, a tiny village near the western border of St. Lawrence County. The weather had been so frigid that Clarissa's neck was badly nipped, and became swollen and blistered. But they were now only thirty odd miles from Canton, and the next day, they completed their trip. They were very tired, but their only casualty was the door of their stove, which had somehow been lost on the way. Even " Tommy " arrived little the worse for wear.[1]

1 Wright to Van Buren, Jan. 28, 1847, Van Buren papers; Wright to Flagg, Feb. 7, 1847, Flagg papers; J. Hinman to Hammond, Feb. 17, 1848, Hammond, *Wright*, pp. 715-7; Wright to H. Moody, Feb. 13, 1847, Wright papers, St. Lawrence University.

At home, they spent the rest of the winter getting resettled and rested, but as soon as the weather permitted Silas undertook to become a fulltime farmer. His long career in politics had not made him rich, but he had accumulated a reasonable amount of property and a little money. His farm was run by several hired hands while he was away on political business at Washington or Albany, and he had interests in several local enterprises, such as grist-mills and sawmills.[2] Also, he had always tended his own vegetable garden. Many stories, more or less apochryphal, but based no doubt on fact, were told of Wright's love of farming and of his insistence, even at the height of his career, on doing a great deal of his farm work himself. Probably the most common tale was the one of the " distinguished visitor " who, arriving at Canton to see Senator Wright, approached a workman to ask where he might be found.

" There is Mr. Wright in the yard, working on the mortar bed," the man informed him.

" But," said the visitor, " I mean the Hon. Silas Wright."

" Well, that is him."

" I mean Senator Wright."

" Well, that is Senator Wright."

At this point the amazed visitor went up to the man at the mortar bed and discovered that the workman had not been pulling his leg, that the great Senator Wright was really hard at work with his helpers.[3]

Actually, Wright was never a full time farmer during the years he held public office, but he enjoyed doing agricultural work and probably did a great deal of " puttering " about his land and buildings whenever he had the time. There was a good deal of Yankee shrewdness in this. After two weeks of hard work in the hay field one summer he wrote to Flagg

2 Wright to Russell, June 18, 1842, Gillet, *Wright*, II, 1328.

3 Hammond, *Wright*, pp. 35-6; for other stories of a similar nature, see *Democratic Review*, V, 417-8, and Gillet, *Wright*, II, 1935-8.

that he had been laboring, " not to accomplish so much with
my own hands as with the hands of others by my presence."
But when he returned from Albany in February, 1847, he was
determined that he was finished with politics, and that he was
going to become a serious farmer. For a man over fifty, who
had had little opportunity for exercise in many years, it was
a difficult transition, but he set at it with all the effort he
could muster. He got to work on the woodpile first. By the
middle of March he could do three times as much work a day
as he had at first. But he had learned that sawing wood was
too much for him and had settled on splitting logs after they
had been cut to proper lengths by others. He was pleased with
his progress, but not completely satisfied. " I get very tired
much before the day is ended," he complained to Flagg.
Shortly before his election as Governor, he had purchased
about a hundred acres of partially cleared land, and the work
of preparing it for the plow was extremely arduous and time
consuming.[4]

He was really trying to remake the pattern of his life. "For
months he [has] been, a most *abstinent tee-totaller!* " wrote
one of his friends in astonishment. As time went on he was
able to accomplish more and more. " I labor steadily and enjoy my food and sleep as no politician can," he wrote happily
to his good friend, Senator John Fairfield.[5] He found little
time for politics, and his reading on such matters was confined
pretty much to a perusal of the *Atlas*. His main object was to
steer clear of all public affairs, for he knew that any statement
he might make, however innocent, would be interpreted in relation to the coming presidential election. " Can I not in some
way convince my friends and my enemies (I speak politically)
that I am not a candidate for the presidency and I do not want

4 Wright to Flagg, Aug. 6, 1843, Mar. 12, 1847, Flagg papers; Jenkins,
Wright, p. 247.

5 Russell to Flagg, Aug. 27, 1847, Flagg papers; Wright to Fairfield,
Aug. 11, 1847, Gillet, *Wright*, II, 1933.

the office if I could get it?" he wrote plaintively to Dix. This was his only worry during these days, but it was an irritating one, because it made it next to impossible for him to do many of the things he wanted to do. When Fairfield invited him to his home at Saco for a session of cod fishing he had to turn the offer down. "I should not dare travel this year, as I should be suspected of doing it for sinister purposes," he wrote, but "after this year I shall be relieved of this embarrassment, and then I hope the time may come, when I can . . . have the pleasure of fishing with you for cod, without the suspicion of being a fisher for men." [6] Alas, this small pleasure was to be denied him.

But in spite of the lengths to which he went he was unable either to stop the use of his name as a presidential possibility or keep silent on the big issues of the day. A new subject, or rather, a new aspect of one that was as old as the Republic, was agitating the public mind, the question of slavery in the territories.

At the time that Wright had left the Senate, the Texas question had been put aside, awaiting the decision of the people at the polls. The election of Polk on a platform calling for the "reannexation" of the Lone Star Republic insured the rapid accomplishment of that object in the spring of 1845. But within a year the fears of men like Wright had been realized. Mexico was unwilling to accept the situation, and when the United States pressed its claim to the left bank of the Rio Grande, and backed that claim with an army under General Zachary Taylor, war resulted. Once undertaken, the conflict was supported by most Northern Democrats, and Wright, as Governor of New York, did his best to "raise an army" for Polk. But as hostilities progressed, and most of New Mexico and California fell into American hands, the slavery problem

6 Wright to Flagg, June 27, 1847, Flagg papers; Wright to Dix, Mar. 22, 1847, Gillet, *Wright*, II, 1924-5; Wright to Fairfield, Aug. 11, 1847, *ibid.*, II, 1933.

began to demand more attention. As early as August 6, 1846, David Wilmot, a Representative from Pennsylvania, introduced an amendment to a bill providing money for the negotiation of peace with Mexico. His amendment, the famous Wilmot Proviso, called for the prohibition of slavery in any territory added to the Union as a result of the " negotiations " mentioned in the bill. Wilmot's Proviso did not pass, but it was not forgotten by many Northerners. Preston King tried to append it to another appropriation bill presented in the House in January, 1847, and in New York, resolutions approving the spirit of the Proviso passed the legislature almost unanimously.[7]

For Wright, King's action spelled trouble. The pudgy Representative was not only a close friend and supporter of the ex-Governor, but also represented Wright's home district in the House. It was inevitable that this former member of Silas' " cabinet " would be regarded in Washington as his present spokeman. King had introduced the Proviso on January 4, 1847, while Wright was still in Albany waiting for sufficient snow to make the trip to Canton. His act worried Wright a great deal. It was not a question of his own position regarding the Proviso but of his supposed connection with King's sponsorship of it that bothered him. He wrote a long letter to King, sending it via their mutual friend, Ransom H. Gillet, in which he warned the Congressman not to say or intimate that his own action was in any way connected with Wright, or that he was acting as his mouthpiece. He was plainly nervous, though to his friends he tried to make light of it. " I have a good laugh every day to see the extent of my agency [at Washington] ... if the letter-writers and newspaper scribblers are to be credited," he wrote to Senator Dix. " I am made to write speeches for King to deliver, as well as to dictate the measures and movements upon which he is to make the speeches." He also expressed his disappointment at

7 For the resolutions, see Gillet, *Wright*, II, 1867.

King's sponsorship of the Proviso. He thought that it should have been left to its original sponsor, Wilmot.[8]

But he had no objection to the Proviso itself; he was indeed enthusiastic in his support of the idea of keeping slavery out of new additions to the United States.

> The great point [his letter to Dix said] is as to the propriety of the movement at all. Upon this point, I have not a doubt. The principle asserted is clearly right, and its assertion now is, in my judgment, not merely expedient, but positively necessary.

He expounded his opinions at some length. In all previous additions of territory to the country, the principle had been entirely different, he rationalized. In the cases of Louisiana, Florida, and Texas, slavery already existed when the annexation took place, but the peculiar institution was illegal in Mexican territory. " Shall we pay the money and use the arms of the Union to acquire new territory, that we may incorporate [slavery] upon it, and thus extend the limits of a universally conceded social and political evil? " The North, he said, always backed the South in the preservation of slavery where it already existed, " but it is as manifest as the light of day, that no part and no party of the free states will consent that territory be purchased or conquered to extend this institution. . . ."

Wright even considered that the Missouri Compromise, which divided the Louisiana Purchase into slave and free areas, was unconstitutional, and curiously enough he based his reasoning on the arguments later advanced by Calhoun and upheld by the Supreme Court in the Dred Scott case, that every state has a right to establish whatever institutions it pleases within its own borders:

> When a State is admitted to the Union . . . it must be admitted upon a footing of perfect equality . . . with the original thirteen States. One of their rights and powers was to establish the

8 *Ibid.*, II, 1872-3; Wright to Dix, Jan. 19, 1847, *ibid.*, II, 1915-8.

> institution of slavery within themselves and to abolish it, at will, and every State now in the Union and every one which shall ever be admitted ... does and must possess that constitutional right and power of the original States, the Missouri Compromise or any other action of Congress notwithstanding.

But he used this unquestionably sound constitutional argument to come to exactly the opposite conclusion from the one reached later by the Court. In the Dred Scott case, in 1857, Chief Justice Taney was to say that this doctrine meant that Congress must not legislate slavery in or out of the territories lest in doing so it limit the future ability of states entering the Union to set up whatever institutions they desired. Thus the Court found unconstitutional the part of the Compromise which prohibited human bondage north of 36° 30'. Ten years earlier, Wright had deduced from the same principle that it was unconstitutional for Congress to declare that slavery could not exist in the northern part of the Louisiana Purchase *after* the territory there had been admitted to statehood.

> All Congress can do ... is to determine whether or not slavery shall be an institution of the territory while it remains a territory of the United States, subject to the government of the laws of the Union.

Therefore the Wilmot Proviso was perfectly in order, but even more, it was "imperatively necessary." "The war cannot be efficiently prosecuted," he wrote to his friend, "unless a distinct negative is put upon the idea that its object is to extend the limits of the institution of slavery. I do not think it is now possible to avoid or prevent a ... decision of the question, and I shall regard a decision against Mr. King as fatal to this administration and its prosecution of the war." [9]

Two months later, from Canton, he wrote again to Dix. "I have no doubt that the principle of the Wilmot Proviso will be adopted ... [for] all the territory hereafter to be added to

9 *Ibid.*

the Union, and if the southern people are unwise enough to follow the fanatical dogmas of Mr. Calhoun upon this point, then . . . the politics of this Union will be geographical . . . a deep misfortune, but one which that statesman has seemed determined for years to force upon the country, or to force it to yield to his sole domination." Wright had not forgotten Baltimore.

During the spring, the press took up his position on the Proviso. Northern papers were divided not so much on whether or not the Proviso was morally correct as whether or not it was expedient. As the *New York Globe,* a Hunker paper, said in criticizing King's amendment, it was a " question of *time* rather than *principle.*" The country should win the war and then worry about how to govern the conquered (or purchased) territory. Wright's name was not brought into the discussion until April, after King's amendment had been defeated. On April 9, the *Globe,* in reply to attacks on its position by papers like the *Evening Post,* which had consistently opposed the extension of slavery, said self-righteously that at least in its stand on the Proviso it was in good Democratic company, including "no less a personage than SILAS WRIGHT."

The *Post* leaped to the defense of Wright, saying, "we have reason to know" that the former Governor favors the immediate passage of the Proviso. The *Globe* retorted to the effect that it also had inside information, straight from "*among the warmest and most sincere friends of Gov. WRIGHT.*"

This futile argument was called to Wright's attention by an acquaintance, James H. Titus, who sent him some clippings from the papers. These distressed the ex-Governor a good deal, for he knew that discussions of this sort were inconsistent with his plans for permanent retirement. He had spoken to Titus in Albany during January about the Proviso, and he now reiterated his stand in phrases similar to those used in his letters to Dix. King was not acting in consultation with him, he said. He wished the St. Lawrence Congressman had not felt compelled to assume the initiative in advancing Wilmot's doctrine, but he was in complete sympathy with the idea of keeping slavery within its present limits, and thought that the subject should be brought to public attention at once.

Wright asked Titus to show his letter to William Cullen Bryant, of the *Post,* but laid a strict ban on its publication.

> I prefer not to have my personal opinions upon any public question made the subject of discussion in the public papers. It is impossible to separate such discussions, in the public mind, from an impression either that the individual himself wishes them promulgated, or that his friends promulgate them because they think they will influence others . . . .

Wright told Titus that he realized his friends were only trying to correct false rumors which had been circulated about his stand, but he hoped that the subject could be disposed of as quietly and unobtrusively as possible. Bryant should say, he wrote, that he knew nothing about the " warmest and most sincere friends of Gov. Wright " to whom the *Globe* had referred, but that he had positive evidence that the former Governor " is opposed in principle to the conquest or purchase of territory, now free, for the purpose of incorporating slavery upon it. . . ." [10]

Other matters also forced their way into Wright's life, and he felt compelled to make public statements about them. In 1846, Polk had vetoed a bill providing money for the forwarding of harbor facilities on the Great Lakes and on certain rivers, an action very unpopular in the Great Lakes region. In July, 1847, a River and Harbor convention was held at Chicago, and Wright was one of the statesmen invited to at-

---

10 Wright to Dix, Mar. 22, 1847, *ibid.,* II, 1924. *New York Globe,* Jan. 22, Mar. 1, 1847; *New York Post,* Apr. 9, 1847; *Globe,* Apr. 10, 1847, *Post,* Apr. 30, 1856. Wright to Titus, Apr. 15, 1847, Gillet, *Wright,* II, 1874-6. Bryant wisely said nothing at all and the discussion of Wright's stand was not resumed until after the former Governor had died. Then Bryant published the letter to Titus. Clipping in Flagg papers.

tend. He did not go, but he wrote a long letter to the committee which had invited him, expressing his views on such public works. His statement was an attempt to distinguish between two types of internal improvements, and represents a modification, or at least a clarification, of his previous position that the federal government should not engage in such undertakings at all. Construction on the Lakes, he said, was perfectly constitutional because it was no different from harbor improvements at any Atlantic port. People who doubted this just had not seen the Great Lakes and did not realize " the magnitude and importance " of these vast bodies of water. But federal funds should only be spent to develop already extant harbors, not to enable a poorly endowed port to compete with a more fortunate area. " My own observation," he added sensibly, " has shown that applications for harbor improvements at the public expense are made and passed within distances of a very few miles, and at locations where . . . a good harbor at either point would secure to the commerce of the lake all the convenience and safety of duplicate improvements. . . . It is the duty of those who urge these improvements to be honest with Congress, and to urge appropriations only at points where these considerations demand them."

When it came to river developments, Wright admitted that he was baffled:

> There are applications for improvements of rivers about which . . . I have no more doubt than about the harbors upon the lakes or the Atlantic coast, and there are those which, in my judgment, come neither within the principle nor the constitutional power; but to draw a line between the two classes of cases I cannot.

The only safe course was to have Congress act on each case individually, but again, the principle of distinguishing between bettering already existing works and developing new ones should be a guide. Congress might aid commerce where it al-

ready existed, but it had not the power to try to create commerce.[11]

In reprinting this letter the *St. Lawrence Republican* called
it the Democratic creed on internal improvements. If it was
not a particularly unusual or brilliant policy it had at least the
virtue of being democratic in spirit, leaving as it did the settlement of doubtful cases to the representatives of the people.
The proper working of such a democratic system required, as
Wright always stressed, certain qualities in the body of voters.
As he wrote in his last public statement, which was delivered
after his death by John Dix, " the history of all civil government [proves] . . . that a well-educated, industrious, and independent yeomanry, are the safest repository of freedom and
free institutions." This axiom, taken straight from Thomas
Jefferson, permeated all Wright's thinking. Especially when
considering agricultural problems was he a disciple of the Sage
of Monticello. During the months after his retirement he had
consistently turned down all invitations to speak or appear at
public functions, but in the summer he did agree to address
the meeting in September of the New York State Agricultural Society at Saratoga. The preparation of his speech was a
labor of love. It is part of the tragedy of his last years that
he did not live to deliver it, though he tried to make it appear
that he did not want to be bothered with it. " I feel about this
address," he wrote to Flagg on the warm July day when he
finished drafting it, " as old Hickory did about his inaugural
address. I had rather hoe corn through the whole of a day hot
as this than to have anything to do with such a matter." What
he did not add was that hoeing corn was one of his greatest
pleasures.[12]

The speech itself is certainly one of his best. It stressed the
importance of agriculture in American life, and called upon

11 Wright to N. Judd and others, May 31, 1847, Gillet, *Wright*, II,
1899-1902.

12 *St. Lawrence Republican*, July 20, 1847; Jenkins, *Wright*, p. 378;
Wright to Flagg, July 8, 1847, Flagg papers.

the farmer to seek his salvation in world markets and free trade. Agriculture, he wrote, is the basis of the American economy, " the great element which spreads the sail and impels the car of commerce, and moves the hands and turns the machinery of manufacture." In order for this vital segment of the system to prosper it must have a " healthful and stable " market. Since the farmers of the United States produce goods " far beyond any possible demand of the domestic market " foreign outlets are essential. Home consumption must not be neglected, but " other elements " should be cherished with equal care.

The recent repeal of the English Corn Laws (which he called an act " of almost superhuman sagacity ") attracted his attention. It is up to American producers, by providing " the best articles, at the fairest prices " to capture the vast new market thus opened. But above all, he thought, " any well-digested system of agricultural education " must stress the interrelationships between farming and manufacturing, commerce and foreign trade policy. " A thorough and continued education in these collateral but highly necessary branches of knowledge ... will prove extensively useful to the American citizen, beyond their application to the production and sale of the fruits of his labor." This education, " equally and impartially disseminated " can put an end to the rivalry between the various units of the economy by teaching them all that " they are all parts of one great and naturally harmonious system of human industry, of which a fair encouragement to any part is a benefit to all."

> The education proposed will do all that can be done to mark
> the true line between natural and healthful encouragement
> to either interest, and an undue attempt to advance any one,
> at the expense of the united system, [will produce] an un-
> natural and artificial relation and action, which cannot fail
> to work disease and injury.[13]

13 The Agricultural Address is printed in Jenkins, *Wright*, pp. 360-78.

Here again is a key to all Silas Wright's thinking. In essence it was based on the Golden Rule, the principle of non-exploitation. As he saw it the great threat in America was the man who sought private gain at the expense of others: the speculator seeking to improve his lands by getting a canal built past his door at public expense, the banker who tied up important legislation with his incessant demands for charters and privileges, the manufacturer who considered only the fact that a high tariff would increase his own profit, the politician to whom office was a prize rather than an obligation. All his life he fought against this spirit of plunder so common in America, and the longer he lived the more unswerving became his determination to yield it no quarter. This was at once the source of his strength and his weakness. It gave his ideas a moral force which the average man was quick to sense and appreciate, but at the same time it made him unfit for the practical aspects of politics which he had once loved and for which he was so well prepared by his apprenticeship in the Albany Regency. Originally he had, without really considering what he was doing, accepted expediency as a necessary and powerful weapon in the battle against exploitation. Long continued observation of " practical " politics, however, convinced him that this was wrong. Thus in 1824, he fought the passage of the New York electoral law because he thought that by so doing he could help attain a larger end, keeping De Witt Clinton and all he stood for out of the White House. But twenty years later he would not condone Texas annexation even to insure the reelection of Van Buren and the preservation of the whole program of Jacksonian democracy which he sincerely considered in danger. Similarly he refused to pardon the convicted Anti-Renters even to try to obtain the triumph of the radical party in New York in 1846.

He knew what he was doing. He saw that the course he insisted on following as Governor would lead to failure. " Defeat in an attempt to carry out and establish honest principles," he wrote a friend in July, 1847, is " the fate too often met by honest men." " Still," he went on, " there has been something very remarkable in the passage of events. The independent treasury has been [re-]established and is in operation. We have succeeded in establishing the most sound and safe financial principles in our new [State] Constitution, and yet the party which . . . was favorable to these reforms, was beaten at the very election which adopted them. All this shows that our principles possess a strength with our people which our men do not." [14]

He felt strongly that the only way to make sure that the policies he stood for were upheld was to advocate them honestly and without regard for their immediate practical political effect. Only in this way, as he had told his brother Pliny many years earlier, would the average citizen be able to " distinguish between the pretender and the real friend " of American institutions.

Who can say that he was wrong? It is true, as he well realized, that no man can act as he wanted to act and still be a successful politician. That was one reason why he wanted to retire, and why he fought so hard against the Governorship in 1844, and why he discouraged all efforts to build him up as a presidential candidate. When he saw, in September, 1844, that his nomination as the Democratic candidate for Governor was inevitable, he was convinced that it would mean eventual defeat, and this was in a way a consolation. " I incline to think it may have been necessary to dispose of me in this way," he wrote to George Bancroft at that time. " Your letter shows, and it is but one of many evidences of a like character to show, that our friends, in all parts of the Union, are permitting themselves to assign to me an importance in future events, which I feel that I am not competent to sustain; and if the change now proposed for me shall show them that, they will be sooner prepared to supply the vacuum with one equal to the occasion they have in their minds . . . . If I could think and feel that I

14 Wright to ?, July 21, 1847, Gillet, *Wright*, II, 1941.

was equal to the call," he went on, " in a private letter to you
I should not assume any mock modesty to hide my impressions,
but I cannot work myself up to the belief that, if I continue
on, I am not at some point, to disappoint the best friends in
the world and ruin or endanger the great cause; and hence
the idea that events may throw me out . . . is not repugnant to
me." [15]

It seems clear that Wright's withdrawal from politics was
an example of moral weakness not moral strength. There is no
doubt a greater courage and wisdom in the action of a Jefferson or a Lincoln, in using party machinery, the symbol of
man's foibles and his baser aspects, to promote his ultimate
benefit. Silas obviously considered his attitude a demonstration
of his own insufficiency, not of any superiority. But he could
not help himself. So he tried to forget the past and become a
farmer. Whether or not he could have held out against the
efforts that were being made to bring him back into politics,
and how he would have conducted himself if he had again
achieved public office, are questions which must remain unanswered.

* * * * *

The summer of 1847 was hot. Wright toiled away day after
day under the broiling North Country sun. The haying season
was upon him late in July, and he put in long hours getting
in his crop. The heat, the hard work, and the sudden abandon-
ment of alcohol after so many years of hard drinking, were too
much for his system. Twice during the summer he suffered
from slight heart attacks, but as the effects passed off quickly,
he said nothing to anyone but Clarissa and kept up his work.
On August 26, he attended the funeral at the Canton Episcopal
church of a friend who had died after a lingering illness. While
walking from the church to the graveyard, he fell in with John
L. Russell. They talked of recent friends who had passed away,

15 Wright to Bancroft, Sept. 11, 1844, Bancroft papers.

and the manner of their decease. Wright mentioned one man who had died shortly before of a heart attack.

" I have two or three intimate friends," he said to Russell, " who are so apprehensive of being carried off in a minute in *this way,* that they cannot enjoy life as long as it lasts. Now I take a very different view of the matter. Death must come in the way appointed. To my mind the escape from lingering pain and sickness, and from the trouble and care devolving upon neighbors, is a blessing—rather than an evil to be feared. . . ."

Russell knew nothing at the time of Wright's attacks, but the seriousness of his tone was impressive. He sensed that Wright believed that his time on earth was limited. That evening, after getting in the last of his crop, Wright worked late polishing his Agricultural Address, but he was up early the next day. After his usual breakfast, sometime between seven and eight o'clock, he went down to the post office for his mail.

The clerk handed him a packet of letters and papers and he sat down, opened a letter from his brother-in-law, Horace Moody, and began to read. Suddenly the clerk noticed that he had put down his mail and risen to his feet, his face ashy pale, his breathing labored. " I feel quite ill," he said simply. Then he sat down.

At that moment, Charles A. Eldridge, a local friend, entered the post office. One look convinced him that something was wrong. " Are you ill? " he asked Silas.

Wright admitted that he was. He felt sharp pains in his head, neck and arms, he said, and a generally oppressive feeling in his chest. Eldridge wanted to go for a doctor, but Wright restrained him, saying that he had had similar seizures and they had passed off. Eldridge, nevertheless, sent the mail clerk for medical aid. By now a crowd was beginning to gather. Wright sat in the post office quietly but in obvious pain. His eyes grew bloodshot and glassy, his breathing irregular. Someone from the nearby drug store brought him some peppermint, but it gave him no relief. As more and more townspeople

crowded into the room, he was forced to repeat over and over
what had happened and how he felt, but he did so patiently.
Little seven-year-old Leslie Russell, who lived across the road
from the Wrights, noticed the crowd on his way to school and
came in to see what was wrong. Silas called to him, asked him
about his studies, patted him on the head and told him to
hurry on and not be late for school. To all the anxious friends
who congregated about him, he spoke cheerfully, assuring
them that he would be all right. Finally, a full hour after his
attack, a physician, Dr. Darias Clark, arrived. He found the
sick man's pulse weak and flickering, his hands cold. He gave
him something to relieve the pain. Then, feeling somewhat
better, Wright got up, picked up his mail, and together with
the doctor and another townsman, walked down the street to
his house.

He lay down on his bed. His clothing was loosened, and Dr.
Clark applied a mustard plaster to his chest. There was nothing else that the doctor could do, so he left the house and went
off to visit another patient. Silas, however, felt no better. The
mustard plaster was too strong, and he asked Clarissa to remove it. She took it off and went into the kitchen to add flour
to it to lessen its strength.

Suddenly she heard a cry from the bedroom. She rushed
back to his side, but too late. He was dead.[16]

*   *   *   *   *

It is difficult to estimate the honest contemporary opinion of
a man from the words of his friends when he dies. Fulsome
praise, exaggerations and platitudes characterize nearly every
comment. When Wright's death was announced eulogies
splashed from the pens of nearly every newspaper editor in the
country. He was called "the Cato of America," and was compared to George Washington, Thomas Jefferson, Andrew
Jackson, Napoleon, Aristides, and (inevitably) Cincinnatus.

16 Russell to Flagg, Aug. 27, 1847, Flagg papers; Jenkins, *Wright*, p. 249;
Gillet, *Wright*, II, 1693-70.

He was extolled as a great statesman, an outstanding politician, a good neighbor, a devoted husband, a man of unusually praiseworthy character, and a genius. " The mind of Silas Wright was distinguished equally for strength, breadth, fertility, depth and clearness," one paper declared. The *Troy Budget* even claimed that he had never been a heavy drinker. " He conformed, in his early days, to established customs," the *Budget* confessed primly, but " it was never true that he ever became intoxicated." [17]

Men of letters also had their say. Whittier wrote a poem, " The Lost Statesman," about his death, and George Bancroft, the great Democratic historian, writing privately spoke of his place in history as one of America's great leaders, a man of and for the common people. Walt Whitman wrote a touching editorial in the *Brooklyn Eagle*. " We confess that we loved Silas Wright as a true democratic friend of the people .... The late governor was a MAN; Alas! we fear we shall indeed never ' look upon his like again ' .... He was a perfectly upright, honest politician. He never betrayed either his friends or his own conscience .... Far, far, beyond the common herd of ' great ' statemen was Silas Wright." [18]

To these were added the remarks of professional politicians. The Northern Democrats who were thinking in terms of the Wilmot Proviso were shocked, for they had been counting on running him for President. " There was more moral and political power united in his person, than in any other American Citizen," wrote David Wilmot himself. " Silas Wright has left behind him no living man in whom is contained the same elements of strength and moral grandeur of character. He was the leader for the crisis. . . ." John A. Dix expressed the feel-

17 For obituaries of Wright, see Gillet, *Wright*, II, 1991-2008; Whitman, *Gathering of the Forces*, II, 185-8.

18 J. Whittier, *Works* (Cambridge edition), pp. 304-5; Bancroft to Bryant, Nov. 3, 1847, Howe, *Bancroft*, II, 27; Whitman, *Gathering of the Forces*, II, 185-8.

ings of the Regency. " To his friends," Dix admitted to Flagg,
" the affliction is severe indeed; but to the country in its present
unhappy condition . . . it is far greater. I see no hope of rallying
the Northern [radical] democracy, unless it be on Mr. Van
Buren." William E. Cramer, a young Democrat who had
known Wright in New York and had recently migrated to
Wisconsin, wrote privately, " Under his banner, the North
and the West were steadily tending together for the first time
in our history."

But perhaps the greatest tribute paid to his memory came
from politicians outside his own group—men who had known
him for years but who were either disinterested in his presidential possibilities or openly hostile to them. Calhoun is supposed
to have exulted, " Burnt out at last " when told that Wright
had died, but this was not the reaction of the majority. " We
have lost poor Wright who had the soundest head combined
with the warmest heart of any statesman within my knowledge," wrote James Buchanan, adding soberly, " Requiescat in
pace! " The President, who was strictly and sincerely neutral
on the question of his own successor, made this comment in
his diary:

> Intelligence reached the City today of the sudden death by
> apoplexy of the Hon. Silas Wright, late Governor of New
> York. He was a great and a good man . . . I was intimate with
> him when he was in Congress. He was my personal . . . and
> [political] friend, and I deeply regret his death.

Up at Saratoga Springs, where he was vacationing, William
L. Marcy learned of Wright's passing and was " much
shocked." He had known him long and intimately, though two
more unlike men would be hard to imagine. Of late they had
not been close. Though Marcy could never countenance the
disregard of practical politics which had characterized the split
in the New York party, he was certainly more nearly a Hunker
than a radical. But Marcy was a keen critic, a man who almost
instinctively judged events in the cold light of utilitarianism,

and his judgment perhaps stands the test of time better than any other. "The death of no other man among us," he wrote two days after Silas passed away, "would have produced a more profound sensation. He was a truly great man and his loss may well be regarded as a public calamity." [19]

19 Wilmot to King, Sept. 25, 1847, Van Buren papers; Dix to Flagg, Aug. 30, 1847, Flagg papers; Cramer to Flagg, Sept. 9, 1847, Flagg papers; Perry, *Reminiscences of Public Men*, 2nd series, p. 187; Buchanan to Bancroft, Sept. 29, 1847, Bancroft papers; Polk, *Diary*, M. Quaife, ed., III, 153, Aug. 29, 1847; Marcy to A. Campbell, Aug. 29, 1847, Marcy papers.

BIBLIOGRAPHY

MANUSCRIPTS. *The papers of the following*:

George Bancroft, Massachusetts Historical Society.
James Gordon Bennett (Diary, 1831), New York Public Library.
Blair family, Library of Congress.
Francis P. Blair and William C. Rives, Library of Congress.
Hermanus Bleecker, New York State Library.
Luther Bradish, New York Historical Society.
William Cullen Bryant—Parke Godwin, New York Public Library.
James Buchanan, Historical Society of Pennsylvania.
——, Library of Congress.
Benjamin F. Butler, New York Public Library (Miscellaneous papers).
Churchill C. Cambreleng, New York Public Library (Miscellaneous Papers).
John J. Crittenden, Library of Congress.
Edwin Croswell, New York State Library (Miscellaneous papers).
George M. Dallas, Historical Society of Pennsylvania.
Hamilton Fish, Library of Congress.
Azariah C. Flagg, New York Public Library.
——, New York State Library (Miscellaneous papers).
Henry D. Gilpin, Historical Society of Pennsylvania.
Samuel L. Gouverneur, New York Public Library.
Michael Hoffman, New York Historical Society (Miscellaneous papers).
Philip Hone (Diary), New York Historical Society.
William L. Marcy, Library of Congress.
——, New York State Library (Miscellaneous papers).
——, New York Public Library (Miscellaneous papers).
——, New York Historical Society (Miscellaneous papers).
Joel R. Poinsett, Historical Society of Pennsylvania.
James K. Polk, Library of Congress (two series).
——, New York Public Library (transcripts).
Horatio Seymour, New York Historical Society (Miscellaneous papers).
Samuel J. Tilden, New York Public Library.
John Tyler, Library of Congress.
Martin Van Buren, Library of Congress.
——, New York Historical Society (Miscellaneous papers).
Gulian C. Verplanck, New York Historical Society.
Robert J. Walker, New York Historical Society (Miscellaneous papers).
Thurlow Weed, New York Historical Society.
Gideon Welles, Library of Congress.
——, New York Public Library.
Levi Woodbury, Library of Congress.
Silas Wright, Library of Congress (Personal Miscellany).
——, St. Lawrence University.
——, New York State Library.

——, New York Historical Society (Miscellaneous papers).
——, New York Public Library (Miscellaneous papers).
——, Collection of Harry F. Landon, Watertown, New York.
Wright—Butler Letters, New York Public Library.

PERIODICALS

Albany Argus, 1823-47.
Albany Evening Atlas, 1844-47.
Albany Evening Journal, 1830-47.
Log Cabin, 1840.
New York Evening Post, 1844-47.
New York Morning News, 1844-46.
Niles' Weekly Register, 1828-46.
Rough Hewer, 1840.
St. Lawrence Republican, 1833-47.
U. S. Magazine and Democratic Review, 1837-46.
Washington Globe, 1837-44.

OTHER PRIMARY SOURCES

Adams, Charles F. (ed.), *Memoirs of John Quincy Adams*, 12 vols. (Philadelphia, 1875).
A Short Appeal from the decrees of King Caucus & the Albany Regency, to the People (n. p., n. d.), New York Historical Society.
Ambler, Charles H. (ed.), "Correspondence of R. M. T. Hunter," *American Historical Association, Report*, 1916, v. II.
——, "Unpublished Letters of Thomas Ritchie," *John P. Branch Historical Papers*, III, 249 ff.
American State Papers—Documents, Legislative and Executive of the Congress of the United States (Finance), v. V (Washington, 1859).
Bassett, John S. (ed.), *Correspondence of Andrew Jackson*, 6 vols. (Washington, 1926-1933).
Beardsley, Levi, *Reminiscences* (New York, 1852).
Benton, Thomas H., *Thirty Years View: 1820-1850*, 2 vols. (New York, 1856).
Bigelow, John (ed.), *Letters of Samuel J. Tilden*, 2 vols. (New York, 1908).
——, *Retrospections of an Active Life*, v. I, (New York, 1909).
——, (ed.), *Speeches and Writings of Samuel J. Tilden*, 2 vols. (New York, 1885).
Boucher, C. S. and Brooks, R. P. (eds.), "Correspondence Addressed to John C. Calhoun, 1837-1849," *American Historical Association, Report*, 1929, v. II.
Brockway, Beman, *Fifty Years in Journalism . . . with an Autobiography* (Watertown, New York, 1891).
Causten, James H., *Remarks on Mr. Wright's Speech on French Spoilation* (n. p., n. d.), Library of Congress.
Colton, Calvin (ed.), *Private Correspondence of Henry Clay* (Boston, 1856).

Dickinson, John R. (ed.), *Speeches; Correspondence, Etc., of the Late Daniel S. Dickinson*, 2 vols. (New York, 1867).

Fitzpatrick, John C. (ed.), "Autobiography of Martin Van Buren," *American Historical Association, Report*, 1918, v. II.

Garrison, George P. (ed.), "Diplomatic Correspondence of the Republic of Texas," *American Historical Association, Report*, 1908, v. II.

Greeley, Horace, *Recollections of a Busy Life* (New York, 1868).

Heilman, Grace E. and Levin, Bernard S. (eds.), *Calendar of the Poinsett papers in the Gilpin Collection* (Philadelphia, 1941).

Jackson, Andrew, "One of General Jackson's Late Letters," *Tennessee Historical Magazine*, v. VIII.

Jameson, J. F. (ed.), "Correspondence of John C. Calhoun," *American Historical Association, Report*, 1899, v. II.

King, Preston, *Oration Delivered at Canton ... July 4, 1848* (Ogdensburgh, 1848).

Lincoln, Charles Z. (ed.), *Messages from the Governors of New York*, v. IV (Albany, 1909).

McGrane, Reginald C. (ed.), *Correspondence of Nicholas Biddle* (Boston, 1919).

Massachusetts Historical Society, *Proceedings*, v. XLII, "Van Buren-Bancroft Correspondence" (Boston, 1909).

Moore, John B. (ed.), *Works of James Buchanan*, 12 vols. (Philadelphia, 1908-11).

Nevins, Allan (ed.), *Diary of Philip Hone* (New York, 1927).

Legislative Documents of the Senate and Assembly of the State of New York, 1830-1833 (Albany, 1830-1833).

Norton, A. B., *The Great Revolution of 1840* (Mt. Vernon, O., 1888).

Ogle, Charles, *The Regal Splendor of the President's Palace* (Boston, 1840).

Perry, Benjamin F., *Reminiscences of Public Men, Second Series* (Greenville, 1889).

Poore, Ben: Perley, *Perley's Reminiscences of Sixty Years in the National Metropolis* (Philadelphia, 1886).

Proceedings of a Convention of Republican delegates ... nominating a candidate for ... Vice President in 1832, with an Address to New York Republicans by their delegates (Albany, 1832).

Quaife, M. M. (ed.), *Diary of James K. Polk, during his Presidency, 1845 to 1849*, 4 vols. (Chicago, 1910).

Rae, John B., "Democrats and the Dorr Rebellion," *New England Quarterly*, IX, 476 ff.

Richardson, J. D. (ed.), *Compilation of the Messages and Papers of the Presidents*, v. III (Washington, 1908).

Rogers, Cleveland, and Black, John (eds.), *Gathering of the Forces*, 2 vols. (New York, 1920).

Samson, William H., *Letters of Zachary Taylor from the Battle-Fields of the Mexican War* (Rochester, 1908).

Seward, Frederick W., *Autobiography of William H. Seward from 1801 to 1834. With a Memoir of His Life* (New York, 1877).

Siousatt, St. George L. (ed.), "Diaries of S. H. Laughlin," *Tennessee Historical Magazine*, v. II.

——, "Letters of James K. Polk to Andrew Jackson Donelson, 1843-1848," *Tennessee Historical Magazine*, v. III.

——, "Letters of James K. Polk to Cave Johnson, 1833-1848," *Tennessee Historical Magazine*, v. I.

Stanton, Henry B., *Random Recollections* (New York, 1887).

Staples, Arthur G. (ed.), *The Letters of John Fairfield* (Lewiston, Me., 1922).

Stevenson, Adlai E., *Something of Men I Have Known* (Chicago, 1909).

Stickney, William (ed.), *Autobiography of Amos Kendall* (Boston, 1872).

Swammerdam, Eustacius (pseud.), *The Lash; or Truths in Rhyme* (n. p., 1840).

Tyler, Lyon G., *Letters and Times of the Tylers*, 2 vols. (Richmond, 1885).

Van Tyne, Claude H. (ed.), *Letters of Daniel Webster* (New York, 1902).

Warden, R. B. (ed.), "Diary and Correspondence of Salmon Portland Chase," *American Historical Association*, Report, 1902, v. II.

Webster, Fletcher (ed.), *The Private Correspondence of Daniel Webster*, 2 vols. (Boston, 1857).

Weed, Harriet A. (ed.), *Autobiography of Thurlow Weed* (Boston, 1883).

Wright, Silas, *Address at Canton New York, July 4, 1839* (Ogdensburgh, 1839).

——, *Speech...at a Mass Meeting of the Democracy of Brooklyn...September 29, 1840* (New York, 1840).

SECONDARY WORKS

Alexander, Holmes M., *The American Talleyrand; The Career and Contemporaries of Martin Van Buren* (New York, 1935).

Ambler, Charles H., *Thomas Ritchie; A Study in Virginia Politics* (Richmond, 1913).

Bacheller, Irving, "My North Country," *Independent*, XC, 467 ff.

Bancroft, Frederic, *Calhoun and the South Carolina Nullification Movement* (Baltimore, 1928).

Barnes, T. W., *Memoir of Thurlow Weed* (Boston, 1884).

Benton, Nathaniel S., *A History of Herkimer County* (Albany, 1856).

Bigelow, John, *The Life of Samuel J. Tilden*, 2 vols. (New York, 1895).

Butler, Harriet Allen (ed.), *William Allan Butler, A Retrospect of Forty Years, 1825-1865* (New York, 1911).

Catterall, R. C. H., *The Second Bank of the United States* (Chicago, 1903).

Christman, Henry, *Tin Horns and Calico* (New York, 1945).

Clark, Bennett C., *John Quincy Adams; "Old Man Eloquent,"* (Boston, 1932).

Clay, Thomas H., and Oberholtzer, Ellis P., *Henry Clay* (Philadelphia, 1910).

Cleaves, Freeman, *Old Tippecanoe; William Henry Harrison and his Time* (New York, 1939).

Coleman, Mrs. Chapman, *The Life of John J. Crittenden*, 2 vols. (Philadelphia, 1873).

Corey, Albert B., *The Crisis of 1830-42 in Canadian American Relations* (New Haven, 1941).

Curti, Merle, "Robert Rantoul, Jr., Reformer in Politics," *New England Quarterly*, V, 264 ff.

Curtis, Gates (ed.), *Our Country and its People ... St. Lawrence County*, 2 vols. (Syracuse, 1894).

Curtis, George T., *Life of James Buchanan*, 2 vols. (New York, 1883).

Deming, Leonard (ed.), *Catalogue of the Principal Officers of Vermont ... 1778 to 1851* (Middlebury, 1851).

Dix, Morgan, *Memoir of John Adams Dix*, 2 vols. (New York, 1883).

Dodd, William E., *Robert J. Walker, Imperialist* (Chicago, 1914).

Donovan, H. D. A., *The Barnburners* (New York, 1925).

Ellis, David M., *Landlords and Farmers in the Hudson-Mohalk Region, 1790-1850* (Ithaca, New York, 1946).

Eriksson, Erick McK., "Official Newspaper Organs and the Presidential Election of 1836," *Tennessee Historical Magazine*, IX.

Flagg, Azariah C., *Banks and Banking in the State of New York* (Brooklyn, 1868).

Forney, John Weiss, *Anecdotes of Public Men*, 2 vols. (New York, 1873).

Fox, Dixon Ryan, *Decline of Aristocracy in the Politics of New York* (New York, 1919).

——, "The Negro Vote in Old New York," *Political Science Quarterly*, XXXII, 252 ff.

Fuess, Claude M., *Daniel Webster*, 2 vols. (Boston, 1930).

Gillet, Ransom H., *Life and Times of Silas Wright*, 2 vols. (Albany, 1874).

Gilpin, Henry D., *An Eulogy on Silas Wright ...* (Philadelphia, 1847).

Gordon, Armistead C., *William Fitzhugh Gordon* (New York, 1909).

Hammond, Jabez D., *History of Political Parties in the State of New-York*, 2 vols. (Cooperstown, New York, 1842-48).

——, *Life and Times of Silas Wright* (Syracuse, 1848).

Harvey, Peter, *Reminiscences of Daniel Webster* (Boston, 1890).

Hough, Franklin B., *A History of St. Lawrence and Franklin Counties, New York ... to the present time* (Albany, 1853).

Howe, M. A. de Wolfe, *Life and Letters of George Bancroft*, 2 vols. (New York, 1908).

Hudson, Frederic, *Journalism in the United States from 1690 to 1872* (New York, 1873).

James, Marquis, *The Life of Andrew Jackson*, one volume edition (New York, 1938).

Jenkins, John S., *History of Political Parties in the State of New York* (Auburn, 1849).

——, *Life of Silas Wright* (Auburn, 1847).

Lambert, Oscar D., *Presidential Politics in the United States, 1841-1844* (Durham, North Carolina, 1936).

Lee, William S., *Father Went to College, the Story of Middlebury* (New York, 1936).

Ludlum, D. McW., *Social Ferment in Vermont, 1791-1850* (New York, 1939).

Lynch, Denis T., *An Epoch and a Man: Martin Van Buren* (New York, 1929).

McCormac, Eugene I., *James K. Polk, A Political Biography* (Berkeley, California, 1922).

McGrane, Reginald C., *The Panic of 1837* (Chicago, 1924).

McGuire, James K. (ed.), *The Democratic Party of the State of New York; A History* ..., 3 vols. (New York, 1905).

Mackenzie, William Lyon, *The Life and Opinions of B. F. Butler and Jesse Hoyt* (Boston, 1845).

——, *The Life and Times of Martin Van Buren* ... (Boston, 1846).

Meyer, Leland W., *Life and Times of Col. Richard M. Johnson of Kentucky* (New York, 1932).

Munsell, Joel, *Annals of Albany*, 10 vols. (Albany, 1850-9).

Murray, David, "Anti-Rent Episode in the State of New York," *American Historical Association, Report*, 1896, v. I.

Olin, J. E., *Silas Wright in National Politics* (Columbia University Master's Essay, typescript, 1916).

Parks, John H., *Felix Grundy, Champion of Democracy* (Louisiana, 1940).

Parton, James, *Life of Horace Greeley* (New York, 1854).

——, *Life of Andrew Jackson*, 3 vols. (New York, 1859-60).

Pearson, Henry G., *James S. Wadsworth of Geneseo* (New York, 1913).

Peck, Charles H., "John Van Buren; a Study in By-Gone Politics," *Magazine of American History*, XVII, 58 ff., 202 ff., 318 ff.

Pierson, George W., *Tocqueville and Beaumont in America* (New York, 1938).

Poage, George R., *Henry Clay and the Whig Party* (Chapel Hill, North Carolina, 1936).

Rammelkamp, C. H., "Campaign of 1824 in New York," *American Historical Association, Report*, 1904, p. 175 ff.

"Recollections of an Old Stager," *Harpers*, XLVII, 753 ff.

Roach, George W., "The Presidential Campaign of 1844 in New York State," *New York History*, XIX, 153 ff.

——, *New York in the Election of 1844* (Columbia University Master's Essay, typescript, 1939).

Roberts, James A., *A Century of the Comptroller's Office—State of New York* (Albany, 1897).

Schlesinger, Arthur M., Jr., *The Age of Jackson* (Boston, 1945).

Smith, Justin H., *The Annexation of Texas* (New York, 1911).

Smith, W. E., *The Francis Preston Blair Family in Politics*, 2 vols. (New York, 1933).

Spencer, Ivor D., "William L. Marcy Goes Conservative," *Mississippi Valley Historical Review*, XXXI, 205 ff.

Stillwell, Lewis D., "Migration From Vermont, 1776-1860," *Proceedings of the Vermont Historical Society, New Series*, V, # 2.

Storrs, Richard S., " Contributions Made to our National Development by Plain Men," *American Historical Association, Report,* 1896, I, 37 ff.

Swift, Samuel, *History of the Town of Middlebury* (Middlebury, 1859).

Taussig, F. W., *Tariff History of the United States,* 6th edition (New York, 1914).

Van Deusen, Glyndon G., *Thurlow Weed; Wizard of the Lobby* (Boston, 1947).

——, *Life of Henry Clay* (Boston, 1937).

Warden, R. B., *Account of the Private Life and Public Services of Salmon Portland Chase* (Cincinnati, 1874).

Weston, Florence, *Presidential Election of 1828* (Washington, 1938).

Wiltse, C. M., *John C. Calhoun, Nationalist* (New York, 1944).

Wilson, S. (ed.), *Albany City Guide; 1844* (Albany, 1844).

Wise, Henry A., *Seven Decades of the Union...A Memoir of John Tyler* ... (Richmond, 1881).

Zahler, Helene S., *Eastern Workingmen and National Land Policy, 1829-1862* (New York, 1941).

INDEX

A

Adams, John Quincy, 32, 38, 52, 54, 67, 72, 205
Albany Argus, 33, 35, 37, 41-2, 80, 100-01, 128, 151, 154, 157-8, 162, 173, 180-1, 186, 227, 238, 280, 294-7, 299-301, 306, 312, 326, 347-8, 362-4, 370, 372, 376, 379
Albany Atlas, 238, 289, 293-4, 300-01, 306, 347-8, 358, 362-4, 370-3, 382, 392
Albany Evening Journal, 13, 80, 83, 88, 92, 173, 194-5, 323, 325n, 356, 358, 378
Albany Regency, 24-5, 33, 35-40, 42-3, 46-7, 49, 51, 59-61, 66, 68, 71-7, 80, 83-6, 90-2, 95, 97, 99, 108, 110, 120-2, 128-9, 137, 158, 159n, 160, 172-5, 180-1, 187-8, 194, 228, 237, 244, 260, 291, 337, 362, 371, 402, 408
Allen, Cornelius, 384
Allen, Horace, 305
Allen, William, 205, 208, 227, 239
American Republican party, 309, 327-8
Anti-Masonic Enquirer, 83
Anti-Masonry, 70-1, 82, 86, 91-2, 377
Anti-Renter, 377
Anti-Rent movement, 309, 319-22, 331-2, 356-61, 376-8, 381-2, 384-6, 388, 402
Archer, William S., 215
Aristides, 406
Auckland, Lord, 88

B

Baltimore Republican, 177-8
Bancroft, George, 151, 172, 203-04, 244, 247, 255, 262, 265n, 268, 278, 307-08, 348, 372-4, 380, 403, 407
Banking, state; attitudes of New York parties on, 1824-7, 24-5, 44-9; Safety Fund system, 121-2; expansion of, 127; suspension of specie payments, 141-3; general banking law of 1839, 172-3; Wright on, 1845, 353
Barnburners and Hunkers, 292
Barrow, Alexander, 215
Beach, Nelson, 386
Beardsley, Samuel, 158n
Bennett, James Gordon, 54, 77, 90, 199-200

Benton, Thomas Hart, 87-8, 125n, 126-7, 137, 165, 218-9, 242, 251-2, 260, 285
Biddle, Nicholas, 107, 111-3, 117, 119-20, 122-3, 127
Bigelow, John, 368
Birney, James, 326-8
Blair, Francis P., 94, 135, 146, 153, 166, 252, 285, 334
Bonaparte, Napoleon, 203, 406
Bouck, William C., 187-8, 199, 203, 230-1, 292-5, 298-307, 329, 333-4, 339, 341, 346, 348, 350, 366, 370-2
Boughton, Dr. Smith, "Big Thunder," 357-8
Bowman, John, 36
Bradish, Luther, 159
Breese, Sidney, 261
Broderick, D. W., 381
Brooklyn Daily Eagle, 368, 407
Brown, Aaron V., 345
Bryant, William Cullen, 347, 368, 398
Buchanan, James, 13, 27, 162, 206, 218, 242, 256-8, 261, 271, 274, 307, 344-5, 370-5, 408
Buck, John, 79
Bucktail party, 24-5, 32-3, 36, 39-40, 44-9, 71, 229, 365
Buel, Jesse, 65
Burr, Aaron, 172
Burt, Thomas M., 181
Butler, Benjamin Franklin, 87, 100, 122n, 137, 180, 197, 250, 252, 262, 265, 268-9, 272-9, 282-4, 341, 345, 349, 372
Butler, Harriet, 345n

C

Calhoun, John Caldwell, 13, 19, 30, 54n, 61-2, 86-8, 93-4, 97-8, 102, 111, 116, 161-2, 165-6, 217, 227, 240-4, 246-9, 253, 259, 262, 264-5, 275n., 278-9, 282, 288-9, 304, 337, 343-4, 395, 397, 408
Cambreleng, Churchill C., 88, 103, 153, 160, 192-3, 341, 381
Caroline, the, 169
Cass, Lewis, 253, 258-9, 261, 265, 271-8, 283, 287-8
Cassidy, William, 293, 362
Chase, Salmon P., 14
Cincinnatus, Lucius Quintus, 406
Clark, Darias, 406
Clay, Cassius M., 324

419

VITA

John Arthur Garraty was born in Brooklyn, New York, July 4, 1920. He attended the New York City public schools, and received his A. B. from Brooklyn College in 1941. From 1941 to 1942 he attended Columbia University and received his A. M. in June of that year. His Master's Essay, prepared in the seminar of Professor Dwight C. Miner was entitled, "Henry Cabot Lodge and American Foreign Policy, 1895-1914."

From 1942 to 1946 Mr. Garraty served in the United States Maritime Service. Upon his discharge he returned to Columbia and in 1948 received his Ph. D. His work for this degree was undertaken in the doctoral seminar of Professor John A. Krout.